D1266057

INTERMEDIATE

The IDEA MAGAZINE FOR TEACHERS® MAILBOX®

2009–2010 YEARBOOK

The Education Center, Inc.
Greensboro, North Carolina

The Mailbox® 2009–2010 Intermediate Yearbook

ISBN10 1-56234-958-9
ISBN13 978-1-56234-958-5
ISSN 1088-5552

Printed in the United States of America.

The Education Center, Inc.
P.O. Box 9753
Greensboro, NC 27429-0753

RRDWI061022353

Contents

www.themailbox.com

Skills for the Season

SKILLS FOR THE SEASON

Off to a Flying Start

Student motivation

Start the year on a positive note with this disc-flying illustration. Take your class outside or to a multipurpose room or gymnasium. Select several students to each take a turn throwing a plastic disc and note the distance traveled each time. Then fly a disc yourself, putting forth so little effort that it practically lands at your feet. Ask students why your throw did not make the disc travel as far as theirs. Help students conclude that an individual's success depends on his effort. Back in the classroom, give each child a copy of page 11 and have him cut apart the quotes and cut out the disc pattern. Instruct him to read each quote and glue his favorite in the space provided on his disc cutout. Then have him write an explanation of how that quote relates to effort and success. If desired, post the cutouts on a classroom display titled "Off to a Flying Start!"

Lesley McGougan, St. Stephen Elementary, Brampton, Ontario, Canada

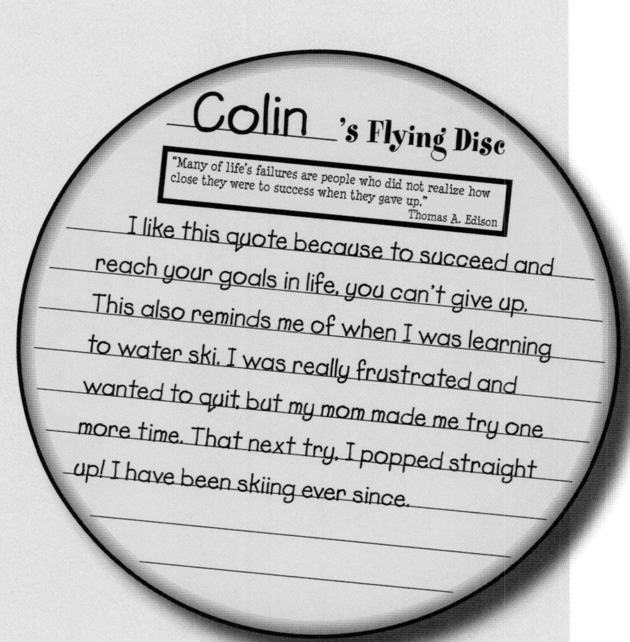

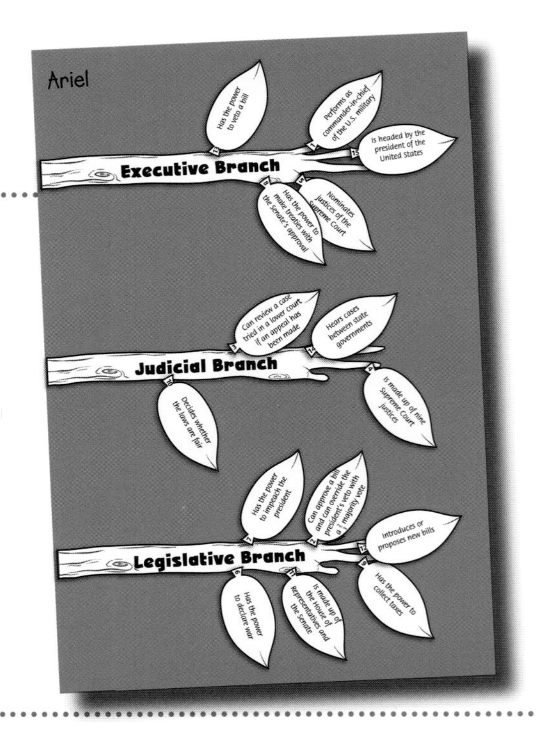

Balancing the Power

Branches of government

Go out on a limb and celebrate Constitution Day (September 17) with this independent research activity! Give each student a copy of page 12 and a sheet of construction paper. Have the student cut out the branch and leaf patterns. Next, have her glue the branches onto the paper, leaving space around each branch. Then instruct her to use her textbook or other available materials to research the roles of each government branch. As she identifies a role, have her glue the leaf to the corresponding branch. If desired, have pairs of students compare their answers.

LaVone Novotny, Liberty Elementary, Caledonia, OH

Patriotic Symbols
Research skills, patriotism

Try this activity close to September 11 to help students develop an understanding of patriotism. Explain that patriotism is love and loyal support for your country. Then display the list shown of symbols that represent the United States. Divide students into small groups and assign each group a symbol to research. Instruct each group to write a short, illustrated essay explaining how its symbol represents patriotism and then present its work to the class. Compile the essays and illustrations into a class book titled "Patriotic Pride!" If desired, allow each group to create a replica of its symbol using arts-and-crafts materials.

Cheryl Rayl, Mayville Elementary, Mayville, MI

Liberty Bell
Statue of Liberty
U.S. flag
U.S. Capitol building
White House
Supreme Court building
Bald eagle
Great Seal of the United States
Jefferson Memorial
Lincoln Memorial
Washington Monument
Uncle Sam

Bald Eagle

The bald eagle was chosen by our founding fathers because it was an animal they thought was unique to the United States. They also thought the bird represented strength, courage, and freedom. The bald eagle is on the Great Seal of the United States, the President's flag, and the one-dollar bill. Bald eagles were added to the Endangered Species List in 1967, but the Bald Eagle Protection Act helped their population, and they were removed from the list in 2007.

I Wish I Had...
Creative writing

Not every child takes a wild, elaborate vacation. So instead of asking kids to write about what they did over the summer, ask them to write about what they did *not* do but wish they had. Encourage students to add sensory details to their writing and use descriptive vocabulary. Allow time for students to share their completed vacation stories with the class.

Neda Issa, Aqsa School, Bridgeview, IL

Morgan

I wish I had gone to Alaska for my summer vacation. We could have seen snow in the middle of July. I bet my mom would have made my little sister wear the winter coat that makes her look like a cream puff. I would have laughed at that! I could have taken pictures of the whales swimming in the water too. What a cool vacation it would have been. Maybe I can convince my parents to take us next year.

Grin and Share It
Getting acquainted

Share with students a list of things that make you smile. Then have each student cut a large circle from a sheet of yellow construction paper and draw a smiley face at the top. Next, instruct him to list on the circle several things that make him smile. Have him count the number of items he listed and include that number in a title at the top of the list. Have students share their completed lists with the class. If desired, collect the papers and post them on a display titled "Things That Make Us Smile!"

Helene Holmes, Butterfield School, Orange, MA

Ten Things That Make Brendan Smile

My dog greeting me at the door
A hug from my mom
A note in my lunchbox from my mom
Watching Saturday morning cartoons
Waking up to the smell of pancakes
Playing with my friends
Scoring a goal at my soccer game
Making good grades
Hearing a good joke
Eating ice cream on a warm day

Name ______________________________

Date ______________

Getting to Know You

Read each number and then follow the directions.

A. 8,462,571.5	If an **8** is in the millions place, then cross out *backpacks*.
B. 7,627,542.35	If a **3** is in the tens place, then cross out *problems*.
C. 9,593,674.025	If a **6** is in the hundreds place, then cross out *tardy*.
D. 36,957.541	If a **1** is in the thousands place, then cross out *big*.
E. 347,562.03	If a **3** is in the hundredths place, then cross out *books*.
F. 97,562.164	If a **9** is in the hundred thousands place, then cross out *some*.
G. 5,362,470.007	If a **7** is in the tens place, then cross out *He*.
H. 6,903,267.405	If a **6** is in the millions place, then cross out *rulers*.
I. 4,807,003.010	If a **0** is in the ten thousands place, then cross out *teachers*.
J. 3,804,057.092	If a **2** is in the thousandths place, then cross out *late*.
K. 48,269.03	If a **0** is in the tenths place, then cross out *pencils*.
L. 532.45	If a **5** is in the tenths place, then cross out *We*.
M. 3.594	If a **9** is in the hundredths place, then cross out *homework*.
N. 168.40	If a **1** is in the hundreds place, then cross out *buses*.
O. 64,981.36	If a **6** is in the thousandths place, then cross out *have*.

He	**We**	**backpacks**	**buses**
late	**homework**	**pencils**	**have**
some	**teachers**	**tardy**	**rulers**
big	**books**	**problems**	

What did one math book say to another math book on the first day of school?
To find out, write each remaining word from the box in order from left to right and top to bottom on the lines below.

________ ________ ________

________ ________________!

Name ______________________________

Date ________________

Works for Me!

Underline the homophone that completes each sentence.

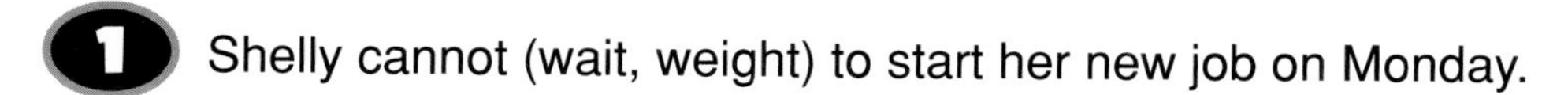
1. Shelly cannot (wait, weight) to start her new job on Monday.

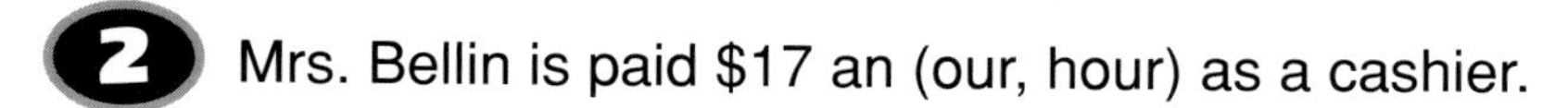
2. Mrs. Bellin is paid $17 an (our, hour) as a cashier.

3. The veterinarian takes care of the (horse, hoarse).

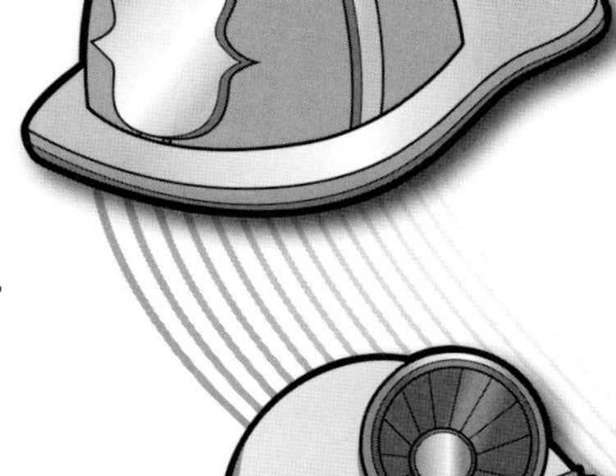

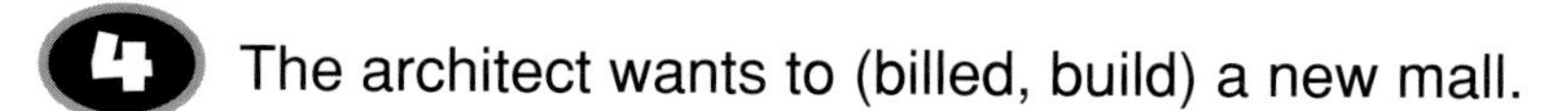
4. The architect wants to (billed, build) a new mall.

5. Steve works at an aquarium and studies (whales, wails).

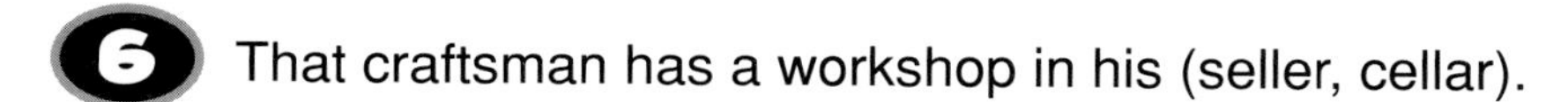
6. That craftsman has a workshop in his (seller, cellar).

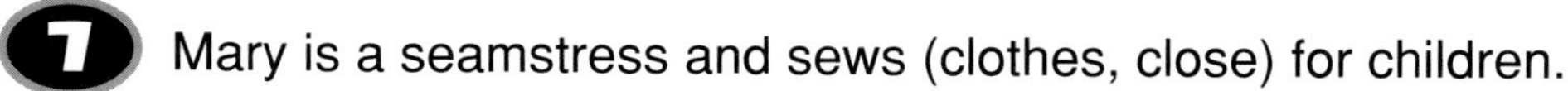
7. Mary is a seamstress and sews (clothes, close) for children.

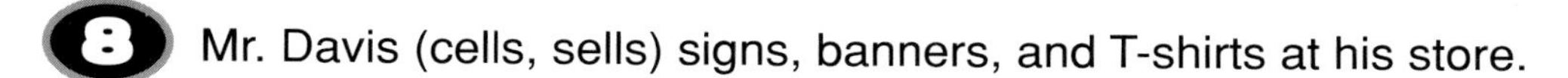
8. Mr. Davis (cells, sells) signs, banners, and T-shirts at his store.

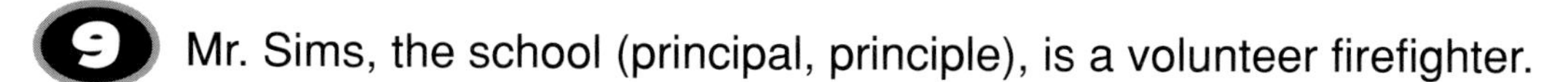
9. Mr. Sims, the school (principal, principle), is a volunteer firefighter.

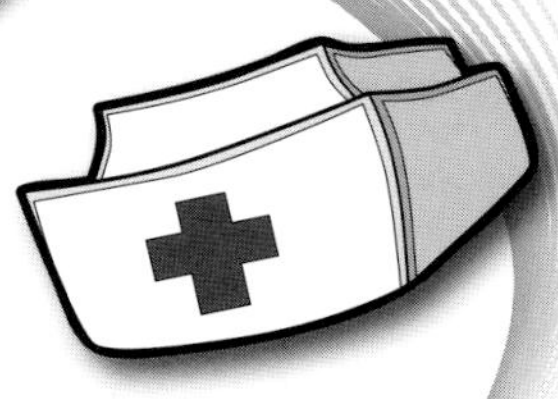

10. Nancy first piloted a (plane, plain) when she was 23 years old.

11. Ms. Gann knew she would be a teacher by the time she was in (forth, fourth) grade.

12. Barney's job is to watch changes in the (whether, weather).

13. The postal worker delivers mail (scent, sent) from all over the world.

14. Mr. Polk (maid, made) the choice to open his own café.

15. Mayor Barton will give tours of the city all next (weak, week).

16. The jeweler sold the man a diamond (wring, ring).

17. The nurse (knew, new) how much medicine to give the child.

18. The banker put the (cache, cash) in the safe.

19. Mrs. Wright (rights, writes) children's books.

20. The newspaper reporter must keep up with (current, currant) events.

Name ____________________

Date ____________________

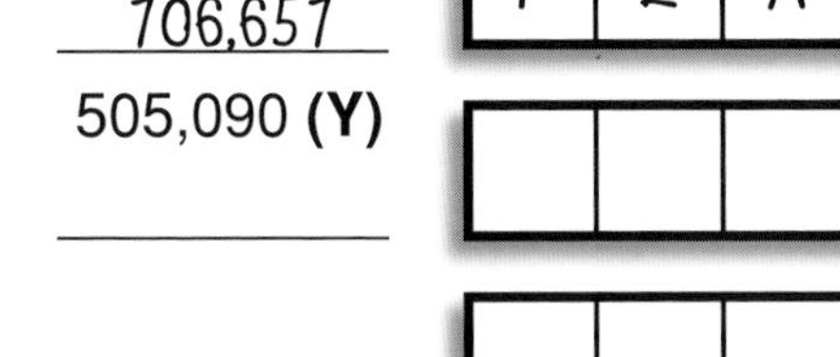

Patriot Day Pride

Write each set of numbers in order from least to greatest. Then write the letters in the same order to reveal a hidden word.

1. 8,010 **(F)** 70,657 **(A)** 8,100 **(L)** 706,657 **(G)**

   8,010 ____ 8,100 ____ 70,657 ____ 706,657 — F L A G

2. 559 **(E)** 51,399 **(M)** 51,600 **(O)** 517 **(M)** 55,009 **(R)** 505,090 **(Y)**

3. 3,469 **(A)** 358 **(S)** 32,994 **(R)** 3,214 **(T)** 320,348 **(S)**

4. 2,254 **(E)** 225 **(F)** 2,253 **(R)** 22,563 **(E)**

5. 6,064 **(T)** 60,067 **(I)** 6,036 **(A)** 606,647 **(N)** 606,067 **(O)** 606 **(N)**

6. 11,324 **(I)** 1,234 **(R)** 13,241 **(D)** 132 **(P)** 112,324 **(E)**

7. 896,680 **(G)** 86,968 **(O)** 896 **(S)** 86,908 **(R)** 889,660 **(N)** 8,696 **(T)**

8. 1,001 **(R)** 10,100 **(V)** 1,100 **(A)** 110 **(B)** 101,101 **(E)**

Write the number from the answer bank that comes between each pair of numbers below. Two numbers will not be used.

9. 79,986 __________ 83,349
10. 24,861 __________ 34,925
11. 117,603 __________ 117,694
12. 1,514 __________ 5,514
13. 39,352 __________ 39,470
14. 119,815 __________ 221,815
15. 303,030 __________ 3,003,003
16. 4,684 __________ 9,005

Answer Bank

119,905	3,780	24,851	117,648
39,387	80,999	330,081	29,880
	5,964	39,001	

Quote Cards and Flying Disc Pattern

Use with "Off to a Flying Start" on page 6.

"I've always believed that if you put in the work, the results will come." Michael Jordan	"The only place success comes before work is in the dictionary." Vince Lombardi
"Don't give up. Don't ever give up." Jim Valvano	"Success doesn't come to you; you go to it." Marva Collins
"It is possible to fly without motors but not without knowledge and skill." Wilbur Wright	"I want to put a ding in the universe." Steve Jobs
"In order to succeed, your desire for success should be greater than your fear of failure." Bill Cosby	"We are what we repeatedly do. Excellence, then, is not an act but a habit." Aristotle
"We can do anything we want to if we stick to it long enough." Helen Keller	"If Columbus had turned back, no one would have blamed him. Of course, no one would have remembered him either." Unknown
"Many of life's failures are people who did not realize how close they were to success when they gave up." Thomas A. Edison	"A dream doesn't become reality through magic; it takes sweat, determination, and hard work." Colin Powell

Branch and Leaf Patterns

Use with "Balancing the Power" on page 6.

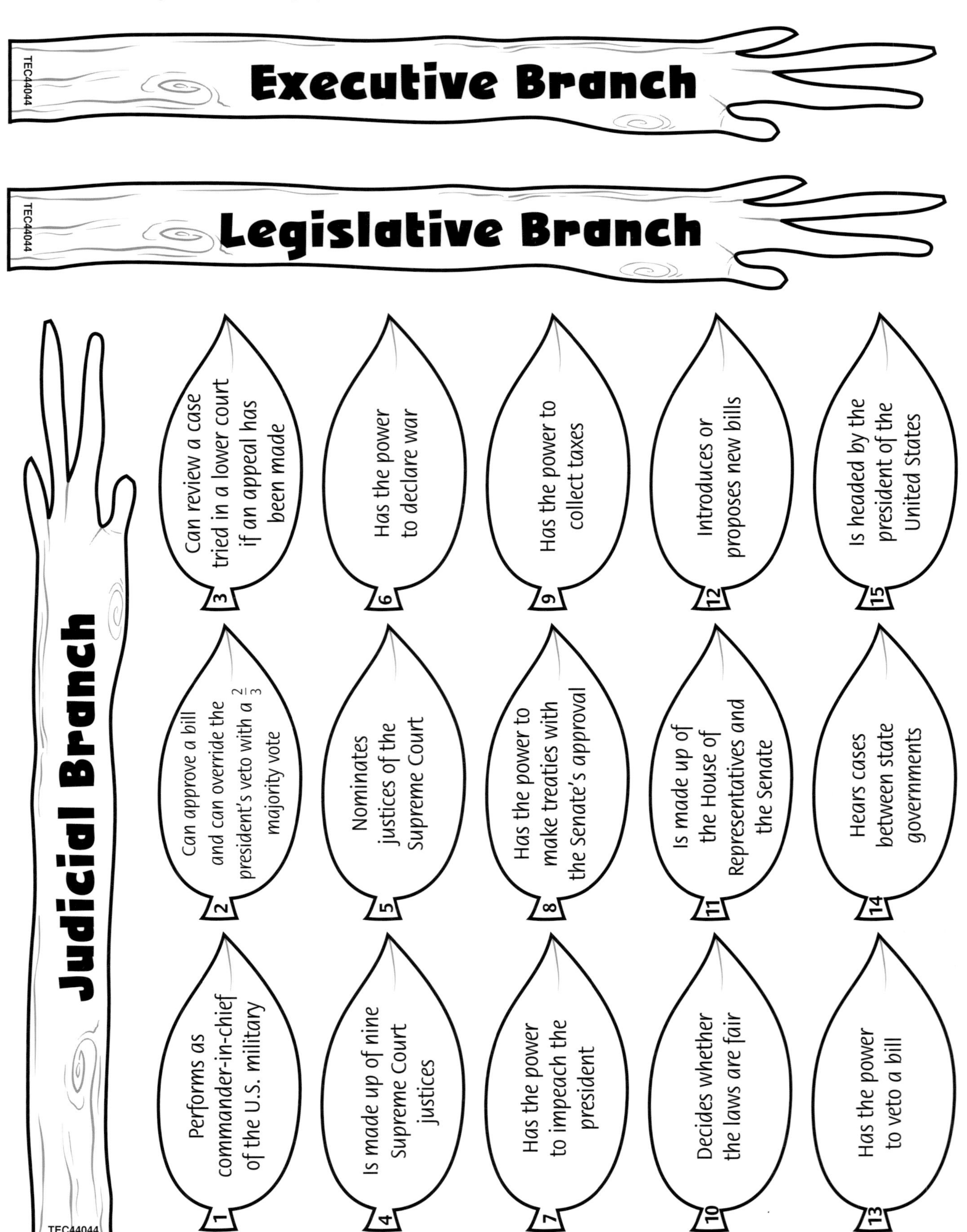

SKILLS FOR THE SEASON

Monster Math
Function tables

This monster-themed activity will have students eager to practice their algebra skills. Give each student a copy of page 18. Instruct him to secretly choose a function and program each row in the table with *x* or *y* values, as shown, making sure to leave several spaces blank. Then he writes an answer key on the back of his page and adds details to the head, arms, and legs to create a one-of-a-kind monster. Finally, each student trades his paper with a partner, completes the table, and checks his answers against the key.

Crissie Stephens, Kelly Edwards Elementary, Williston, SC

Touchdown!
Reviewing any subject

Make reviewing content-area material more fun with this game. Decorate a large sheet of bulletin board paper to resemble a football field. Then divide the class into two teams and stick on the 50-yard line a football cutout for each team. Next, ask each team a question in turn. If a team answers correctly, move its football ten yards toward its end zone. If the answer is incorrect, the team's football stays where it is. When one team's football reaches the end zone, the team scores a touchdown *(seven points)*. Then move both footballs back to midfield for another round of play.

Brenda Williamson
Murray-LaSaine Elementary
Charleston, SC

Sweet Statistics

Mean, median, mode, and range

For Halloween math, draw a number line on the board and label it as shown. Have each student label a sticky note with the name of his favorite candy and the number of letters in the candy's name. Then have him place his note on the board to create a line plot as shown. Use questions 1–6 on page 19 to discuss students' data. To conclude the activity, have each student complete a copy of page 19 and compare his answers with a partner's.

Bonnie Baumgras, Las Vegas, NV

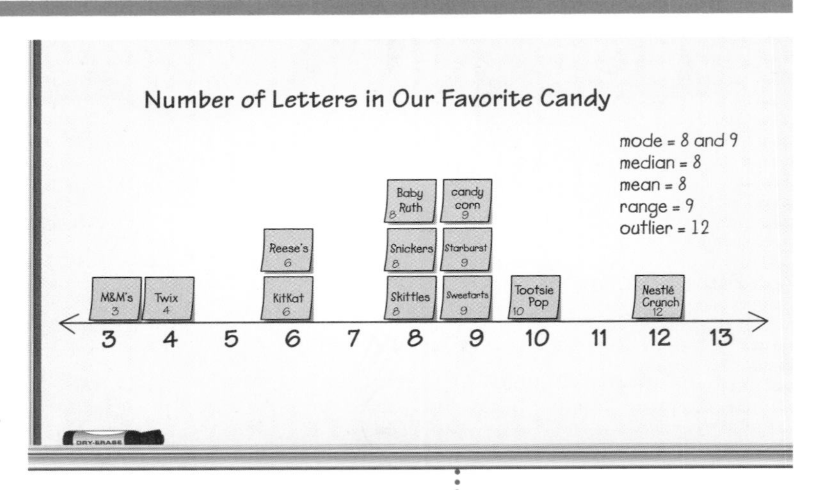

Off We Go!

Identifying geographic features

Celebrate Geography Awareness Week the third week in November with a scavenger hunt across the United States. Post a list of geographic terms, such as the ones shown. Challenge each student pair to use a physical map of the United States to plan a route that includes as many of the listed features as possible. Then have students write their itineraries and share them with the class, instructing one partner to read and the other to trace the route on a wall map. Adapt this activity for use with state or world maps or to include any grade-specific geographic terms.

Pat Twohey, Smithfield, RI

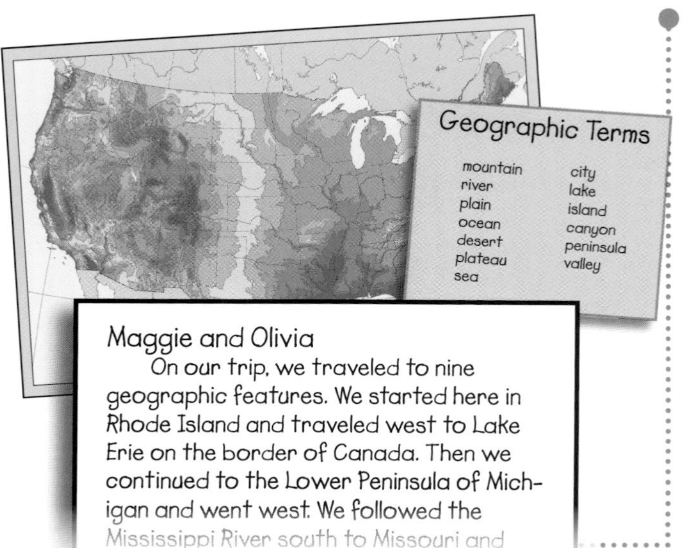

Disgusting Dishes

Writing with adjectives

Jazz up writing time by having students pen descriptions of their least favorite Thanksgiving foods. First, ask each student to list adjectives that describe the dish she dislikes the most. Then have her use the list to write a detailed paragraph about the food without naming it. Have students read their descriptions aloud and allow the class to guess the mystery foods.

Kathy Gardiner, Fredericktown Intermediate, Fredericktown, OH

Caroline

stinky, green, stringy
bland, mushy, swampy

My least favorite Thanksgiving dish is a swampy green color. It smells really stinky like leftover garbage. When I eat it, it feels stringy and tastes bland. In the bowl it just looks mushy. No matter how much I tell my mom I don't like it, it keeps showing up every year.

Green bean casserole!

Name ______________________________

Date ____________________

Pronoun Patches

Write a pronoun from the scarecrow's patches to complete each sentence.
Color the patch after it is used.

1. The squirrel took the acorn and buried __________ under the tree.
2. When Will's mom took __________ to the harvest festival, we had so much fun.
3. Zac asked __________ mom to come along.
4. Amelia and Doug said __________ had never been on a hayride before.
5. Maggie decided to gather pinecones for __________ school project.
6. Caitlin wore __________ straw hat.
7. Since pumpkins can roll, we had to be careful when we carved __________.
8. My mom says __________ loves all the fall colors.
9. Ms. Thomas gave me a ride on __________ tractor.
10. My friend and __________ earn money by raking leaves for our neighbors.
11. __________ put our heads in the cold water to bob for apples.
12. Joey gave out invitations for __________ harvest party.
13. My family sells pumpkins that are grown in __________ garden.
14. After I bake all the pies, I will give __________ to my friends.
15. Farmer Fred says __________ will have a good harvest this year.

 • Key p. 307

Name ____________________

Date ____________________

All Wrapped Up

Write the letter of the word that completes each statement.

1. A scale is used to measure __________.
2. The mummy weighs about 150 __________.
3. The wing of a bat measures about 10 __________.
4. A ruler is used to measure __________.
5. To wrap the mummy, you need about 10 __________ of bandages.
6. The mummy is about 6 __________ tall.
7. A cup is used to measure __________.
8. The mummy drinks 16 ounces, or a __________, of milk every day.
9. In two days, the mummy drinks a __________ of milk.
10. A __________ can weigh about 4 pounds.
11. In her large kettle, the old woman made 2 __________ of her magical brew.
12. The mummy drank a __________ of the old woman's brew.
13. A __________ weighs many tons.
14. The bat flew 3 __________ from the cave to the cemetery.
15. A feather from a black crow weighs less than a(n) __________.

H. feet
D. weight
N. jack-o'-lantern
I. gallons
U. haunted house
S. pounds
E. yards
G. inches
F. miles
J. quart
R. capacity
L. length
B. ounce
O. pint
M. cup

Who did the mummy take to the dance?

To solve the riddle, write each letter from above on its matching numbered line or lines below.

__ __ __ "__ __ __ __ __ - __ __ __ __ __ __"
6 11 2 3 6 8 13 4 14 7 11 5 10 1

Name________________________

Date________________________

Bogus Birds

Read each statement. If the statement is a fact, color the turkey with the matching number. If the statement is an opinion, do not color the turkey.

1. Farmer Fred has owned his farm for 15 years.
2. More people should be vegetarians.
3. The best-tasting turkeys are raised on Farmer Fred's farm.
4. Farmer Fred wears boots and a straw hat.
5. The barnyard is too noisy during the day.
6. The largest turkey on the farm weighs 40 pounds.
7. There are 15 turkeys on Farmer Fred's farm.
8. The best way to cook a turkey is to fry it.
9. Last summer Farmer Fred won a ribbon for his turkeys.
10. Turkeys are silly-looking birds.
11. The farmer's dog sleeps on the porch.
12. Farmer Fred should eat a hamburger instead of turkey for Thanksgiving.
13. Turkeys do not have pretty feathers.
14. Farmer Fred drives a blue tractor.
15. Thanksgiving is always in November.

 • Key p. 307

Name ______________________________

Date ______________

Monster Math

 Note to the teacher: Use with "Monster Math" on page 13.

Name ____________________

Date ____________________

Costume Calculations

Fill in the blanks with the number of letters in each costume's name. Then complete the line plot and answer the questions.

5 clown

___ vampire

___ hippie

___ cowboy

___ princess

___ ninja

___ cheerleader

___ pirate

___ superhero

___ football player

___ black cat

___ doctor

___ chef

___ nurse

___ rock star

___ skeleton

___ knight

___ ladybug

___ zombie

___ fairy

Number of Letters in Each Costume's Name

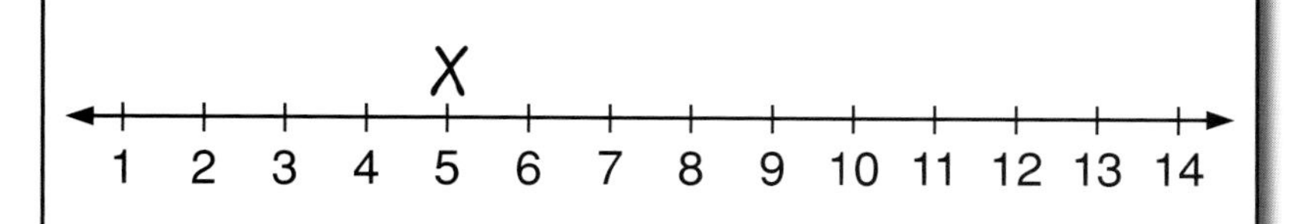

1. What do you notice when you observe the line plot? ____________________
2. What is the mean for the set of data? ____________________
3. What is the mode for the set of data? ____________________
4. What is the median for the set of data? ____________________
5. What is the range for the set of data? ____________________
6. Is there an outlier in the set of data? If so, what is it? ____________________
7. If you take the outlier out, does the mean change? If so, how? ____________________
8. If you take the outlier out, does the mode change? Why or why not? ____________________
9. If you take the outlier out, does the median change? Why or why not? ____________________
10. If a new costume were added to the list, how many letters do you think it would have in its name? ____________________

SKILLS FOR THE SEASON

Designer Duds
Possible outcomes

Students learn to make organized lists using their own lines of elf clothing. Have each student use a copy of the elf clothing patterns on page 26 to design three hats, two pairs of shoes, and four vests for his collection. Next, have the child cut out the patterns and create possible combinations, listing each one as shown. To extend the lesson, ask the student to remove one item, such as a vest, and recalculate the possible combinations.

Brooke Beverly, Dudley Elementary, Dudley, MA

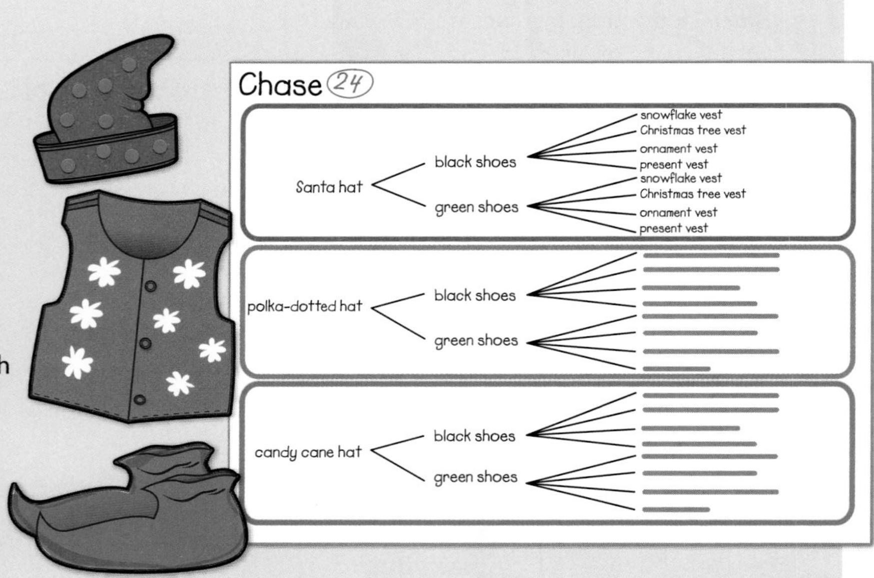

Let's Go Shopping!
Multiplying by percents

For this seasonal shopping activity, gather a class supply of store flyers and program index cards with discount percentages. Next, announce a set amount of money each student is allowed to spend. Give students time to browse the ads and choose items they could buy without exceeding the set amount. Then randomly distribute the programmed coupons. Have each child find each item's discounted price and calculate her total savings. If time allows, have students trade coupons and go shopping again!

Tracy Gatto, Robert Vernam School, Arverne, NY

Recycled Greetings

Prepositional phrases

Want to put those used holiday greeting cards to use? Try this! Have each student cut apart a card and discard the back portion. Instruct the child to study the picture on the front of his card. Then, on a sheet of paper, have him write five sentences, each containing a prepositional phrase that describes the picture on the card. Next, have each student circle the prepositional phrases. Then collect and display the pictures. Finally, have each student share his sentences and challenge his classmates to spot his card.

Anne Williams, Twin Hickory Elementary, Glen Allen, VA

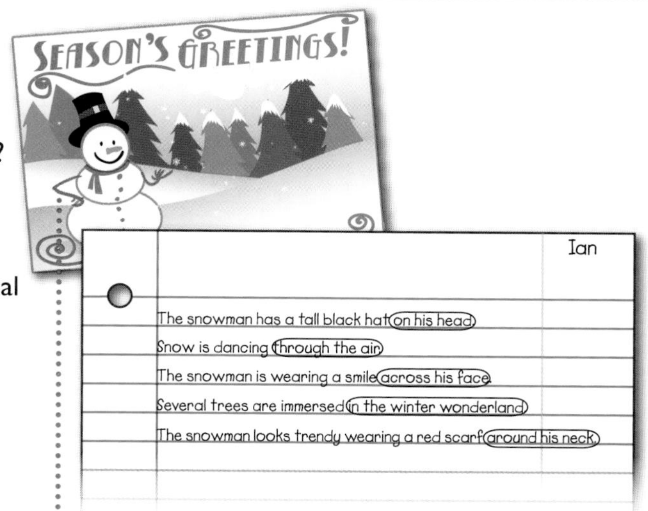

Time for a Change!

Collecting and graphing data

Take resolution-making to a whole new level with this graphing activity. To begin, ask each student to write a New Year's resolution (anonymously) on a slip of paper. Then collect the resolutions and give each child a copy of page 27. Next, read a resolution aloud and have students decide which category on the tally chart the resolution belongs in. Guide each child to make a tally mark beside the corresponding category. After all the resolutions have been tallied, have each student create a pictograph to represent the class data.

Susan Rakay, Academy of Southfield, Southfield, MI

This year, I am going to be nicer to my little brother.

Final Answer?

Reviewing any subject

Celebrate Trivia Day (January 4) with a challenge to write trivia questions that review curricular facts. First, select a unit or topic to review. Next, show students the question format from a familiar trivia game. Then have each student write on an index card a trivia question about the topic, jotting the answer on the back. Collect the cards. To play, divide the class into two teams. In turn, ask each team a trivia question and give students 15 seconds to come up with an answer. If the team is correct, award a point. If the team is incorrect, give the other team a chance to name the correct answer and steal the point. After all the questions have been asked, declare the team with more points the day's trivia champs!

What is the name for a behavior or body part that helps an animal survive in its environment?

a) camouflage
b) mimicry
c) adaptation
d) instinct

adaptation

Name ____ **Ordered pairs**

Date ______________________

Time for Traditions

Plot each coordinate pair. Connect the points, in order, to reveal a popular Hanukkah toy. Then unscramble the letters to tell how to play.

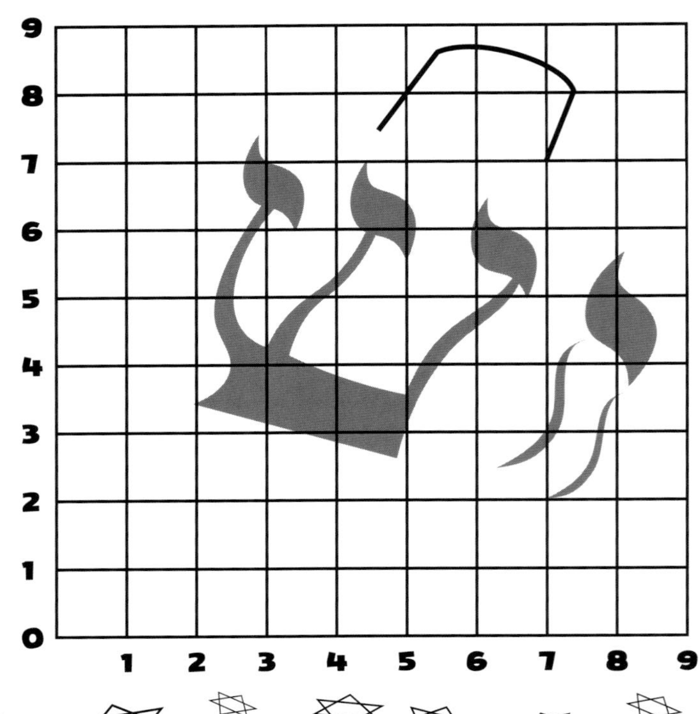

(6, 7), (3, 8), (1, 3), (6, 2), (8, 7), (7, 7)
(8, 7), (9, 5), (7, 1), (6, 2), (4, 0)
(1, 3), (4, 0), (7, 1)

How to play this Hanukkah game:

I D S D H E E T R P E N L I

___ ___ ___ ___

___ ___ ___

___ ___ ___ ___ ___ ___ ___ !

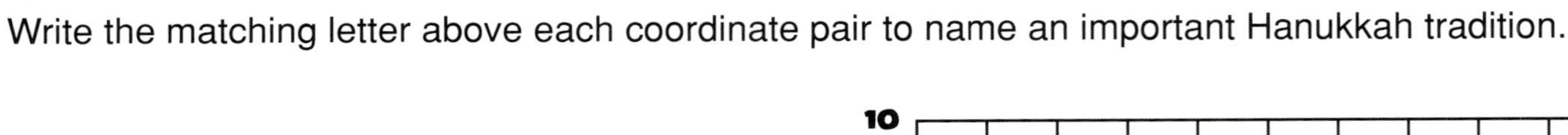

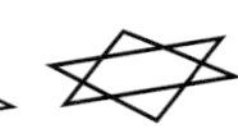
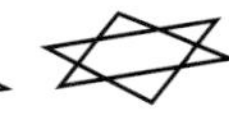

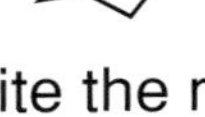

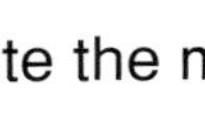
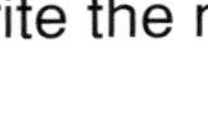

Write the matching letter above each coordinate pair to name an important Hanukkah tradition.

___ (1, 1) ___ (5, 3) ___ (1, 9) ___ (7, 2) ___ (2, 6) ___ (5, 3) ___ (3, 5) ___ (1, 9)

___ (8, 8) ___ (9, 1) ___ (7, 5)

___ (4, 7) ___ (5, 6) ___ (3, 5) ___ (6, 5) ___ (3, 7) ___ (7, 8) ___ (4, 9)

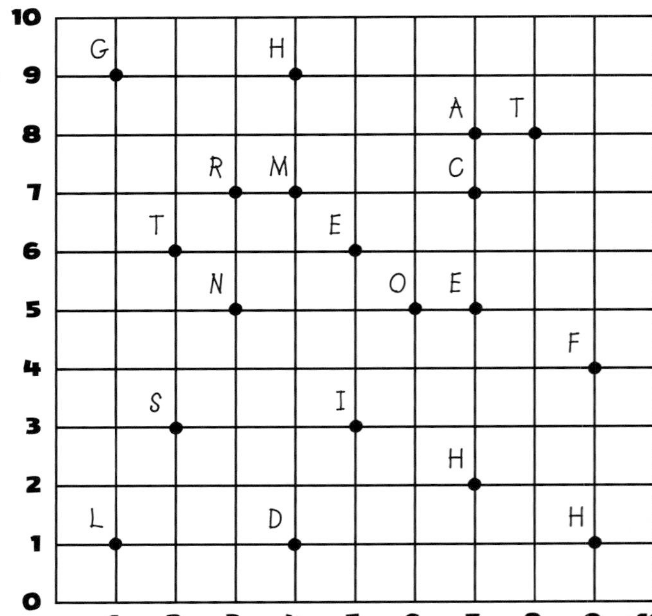

Bonus Box: Using the bottom grid, write the coordinate pairs that spell the following Hanukkah-related words: *eight nights, oil, candles, shamash,* and *gifts.*

Name ____________________________________

Date ______________________

Down the Snowy Slope

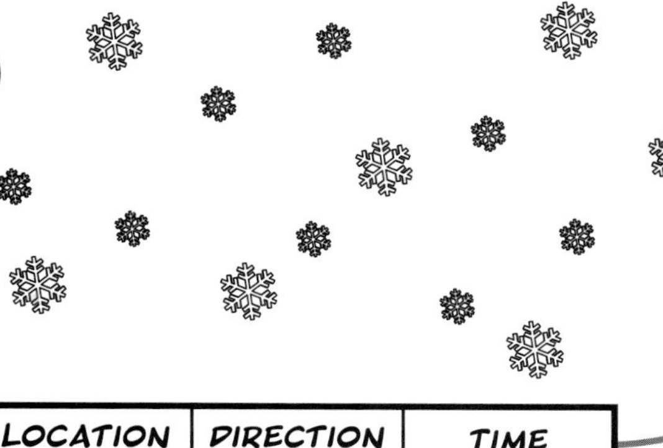

Circle the preposition and underline the prepositional phrase in each sentence. Then check the box that tells what the preposition describes.

	LOCATION (where something is)	DIRECTION (where something is going)	TIME (when something takes place)
1. Snow had fallen throughout the night.			
2. John and Kari dashed into a winter wonderland.			
3. They started making a giant snowman, rolling snowballs up the hill.			
4. They kept rolling snowballs until noon.			
5. Then they propped the colossal snowballs beside a tree.			
6. Kari and John ran back to their house.			
7. After that, a curious squirrel appeared.			
8. The squirrel jumped on a snowball, and the snowball began rolling.			
9. The snowball rolled faster, whizzing down the hill.			
10. Before long, Kari and John saw what was happening.			
11. The snowball and the squirrel were rolling toward the icy pond.			
12. Kari hoped the snowball would stop at the pond's edge.			
13. It didn't; the snowball plopped in the water.			
14. For several seconds, John and Kari scanned the water's surface.			
15. Then they saw the snowball and the wet squirrel floating to the surface.			

Key p. 307

Name ______________________________

Date ______________

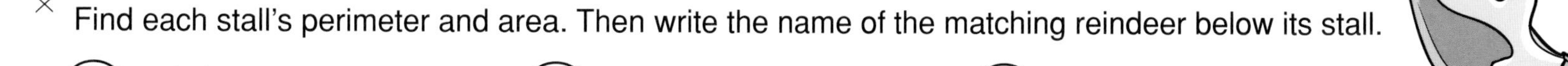

Reindeer Renovations

Find each stall's perimeter and area. Then write the name of the matching reindeer below its stall.

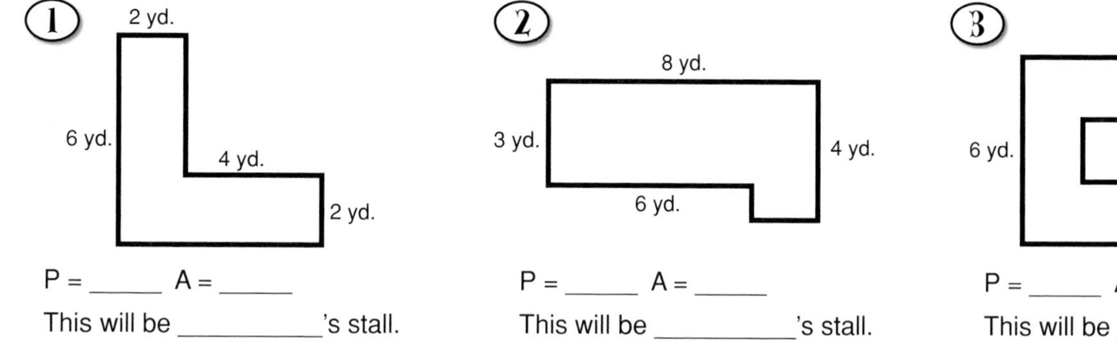

1. P = _____ A = _____
   This will be __________'s stall.

2. P = _____ A = _____
   This will be __________'s stall.

3. P = _____ A = _____
   This will be __________'s stall.

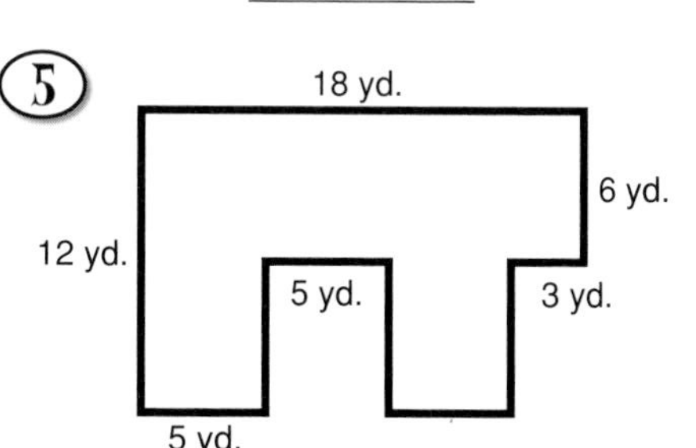

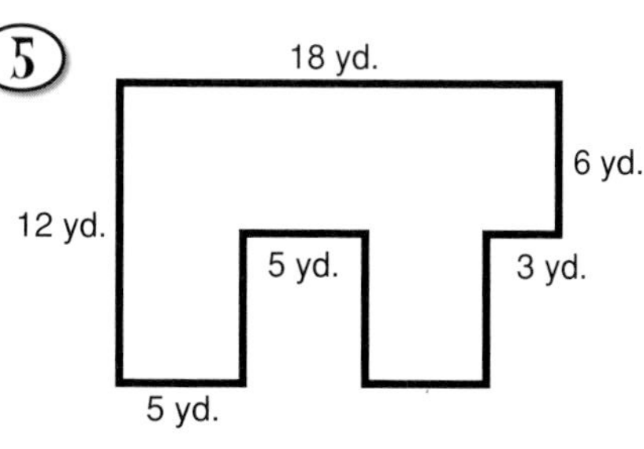

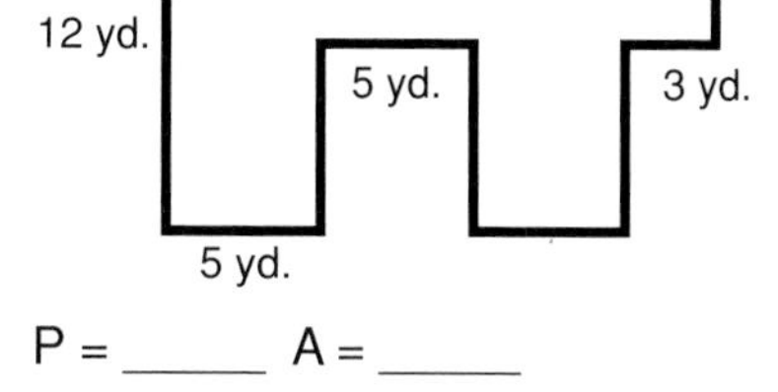

4. P = _____ A = _____
   This will be __________'s stall.

5. P = _____ A = _____
   This will be __________'s stall.

6. P = _____ A = _____
   This will be __________'s stall.

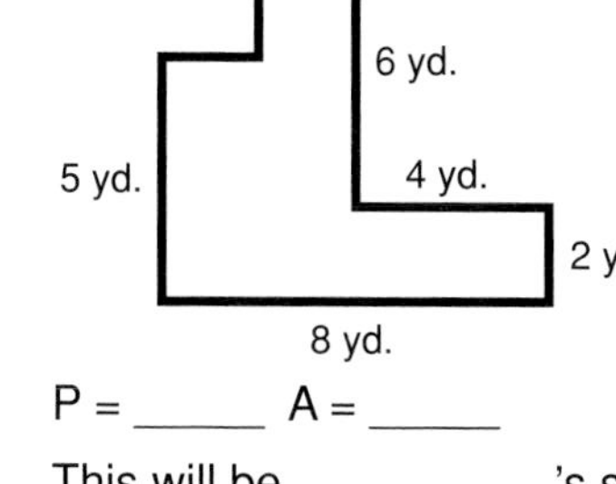

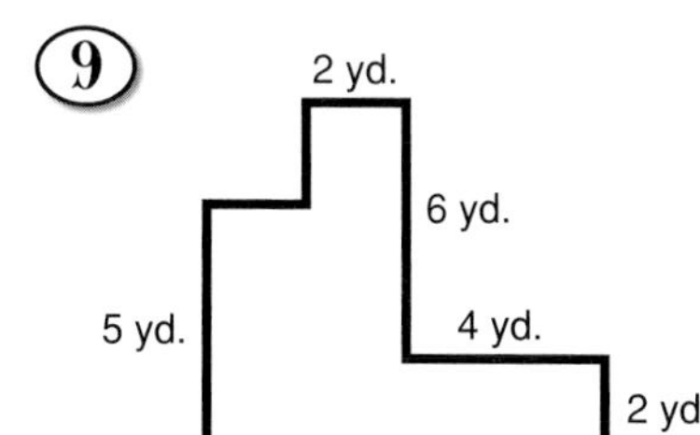

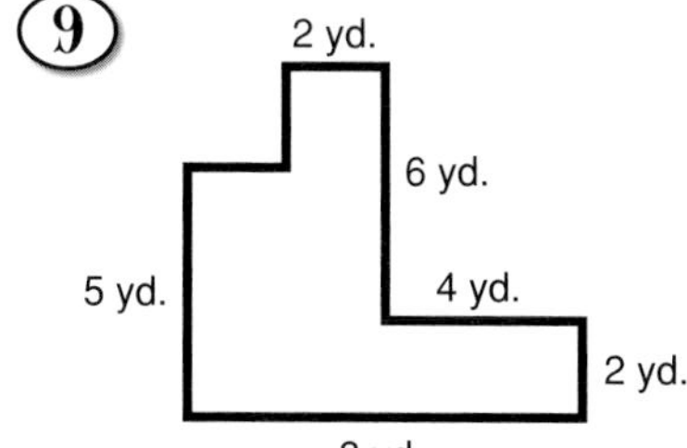

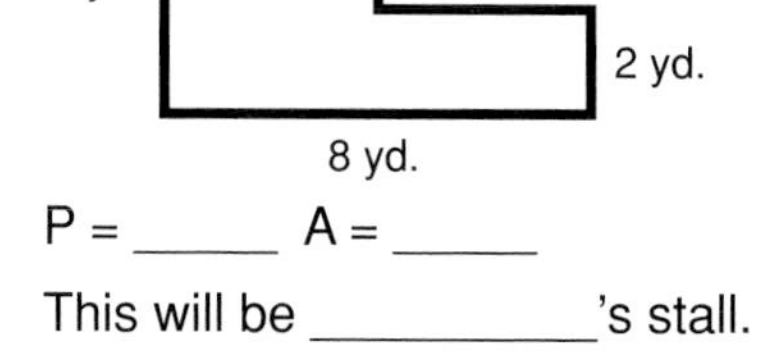

7. P = _____ A = _____
   This will be __________'s stall.

8. P = _____ A = _____
   This will be __________'s stall.

9. P = _____ A = _____
   This will be __________'s stall.

Dasher	P = 48 yd.
Comet	A = 26 yd.^{2}
Dancer	P = 40 yd.
Cupid	P = 32 yd.
Prancer	A = 20 yd.^{2}
Donner	A = 81 yd.^{2}
Vixen	P = 72 yd.
Blitzen	A = 23 yd.^{2}
Rudolph	P = 38 yd.

Name ____________________

Date ____________________

Marching for Freedom

Read the passage. Then use the boldfaced words to complete the puzzle below.

Bonus Box: Use the boldfaced words to write a poem about Martin Luther King Jr.

Martin Luther King Jr. was a leader of the civil rights **movement** in the 1950s and 1960s. He believed no one should **discriminate** because of race. King was a **dynamic** speaker. In his speeches, he would **advocate** that all people should have equal rights. Martin Luther King's goal was to **abolish** unfair laws in the southern states. King and other civil rights leaders organized peaceful **protests.** King helped **unite** people to work toward civil rights for all. On April 4, 1968, Martin Luther King was **assassinated.** People from all over the world **mourned** his death.

Across

2. acts of strong objection
3. to treat someone differently for reasons other than that person's character
5. felt great sadness
7. to speak in favor of something
8. killed

Down

1. people working together for one purpose
3. powerful, energetic
4. to bring to an end
6. to bring together

 Key p. 307

Elf Clothing Patterns

Use with "Designer Duds" on page 20.

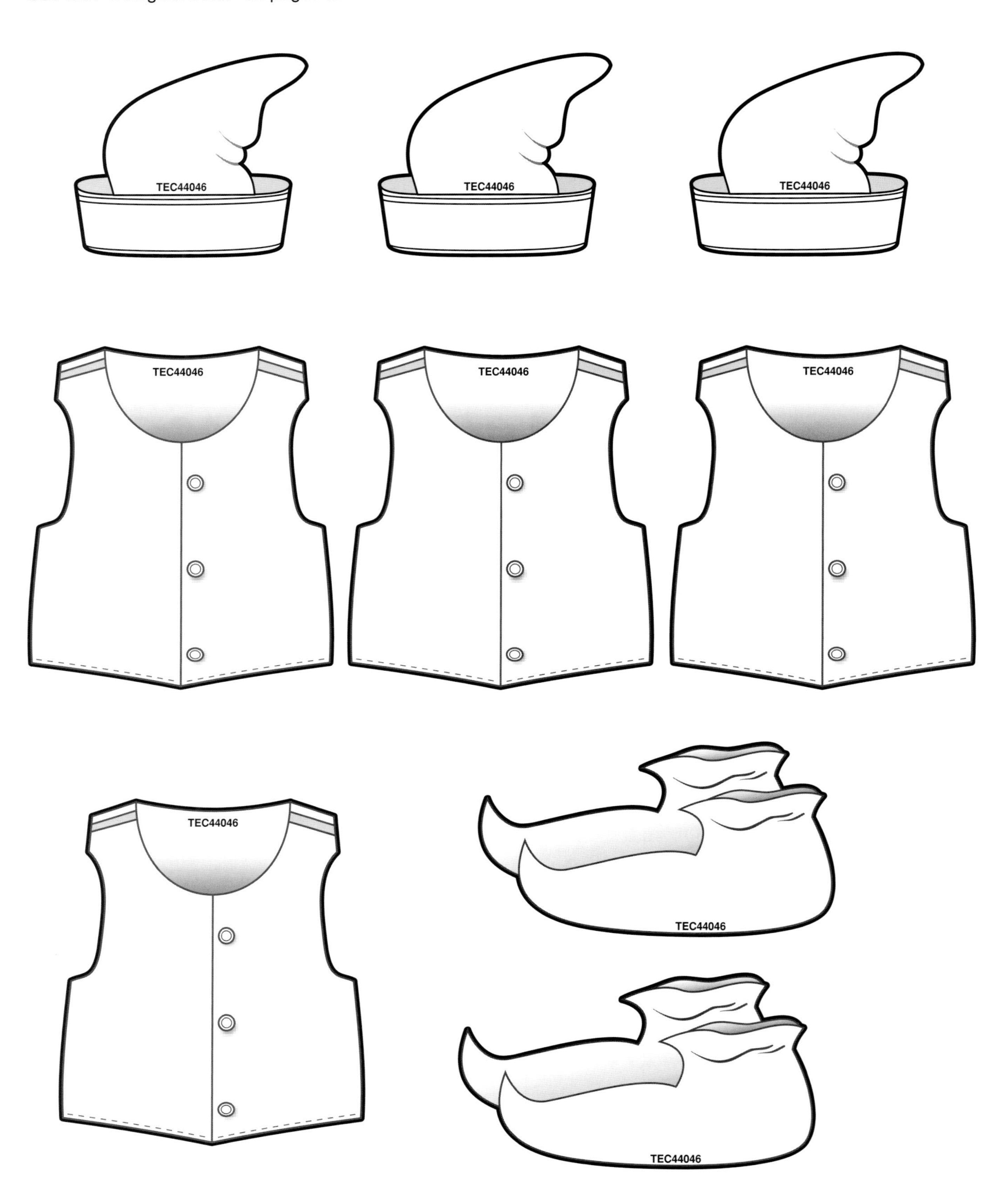

Name ______________________________

Date ______________________

Time for a Change!

Tally Chart for Types of New Year's Resolutions

RESOLUTION CATEGORY	NUMBER OF STUDENTS
improve work habits	
improve character	
become more healthy	
become more organized	
other	

HAPPY NEW YEAR! HAPPY NEW YEAR! HAPPY NEW YEAR!

____

title

y axis label

Key

= ______________

category category category category category

____

x axis label

Note to the teacher: Use with "Time for a Change!" on page 21.

SKILLS FOR THE SEASON

Flip the Flap

Research

Looking for an idea to commemorate Black History Month? Have each child research an important Black American, identifying the most important event in the person's life, two personality traits, and an interesting fact. Then have the child trim two sheets of construction paper to make nine-inch squares. Next, the student folds one square along both diagonals. He cuts along each diagonal, starting at the center and stopping one inch from each corner. He folds up each flap and trims the tip, leaving a square space in the center. Then the child labels the flaps, as shown, and glues the paper's edges onto the second square. Under each flap, the student records the matching facts. In the center space, he draws the person and then shares his work with a partner.

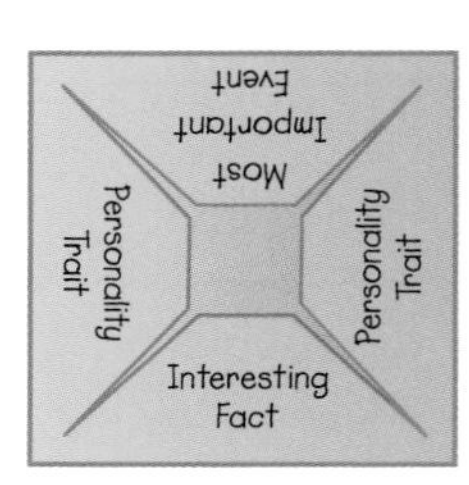

Presidential Fractions

- 1/5 Tyler, Grant
- 2/7 Jackson, Lincoln, Johnson, Harding, Kennedy, Johnson, Clinton
- 1/4 Polk, McKinley, Taft, Ford, Bush, Bush
- 3/10 Washington
- 1/3 Jefferson, Arthur, Cleveland, Wilson, Truman, Carter
- 3/8 Van Buren, Harrison, Fillmore, Buchanan, Garfield, Harrison
- 2/5 Adams, Adams, Taylor, Hayes, Nixon
- 3/7 Madison
- 4/9 Roosevelt, Roosevelt
- 1/2 Monroe, Pierce, Coolidge, Hoover, Eisenhower, Reagan
- 3/5 Obama

Presidential Puzzler

Comparing, ordering fractions

Celebrate Presidents' Day with this cross-curricular activity. To begin, post a list of the U.S. presidents' names. Next, have each pair of students create a fraction to describe the part of each surname that is made up of the vowels *a, e, i, o,* and *u.* Then guide the duo to compare and order the fractions. Finally, have the partners arrange the presidents' names in order from smallest fraction to largest.

adapted from an idea by Jennifer Otter, Oak Ridge, NC

Heartbreaker

Review game

For this fun-to-play class game, program heart-shaped cards with point values from 5 to 100. Program four more heart-shaped cards "Heart-breaker!" and shuffle the cards. Then divide students into two teams and announce a question from a current unit of study. The first group to correctly answer the question draws a card and earns the number of points listed. If the team draws a heart-breaker card, subtract half of the team's points. Continue playing until one team reaches a predetermined number of points.

Mary Baker, Yuma, CO

Detail Oriented

Identifying facts and opinions

Here's a ready-to-use idea that puts the focus on Women's History Month. Have each child number a paper from 1 to 22. Next, read the statements from page 33 aloud one at a time, pausing for each child to write "fact" or "opinion" on her paper. Then discuss the correct answers.

Easy as Pi!

Geometry, circles

March 14, Pi Day, is the perfect day to review important circle concepts. To begin, have each child cut out the pie shapes from a copy of page 34. Then guide the student to follow the directions shown for each pie shape. To extend the activity, have each student fold over about one-third of each pie to create and then measure a chord.

Gail Peckumn, Jefferson, IA

Steps:

1. Fold a pie in half and open it back up.
2. Fold the pie in half again, in the opposite direction. Open the pie back up.
3. Draw a black dot in the center. Trace a diameter in red. Trace a radius in blue.
5. Measure the pie's radius and diameter in centimeters. Record each length.
6. Multiply the diameter by 3.14, pi, to find the pie's circumference. Record the circumference.
7. Repeat with the rest of the pies.

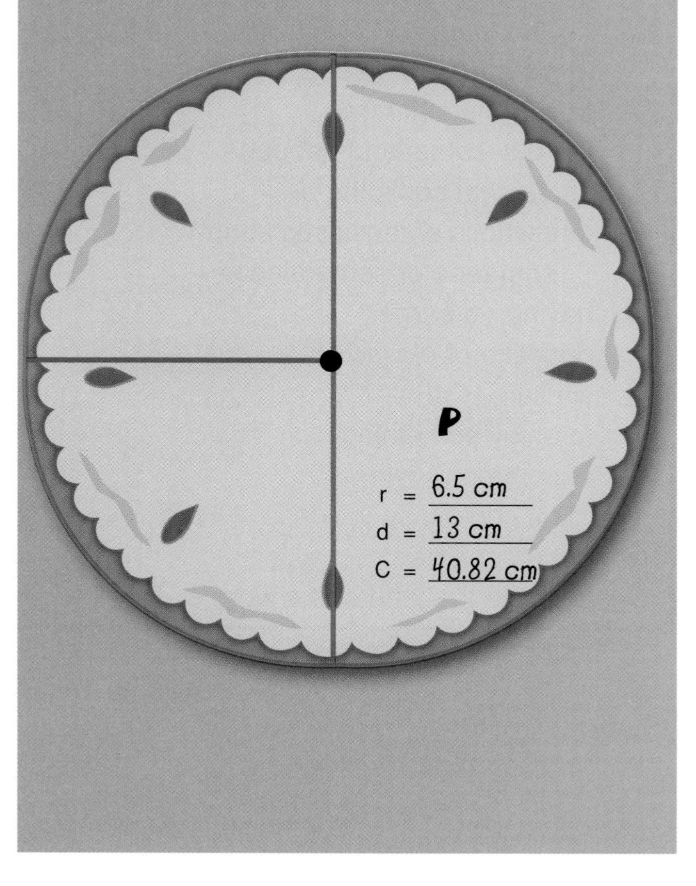

Name ______________________________

Date ____________________

First in Flight

To name two famous Black Americans who traveled in space, write each circled letter on the matching numbered line or lines below.

On the lines, write the word that matches both clues.

1. side of a river
   place to deposit money
2. to obstruct
   treat made by cooking fruit
3. marine mammal with flippers
   to tightly close something
4. used to measure length
   leader of a country
5. to put in a certain place
   twig
6. place for washing hands
   opposite of *float*

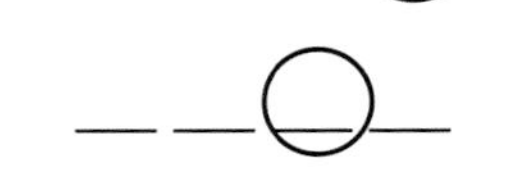

7. 16 ounces
   to hit hard

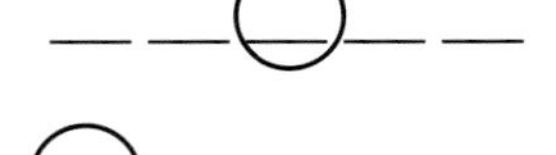

8. third month of the year
   to step together in rhythm
9. surface of the earth
   rubbed into smaller pieces

10. newspapers and magazines
    to push or squeeze

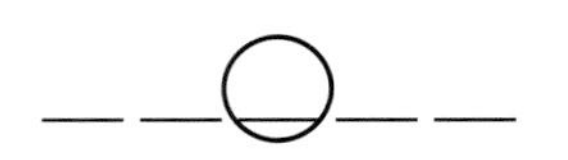

11. fruit of the palm tree
    the day something happens

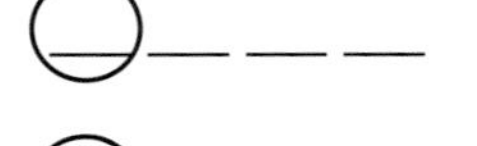

12. object that cools the air
    one who is enthusiastic about
    someone or something

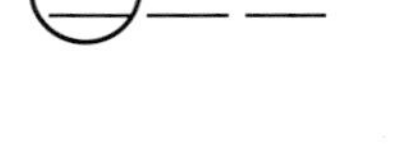

13. having no barrier
    opposite of *closed*

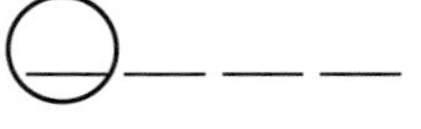

14. similar
    to enjoy something

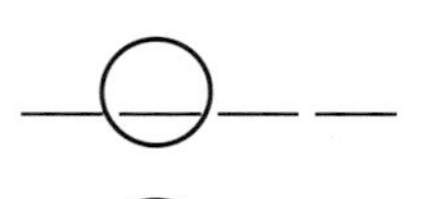

15. uncommon
    meat cooked so inside is still red

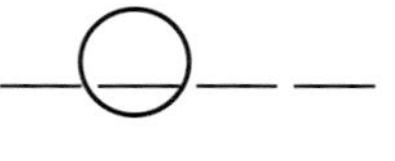

16. period of time
    to name the letters of a word

First Black American to travel in space
(aboard the space shuttle
Challenger, 1983)

___ ___ ___ ___ ___ ___.
9 7 14 13 6 3

___ ___ ___ ___ ___ ___ ___ ___ ___.
1 16 7 12 13 4 11 2 4

First Black American woman to travel in space
(aboard the space shuttle
Endeavor, 1992)

___ ___ ___ ___.
8 15 10 5

___ ___ ___ ___ ___ ___ ___
2 10 8 14 3 13 6

Word Bank

RARE	JAM	POUND	RULER
PRESS	OPEN	STICK	BANK
SINK	GROUND	DATE	FAN
SPELL	SEAL	MARCH	LIKE

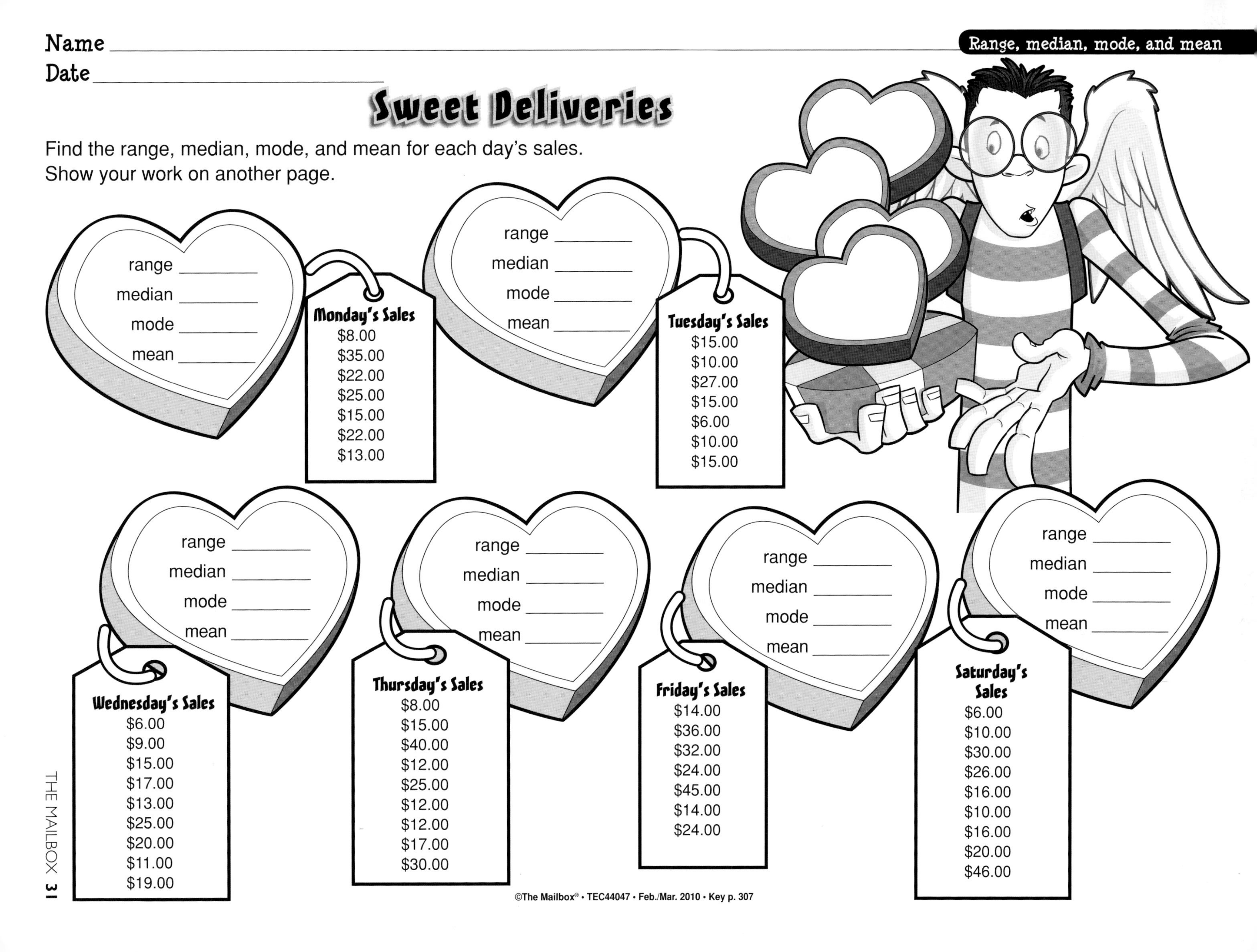

Name ____________________

Date ____________________

Sweet Deliveries

Find the range, median, mode, and mean for each day's sales.
Show your work on another page.

Monday's Sales
$8.00
$35.00
$22.00
$25.00
$15.00
$22.00
$13.00

range ______
median ______
mode ______
mean ______

Tuesday's Sales
$15.00
$10.00
$27.00
$15.00
$6.00
$10.00
$15.00

range ______
median ______
mode ______
mean ______

Wednesday's Sales
$6.00
$9.00
$15.00
$17.00
$13.00
$25.00
$20.00
$11.00
$19.00

range ______
median ______
mode ______
mean ______

Thursday's Sales
$8.00
$15.00
$40.00
$12.00
$25.00
$12.00
$12.00
$17.00
$30.00

range ______
median ______
mode ______
mean ______

Friday's Sales
$14.00
$36.00
$32.00
$24.00
$45.00
$14.00
$24.00

range ______
median ______
mode ______
mean ______

Saturday's Sales
$6.00
$10.00
$30.00
$26.00
$16.00
$10.00
$16.00
$20.00
$46.00

range ______
median ______
mode ______
mean ______

 Key p. 307

Name ____

Date ______________________

A FINE LINE

Shade the coin next to each correct answer.

1. ∠KEH is
- ◯ obtuse
- ◯ right
- ◯ acute

2. ∠QNM is
- ◯ right
- ◯ acute
- ◯ obtuse

3. ∠BEI is
- ◯ acute
- ◯ obtuse
- ◯ right

4. ∠QNO is
- ◯ obtuse
- ◯ acute
- ◯ right

5. ∠ABQ is
- ◯ obtuse
- ◯ right
- ◯ acute

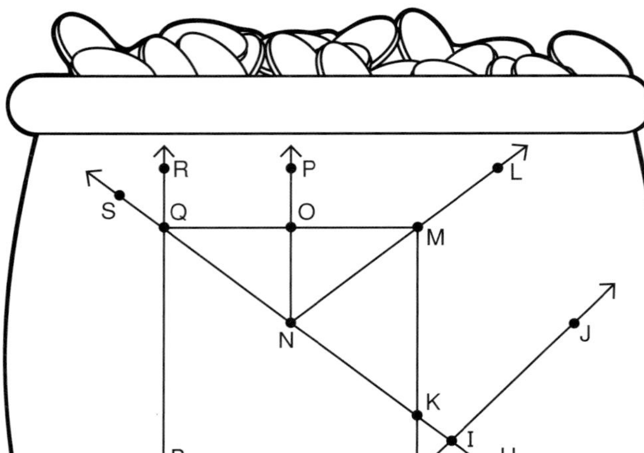

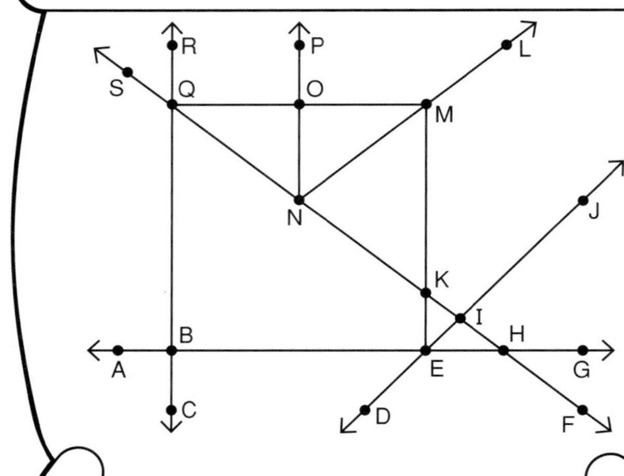

6. ∠EHI is
- ◯ acute
- ◯ obtuse
- ◯ right

7. ∠IHG is
- ◯ right
- ◯ obtuse
- ◯ acute

8. ∠QBE is
- ◯ acute
- ◯ obtuse
- ◯ right

9. $\overline{ME}$ and $\overline{BH}$ are
- ◯ parallel
- ◯ perpendicular
- ◯ intersecting

10. $\overline{ME}$ and $\overline{QB}$ are
- ◯ perpendicular
- ◯ parallel
- ◯ intersecting

11. $\overrightarrow{KF}$ and $\overrightarrow{EG}$ are
- ◯ parallel
- ◯ perpendicular
- ◯ intersecting

12. $\overleftrightarrow{RC}$ and $\overleftrightarrow{AG}$ are
- ◯ intersecting
- ◯ parallel
- ◯ perpendicular

13. Name four line segments. ____

14. Name four rays. ____

15. Name two lines. ____

Women's History: Fact or Opinion?

1. Sixteen-year-old Sybil Ludington was a Revolutionary War heroine. She rode 40 miles in the dark to round up her father's troops.
2. It would have been exciting to go to the first women's rights meeting in Seneca Falls, New York, in 1848.
3. Sojourner Truth was the first black woman to give antislavery speeches.
4. Clara Barton, the best nurse of the Civil War, worked on the battlefields.
5. Loreta Velazquez wrote the book *The Woman in Battle* about being a soldier in the Civil War.
6. In 1889, Jane Addams and Ellen Gates Starr started Hull House to help poor people.
7. Marie Curie was the greatest female scientist of the late 1800s.
8. It is so sad that Susan B. Anthony died 14 years before the 19th amendment was passed.
9. In 1912, Juliette Gordon Low started the first Girl Scout patrol in the United States.
10. Nellie Tayloe Ross should have been proud to become the first female governor in 1925.
11. Amelia Earhart, the bravest pilot of the 1920s, was the first woman to fly across the Atlantic Ocean alone.
12. Mary McLeod Bethune, founder of the National Council of Negro Women, worked with four different presidents.
13. Despite losing her sight and hearing as a baby, Helen Keller wrote books that have been translated into over 50 languages.
14. Grace Murray Hopper helped develop COBOL, a key computer programming language.
15. The most interesting book Rachel Carson wrote was *Silent Spring.*
16. Shirley Chisholm, the first woman from a major party to run for president, was also the first black woman to serve in Congress.
17. Antonia Coello Novello was the first woman and the first Hispanic American to serve as Surgeon General.
18. Everyone was surprised when Sandra Day O'Conner became the Supreme Court's first female justice.
19. In 1993, brave Ellen Ochoa boarded the shuttle *Discovery* and became the first Hispanic American woman to travel in space.
20. Rosa Parks was awarded the Presidential Medal of Freedom in 1996.
21. Condoleezza Rice, United States secretary of state from 2005 to 2009, must have loved teaching because she won a teaching award in 1984.
22. Hillary Rodham Clinton is the first wife of a former president to be elected to public office.

Note to the teacher: Use with "Detail Oriented" on page 29.

Pie Circles

Use with "Easy as Pi!" on page 29.

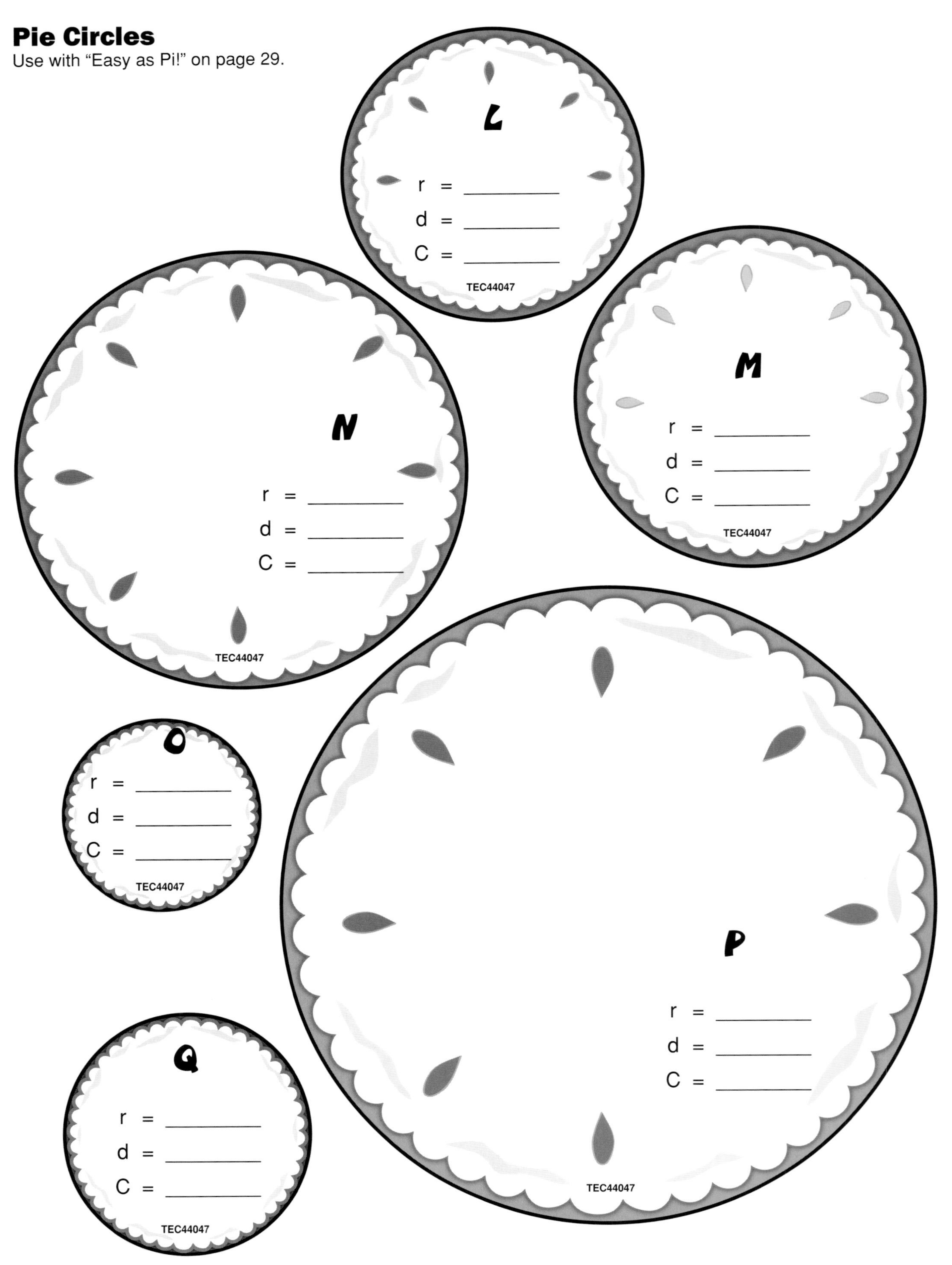

Skills for the Season

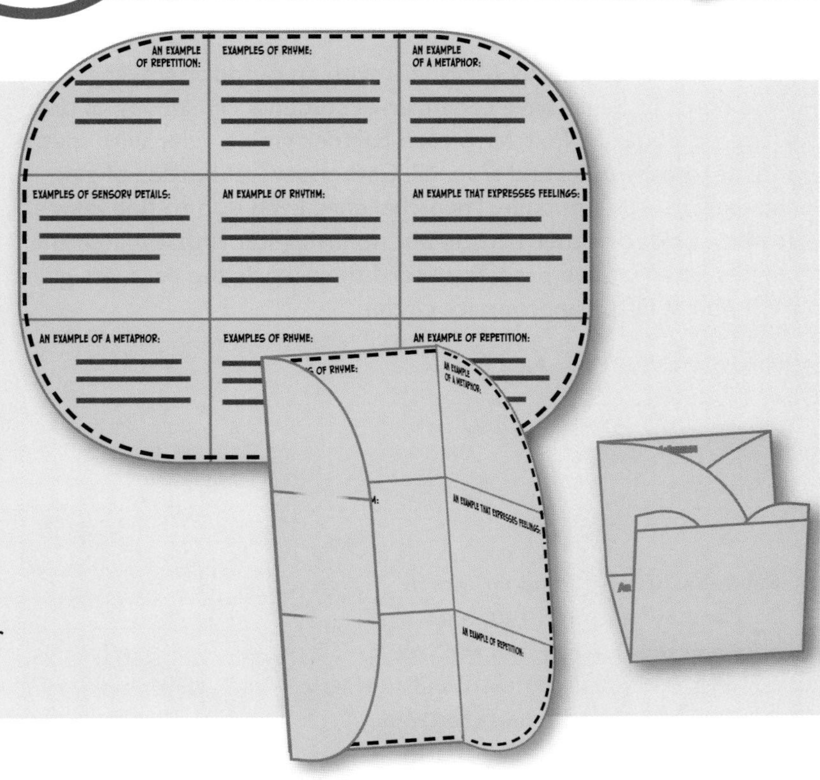

A Poetic Primer

Poetic elements

Here's an idea for early finishers that's perfect for National Poetry Month in April. Collect several books of poetry and make a class supply of page 40. When a child finishes her work early, she cuts out the pattern on the page and chooses a book. Next, she finds and records examples of the poetic elements and devices listed on the pattern. Then the student flips the pattern, copies her favorite poem, and adds a border of important images or words from the poem. Finally, she folds the pattern as shown and takes the primer home to share with her family.

Punny Transitions

Multiple-meaning words

For National Humor Month (April), read several jokes that feature puns, or plays on words. Next, guide students to analyze the pun in each joke and then brainstorm multiple-meaning words they can use to write jokes of their own. Give each pair of students three index cards and have the duo write a joke that features a pun on each one. When students finish, collect their cards and keep them handy. Throughout the month, read a few of their jokes aloud each time students line up.

WHERE DO FISH KEEP THEIR MONEY?

IN THE RIVER BANK!

Why is it so hard for a Dalmatian to hide?

(Because it's always spotted.)

How can you stop a bull from charging?

(Take away its credit card.)

Why do bears have fur coats?

(Because they'd look silly if they were bare.)

Multiple-Meaning Words Perfect for Puns

bank	bark	batter
bill	bright	charge
dough	dry	fan
foot	left	mammoth
racket	sentence	shed
spring	star	watch

For Good Measure
Measurement

Celebrate Earth Day (April 22) with an outdoor scavenger hunt! To begin, have each pair of students clip a copy of page 41 to a clipboard. Next, have each partner grab a ruler with metric and customary units and a pencil. Gather several bottles of glue and lead students outside. Then challenge each duo to find leaves, stones, sticks, or other natural but nonliving items that match the lengths listed on the page. To record their work, the partners glue each object in the appropriate circle.

Jennifer Otter, Oak Ridge, NC

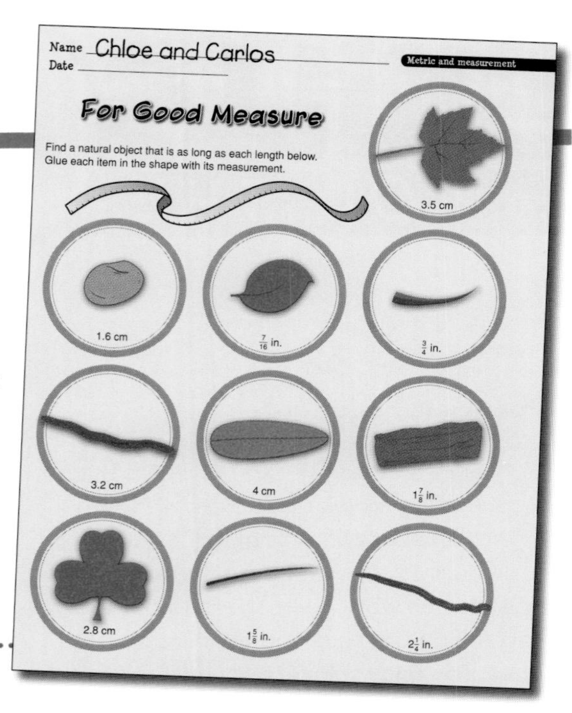

Coordinate Range	Asian-Pacific Country
between 20° north and 60° north and 60° east and 140° east	China
between the Equator and the Tropic of Cancer and 100° east and 120° east	Vietnam
between the Equator and the Tropic of Cancer and 120° east and 140° east	Philippines
between the Equator and 40° north and 60° east and 100° east	India
on the Tropic of Cancer and between 120° east and 140° east	Taiwan

Global Grid
Latitude and longitude

This map-reading idea is just right for Asian-Pacific American Heritage Month (May). Give each small group of students a world map with latitude and longitude lines. Next, read aloud the coordinate range of an Asian-Pacific country, such as those shown. Then guide students to find the coordinates and name the country or countries that lie within the coordinates. To follow up, have each student choose five more Asian-Pacific countries and list each one's coordinate range.

¡Viva México!
Research

Commemorate the anniversary of Cinco de Mayo with this research center. For the center, gather resources about Mexico, gray or tan construction paper, a ruler, scissors, glue, and a list of topics such as those shown. A student chooses a topic about Mexico and researches it. Then he cuts out two 4" x 4" construction paper squares and trims the edges so they look like blocks from an ancient Mexican pyramid. On one block, the student lists his topic, sources, and his name. On the other block, the child summarizes his research. Then each student arranges his blocks on a board to create a step pyramid as shown.

Topics About Mexico

agriculture	art	climate
economy	education	family life
flag	government	holidays
industry	landforms	landmarks
music	natural resources	population
regions of Mexico	traditional clothing	Spanish conquest

Name ______________________________

Date ____________________

Fun and Games

Write a fraction in each blank to answer each question. Write each fraction in its simplest form.

1. The royal jester, Jack, plants 15 phony mice in different rooms in the castle. There are 50 rooms.

   What is the probability the prince will walk into a room that has a fake mouse? _______
   What is the probability he will walk into a room without a fake mouse? _______

2. Jack loves to juggle hard-boiled eggs. The princess replaces some of the hard-boiled eggs with fresh ones. There are 10 hard-boiled eggs and 6 fresh eggs.

   What is the probability Jack will grab a fresh egg? _______
   What is the probability he will grab a hard-boiled egg? _______

3. The prince sticks buzzers under 3 of the chairs in the hall. There are 12 chairs in all.

   What is the probability the princess will sit on a chair without a buzzer? _______

   What is the probability she will sit on a chair with a buzzer? _______

4. Jack puts 5 garlic gumballs in the king's candy jar. There are already 11 grape, 9 gooseberry, and 10 guava gumballs in the jar.

   What is the probability the king will get a garlic gumball? _______
   What is the probability he will get a guava gumball? _______

5. Jack sneaks chocolate-covered ants into the queen's chocolates. Now there are 14 chocolate-covered raisins, 13 chocolate-covered peanuts, and 9 chocolate-covered ants in the bowl.

   What is the probability the queen will not get an ant? _______
   What is the probability she will get an ant? _______

6. The princess stuffs paper into the toes of 4 of the prince's shoes. The prince has 12 pairs of shoes.

   What is the probability he will choose a shoe stuffed with paper? _______
   What is the probability he will not choose a shoe stuffed with paper? _______

7. For his grand finale, Jack juggles 3 eggs, 6 golf balls, 2 apples, and an orange.

   If he drops one item, what is the probability it will be an egg? _______
   What is the probability it will be a golf ball? _______
   What is the probability he will not drop one of the eggs? _______
   What is the probability he will drop the orange? _______

Name ______________________________
Date ______________________

Earth Friendly?

Use a subordinating conjunction from below to recycle (rewrite) each pair of sentences as a complex sentence. Use each conjunction only once.

1. Lola Lavish could walk to work. She drives her car.
   Although Lola Lavish could walk to work, she drives her car.
2. Ben Queasy added worms to his compost. He realized worms aren't gross.
   ____
3. A tree in Ima Saver's yard died. She planted a new one.
   ____
4. Ben started recycling. There is less trash to take out on trash day.
   ____
5. Lola prefers to drive by herself. She could save gas by carpooling.
   ____
6. Ima gets a plastic shopping bag. She reuses it.
   ____
7. Ima wants to make a difference. She rides the bus instead of driving.
   ____
8. Ben plans his errands. He doesn't waste gas driving all over town.
   ____
9. Ima walks to work nearly every day. She rides her bike some days.
   ____
10. Lola doesn't seem to care about the environment. She just isn't sure what to do first. ______________________________

I know you're wiggly, but this is ridiculous!

SUBORDINATING CONJUNCTIONS

AFTER	ALTHOUGH	AS	AS LONG AS
BECAUSE	BEFORE	IF	SINCE
SO THAT	THAT	THOUGH	UNLESS
UNTIL	WHEN	WHERE	WHILE

Name ____________________

Date ____________________

In Memory

Shade the circle next to the best answer.

1. Which word is a synonym for *decide?*
Ⓠ single Ⓡ choose Ⓢ refuse

2. Which word is a synonym for *guess?*
Ⓒ believe Ⓓ prove Ⓔ speculate

3. Which word is an antonym for *accept?*
Ⓖ get Ⓗ reject Ⓘ lose

4. Which of these is a synonym for *trust?*
Ⓐ confidence Ⓑ hope Ⓒ suspicion

5. Which of these is an antonym for *warm?*
Ⓐ tepid Ⓑ chilled Ⓒ hot

6. Which word is an antonym for *calm?*
Ⓢ clear Ⓣ composed Ⓤ flustered

7. Which word is a synonym for *tired?*
Ⓣ weary Ⓤ energized Ⓥ old

8. Which of these could be used to replace *brave?*
Ⓑ fearful Ⓒ adventurous Ⓓ heroic

9. Which of these is an antonym for *strong?*
Ⓔ husky Ⓕ rugged Ⓖ delicate

10. Which of these is an antonym for *help?*
Ⓦ assist Ⓧ support Ⓨ hinder

11. Which word is a synonym for *teamwork?*
Ⓖ cooperation Ⓗ togetherness Ⓘ unite

12. Which word is an antonym for *famous?*
Ⓡ popular Ⓢ anonymous Ⓣ renowned

Bonus Box: On another sheet of paper, name an antonym and three synonyms for each of the following words: *proud, give, soldier,* and *war.*

Which famous speech is often read on Memorial Day?

To find out, write the shaded letters from above on the matching line or lines below.

__ __ __   __ __ __ __ __ __ __ __ __ __   __ __ __ __ __ __ __
7 3 2   11 2 7 7 10 12 5 6 1 9   4 8 8 1 2 12 12

Poetry Primer Pattern

Use with "A Poetic Primer" on page 35.

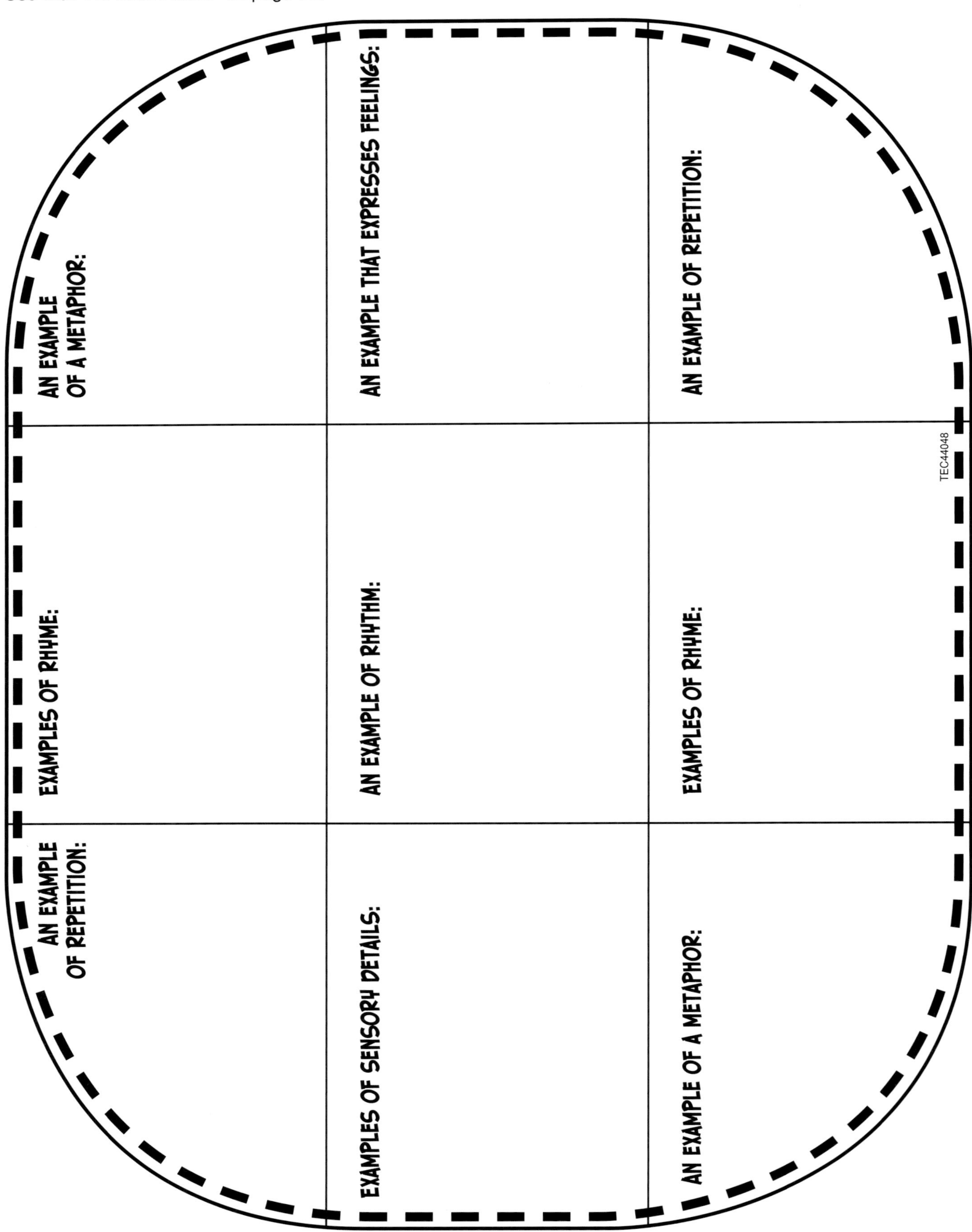

Name ______________________________

Date ____________________

For Good Measure

Find a natural object that is as long as each length below.
Glue each item in the shape with its measurement.

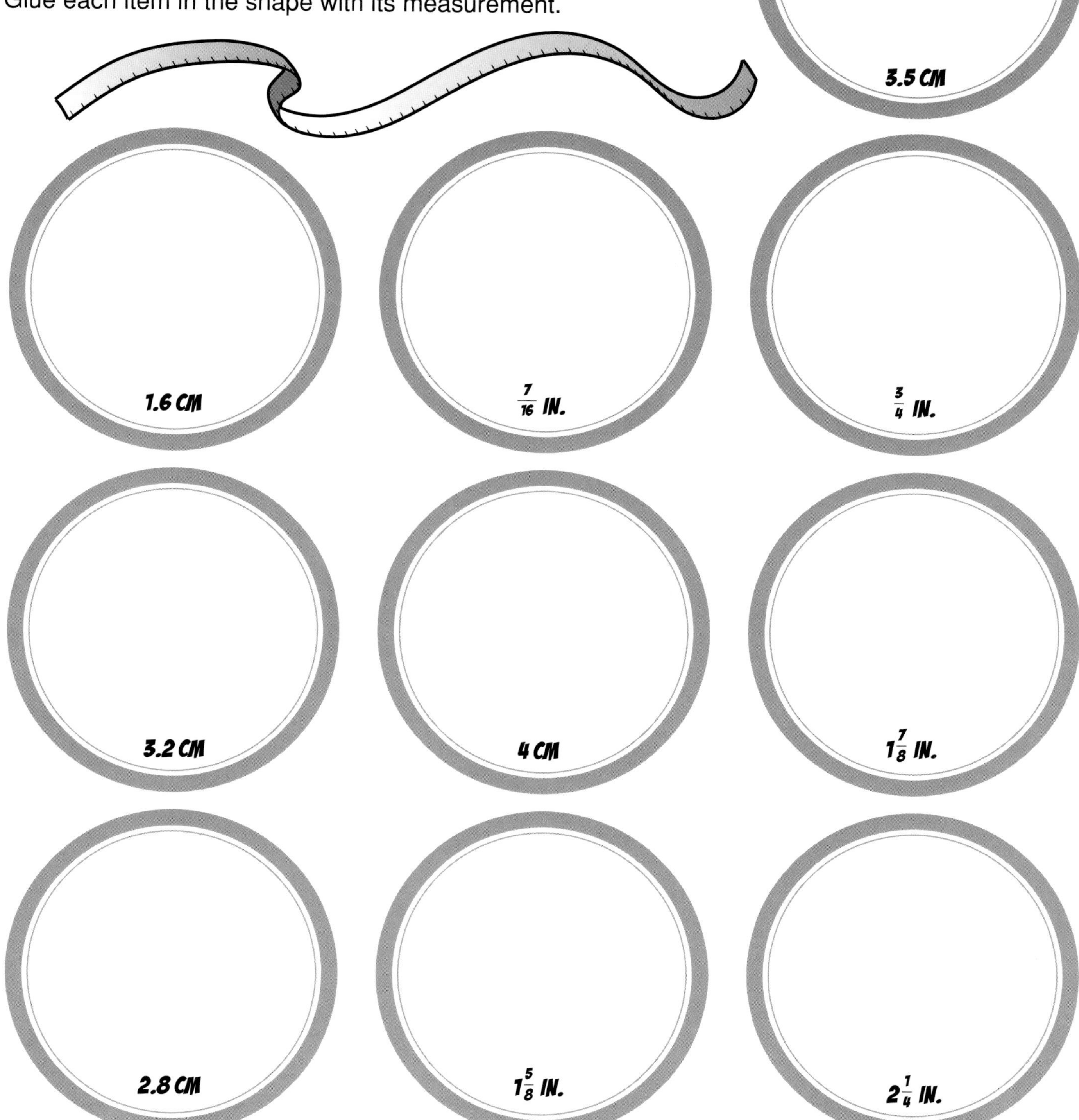

Note to the teacher: Use with "For Good Measure" on page 36.

SKILLS FOR THE SEASON

See You in the Funny Pages!

Figurative language

For this amusing end-of-the-year review, collect the comics from several editions of your daily or Sunday newspaper. Then place them at a center along with construction paper sheets labeled "Hyperbole," "Idiom," "Metaphor," "Simile," and "Personification." A pair of students reads the comics looking for figurative language. When the partners find an example, they cut out the frame or frames and tape them to the appropriately labeled sheet. After all students have visited the center, share each poster with the class. Then tuck the posters away and pull them out next year when it's time to teach figurative language!

Christine Hamilton, Bear Creek Intermediate, Keller, TX

Look What We've Discovered!

End of the year

Showcase students' progress with this global display! Post an enlarged copy of the explorer pattern from page 47. Then guide each child to describe in a paragraph the most interesting or challenging topic he "discovered" this year. Have each student decorate a construction paper circle to represent a globe and add it, along with his paragraph, to the display.

Julia Alarie, Williston, VT

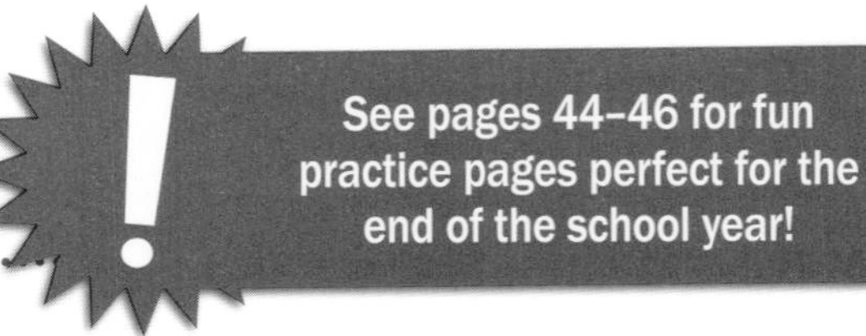
See pages 44–46 for fun practice pages perfect for the end of the school year!

Summertime Review

Mixed review

Here's a quick idea for a seasonal class review! Cut two sheets of construction paper into 3" x 2" cards. Then draw suns on 15 cards, beach umbrellas on ten cards, palm trees on eight cards, and flip-flops on the last three cards. Display the code shown and shuffle the cards. Next, divide students into two or more teams and ask a review question. Have the student who answers the question correctly draw a card from the pile. Award her team points according to the code; then ask the next question. When time is up, total the points. The team with the most points wins.

Lilibeth Brewer, St. Patrick School, Sacramento, CA

Summertime Review Point Code

sun = 1 point
beach umbrella = 2 points
palm tree = 3 points
flip-flops = Steal all the points from another team.

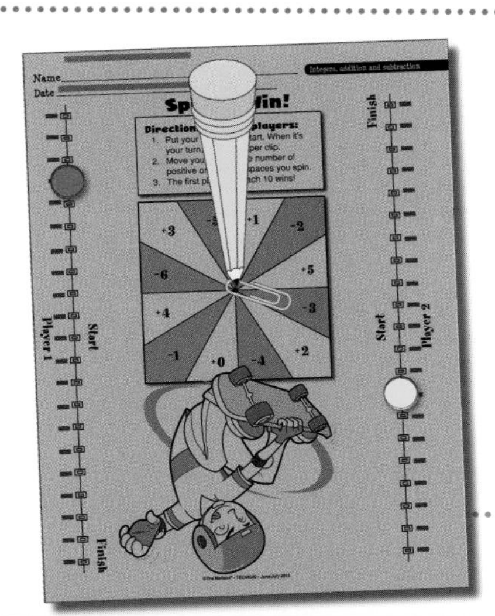

Integer Race

Integers, addition and subtraction

Want to give students an end-of-the-year math challenge? Try this partner game! Give each pair of students a copy of the gameboard from page 48, two game markers, a paper clip, and a pencil. Then guide the partners to follow the directions on the page.

Debbi Berris, Poinciana Day School, West Palm Beach, FL

Batters Up!

Prewriting, persuasive writing

This prewriting activity is based on America's favorite summer pastime! To prepare, program paper circles with persuasive prompts such as those shown. Put the prompts in a bag and divide your class into two teams. Next, have a student draw a circle from the bag and "pitch" the prompt to the other team. Give the team 15 seconds to name a supporting fact or example. If the team gives an example that supports the prompt, the team scores a home run and the other team steps up to bat. If the team does not give an example or its example does not support the prompt, the team strikes out, and the other team steps up to bat. The team with the most runs wins the game. After the game, return the circles to the bag and have each small group draw a prompt and draft a persuasive response.

Terry Healy, Marlatt Elementary, Manhattan, KS

Summer vacation is more fun for children than for parents.

It's a good idea to ban water balloon fights at school.

Persuasive Prompts

Swimming in a lake is more fun than swimming in a swimming pool.
Summer vacation is more fun for children than for parents.
Baseball and softball are the best summer games.
It's a good idea to ban water balloon fights at school.
The worst part of summer is not seeing your school friends.
Tennis is the best sport to play in the summer.

Name ____________________

Date ____________________

SURF, SAND, AND SUN

Surf Shore 348 miles

Wave Side 579 miles

Key East 965 miles

Swim City 888 miles

Use the beach signs to help you answer each question. Then circle your answer in the puzzle.

1. How much farther is it to Swim City than to Wave Side? 309 miles
2. It takes you three days to drive to Swim City. On average, about how many miles do you drive each day? ______
3. You take a round trip to Key East. Then you take a round trip to Wave Side. How many miles do you travel altogether? ______
4. On your first day of vacation, you travel $\frac{2}{3}$ of the way to Surf Shore. How many more miles do you have to go? ______
5. What is the average distance to the beaches? ______
6. How many more miles is it to the farthest beach than to the closest beach? ______
7. You take two round trips to Surf Shore. How many total miles do you travel? ______
8. You travel 438 miles on the first day and 379 miles on the second day. How many more miles do you have to travel to get to Key East? ______
9. It takes you three days to drive to Wave Side. On average, how many miles do you travel each day? ______
10. At the beach shop, you buy sunblock for $3.75, a towel for $8.99, flip-flops for $4.80, and snacks for $5.45. How much do you spend in all? ______
11. How far would you travel if you made a round trip to Surf Shore and then a round trip to Key East? ______
12. You drive one-fourth of the distance to Swim City. How far have you traveled? ______
13. Your car travels 64 miles on two gallons of gas. About how many gallons of gas will you need to drive to Key East? ______
14. Your car goes 24 miles on one gallon of gas. Gas costs $3.29 per gallon. How much will it cost you to drive to Swim City? ______

3	0	4	5	3	0	9
2	3	1	4	8	2	1
6	1	2	1	7	3	2
2	6	1	7	2	9	2
6	7	1	3	9	2	2
1	1	6	8	6	9	5
1	9	5	2	2	9	9
3	3	3	0	8	8	4

Name ______________________

Date ______________________

Step Right Up!

Read each problem. Circle *yes* if the answer is reasonable or *no* if it is not. Then explain your answer on another sheet of paper.

Problem		
1. On the first day of the carnival, there are 179,205 visitors. If attendance is about the same for six days, is it reasonable to predict that at least 600,000 people will visit the carnival? Explain.	**yes**	**no**
2. Justin has $25.00. He can buy three tickets for $4.00. Is it reasonable to say Justin can buy 25 tickets? Explain.	**yes**	**no**
3. A group of 36 children go to the dog and pony show. Of those children, $\frac{2}{3}$ buy popcorn. Would it be reasonable to say that about 26 children buy popcorn? Explain.	**yes**	**no**
4. The distance from John's house to the carnival is 5 miles. He calculates that to be 15,000 feet. Is his calculation reasonable? Explain.	**yes**	**no**
5. Abbie is the 416th person waiting in line to ride the Ferris wheel. The wheel holds 52 people, and each ride lasts 4 minutes. Is it reasonable to say Abbie will get on the ride in about 30 minutes? Explain.	**yes**	**no**
6. The lemonade stand crew sells 20 gallons of lemonade each hour. Is it reasonable to say they will sell close to 160 quarts in 8 hours? Explain.	**yes**	**no**
7. Macy sets up the balloon-popping game. She spaces the balloons 5 inches apart. She thinks she can fit about 50 balloons in a row across a 20-foot board. Is her estimate reasonable? Explain.	**yes**	**no**
8. On Monday, 2,360 children go to the carnival. Of those children, 600 slide down the Superslide. Is it reasonable to say that about $\frac{1}{4}$ of the children at the carnival on Monday go down the slide? Explain.	**yes**	**no**
9. Kaden thinks he will sell one ton of fries at the carnival over 6 days. Frozen fries come in 5-pound bags. Each day, Kaden uses 40 bags of fries. Is Kaden's estimate reasonable? Explain.	**yes**	**no**
10. Gena thinks she will sell 125,000 bags of cotton candy. She has one box of 700 cotton candy bags. She orders 105 more boxes of cotton candy bags. Is it reasonable to say that Gena will have enough cotton candy bags? Explain.	**yes**	**no**

Bonus Box: Solve each problem on another sheet of paper. Compare your answers with the estimates given.

Name ____________________

Date ____________________

SUMMER'S CALLING!

Read each sentence. Circle the verb form that completes each sentence.

1. On the last day of school, teachers and students _______ the hours until summer vacation begins. **W)** count **S)** counts	**2.** Anyone walking down the halls _______ the excitement in the air. **O)** feels **I)** feel	**3.** Colin and Grant _______ their favorite memories from the school year. **D)** shares **H)** share
4. Ms. Jones and Ms. Cox _______ our textbooks. **T)** collect **R)** collects	**5.** Each of us _______ open our report card. **A)** rips **E)** rip	**6.** Instead of eating in the cafeteria, Jack and Sophie _______ pizza. **M)** orders **D)** order
7. Michael and Avery _______ pepperoni pizza, and Sara has cheese. **L)** has **T)** have	**8.** Everyone _______ a letter to give next year's class advice! **E)** write **R)** writes	**9.** Ms. Jones _______ shaving cream on our desks so we can clean them. **T)** sprays **O)** spray
10. At recess, the boys and the girls _______ each other to a game of kickball. **N)** challenge **S)** challenges	**11.** Everybody at school _______ about their summer plans. **T)** talks **G)** talk	**12.** After recess, the fourth and fifth graders _______ in a talent show. **S)** perform **R)** performs
13. Before we leave for the day, our class _______ for its last picture. **A)** pose **E)** poses	**14.** Once all the students leave, the teachers and the principal _______ a sigh of relief. **Y)** breathes **T)** breathe	**15.** After school, the custodians and the teachers _______ the desks and chairs. **S)** stack **W)** stacks

Why did the teacher go to the beach?

To solve the riddle, write each circled letter from above on its matching numbered line or lines below.

__ __ __ (12 3 13) __ __ __ __ __ __ (1 5 10 7 13 6) __ __ (11 2)

__ __ __ __ (4 13 15 7) __ __ __ (14 3 13) __ __ __ __ __! (1 5 9 13 8)

Explorer Pattern

Use with "Look What We've Discovered!" on page 42.

Names ______________________________

Date ______________________________

Spin to Win!

Directions for two players:

1. Put your marker on Start. When it's your turn, spin the paper clip.
2. Move your marker the number of positive or negative spaces you spin.
3. The first player to reach 10 wins!

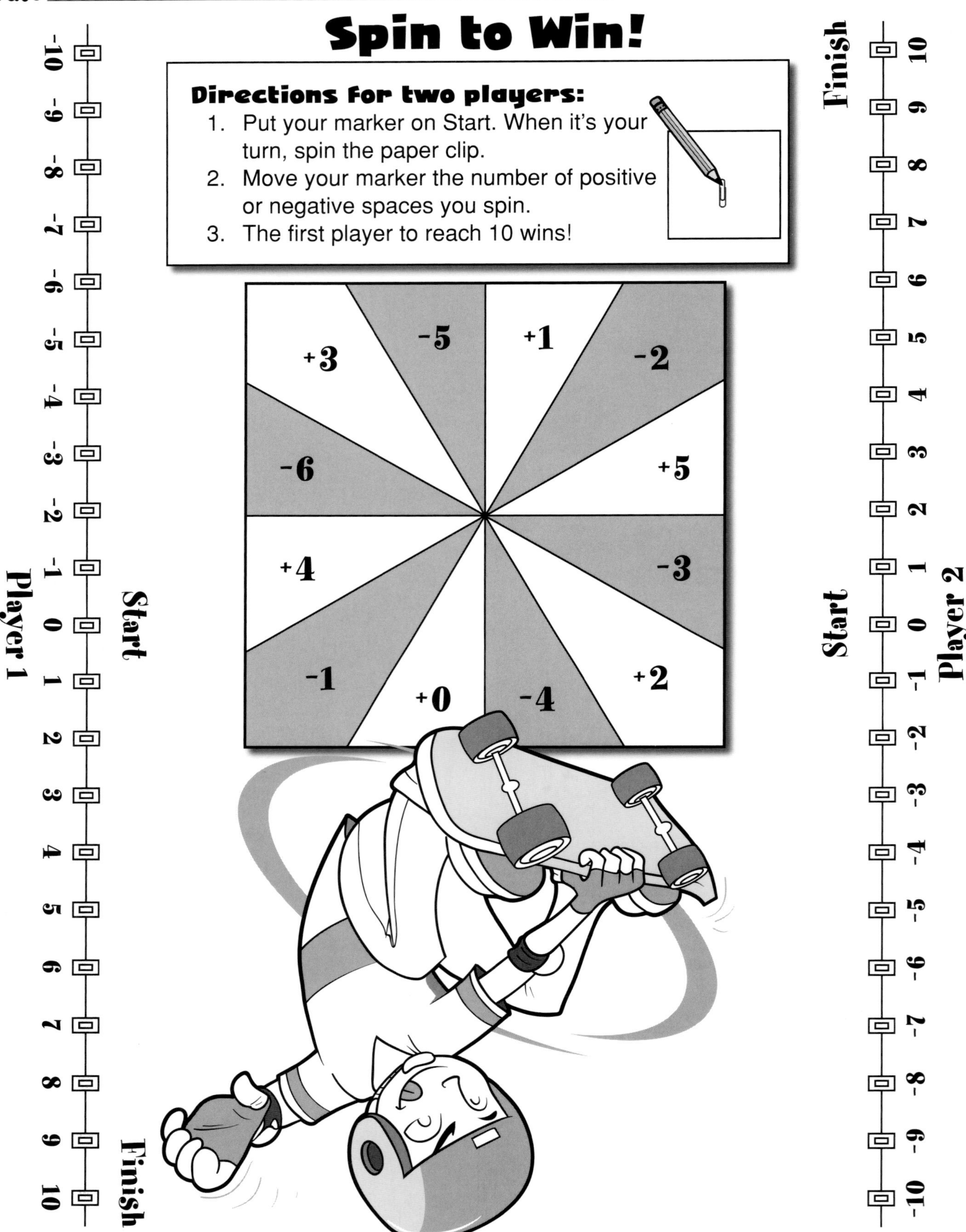

 Note to the teacher: Use with "Integer Race" on page 43.

Classroom Displays

CLASSROOM DISPLAYS

Welcome students to your room with this inspirational display. Make a class supply of the guitar pattern from page 52. Write each student's name on a guitar and post the guitars on a board along with large music notes labeled with words of encouragement. If desired, also post an enlarged copy of the guitar pattern.

Lisa Hall, Waller Mill Elementary, Williamsburg, VA

To give students a preview of the year ahead, make a large theater sign similar to the one shown. Add a border of large yellow circles (lights) and a colorful copy of the spotlight pattern from page 52. Then post four major topics that will be covered this year. If desired, change the features each grading period to build student excitement.

Kelli Higgins, P. L. Bolin Elementary, East Peoria, IL

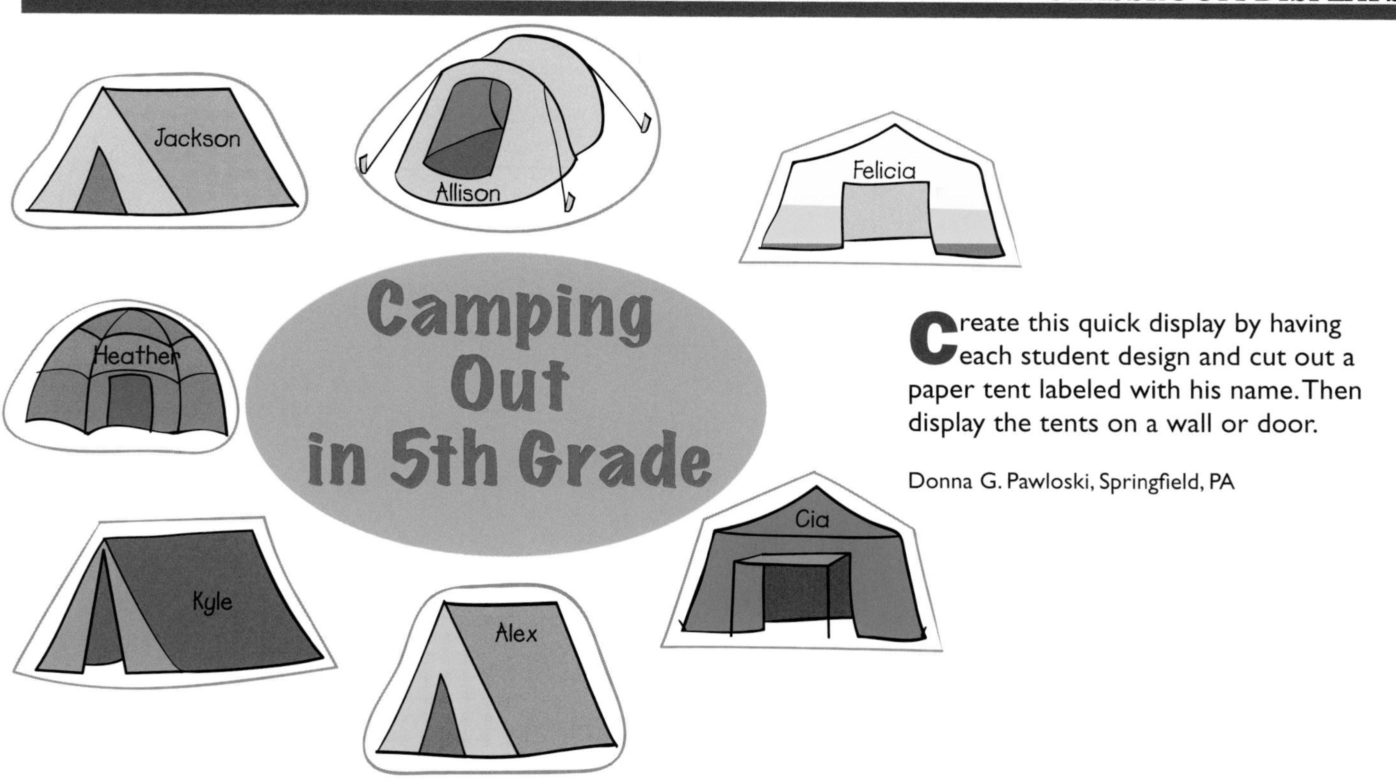

Create this quick display by having each student design and cut out a paper tent labeled with his name. Then display the tents on a wall or door.

Donna G. Pawloski, Springfield, PA

Give a "seal of approval" to character education by enlarging a copy of the seal pattern from page 52. Next, cut out several large paper circles and program each one with a positive character trait. Each week, highlight a different trait by pinning it on the seal's nose.

Natalie McGregor, Grenada Upper Elementary, Grenada, MS

Guitar, Spotlight, and Seal Patterns

Use the guitar pattern with "Start Off on the Right Note!" on page 50, the spotlight pattern with "Coming Soon to a Classroom Near You" on page 50, and the seal pattern with "Good Character Earns the Seal of Approval" on page 51.

CLASSROOM DISPLAYS

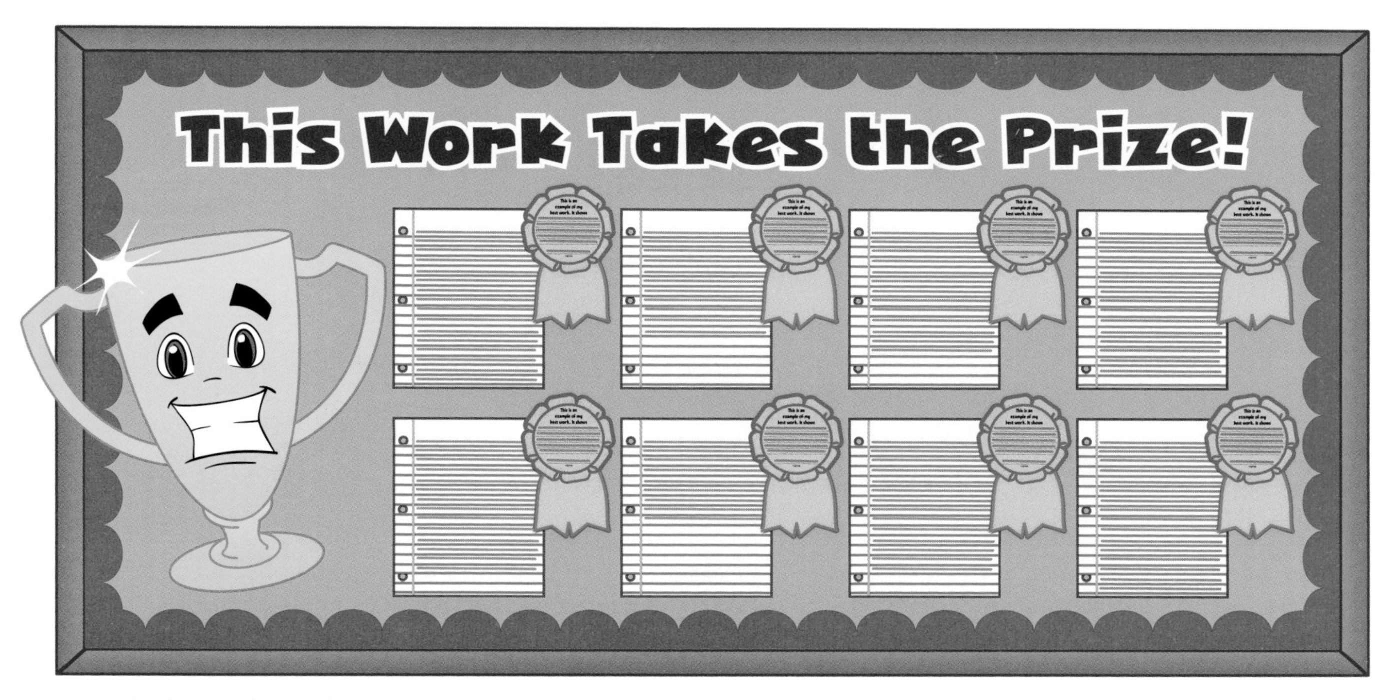

To display students' finest work, have each child choose an example of his work that shows his best efforts. Then have him fill out a copy of the blue ribbon pattern on page 54 and post it along with his work on a board decorated as shown.

Colleen Dabney, Williamsburg, VA

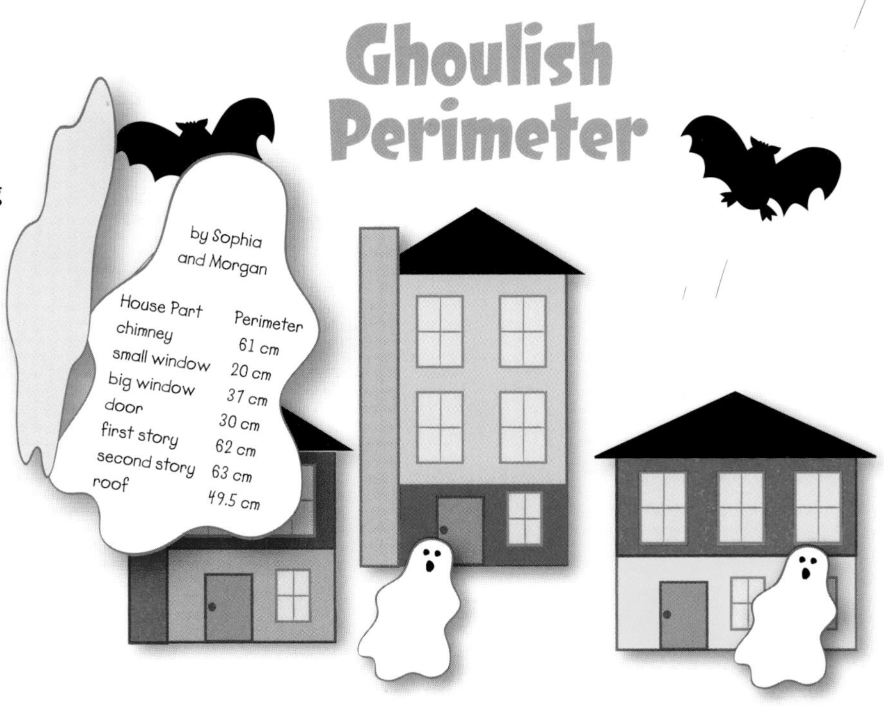

For this interactive display, have each pair of students create a haunted house using construction paper squares, rectangles, and triangles. The pair determines the perimeter of each part of the house, records the measurements inside a ghost-shaped card, and posts its work on a board. As time allows, a student visits the board and chooses a house. Then she measures each part's perimeter and peeks inside the card to check her work.

Crissie Stephens
Kelly Edwards Elementary
Williston, SC

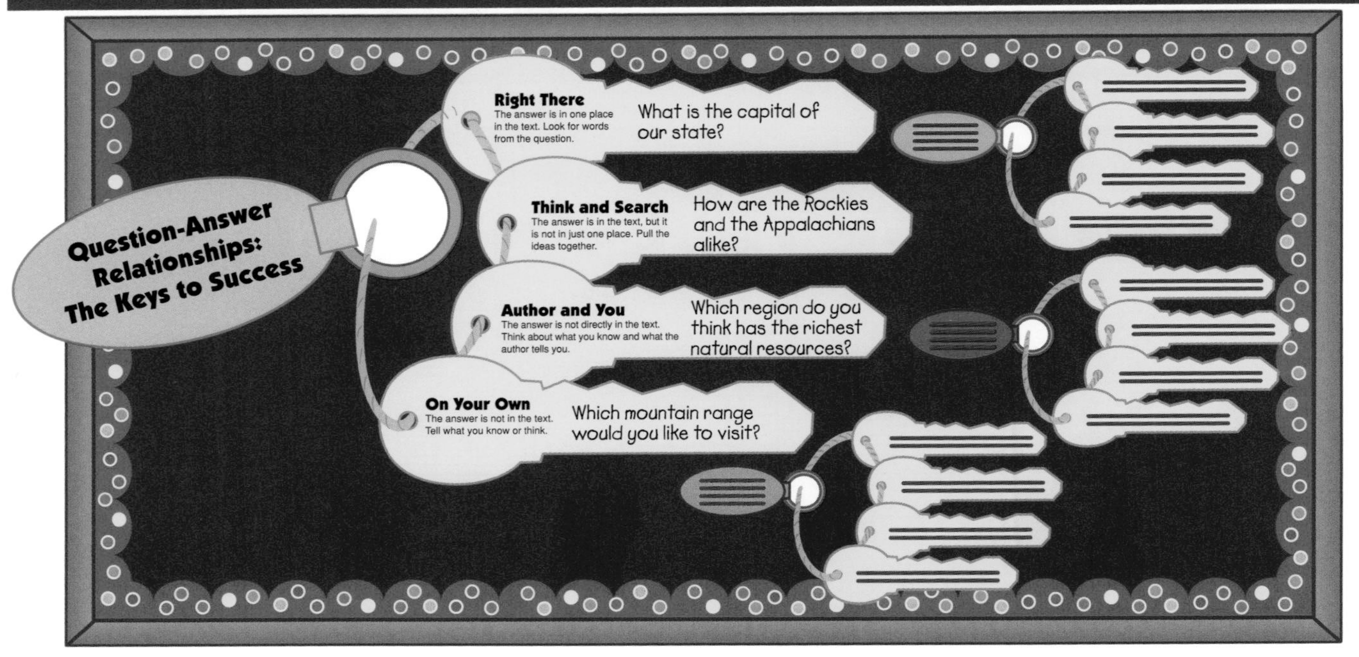

Connect enlarged copies of the key chain and key patterns from page 55 with yarn and post them. Next, give each small group of students a copy of page 55 and guide them to find an example of each question-answer relationship (QAR). The students record each example on the corresponding key and then sign their names on the key chain. They cut out the patterns, punch a hole in each piece, tie the pieces together with yarn, and add their work to the board.

adapted from an idea by Colleen Dabney, Williamsburg, VA

Blue Ribbon Pattern

Use with "This Work Takes the Prize!" on page 53.

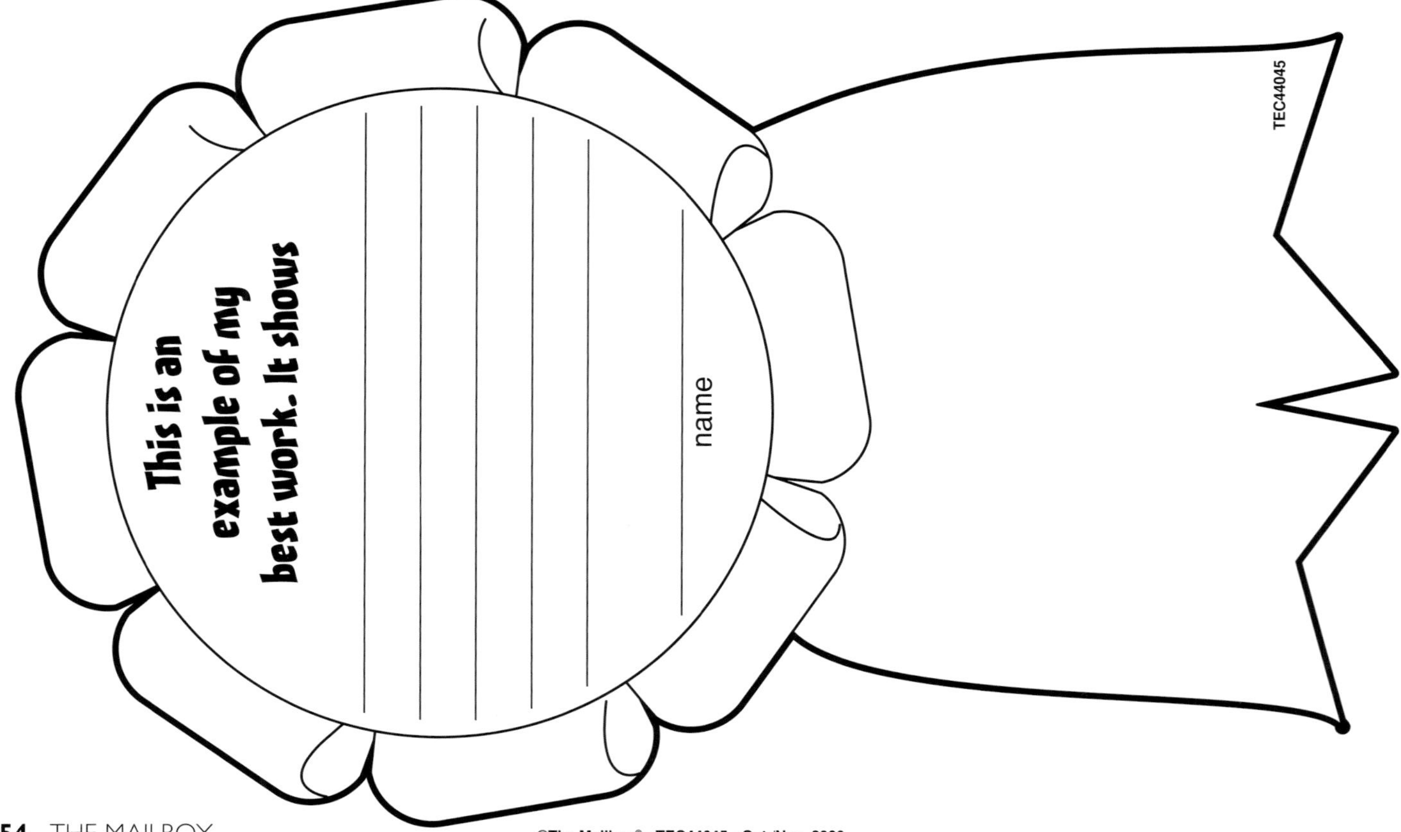

Use with "Question-Answer Relationships: The Keys to Success" on page 54.

Question-Answer Relationships: The Keys to Success

TEC44045

Right There

The answer is in one place in the text. Look for words from the question.

Think and Search

The answer is in the text, but it is not in just one place. Pull the ideas together.

Author and You

The answer is not directly in the text. Think about what you know and what the author tells you.

On Your Own

The answer is not in the text. Tell what you know or think.

CLASSROOM DISPLAYS

For this display, each student describes winter or a special winter holiday on a copy of page 58. The child writes a variety of descriptive sentences as guided by the number of blanks and the ending punctuation for each line. Then she decorates the tree and cuts it out.

Cynthia Holcomb, San Angelo, TX

The Life and Timeline of Dr. Martin Luther King Jr.

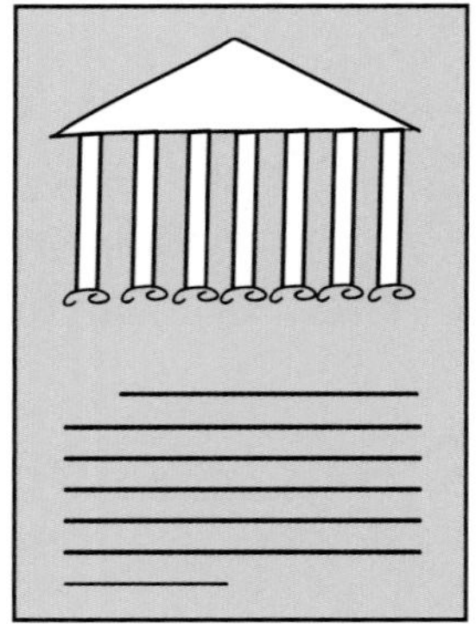

To honor this important civil rights leader, guide each pair of students to research a significant event relating to Dr. King. Then have the partners summarize and illustrate the event on a mini poster. After each duo shares its work, display the posters side by side in chronological order.

Amy Barsanti, Pines Elementary, Plymouth, NC

Timeline Events

- Dr. King's Youth
- Dr. King's Education
- Montgomery Bus Boycott
- Supreme Court Ruling About Montgomery Bus System
- Southern Christian Leadership Conference
- Protesting Discrimination in Birmingham
- March on Washington
- Nobel Peace Prize
- Civil Rights Act of 1964
- Voting Rights Act of 1965
- Chicago Civil Rights Campaign
- Poor People's Campaign
- Dr. King's Assassination
- Dedication of Martin Luther King Jr. National Historic Site
- Martin Luther King's Birthday Becomes Federal Holiday
- National Civil Rights Museum Opens

Here's a seasonal idea that doubles as a math center! First, have each student label a snowball-shaped card with an angle and sign his name. Next, the child measures the angle and records the measurement inside the card. Post students' cards with an enlarged copy of the penguin pattern below. A student makes a chart labeled as shown. He chooses a snowball, lists the snowball-maker's name, and estimates the angle measurement. Then he lifts the flap, checks his estimate, and calculates the difference, repeating with other snowballs as time allows.

adapted from an idea by Rebecca Juneau, Highland Elementary, Lake Stevens, WA

Penguin Pattern

Use with "What's the Angle?" on this page.

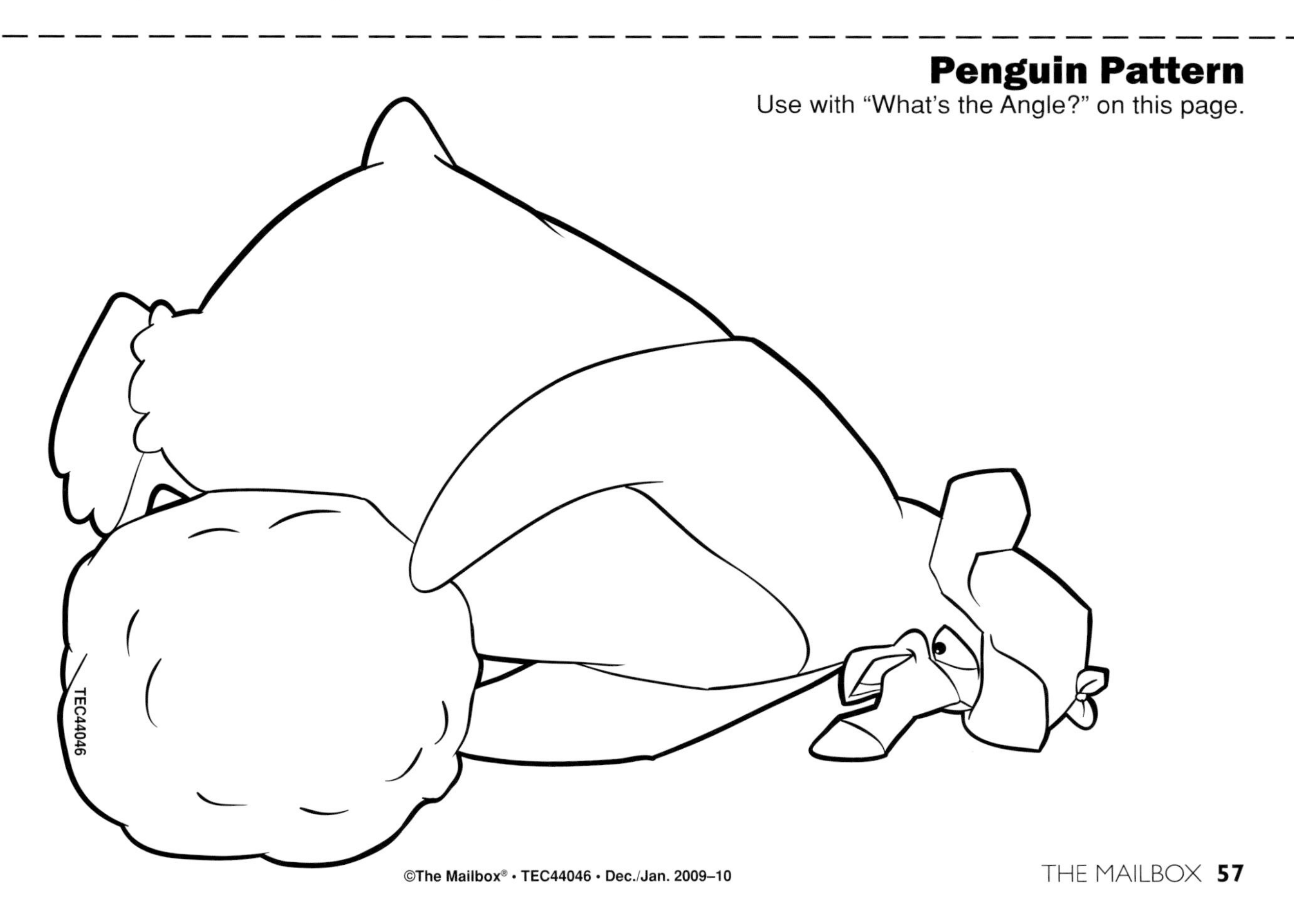

Tree Pattern

Use with "Wintry Descriptions" on page 56.

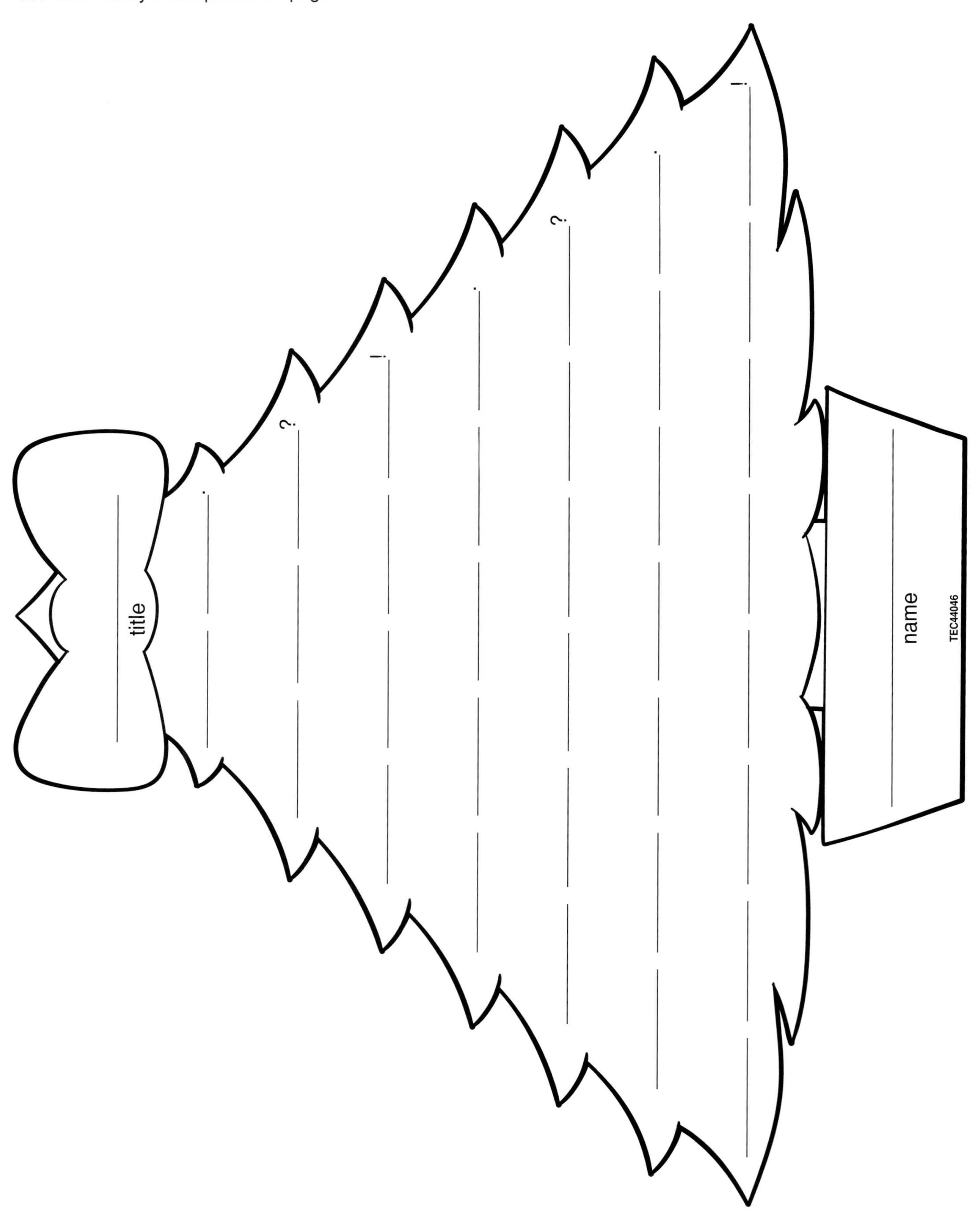

CLASSROOM DISPLAYS

Get students to trade in tired, overused words for fresh, precise ones! Program copies of the old car pattern from page 61 with words your students use too much. Cut out each car and post it on a board decorated as shown. Then lead students to brainstorm substitutes for the words, writing each new word on a cutout copy of the new car pattern from page 61 and adding it to the board.

adapted from an idea by John Hughes, Deerfield Elementary, Cedar Hills, UT

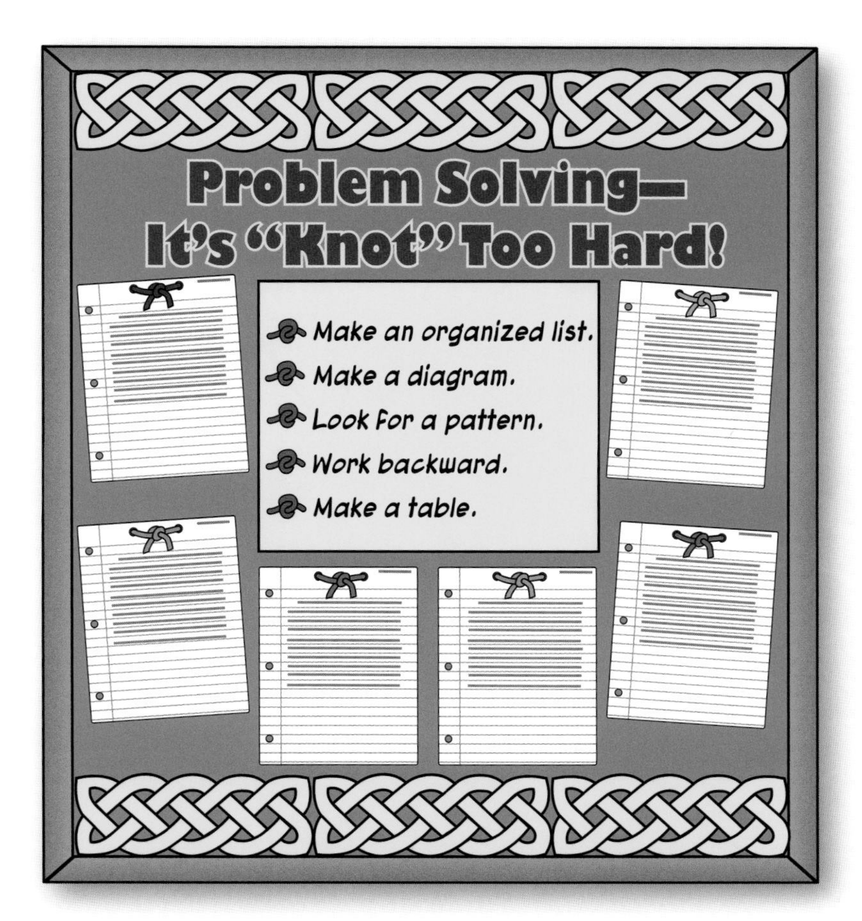

For this motivating math display, post problem-solving strategies such as those shown. Then have each student solve a two-step math problem and explain how she solved it. Have her punch two holes in the top of her page, thread a length of thick yarn through the holes, and tie the yarn in a big knot before adding her work to the display.

Kim Minafo, Cary, NC

Here's a seasonal display that's right on target! Program cutout copies of the heart pattern from the bottom of this page with various fractions. Then give each student a heart and challenge her to list fractions, decimals, and percentages that are equal to the fraction. Post students' work on a board decorated as shown.

Colleen Dabney, Williamsburg, VA

Heart Pattern

Use with "We ❤ Fractions" on this page.

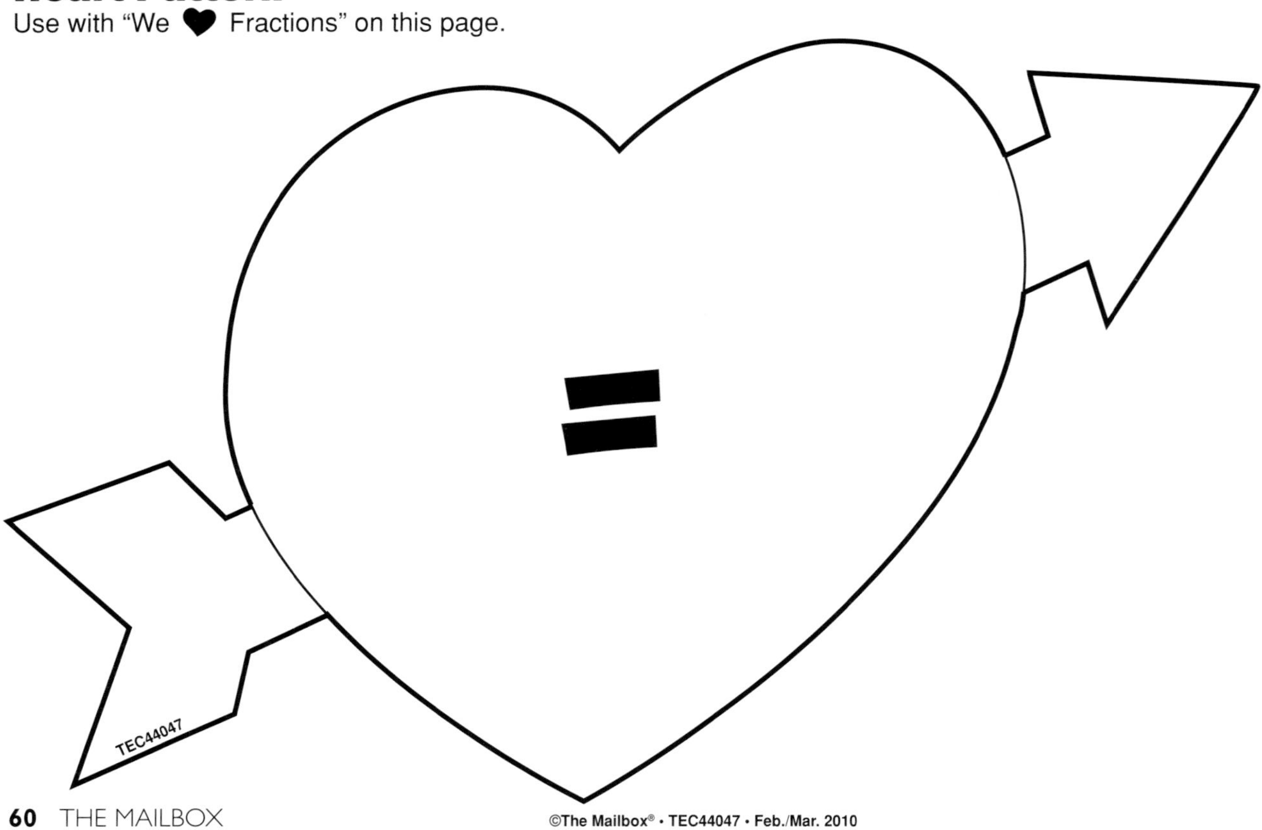

Old and New Car Patterns

Use with "Trade-Ins Welcome!" on page 59.

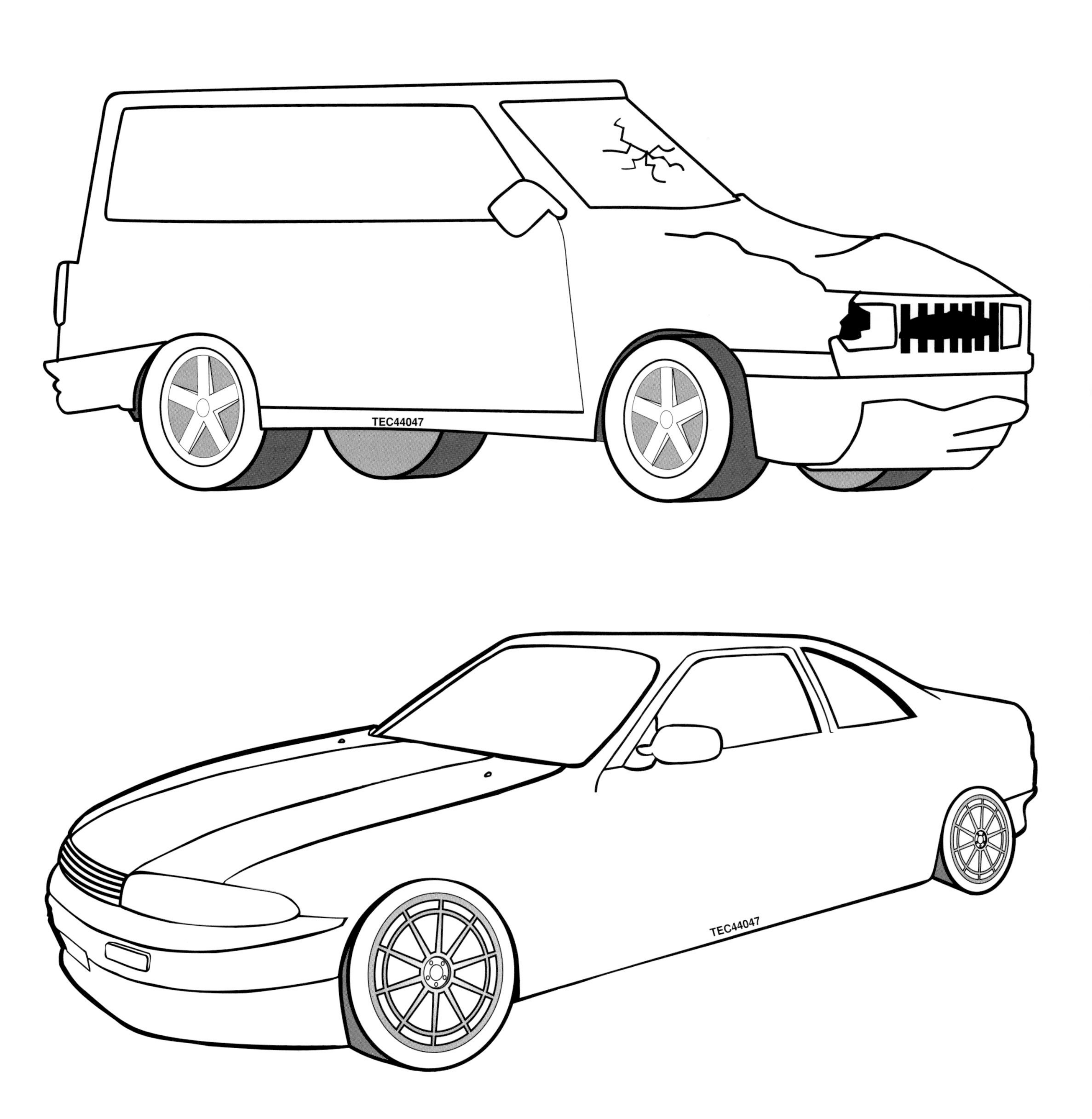

CLASSROOM DISPLAYS

For this Earth Day display, have students bring in recycling symbols from labels and boxes. Next, draw a large recycling symbol on poster board and have students glue on the emblems in collage fashion. Then cut out and assemble the symbol on a board. If desired, also post examples of items your community recycles along with the amount of time each item will sit in a landfill if it's not recycled.

Stephanie Green, Sewell Elementary, Sachse, TX

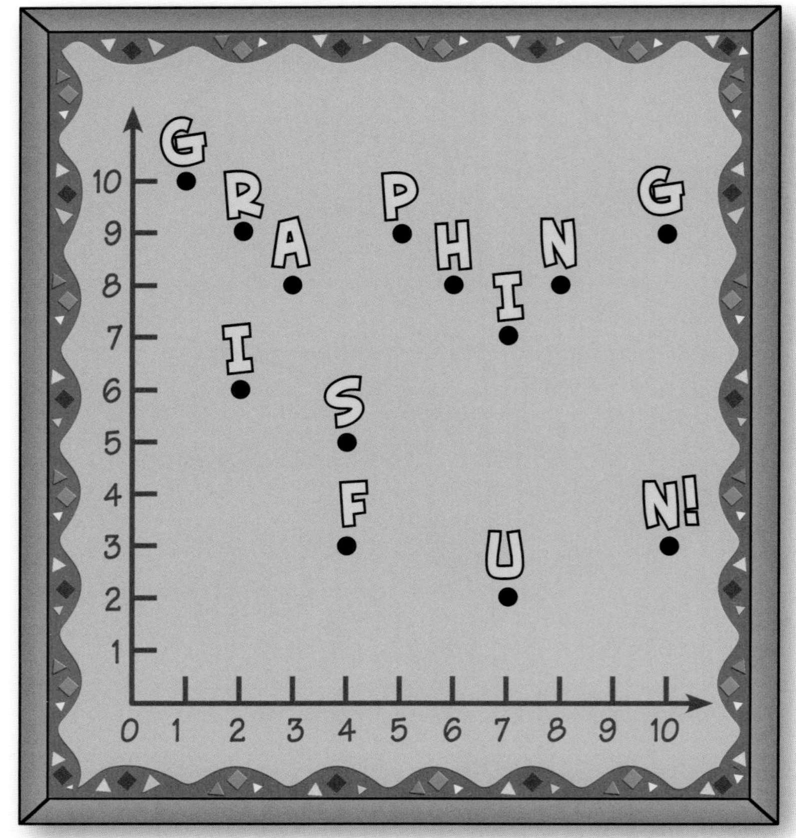

Turn your bulletin board into a coordinate plane, numbering each axis as shown. Then plot points that spell out an engaging or seasonal sentence and challenge students to list its ordered pairs.

Colleen Dabney, Williamsburg, VA

Singing Classmates' Praises

For this display, post samples of students' best work. Then provide copies of the music note pattern from page 64. When a student finishes a task early, have him read a classmate's posted work and jot comments or compliments on a music note. Then post each student's comments around the appropriate work.

Becky Juneau, Highland Elementary, Lake Stevens, WA

Shortly before a field trip, label an enlarged copy of the UFO pattern from page 64 with the trip's destination, date, important reminders, and permission slips' due date. Post the UFO on a board decorated as shown. Then, after the field trip, change "Will Be" in the title to "Was." Have each student summarize the trip on a copy of the UFO pattern and add her work to the board.

Colleen Dabney, Williamsburg, VA

Music Note Pattern

Use with "Singing Classmates' Praises" on page 63.

UFO Pattern

Use with "This Field Trip Will Be Out of This World!" on page 63.

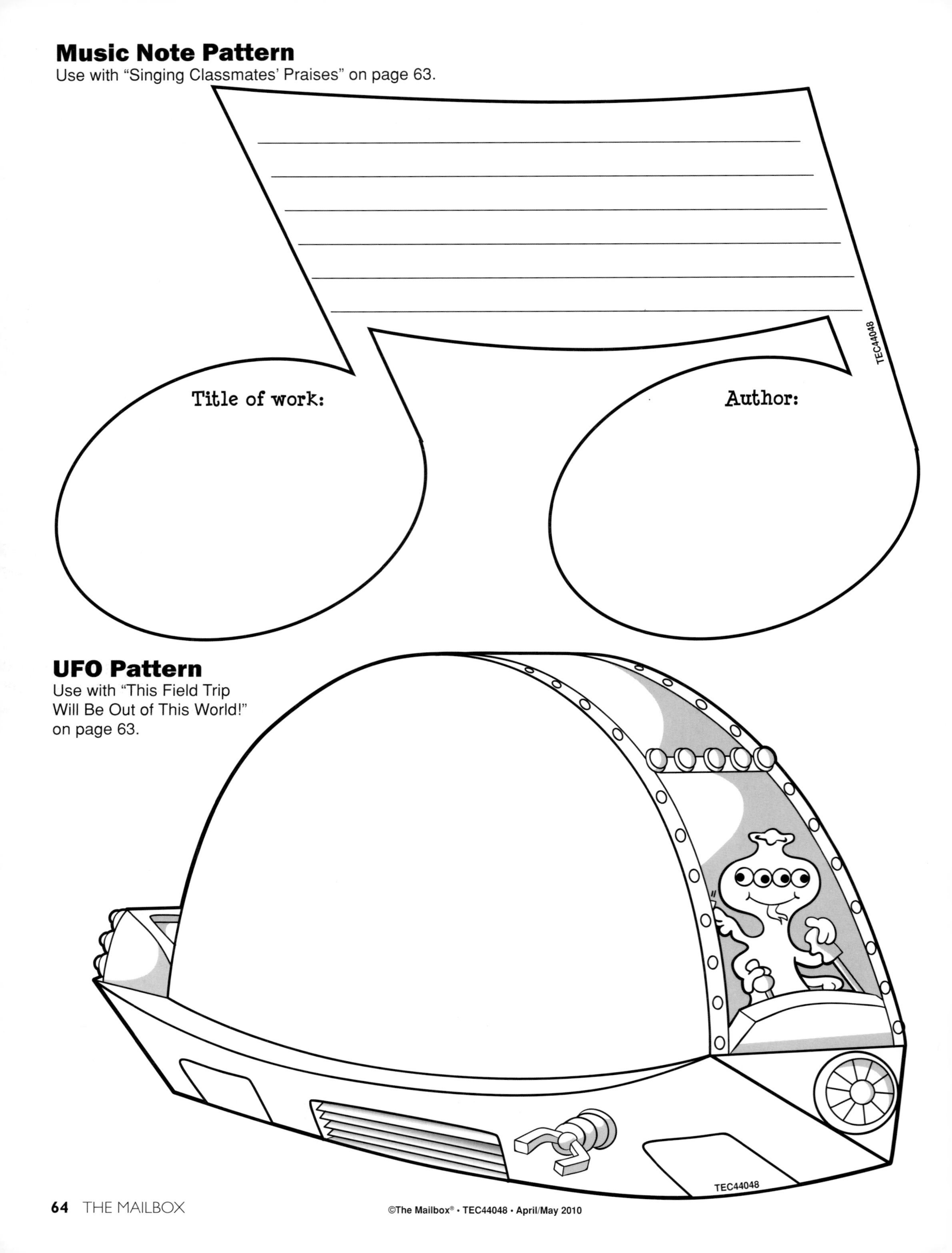

CLASSROOM DISPLAYS

Invite this year's class to leave important tips for your next class with this idea. Have each student personalize a T-shirt pattern and then write suggestions on it to help next year's students have a great year. Clip students' T-shirts on wire hangers and pin them to the board with pushpins. This makes a great year-end and back-to-school display.

Michelle Cooper, Franklin Elementary, Franklin, NJ

To showcase students' recommendations for great summer reading, title a board as shown and attach an inexpensive pair of flip-flops. (Wrap a piece of tape around each flip-flop's thong and pin the tape's ends to the board.) Then have each student describe her favorite book on a copy of a flip-flop pattern from page 66 and post her work as shown.

Kristi N. Ballash, South Harnett Elementary, Bunnlevel, NC

Flip-Flop Patterns

Use with "Books You'll Flip For!" on page 65.

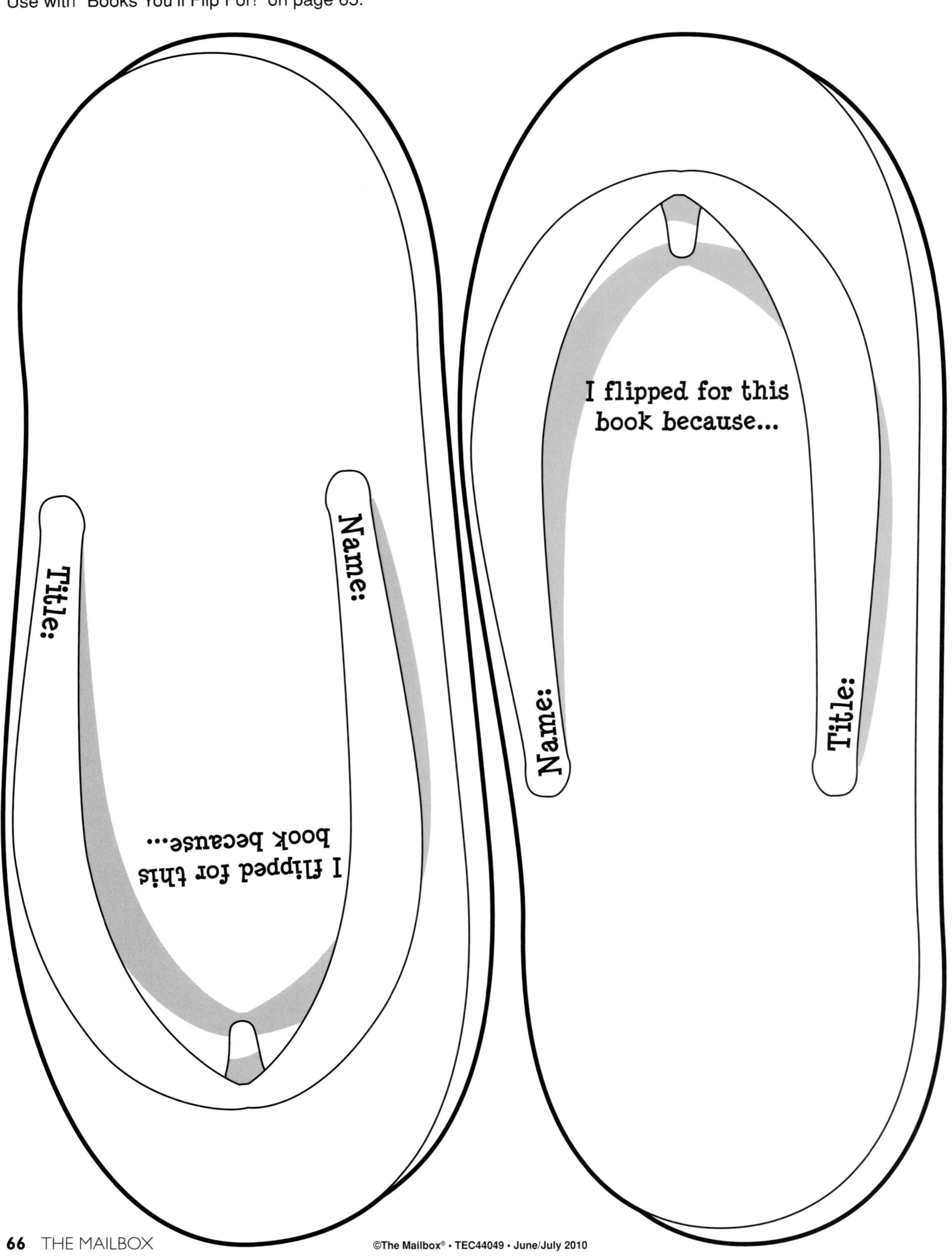

Reading and Language Arts

Language Arts TIPS & TOOLS

Right at Home

Sequencing

Use this activity to bring sequencing home to students the next time they read informational text with a sequential structure. Each child trims one end of two 5" x 8" unlined index cards as shown and labels one with his name and the other with the selection's title and author's name. After he decorates the cards to look like the front and back of a house, he accordion-folds a 6" x 18" piece of white paper into four sections. Then he unfolds his paper and labels each section, in order, with a one-sentence summary and a matching illustration of a major event or step. Finally, he glues the house-shaped cards to the backs of his strip's first and last sections. Now he will feel right at home with sequencing!

Kim Minafo, Apex, NC

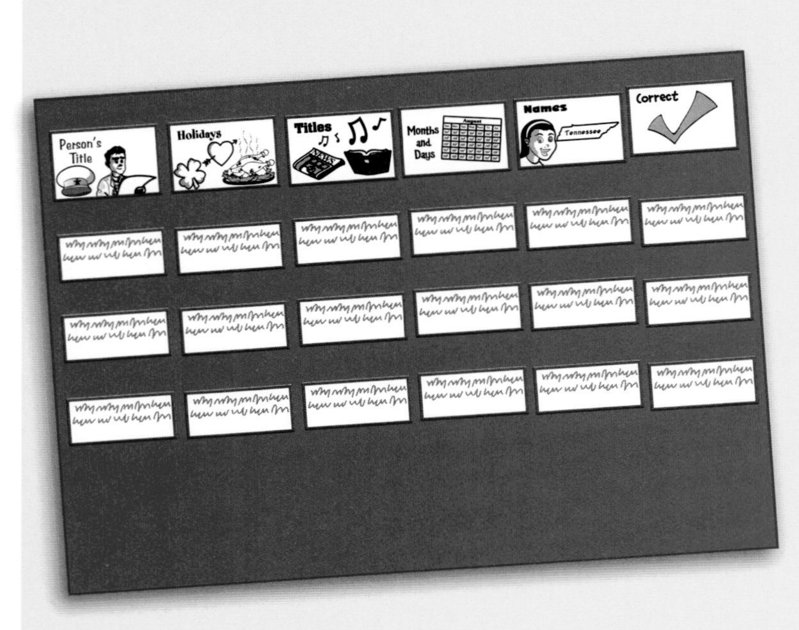

Sentence Sort

Capitalization

To give students practice using capitalization rules, provide each student with a large sheet of construction paper and a copy of the cards from page 72. A student cuts apart the cards and glues the larger cards across the top of her construction paper as shown. Next, she reads each numbered card and decides whether the sentence contains a capitalization error. If she finds an error, she corrects it on the card. Then she glues the card in the appropriate column. If no capitalization changes are needed, she glues the sentence under the "Correct" heading. If desired, have each student compare her chart with a partner's.

Jennifer Otter, Oak Ridge, NC

What's the Big Idea?
Main idea

Give each student a notecard and ask him to write a category on the back of it, such as "colors." On the front, instruct the student to write four words that are associated with his category. Then have him trade cards with a partner to see whether she can guess the category based on the four words. Next, have each student choose a main idea, write it on a new card, write on the back of the card four detail sentences that support the idea, and then trade cards with a partner. Direct each student to read his partner's sentences and try to identify the main idea. If time allows, have each student trade with another partner.

Rebecca Juneau, Highland Elementary, Lake Stevens, WA

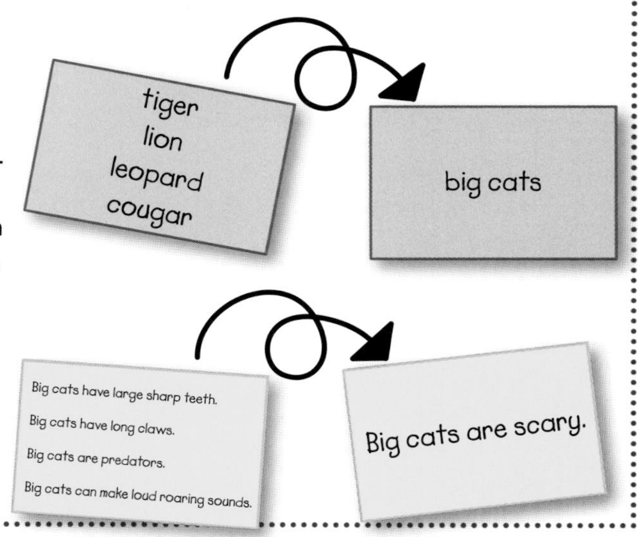

CUPS?
Conventions

Assess your students' skills in capitalization (*C*), usage (*U*), punctuation (*P*), spelling (*S*), and sentence sense (*?*) with this point-earning activity. Write ten spelling or vocabulary words on the board. Then give each child a copy of page 73. Have each student write ten sentences on her paper, using each spelling or vocabulary word once. When she is finished, have her reread each sentence, check it for each convention, and make any needed corrections. Then collect the papers and award two points for each correctly used convention, up to ten points per sentence. For a fun twist, challenge students to write all ten sentences about a theme, such as fall.

Wendy Whitney Scherer, River Ridge School District, Patch Grove, WI

Guide Word Game
Spelling, vocabulary

This fun alphabetical order activity requires students to use their vocabulary skills. To begin, arrange students in groups of three or four and give each group a sheet of paper and a pencil. Then write two guide words on the board. Give group members one minute to list as many words as possible that come between the guide words. When time is up, have each group read its list aloud for the class to verify. Award one point for each correct word and declare the group with the most points the winner of the round. At first, choose words that require alphabetizing to the first letter. For additional rounds, increase the difficulty by using words that require looking at the second, third, or fourth letters.

Ann Fisher, Toledo, OH

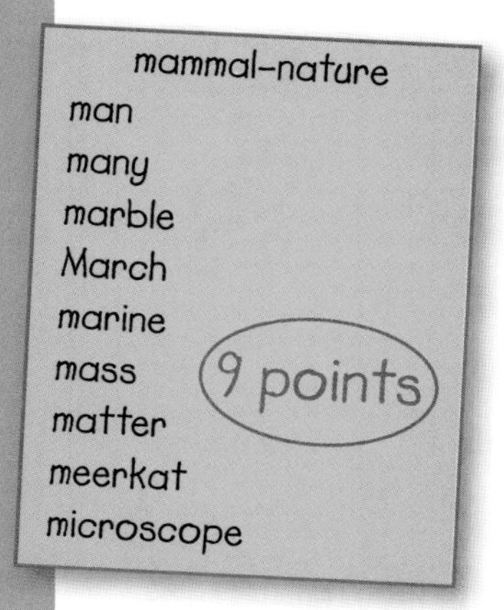

Name ______________________

Date ______________________

LOOK INTO THE FUTURE

Title: ______________________

	Event	Prediction	Outcome
Beginning			
Middle			
End			

Glimpse Ahead Glasses

ACME

Note to the teacher: As each student reads a story, have him write an event from the corresponding section of the text, a prediction of what might happen next, and then a summary of what actually happens.

Name ______________________

Date ______________________

Princess Cookie Crumb

Circle the common nouns in each story section. Then write each proper noun in the spaces provided.
Hint: The number at the end of the section tells how many common nouns should be circled.

Proper Nouns in Section A

Proper Nouns in Section B

[A] There is trouble in the Cookie Kingdom. Princess Crumb has fallen into a deep sleep. The only way to wake her is with a mixture made from special cookies. The princess must be saved in less than two hours, or she will sleep forever. King Crumb grabs his cell phone and calls Captain Snicker and his pal, Doodle. He tells them which cookies they must find.

Captain Snicker flies off to find a butter cookie. He heads straight to Sweden. He arrives at a bakery and buys a butter cookie. He yells to the bakery owner, "Thank you!" Then he takes off for China.

Once in China, Captain Snicker begins searching for a fortune cookie. He flies around the Great Wall of China. He sees several dessert stands. He buys a fortune cookie in Beijing and heads back to the Cookie Kingdom. (17)

[B] Meanwhile, Doodle picks up a shortbread cookie in Scotland. Then he zips off to the North Pole to buy an icebox cookie. From the North Pole, Doodle heads to America. He spots a bag of chocolate chip cookies near the Statue of Liberty. He grabs the bag and flies back to the Cookie Kingdom.

With only minutes to spare, Captain Snicker and Doodle present their cookies to the king. The king crushes the cookies and sprinkles them over his daughter. Princess Crumb awakens. Captain Snicker and Doodle save the princess, and things in Cookie Kingdom are right once again. (13)

Capitalization Cards

Use with "Sentence Sort" on page 68.

Names

Holidays

Months and Days

Titles

People's Title

Correct

1. Jake went to wyoming to visit his grandmother.

2. On thanksgiving day, my family cooks turkey.

3. I have a soccer game every saturday.

4. I bought a new cookbook called *creative cupcakes*.

5. Did you see principal Williams at school?

6. We ate at the Pizza Shack last night.

7. On the fourth of july, we celebrated with fireworks.

8. My hamster, squeaky, loves to run on his wheel.

9. In june, we went to the beach.

10. Sarah's favorite teacher was mrs. Cox.

11. Our class's favorite book is called *school days*.

12. I live on Southbrook Lane.

13. My class sang "happy birthday" to me today.

14. Last summer I went to new york city.

15. My best friend is Mya.

16. I like the month of september best.

17. We had a valentine's day party at school today.

18. I had a sore throat, so I went to see dr. Jones.

Name ____________________

Date ____________________

CUPS?

Write each spelling or vocabulary word on a blank. Then use each word in a complete sentence. Evaluate your sentences by placing a check in the upper corner of each matching box.

C Capitalizes necessary words

U Uses the word correctly

P Punctuation is correct.

S Spelling is correct.

? Does the sentence make sense?

1. ____________ ______________________________

2. ____________ ______________________________

3. ____________ ______________________________

4. ____________ ______________________________

5. ____________ ______________________________

6. ____________ ______________________________

7. ____________ ______________________________

8. ____________ ______________________________

9. ____________ ______________________________

10. ____________ ______________________________

Total points: ____________

	C	U	P	S	?
1					
2					
3					
4					
5					
6					
7					
8					
9					
10					

Note to the teacher: Use with "CUPS?" on page 69.

Language Arts TIPS & TOOLS

Easily Confused Homophones	
ant, aunt	its, it's
ate, eight	knight, night
bear, bare	knot, not
blue, blew	loan, lone
bored, board	miner, minor
die, dye	oar, ore, or
hole, whole	sent, scent, cent
hour, our	their, there, they're

Use the "Write" One!
Homophones

To give students entertaining practice using homophones correctly, post a list of easily confused homophones, such as those shown. Next, have each student choose a set of words and write a silly sentence using both or all three words. Have the child write his sentence on an index card, underline each homophone, and illustrate the sentence. Collect students' cards, punch holes in them, and bind them with a binder ring to make a fun class reference titled "Write the Right Word!"

Leigh Anne Newsom, Cedar Road Elementary, Chesapeake, VA

I Spy a Vivid Verb!
Descriptive verbs

Set up this ongoing activity by gluing a copy of the directions card from page 77 onto a large envelope. Then place in an accessible spot the envelope and a supply of binocular cards from page 77. When a student finds a vivid verb in her reading, have her complete a binocular card and drop the card in the envelope. At the end of each week, draw several cards from the envelope. Have each student share her work. Then add each verb to your word wall, reminding students to be on the lookout for descriptive verbs when they read and to use these verbs when they write!

Colleen Dabney, Williamsburg, VA

Super Spelling Contract
Spelling

Here's an idea for spelling practice that students will look forward to using over and over! Program a copy of page 78 with the number of activities you want students to complete. Then, at the beginning of the week, give each child a copy of the programmed page along with his list of spelling words. Have the student follow the directions on the page to practice his words all week long!

adapted from ideas by Shauna T. Harris, Dean Allen Elementary, Las Vegas, NV, and Linda Biondi, Pond Road Middle School, Robbinsville, NJ

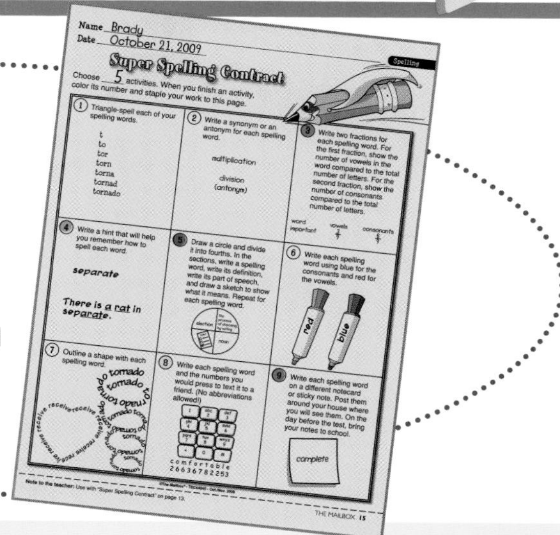
Name Brady
Date October 21, 2009

Spelling

Super Spelling Contract

Choose 5 activities. When you finish an activity, color its number and staple your work to this page.

1. Triangle-spell each of your spelling words.
   t / to / tor / torn / torna / tornad / tornado
2. Write a synonym or an antonym for each spelling word.
   multiplication / division (antonym)
3. Write two fractions for each spelling word. For the first fraction, show the number of vowels in the word compared to the total number of letters. For the second fraction, show the number of consonants compared to the total number of letters.
   word: important | vowels | consonants
4. Write a hint that will help you remember how to spell each word.
   separate
   There is a rat in separate.
5. Draw a circle and divide it into fourths. In the sections, write a spelling word, write its definition, write its part of speech, and draw a sketch to show what it means. Repeat for each spelling word.
   election | noun
6. Write each spelling word using blue for the consonants and red for the vowels.
   red | blue
7. Outline a shape with each spelling word.
   tornado | receive
8. Write each spelling word and the numbers you would press to text it to a friend. (No abbreviations allowed!)
   comfortable 26636782253
9. Write each spelling word on a different notecard or sticky note. Post them around your house where you will see them. On the day before the test, bring your notes to school.
   complete

Note to the teacher: Use with "Super Spelling Contract" on page 13.

THE MAILBOX 15

Step-by-Step
Questioning

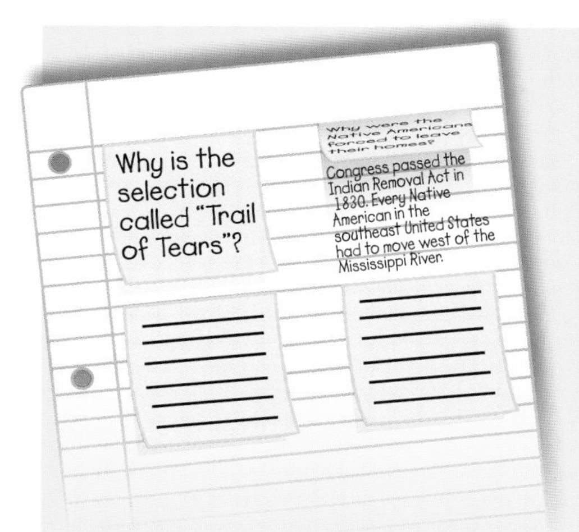

Want your students to ask questions as they read? Try this! Lead each student to preview a short fiction or nonfiction selection. Next, have the child jot on a sticky note a question about the selection and stick her note near the selection's beginning. Then the student begins reading, stopping after each paragraph to write a question. After reading, the child sticks her notes on a sheet of paper, reviews the questions, and records each answer under the matching note. Then she shares her work in a small-group discussion about the selection.

Dawn Little, Laytonsville, MD

Really Big Brochures
Nonfiction text features

Use this activity to build students' experience with informational text. First, collect a variety of nonfiction materials. Next, give each small group of students a text and a sheet of poster board. Have the group fold its poster board in thirds and label the inside sections with the questions below, filling in each blank with the type of its assigned text. Then guide the group to study its text's features, answer each question, and add illustrations to create a brochure that advertises its text. Set aside time for each group to present its finished product before posting the projects as handy references.

Kim Minafo, Resurrection Lutheran School, Cary, NC

Why do we read __________?
What are the features of a(n) __________?
What information can we find in a(n) __________?

Nonfiction Texts

textbook	newspaper
nonfiction trade book	owner's manual
biography	cookbook
dictionary	catalog
thesaurus	assembly instructions
encyclopedia	game directions
magazine	pamphlet

Name ____

Date ______________________

In a Nutshell

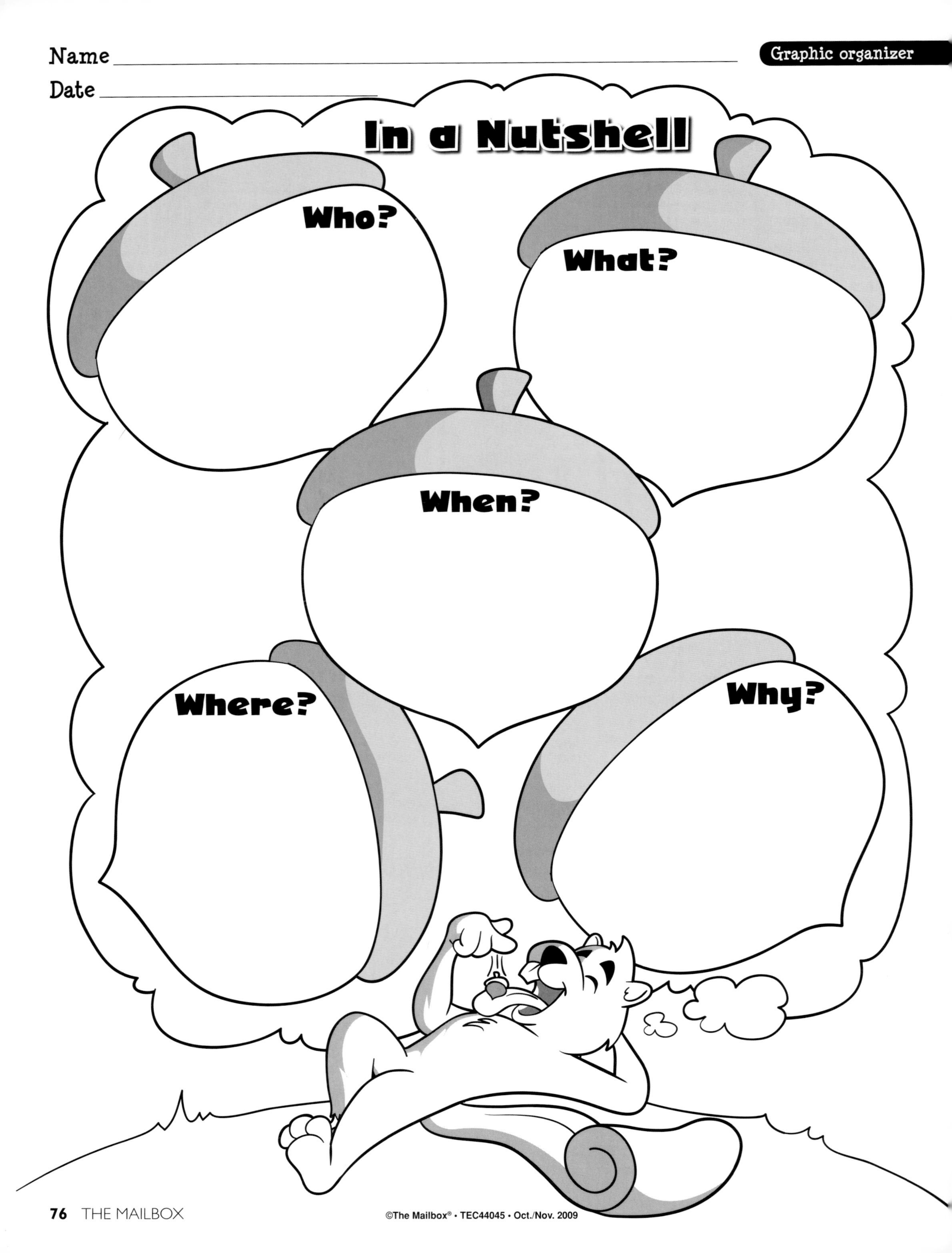

Binocular Cards and Directions Card

Use with "I Spy a Vivid Verb!" on page 74.

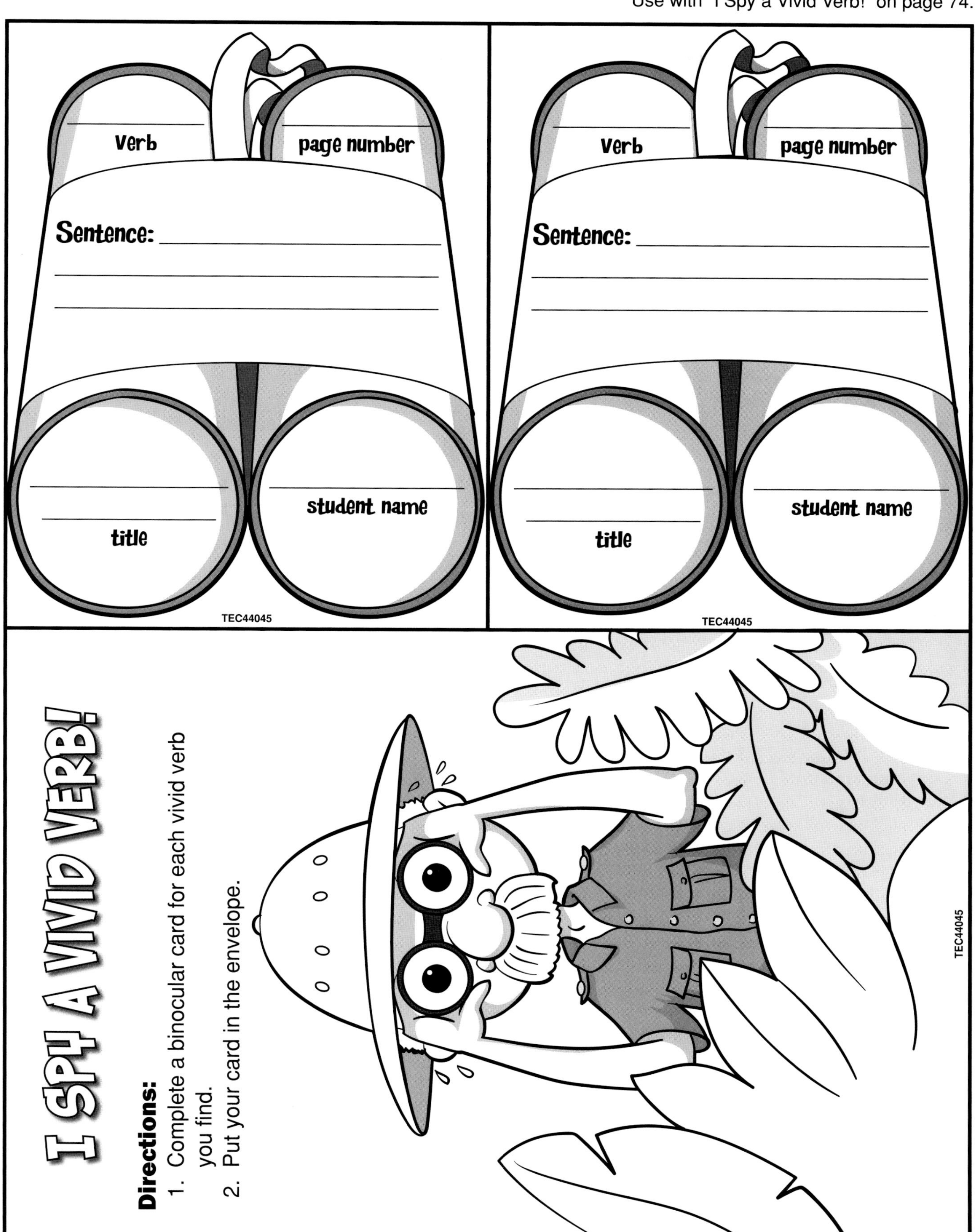

Name ____________________

Date ____________________

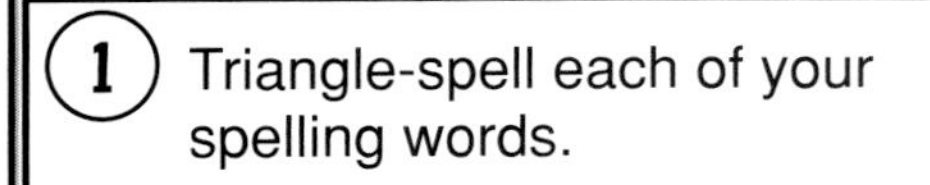

Choose _____ activities. When you finish an activity, color its number and staple your work to this page.

1 Triangle-spell each of your spelling words.

t
to
tor
torn
torna
tornad
tornado

2 Write a synonym or an antonym for each spelling word.

multiplication

division
(antonym)

3 Write two fractions for each spelling word. For the first fraction, show the number of vowels in the word compared to the total number of letters. For the second fraction, show the number of consonants compared to the total number of letters.

word	vowels	consonants
important	$\frac{3}{9}$	$\frac{6}{9}$

4 Write a hint that will help you remember how to spell each word.

separate

There is a rat in separate.

5 Draw a circle and divide it into fourths. In the sections, write a spelling word, write its definition, write its part of speech, and draw a sketch to show what it means. Repeat for each spelling word.

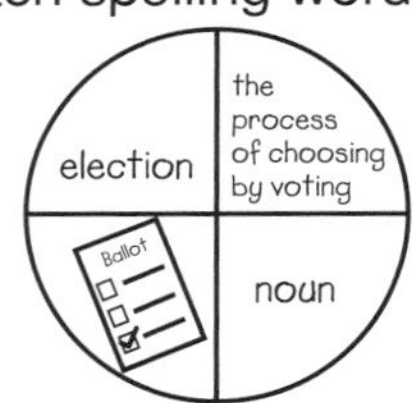

6 Write each spelling word using blue for the consonants and red for the vowels.

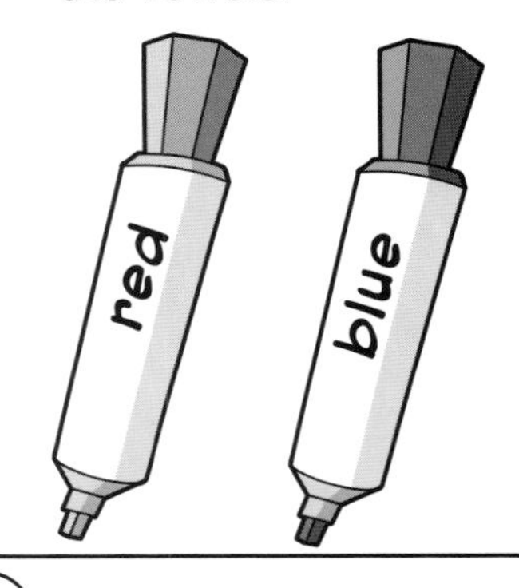

7 Outline a shape with each spelling word.

8 Write each spelling word and the numbers you would press to text it to a friend. (No abbreviations allowed!)

c o m f o r t a b l e
2 6 6 3 6 7 8 2 2 5 3

9 Write each spelling word on a different notecard or sticky note. Post them around your house where you will see them. On the day before the test, bring your notes to school.

Note to the teacher: Use with "Super Spelling Contract" on page 75.

Game Cards and Answer Key

Use with "On Your Mark!" on page 80. Mount on construction paper a copy of the game mat on page 80 and a copy of the cards and answer key below. If desired, laminate the pages before cutting the cards apart.

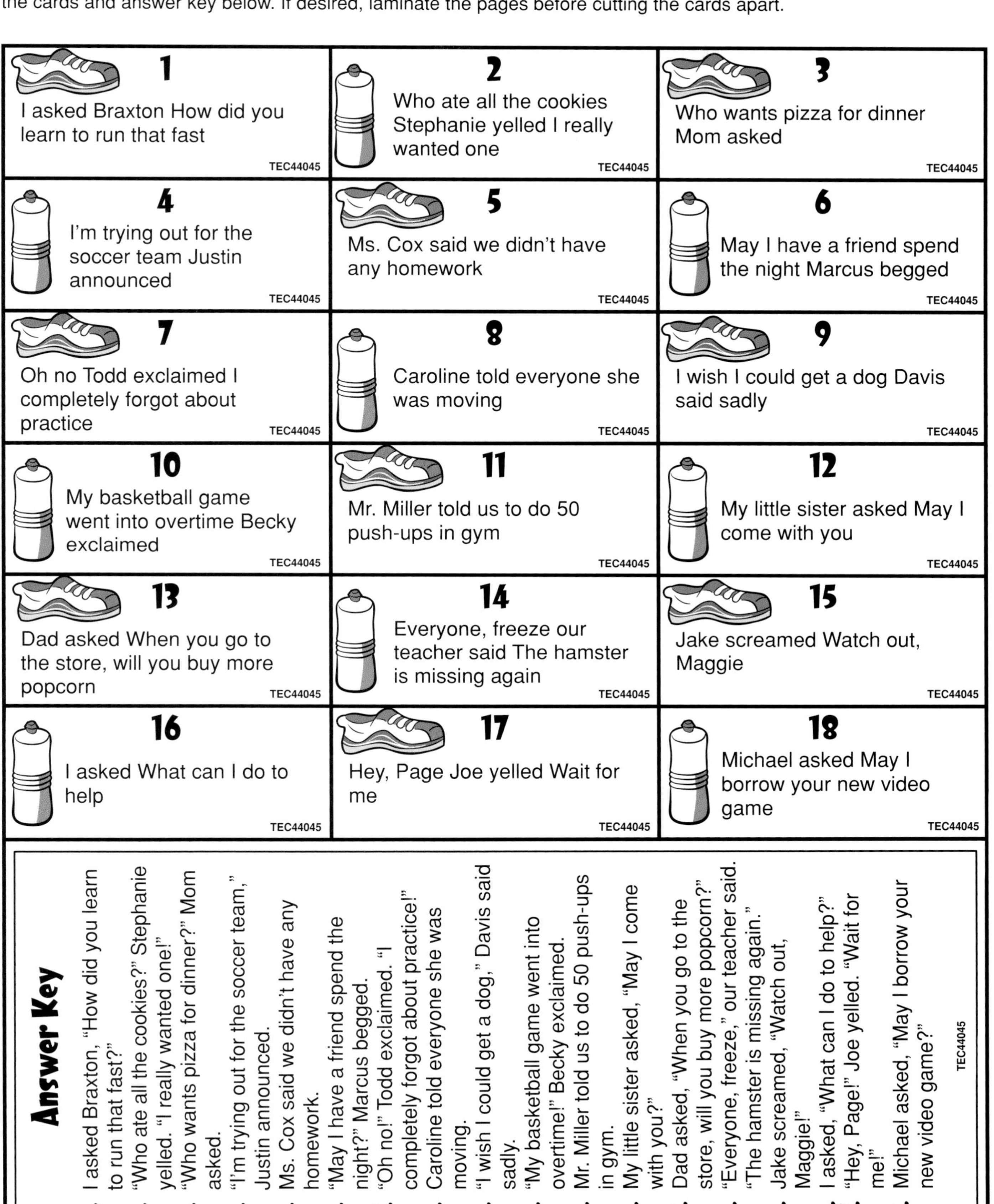

1 I asked Braxton How did you learn to run that fast TEC44045

2 Who ate all the cookies Stephanie yelled I really wanted one TEC44045

3 Who wants pizza for dinner Mom asked TEC44045

4 I'm trying out for the soccer team Justin announced TEC44045

5 Ms. Cox said we didn't have any homework TEC44045

6 May I have a friend spend the night Marcus begged TEC44045

7 Oh no Todd exclaimed I completely forgot about practice TEC44045

8 Caroline told everyone she was moving TEC44045

9 I wish I could get a dog Davis said sadly TEC44045

10 My basketball game went into overtime Becky exclaimed TEC44045

11 Mr. Miller told us to do 50 push-ups in gym TEC44045

12 My little sister asked May I come with you TEC44045

13 Dad asked When you go to the store, will you buy more popcorn TEC44045

14 Everyone, freeze our teacher said The hamster is missing again TEC44045

15 Jake screamed Watch out, Maggie TEC44045

16 I asked What can I do to help TEC44045

17 Hey, Page Joe yelled Wait for me TEC44045

18 Michael asked May I borrow your new video game TEC44045

Answer Key

1. I asked Braxton, "How did you learn to run that fast?"
2. "Who ate all the cookies?" Stephanie yelled. "I really wanted one!"
3. "Who wants pizza for dinner?" Mom asked.
4. "I'm trying out for the soccer team," Justin announced.
5. Ms. Cox said we didn't have any homework.
6. "May I have a friend spend the night?" Marcus begged.
7. "Oh no!" Todd exclaimed. "I completely forgot about practice!"
8. Caroline told everyone she was moving.
9. "I wish I could get a dog," Davis said sadly.
10. "My basketball game went into overtime!" Becky exclaimed.
11. Mr. Miller told us to do 50 push-ups in gym.
12. My little sister asked, "May I come with you?"
13. Dad asked, "When you go to the store, will you buy more popcorn?"
14. "Everyone, freeze," our teacher said. "The hamster is missing again."
15. Jake screamed, "Watch out, Maggie!"
16. I asked, "What can I do to help?"
17. "Hey, Page!" Joe yelled. "Wait for me!"
18. Michael asked, "May I borrow your new video game?"

TEC44045

Punctuating dialogue
ON YOUR MARK!
FINISH
You get a burst of energy. Move ahead one space.
You're out of breath. Move back one space.
GO!
Directions for two players:
1. Shuffle the cards and stack them facedown.
2. In turn, draw a card. Write the sentence on your paper and punctuate it correctly.
3. Have your partner check the key. If you are correct, move your marker according to the symbol on your card. If you are incorrect, your turn is over.
4. Place the card at the bottom of the stack.
5. The first player to reach Finish wins.
= Move ahead one space.
= Move ahead two spaces.
Your shoe comes untied. Move back one space.
START

Names ______________________________

Date ________________

Dance Off

A Game for Two Players

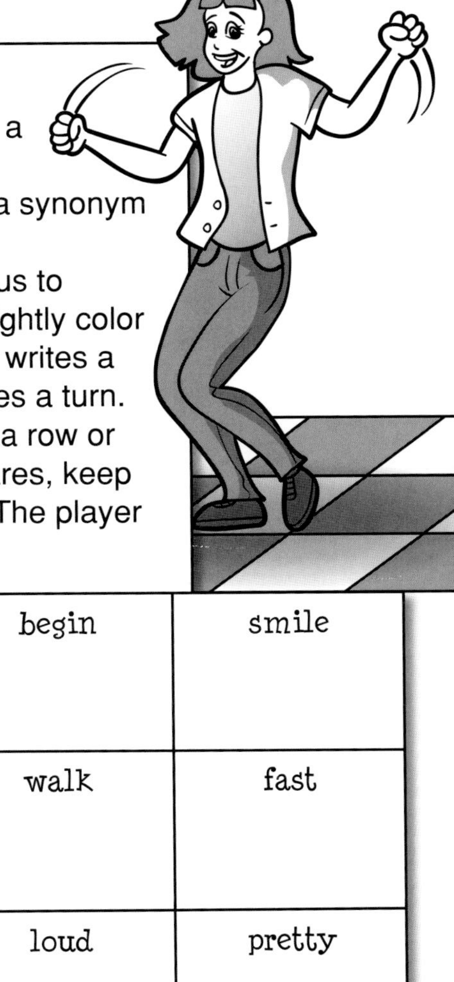

Directions:

1. Choose a crayon or colored pencil that is a different color than your partner's.
2. In turn, select a word on the page. Write a synonym in its box.
3. Your partner uses a dictionary or thesaurus to check your synonym. If you are correct, lightly color the box. If you are incorrect, your partner writes a correct synonym, colors the box, and takes a turn.
4. The first player to connect six squares in a row or column wins. If no one connects six squares, keep playing until all the squares are colored. The player with the most colored squares wins.

yell	mad	amazed	run	begin	smile
smart	short	hungry	persuade	walk	fast
big	draw	hot	kind	loud	pretty
error	happy	nervous	laugh	easy	repair
jump	throw	wet	rip	scared	cold
bad	small	end	tired	thin	look

Note to the teacher: Give each student pair a copy of the page and two different-colored crayons or pencils.

Language Arts Tips & Tools

How many titles can you list that begin with the letter S?

How's It Written?

Punctuating titles

This twist on The Game of Scattergories gives students practice punctuating titles. To begin, have each pair of students divide a sheet of paper into four columns and label them as shown. Next, announce a letter and challenge partners to list titles that begin with that letter. After 30 seconds, have each student pair share its list. Then award one point for each unique and correctly punctuated title. The pair with the most points wins.

Patricia Twohey, Smithfield, RI

Books	Magazines or Newspapers	Movies, Plays, Musicals, or TV Shows	Poems or Songs
Stone Fox	Sports Illustrated Kids	So You Think You Can Dance	"Skip to My Lou"
	Sun News		"Simple Simon"

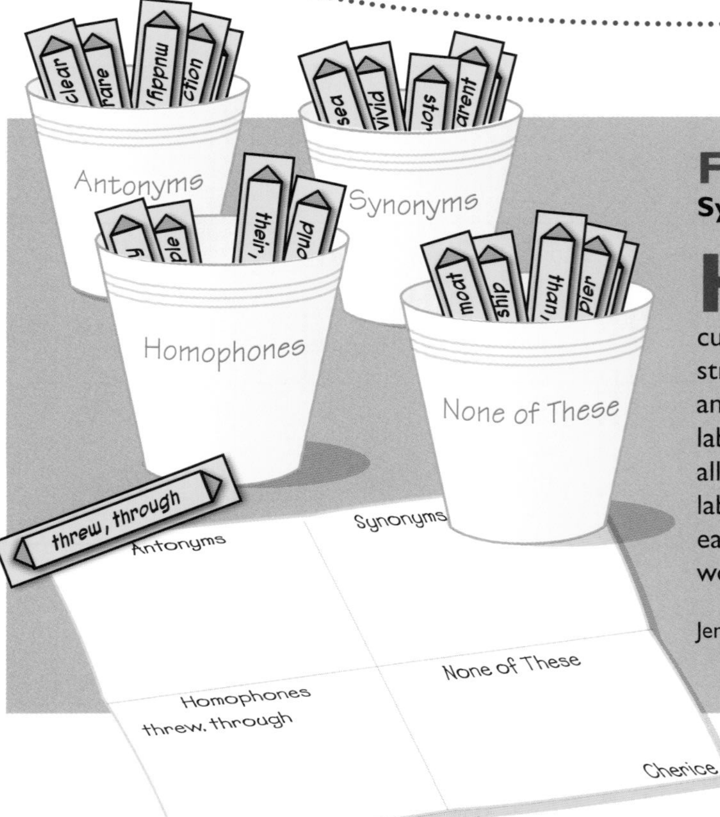

Four Cups

Synonyms, antonyms, and homophones

Help students build vocabulary skills with this simple sorting center. In advance, label four disposable cups as shown and then cut apart a copy of the word pair strips and answer key on page 87. A student draws a strip and reads both words. She puts the strip in the cup whose label describes the word pair. When the child has sorted all the cards, she folds a sheet of paper into fourths and labels the sections to match the cups. Then she records each word pair in the appropriate section and checks her work using the key.

Jennifer Otter, Oak Ridge, NC

Name That Letter

Spelling

The word is multiplication.

clap, clap, clap, clap

For fun spelling practice, divide your class into two teams and have each team form a straight line. Announce a spelling word for the first student on each team. Then clap to indicate the position of a letter in the word. For example, if the word is *carnival,* clap five times to indicate the letter *i*. The first student to say the correct letter earns a point for his team. Then both players go to the end of the line and the next players compete with another word. When time's up, the team with more points wins!

Brenda Tweed, Pigeon Forge, TN

Breaking It Down

Story elements

Increase students' focus during reading time by having them create book guides as they read. To begin, have each student fold a sheet of paper into thirds and label the front and back as shown. Next, instruct the child to keep the guide on his desk as he reads so he can illustrate and describe the story's elements. At the end of the reading session, have the student fold his guide and use it as a bookmark. Then he'll be ready to get right back to work the next day.

Kami Allers, Cross Creek Charter Academy, Byron Center, MI

Getting the POQ (Point of the Question)

Answering questions

I'm going to the basketball game tonight at seven o'clock.

What time are you going to tonight's basketball game?

Here's a great idea for reminding students to answer questions in complete, informative sentences. Whisper a simple question to a student volunteer and guide her to answer it in a complete sentence that restates the question. Next, have the class use the child's answer to figure out the question you asked. If the class guesses correctly, announce that the volunteer got the POQ and call on a different student. If the class's guess is incorrect, lead the student to rephrase her answer and have the class guess again. After several rounds, have students answer reading comprehension questions, making sure each answer includes the POQ!

Michele Anszelowidz, Forest Lake Elementary, Wantagh, NY

Name ______________________________

Date ____________________

READ ALL ABOUT IT!

On each newspaper, describe something the main character does in the story. Then tell why he or she does it.

____
story title

____
main character

The Character Times
What the character does:

Why the character does it:

The Character Times
What the character does:

Why the character does it:

The Character Times
What the character does:

Why the character does it:

The Character Times
What the character does:

Why the character does it:

The Character Times
What the character does:

Why the character does it:

The Character Times
What the character does:

Why the character does it:

Name ______________________________

Date ______________________

What's Your Move?

Use a ruler to connect each cause with its matching effect.

Cause		Effect
1. The shortstop dropped the ball;		we'll have to drink water.
2. We have to raise $200 for our class trip,	C K C B H	she tells tons of knock-knock jokes.
3. Since Paige found that book of jokes,	E P	so he'll have to make a new plan.
4. When our bus broke down,	G A H	Diana is the best shooter on the team.
5. Because he left the spelling list at school,	L C S V K	so they ride the same bus.
6. Since we all turned in our permission slips,	D F O	we need to leave by 7:00.
7. The tournament begins at 9:00;	T	we had to cancel our game.
8. Lauren just captured Jared's queen,	M A U	our whole class is going to the play.
9. The Bears' best player is sick,	Q E T N	as a result, Riley is safe on first.
10. Because she shoots baskets every day,	R J	so the Tigers think they'll win the match.
11. There are no more sodas;	I E M	Luke didn't review his words last night.
12. Hunter and Chloe are next-door neighbors,		so we are having four bake sales.

To find out Lauren's next move, write each letter that is not crossed out in order from left to right and top to bottom on the lines below.

__ __ __ __ __ __ __ __ __ __ __!

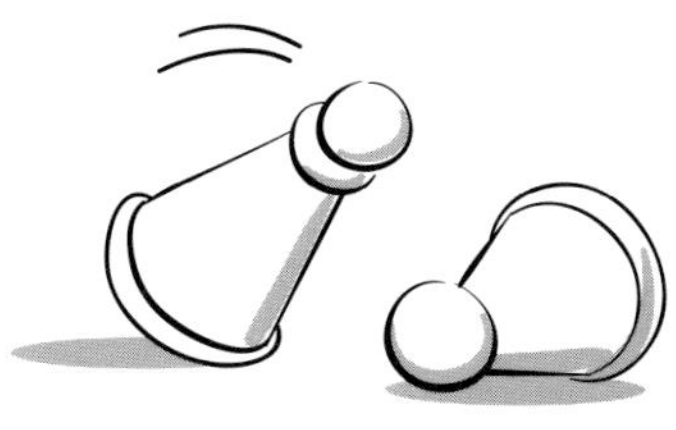

Name ______________________

Date ______________

Choose the idiom that best matches each situation. Write the idiom's letter on the line next to each item.

_____ **1.** Julia walks into her room and finds her brother, Josh, reading her journal.

_____ **2.** Coach Winter tells Craig that if he misses this free throw, they'll lose the game. Craig calmly walks right up to the line and shoots the ball.

_____ **3.** Emma trips on the sidewalk and drops her books. When she leans down to pick them up, she finds ten dollars.

_____ **4.** Ethan says he always puts his name on his paper. When Mrs. Brown holds up three nameless papers, Ethan has to admit they are all his.

_____ **5.** Brook wishes her parents would give her a new bike like Sara's.

_____ **6.** Tanner knows that Sean is buying a new CD for Cole's birthday. On their way home from school, Tanner tells Cole that Sean is giving him the CD.

_____ **7.** Alexa loses an earring on the playground. Katie and Alexa search for hours but never find the earring.

_____ **8.** Justin tries out for the lead role in the play. He can hardly wait to find out whether he will get the part.

_____ **9.** Since Bailey is new to our school, he doesn't know very many people.

_____ **10.** Vanessa screams and jumps out of her seat when she gets a paper cut.

_____ **11.** Mr. Adams scolds students who goof around in the hall, but his students know he's one of the nicest teachers at the school.

_____ **12.** Tristan's hands are so cold he can't tie his shoelaces.

A. If the shoe fits, wear it.
S. Every cloud has a silver lining.
M. He is all thumbs.
G. She makes a mountain out of a molehill.
U. It is like trying to find a needle in a haystack.
H. He is caught red-handed.
W. He is as cool as a cucumber.
J. His bark is worse than his bite.
P. He lets the cat out of the bag.
Y. He feels like a fish out of water.
O. She is green with envy.
I. He is sitting on pins and needles.

To complete this idiom, write each letter from above on its matching numbered line or lines below. Then write what you think it means.

When I say, "__ __ __ __," __ __ __ __ __ __, "__ __ __ __ __ __ __?"

(11 7 12 6) (9 5 7) (3 4 9) (1 5 2) (1 8 10 1)

____

Word Pair Strips and Answer Key

Use with "Four Cups" on page 82.

tree, flower TEC44046

pear, pier TEC44046

ocean, sea TEC44046

muddy, clean TEC44046

stationary, stationery TEC44046

frequent, rare TEC44046

story, tale TEC44046

night, day TEC44046

threw, through TEC44046

than, then TEC44046

clear, transparent TEC44046

fact, fiction TEC44046

their, they're TEC44046

sea, ship TEC44046

boat, moat TEC44046

colorful, vivid TEC44046

grimy, dirty TEC44046

cloudy, clear TEC44046

principal, principle TEC44046

wood, would TEC44046

Answer Key

Synonyms
- clear, transparent
- colorful, vivid
- grimy, dirty
- ocean, sea
- story, tale

Homophones
- principal, principle
- stationary, stationery
- their, they're
- threw, through
- wood, would

Antonyms
- cloudy, clear
- fact, fiction
- frequent, rare
- muddy, clean
- night, day

None of these
- boat, moat
- pear, pier
- sea, ship
- than, then
- tree, flower

TEC44046

Sentence Cards

Use with "Face Off!" on page 89. Mount copies of pages 88 and 89 on sturdy paper. If desired, laminate the pages before cutting out the cards and answer key.

1 The **thermostat** must be set too low; it's really cold in here!
TEC44046

2 How am I supposed to get **traction** on ice?
TEC44046

3 The horn's **abrupt** blast made me lose my balance!
TEC44046

4 Someone should have **forewarned** me about the cold.
TEC44046

5 Is this a **tripartite** game?
TEC44046

6 If that puck hits me in the face, it could cause **monocular** pain.
TEC44046

7 I'm not afraid of the puck, though; it's an **inanimate** object.
TEC44046

8 This game is going to be a **spectacle!**
TEC44046

9 I'll **contradict** anyone who says field hockey and ice hockey are the same.
TEC44046

10 Will I get warm in the **foreseeable** future?
TEC44046

11 After sliding around on all this frozen water, I may become **aquaphobic.**
TEC44046

12 Isn't there an **asterisk** on the program to tell when this game will end?
TEC44046

13 I wish someone would **intervene** in this game!
TEC44046

14 The **cacophony** of the crowd makes it hard to think.
TEC44046

15 Is one **quadrant** of the floor less slippery than the rest?
TEC44046

16 This must be a **conspiracy** to make us look silly.
TEC44046

ANSWER KEY FOR "FACE OFF!"

1. hypothermia, thermal, thermometer, thermos
   device that controls the temperature
2. attract, attraction, contract, track
   ability to grip a surface
3. disrupt, erupt, interrupt, rupture
   sudden
4. before, forecast, forward, warn
   given early warning
5. part, triangle, trio, triple
   having three parts
6. binocular, monocle, ocular, one
   affecting just one eye
7. animal, animated, animation, inactive
   not living
8. expect, obstacle, spectacular, spectator
   something entertaining to watch
9. contrary, contrast, dictate, predict
   argue the opposite
10. able, before, forecast, see
    known in advance
11. aquarium, aquatic, claustrophobia, phobia
    afraid of water
12. asteroid, astrology, astronomy, star
    star symbol used to show extra information
13. convene, interfere, interject, interrupt
    to change the way something happens
14. megaphone, phone, phonics, symphony
    harsh, unpleasant sounds
15. quadrilateral, quadruple, quadruplet, quarter
    one of the four quarters
16. conspire, expire, inspire, spirit
    plot

TEC44046

Analyzing complex words

FACE OFF!

DIRECTIONS:

1. Stack the cards facedown.
2. Draw a card. Read the sentence. List words that have root words related to the boldfaced word. Then tell what you think the boldfaced word means.
3. Check the key. For every word you listed that is on the key, score one point. If your definition is correct, score two points.
4. After drawing all the cards, add up your points. Use the table to rate the level of your play.

1–23 points:	Welcome to the Bantam League.
24–47 points:	You're a Minor Leaguer.
48–71 points:	You've made it to the Majors!
72–96 points:	Congratulations; you are a Pro!

Reading and Language Arts TIPS & TOOLS

Making the Curve
Analyzing challenging words

Want your independent readers to analyze challenging words in their reading instead of skipping them? Try this! Post a sign similar to the traffic sign shown and explain that when a driver comes to a sharp turn, she slows down and keeps her eyes on the road. Like the driver, a reader who comes to a challenging word should slow down and look for clues, making sure she understands the word's meaning. If desired, have each student write challenging words from her reading on small sticky notes and put them on the sign so you can see which words are giving your students the most trouble.

adapted from an idea by Sandy Ross, Woolls Intermediate School, Hondo, TX

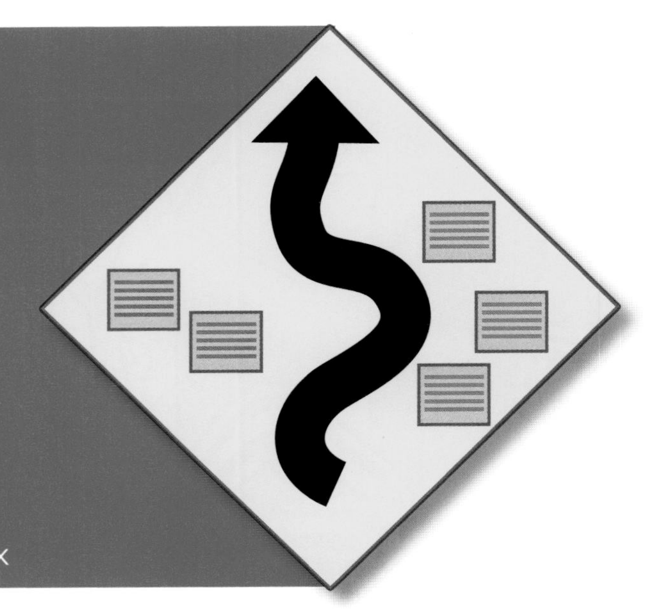

Novel ABCs
Distinguishing important and minor details

These alphabet books are perfect for literature circles! To begin, have each small group cut 13 sheets of paper in half and label each page with a different letter pair. The students identify a detail from a current novel and decide whether it's important or minor. If the detail is important, the students describe it on the page with the matching letter pair. Next, they illustrate the detail and tell why it's important. If the detail is minor, the students simply write a sentence about it on the page. Each group can leave up to five pages blank for letters without matching details. When students finish, they create a construction paper cover, order the pages, and staple them inside.

Melissa Barbay, Devers Elementary, Devers, TX

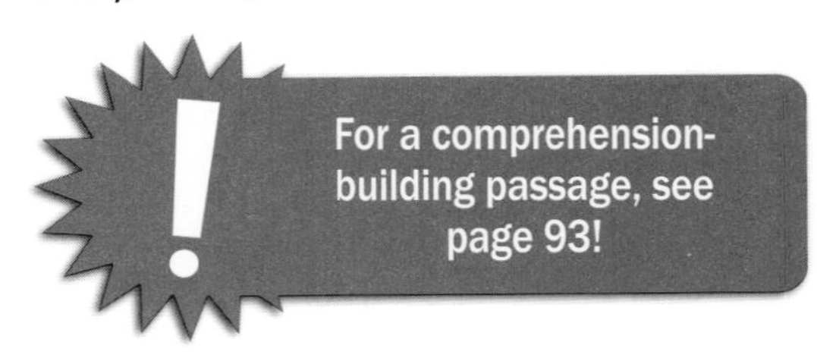

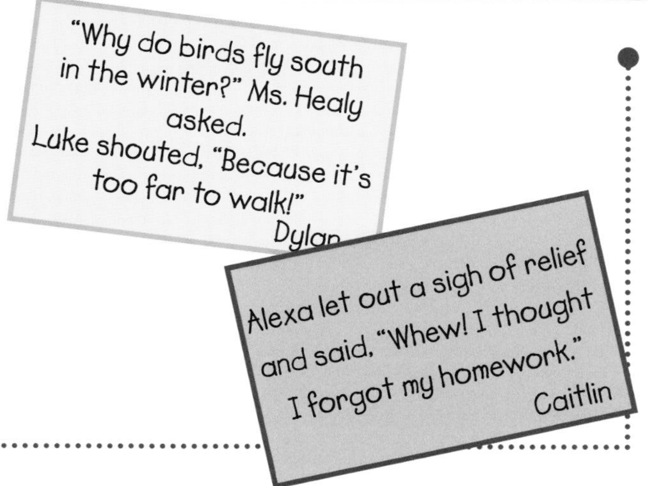

Quotable Moments

Punctuating dialogue

For this simple idea, give each student an index card. Next, guide the child to listen for and record five interesting things you or his classmates say during the day, using correct punctuation. Shortly before the dismissal bell, collect students' work and read aloud a sampling of quotations. Then use the cards to get a quick picture of each student's punctuation skills.

Terry Healy, Marlatt Elementary, Manhattan, KS

On a Roll

Responding to literature

Make sure each student's independent reading is productive with this response log. Have the child accordion-fold a two-sided copy of page 97 to make a reading log, as shown. Have the student keep the log handy during silent reading or when reading at home. Guide the child to jot notes on his log before, while, and after he reads. Then set aside time for students to discuss their reading in small groups.

Karen Slattery, Dundas, Ontario, Canada

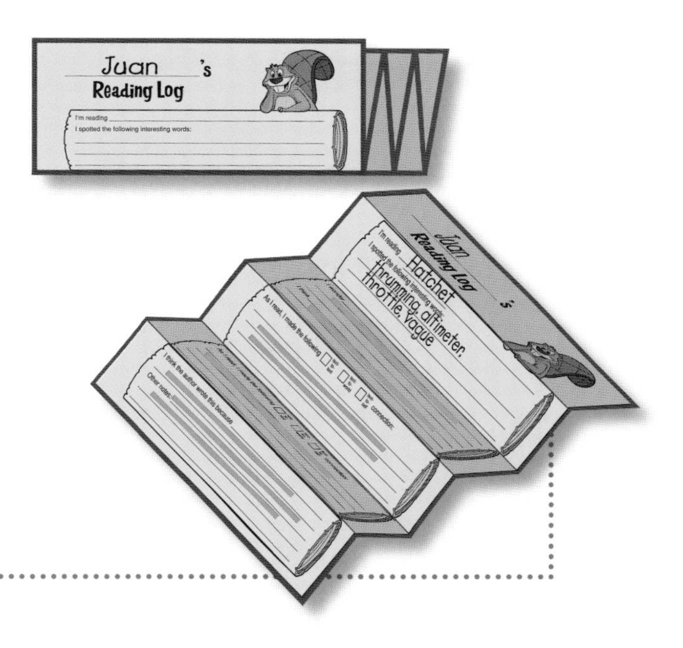

Ace Speller

Spelling

To engage students in practicing their spelling words, have each child create a code as guided on a copy of page 98. Next, have the student write coded versions of her spelling words, arranging the words in a random order on the page. Then have each child trade papers with a partner and decipher her partner's words. If desired, have each student complete the page at home and challenge her parent or guardian to decode the words.

Tracey Stuart, Oregon, WI

Name
Date

Graphic organizer

Rich Relationships

Main Character

Title

N
W E
S

Supporting Characters

How does the main character act toward and feel about others?

•

•

•

•

How do other characters act toward and feel about the main character?

•

•

•

•

What does this tell you about the character?

•

•

Note to the teacher: Have each student use the organizer to analyze the main character through his or her interactions with other characters.

Name ______________________________ Date ______________

What a Ride

It was March 2. We were headed across the state to watch my sister's basketball team play. Her team had made it to the first round of the state playoffs, and this game was do or die.

When Mom planned our route, she noticed a shortcut over Flint Peak that would save us two hours. We usually avoided Flint Peak in the winter, but it was almost spring, it hadn't snowed in a couple of weeks, and it was a warm day. Since the shortcut gave us extra time, we stopped for lunch in town before we left.

The first thing we saw on the shortcut was a sign that read, "Road closed November 15 through March 1 due to icy conditions."

"What do you think, Diana?" Mom asked me.

"I don't know, Mom. That's a little scary."

"The road looks fine. It is open today, and we don't really have time to turn around and go the other way," Mom said, thinking out loud. "That settles it. We're going!"

Before long, we realized why the road had been closed. It was a narrow, curvy dirt road. We already knew that, but as soon as we started driving up, we saw that snow and ice covered nearly the whole road. We slid a little here and there, but Mom kept the car under control.

We smiled at each other as we cruised down the last incline. The sun was shining. The road looked wet but not icy. We had made it!

When we saw the truck ahead sitting at an odd angle beside the road, it was too late. As Mom started to go around, we realized the road wasn't just wet—it was flooded. The truck was stuck in the mud, and, by that time, so were we!

We sat in the middle of the road for about an hour before a friendly couple came by and pulled our car out of the mud. We still could have made it to the game, but we didn't want to go any farther. So we headed back over Flint Peak, listened to the game on the radio, and vowed to never again take a road like that on the first day it opens!

Circle the letter of the best answer.

1. What is the main purpose of the selection?
- **A.** to warn drivers not to drive on icy roads
- **B.** to share an interesting experience
- **C.** to describe a springlike day

2. Why did the author write that "it was almost spring"?
- **A.** to let the reader know it was still winter
- **B.** to let the reader know flowers were blooming
- **C.** to let the reader know the road was safe

3. Which word best describes the trip?
- **A.** adventurous
- **B.** worrisome
- **C.** terrifying

4. In the first paragraph, what does "this game was do or die" mean?
- **A.** The team performed best when the pressure was on.
- **B.** The team always won its games.
- **C.** The team had to win the game to advance.

5. Which event happens before Mom starts to go around the truck?
- **A.** A friendly couple pulled their car out of the mud.
- **B.** They sat in the middle of the road for an hour.
- **C.** A truck got stuck in the mud.

Name ____________________
Date ____________________

AS BUSY AS A BEE

...and then you turn left...

Pick ___ activities to do.
When you finish an activity, color its number.

1 Draw pictures to show what each simile actually means. • The raindrops feel like feathers. • My cereal is as soggy as pudding. • The gecko's tongue moves like a yo-yo. • This cookie is as hard as a rock!	**2** Copy each sentence starter. Add a simile to finish each sentence. Grace runs ___. The dancer spins across the stage ___. Jared's snake slithers ___. My handwriting looks ___.	**3** Choose five objects. Write a simile to describe each one.  When the speaker comes on, it's as loud as a hive of bees.
4 Draw pictures to show what each metaphor actually means. I'm an ice cube frozen to the team bench. Her smile was a ray of sunshine. The playground can be a zoo. The rain, a welcome visitor, started falling last night.	**5** List three things each metaphor below could describe. The ___ is a rock concert of color. The creeping ___ is syrup oozing over a stack of pancakes. ___ sprints by, a cheetah on the chase.	**6** Fold a sheet of paper in half vertically. Draw a self-portrait on one side. On the other side, list six or more similes and metaphors that describe you. Stand your work to display it. 
7 Complete each sentence with a simile or a metaphor. When I was five, I ___. When I was in second grade, I ___. When I am 14, I will ___. When I get my driver's license, I will drive ___.	**8** Copy the adjectives below. For each one, name an animal, place, or thing that has that quality. Then use each one as a simile or metaphor in a sentence. SMOOTH rough quiet SHY shiny smelly	**9** Describe a new breakfast cereal using three similes and three metaphors. Design the front panel of the cereal package. Include your similes, metaphors, and pictures. 

Independent Practice Grid: Program the student directions with the number of activities to be completed. Then copy the page for each student.

Name ______________________________

Date ____________________

BEFORE and After

Match each prefix or suffix with its meaning. Write the letter on the blank.

1. *-able*	______	**A.**	before
2. *mis-*	______	**B.**	one who
3. *-en*	______	**C.**	not
4. *pre-*	______	**D.**	wrong
5. *-less*	______	**E.**	again
6. *un-*	______	**F.**	under
7. *-er*	______	**G.**	made of
8. *re-*	______	**H.**	full of
9. *-ful*	______	**I.**	without
10. *sub-*	______	**J.**	can do

Circle the prefix or suffix from above in each sentence. Then write *T* if the statement is true or *F* if the statement is false.

__F__ **11.** A misleading arrow shows the way.

______ **12.** Alli is breathless because she just ran a mile.

______ **13.** As a blogger, Josh does not need access to the Internet.

______ **14.** John's mother warns him to be careful as he pours the milk.

______ **15.** Amy is eager to see the previews after the movie.

______ **16.** Ty studies for the math test by reviewing the chapter.

______ **17.** To get on the subway, we go up the stairs.

______ **18.** Anna misunderstood her dad and got lost.

______ **19.** Tanner is unable to spell *bromeliad* and wins the spelling bee!

______ **20.** My grandfather carves wooden flutes and sells them.

______ **21.** If a starfish loses an arm, it can regenerate it.

______ **22.** Vicky turns the oven off to preheat it.

Name ____

Date ______________________

Making Wise Choices

Which resource would be the **best** place to look for the answer to each question? Circle the letter in the matching column.

Encyclopedia	Dictionary	Thesaurus	
R	S	T	1. What does *calorie* mean?
M	D	T	2. What is a synonym for *healthy?*
I	G	H	3. Why do our bodies need vitamins?
M	N	O	4. What is another word for *eat?*
D	E	F	5. How do you spell the adjective form of *nutrition?*
A	P	C	6. How many calories should a person eat in one day?
T	U	V	7. How do you pronounce *carbohydrate?*
F	G	H	8. What are the benefits of drinking milk?
P	Q	R	9. Should you cut fat out of your diet altogether?
W	C	S	10. Is there more than one meaning for *diet?*
K	L	N	11. What is an antonym for *healthy?*
Y	B	T	12. Which foods are high in protein?
G	H	I	13. Can *cook* be used as a noun and a verb?
D	A	B	14. How many servings of vegetables should you eat each day?
O	R	W	15. What is the past tense of *eat?*

To complete the sentence, write each circled letter from above on its matching line or lines below.

If you add up all the time you spend eating in a year, you will find that

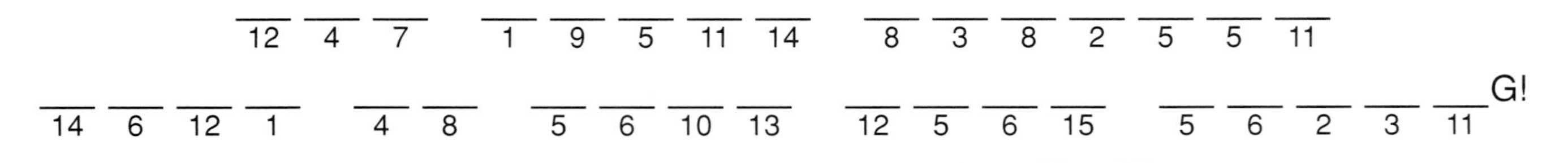

Bonus Box: Find the answer to each question above.

_______________________________'s

Reading Log

I'm reading ______________________________

I spotted the following interesting words:

____

____

____

I wonder ______________________________

____

____

I think ______________________________

____

____

As I read, I made the following ☐ text-to-text ☐ text-to-world ☐ text-to-self connection:

____

____

____

____

As I read, I made the following ☐ text-to-text ☐ text-to-world ☐ text-to-self connection:

____

____

____

____

I think the author wrote this because ______________________________

____

Other notes: ______________________________

____

____

Note to the teacher: Use with "On a Roll" on page 91.

Name ______________________________

Date ______________________

Ace Speller

Fill in the chart with different letters to create a code. Then use the code to encrypt, or write in code, each of your spelling words.

a	b	c	d	e	f	g	h	i	j	k	l	m

n	o	p	q	r	s	t	u	v	w	x	y	z

	Coded Words	Decoded Words
1		
2		
3		
4		
5		
6		
7		
8		
9		
10		
11		
12		

These words have been deciphered by ______________________________.

 Note to the teacher: Use with "Ace Speller" on page 91.

Names ______________________

Date ______________________

WHAT'S THE SCOOP?

adjective
pronoun
verb
preposition
adverb
pronoun
noun
adverb
adjective
verb
preposition
noun

PLAYER 1

A Yummy Game for Two Players

DIRECTIONS:

1. Choose a sundae.
2. In turn, roll a die to determine the part of speech you will look for. Find a word in your list of sentences that is that part of speech.

   roll of 1 = noun roll of 4 = adjective
   roll of 2 = verb roll of 5 = adverb
   roll of 3 = pronoun roll of 6 = preposition
3. If you are correct, write the word in a matching ice cream scoop. Have your opponent use a dictionary to check your answer.
4. If you have already filled the scoops for the part of speech, your turn is over.
5. The first player to correctly fill in all his sundae's scoops wins.

Player One's Sentence List

- Strawberry Splash loves every kind of ice cream.
- She easily wins every ice cream–eating contest in the state.
- She gazes at the supersundae in the enormous dish.
- Strawberry can see herself devouring it in no time.
- The sundae is piled high with ice cream, and a yummy cherry sits on top.
- Strawberry quickly grabs her favorite spoon.
- Then she looks around to see who she will race.
- She spots Rocky across the room and sizes up her competition.

Player Two's Sentence List

- Rocky Rhodes is crazy about ice cream.
- Chocolate chip cookie dough is his very favorite flavor.
- He is surprised he will face Strawberry in an ice cream–eating duel.
- Rocky is confident and expects to be the new champion.
- Strawberry is good, but unfortunately, she holds only one spoon.
- Rocky smiles and happily shows his secret weapons.
- He holds an oversize spoon in each hand.
- The crowd sits silently, waiting for the challenge to start.

Reading and Language Arts TIPS & TOOLS

Spur of the Moment
Speaking

Give your students a taste of extemporaneous speaking by practicing with low-stress speech topics. In advance, program paper strips with speech topics, such as the ones shown, and place them in a bag. Next, have each student draw two strips, choose one, and return the other. Then have the student label three index cards as shown. Give each child five minutes to plan a short speech about his topic, listing key words and phrases on each card. Finally, have him announce his topic and present his one- to three-minute speech.

Beth Gress, Granville, OH

Extemporaneous Topics

Is homework necessary? Why or why not?
Which animal makes the best pet? Explain.
What is the best thing ever invented? Why?
Which of your five senses is most important to you? Explain.
Does advertising influence people's food choices? Explain.
Who inspires you most? Explain.
Which season is the most fun? Explain.
Why is a dog often called man's best friend?
What is a good summer job for kids? Explain.
Is ice cream only a summer treat? Why or why not?

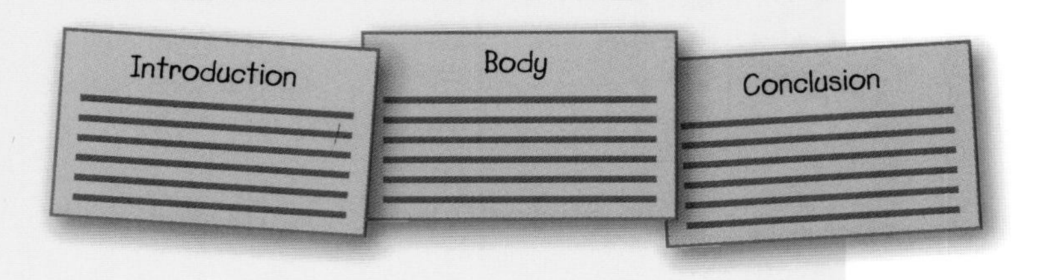

What's the Meaning?
Word study

Looking for a fun way to get kids interested in figuring out challenging words? Try this! Post a list of unusual nouns, such as those shown, and have each student fold a sheet of paper in half two times to form four sections. Next, have the child unfold the paper and write one of the nouns in the first section. In the next section, the student makes a prediction about the word's meaning. In the third section, she draws a picture of what she thinks the noun looks like. In the last section, the student uses the unfamiliar word in a sentence. Then she looks up the noun in a dictionary or an encyclopedia, flips her paper, and repeats the steps with the actual definition.

Isobel L. Livingstone, Rahway, NJ

Unusual Nouns

aioli	bauble	buoy
clavier	doily	dollop
fez	kumquat	nosh
parasol	tocsin	tome
wapiti	weskit	zephyr

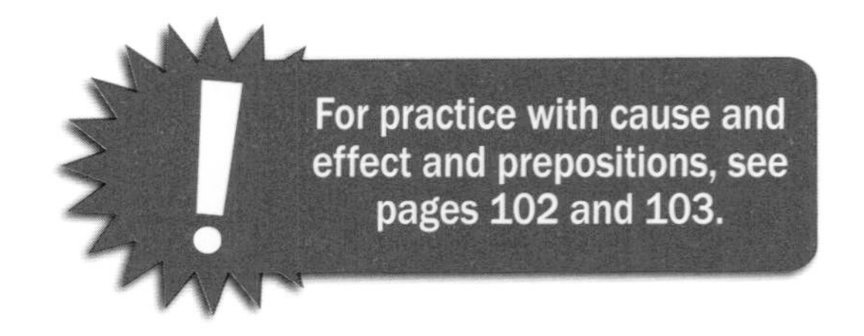

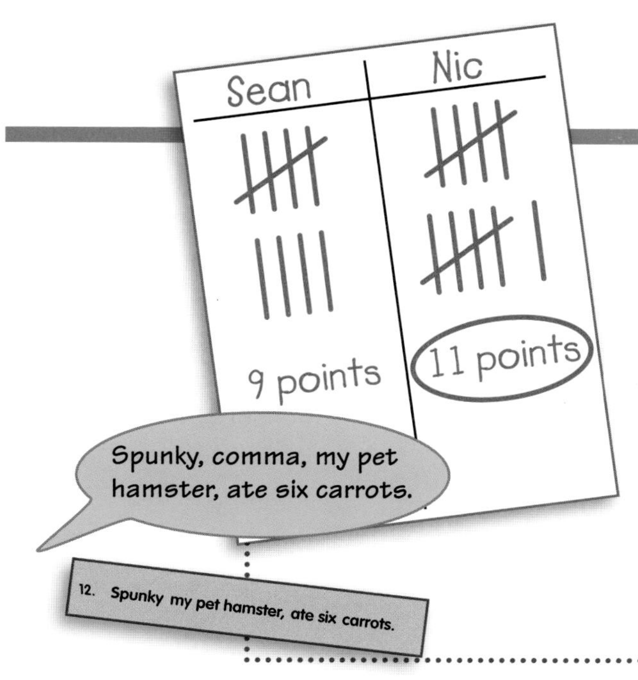

Something's Missing!

Punctuation review

For this fun punctuation game, give each pair of students a copy of the game cards and answer key on page 105. Have the partners cut apart the cards and stack them face-down. In turn, one student draws a card, reads the sentence, and adds the correct punctuation. His partner checks the answer key. If the answer is correct, he earns a point and his partner takes a turn. If it's not correct, he does not earn a point and his turn is over. After all the cards have been played, the player with more points wins.

Jennifer Otter, Oak Ridge, NC

Roots and Results

Cause and effect

To help students make real-world and literary connections between causes and effects, give each student a copy of the chart on page 106. Have the child record in each row an example of characters or people who see eye to eye. Then guide the child to describe the effect of the characters or people getting along. Next, have the student repeat the steps with examples of people or characters who disagree. To follow up, have each child respond to one of the prompts shown.

Jennifer Davis Bowman, DuBois Academy, Cincinnati, OH

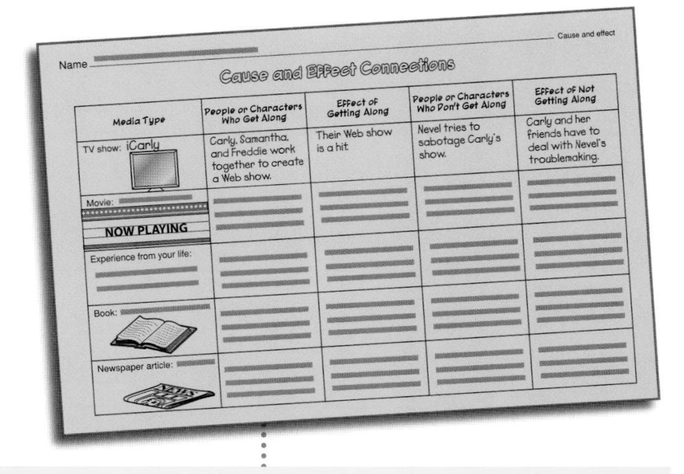

Cause and Effect Connections

Media Type	People or Characters Who Get Along	Effect of Getting Along	People or Characters Who Don't Get Along	Effect of Not Getting Along
TV show: iCarly	Carly, Samantha, and Freddie work together to create a Web show.	Their Web show is a hit	Nevel tries to sabotage Carly's show.	Carly and her friends have to deal with Nevel's troublemaking.
Movie:				
Experience from your life:				
Book:				
Newspaper article:				

- What happened the last time you were involved in a disagreement?
- What positive effects can come from a disagreement? Explain.
- Who is it the easiest for you to get along with? Why?

Read All About It!

Identifying information

Add the fun of a scavenger hunt to reading for information. In advance, cut out one newspaper sports article for every four students. Then post the list of details shown and give each small group an article. Next, challenge the group to read the article and find each detail on the list. Have the students highlight the detail in the article and create a T chart to record their work. As time allows, have each group share the highlights of its article with the class.

Diane Marshall, Salem, AL

Name ______________________________

Date ______________________

ONE THING LEADS TO ANOTHER

WORDS THAT POINT TO THE CAUSE

- if
- due to
- for this reason
- because
- since

WORDS THAT POINT TO THE EFFECT

- so
- therefore
- consequently
- as a result
- then

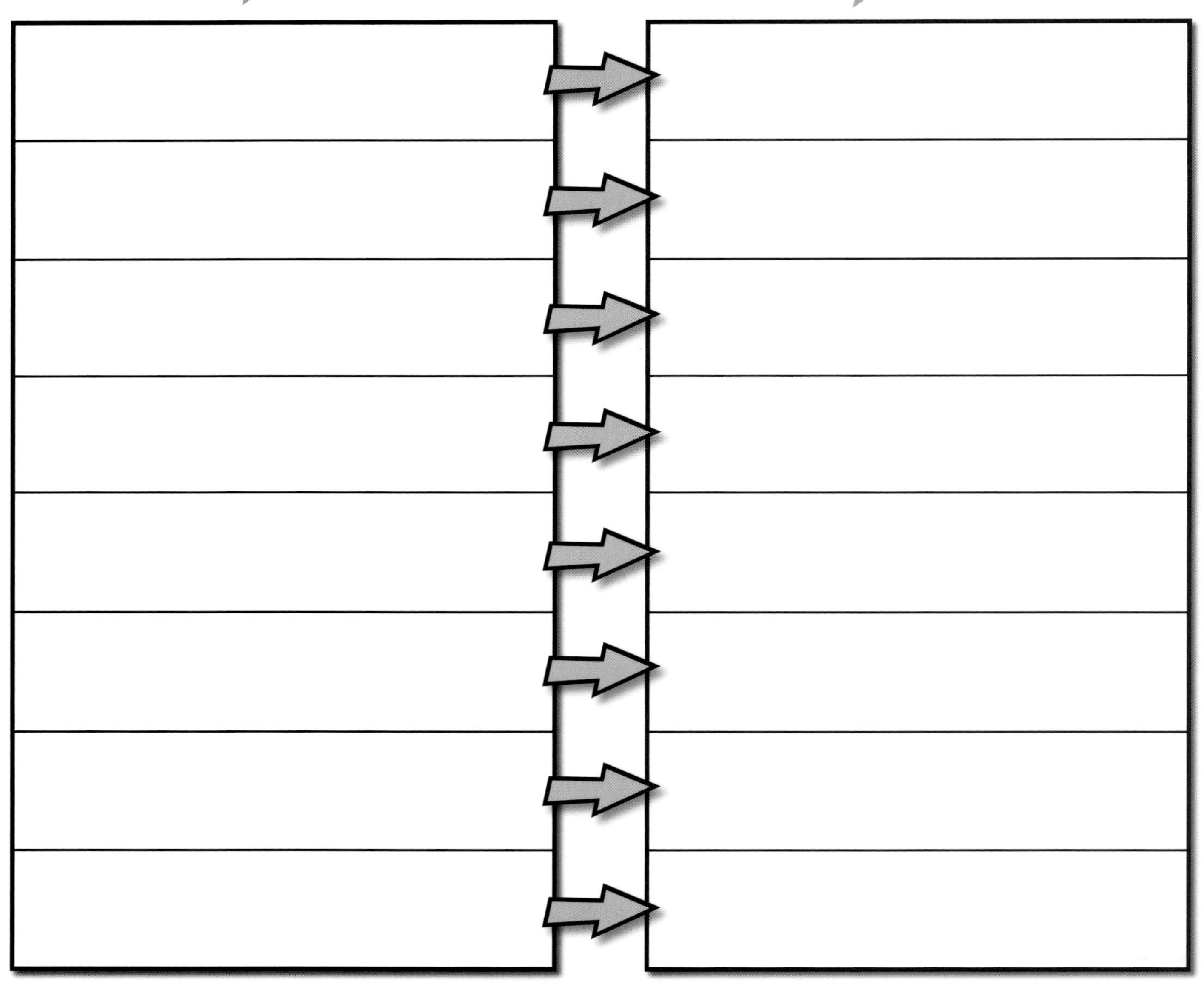

Note to the teacher: Have each student use a copy of the organizer to identify cause and effect when reading.

Name ______________________________

Date ______________________________

Pick ___ activities to do.
When you finish an activity, color its number.

1 Create a word search using the prepositions below.

above	in
against	into
along	of
behind	on
by	over
down	under
from	with

2 Draw a three-column chart to show which prepositions below tell when, which ones tell where, and which ones tell either when or where.

across	near
after	outside
around	since
before	throughout
beneath	till
beside	until
during	within

3 Unscramble each preposition below.

A. toin	G. noot
B. tuoab	H. heanrdnuet
C. eewebtn	I. inebhd
D. rinugd	J. tisoude
E. rdnue	K. stap
F. socras	L. oelbw

4 Create a poster that shows ten compound prepositions, such as "according to" and "in back of."

5 Write eight prepositional phrases. Use the prepositions and nouns or noun phrases below.

6 Finish each prepositional phrase below. Circle the preposition.

___ the street
___ the river
___ my friends
___ dinner
___ the ladder
___ the edge
___ school
___ the author

7 Write eight prepositional phrases using the prepositions shown. Draw an arrow from each preposition to its object.

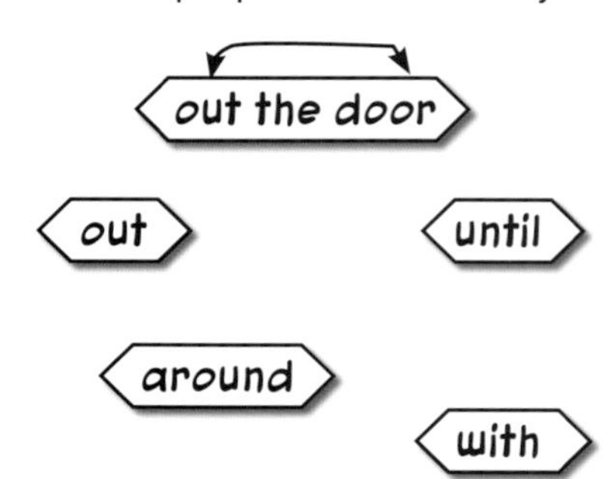

8 List ten prepositional phrases from your reading. Circle each preposition.

9 Write eight prepositional phrases using the noun objects below. Then illustrate each phrase.

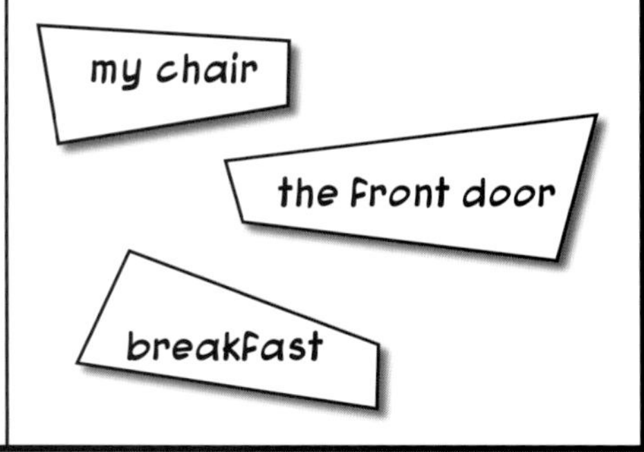

Independent Practice Grid: Program the student directions with the number of activities to be completed. Then copy the page for each student.

Name ______________________

Date ______________

LOOK HIGH AND LOW!

Color the boxes according to the code.

What do you always overlook?

To find out, identify the word hidden in the puzzle.

Your ____________________!

COLOR CODE

present tense verb = red
past tense verb = yellow
future tense verb = green

gave	go / ate	fly	wrote	blow	open	type	tasted	knew	skipped	hike	swim
smiled	hid / run	try / were	made	will play	will sleep	will breathe	drew	move	shake	will make	will draw
washed	shout	flew / see	froze	will run	tear	will fly	sanded	packed	took	will go	catch
liked	break	work	rode	will eat	cook	will see	eat	fold	spoke	will learn	will practice
dive	play	bake	give	will walk	will write	will ride	ran	blew	washed	will open	take
hide	call	fall	skip	grow	look	sleep	speak	fold	come	will say	will bake

Bonus Box: On another page, write the past tense form of each present tense verb.

Game Cards and Answer Key

Use with "Something's Missing!" on page 101.

1. Dad bought popcorn and I bought soda. TEC44048	2. The cheering crowd shouted, Go, team! TEC44048
3. If you arrive late you will miss your flight. TEC44048	4. Sydney bought plates cups and napkins for her party. TEC44048
5. Wait I'm coming. TEC44048	6. If you've seen my favorite jacket would you tell me where? TEC44048
7. Trevor it's your turn. TEC44048	8. Gosh I forgot! TEC44048
9. Wow you're doing great! TEC44048	10. If you need more time please raise your hand. TEC44048
11. Stop, thief TEC44048	12. Spunky my pet hamster, ate six carrots. TEC44048
13. Mom asked "What time will you be home?" TEC44048	14. I bought syrup ice cream and whipped cream. TEC44048
15. Anna will you take out the garbage TEC44048	16. Maddie helped wash the car but then she had to leave. TEC44048
17. When you finish your test turn your paper over. TEC44048	18. "That's my dog! Blake said. TEC44048
19. Im not sleepy. TEC44048	20. Luke my best friend gave me the coolest present. TEC44048

ANSWER KEY FOR "SOMETHING'S MISSING"

1. Dad bought popcorn, and I bought soda.
2. The cheering crowd shouted, "Go, team!"
3. If you arrive late, you will miss your flight.
4. Sydney bought plates, cups, and napkins for her party.
5. Wait! I'm coming.
6. If you've seen my favorite jacket, would you tell me where?
7. Trevor, it's your turn.
8. Gosh, I forgot!
9. Wow, you're doing great!
10. If you need more time, please raise your hand.
11. Stop, thief!
12. Spunky, my pet hamster, ate six carrots.
13. Mom asked, "What time will you be home?"
14. I bought syrup, ice cream, and whipped cream.
15. Anna, will you take out the garbage?
16. Maddie helped wash the car, but then she had to leave.
17. When you finish your test, turn your paper over.
18. "That's my dog!" Blake said.
19. I'm not sleepy.
20. Luke, my best friend, gave me the coolest present.

TEC44048

Name ______________________________

Cause-and-Effect Connections

Media Type	People or Characters Who Get Along	Effect of Getting Along	People or Characters Who Don't Get Along	Effect of Not Getting Along
TV show:				
Movie: NOW PLAYING				
Experience from your life:				
Book:				
Newspaper article: NEWS				

Note to the teacher: Use with "Roots and Results" on page 101.

Analogy Cards

Use with "Tuning Up" on page 108. Mount on construction paper the game mat on page 108 and the cards and answer key below. If desired, laminate the pages before cutting out the cards and answer key.

1. *Enjoyable* is to *fun* as *monotonous* is to _______. TEC44048	2. *Fast* is to *rapid* as *careful* is to _______. TEC44048	3. *Bicycle* is to *spokes* as *school* is to _______. TEC44048	4. *Team* is to *player* as *flock* is to _______. TEC44048
5. *Glad* is to *joyless* as *soft* is to _______. TEC44048	6. *Minute* is to *seconds* as *tree* is to _______. TEC44048	7. *Lucky* is to *fortunate* as *calm* is to _______. TEC44048	8. *Book* is to *read* as *basketball* is to _______. TEC44048
9. *Read* is to *peruse* as *run* is to _______. TEC44048	10. *Hot* is to *freezing* as *bottom* is to _______. TEC44048	11. *Couch* is to *sit* as *nose* is to _______. TEC44048	12. *Solitary* is to *alone* as *dusky* is to _______. TEC44048
13. *Cookie* is to *chocolate chip* as *book* is to _______. TEC44048	14. *Broom* is to *sweep* as *pencil* is to _______. TEC44048	15. *Friend* is to *enemy* as *generous* is to _______. TEC44048	16. *Room* is to *windows* as *mouth* is to _______. TEC44048
17. *Cloudy* is to *clear* as *hungry* is to _______. TEC44048	18. *Ruler* is to *measure* as *crayon* is to _______. TEC44048	19. *Soundless* is to *noisy* as *inactive* is to _______. TEC44048	20. *Steps* are to *climb* as *teeth* are to _______. TEC44048

Answer Key for "Tuning Up"

Word to Synonym
1. boring
2. cautious
7. peaceful
9. sprint
12. dark

Word to Antonym
5. scratchy
10. top
15. stingy
17. full
19. busy

Whole to Part
3. students
4. bird
6. leaves
13. page
16. teeth

Object to Use
8. dribble
11. smell
14. write
18. color
20. chew

TEC44048

Tuning Up

Directions:
1. Divide a sheet of paper into four sections. Label each section with an analogy relationship from below.
2. Draw a card and read the first word pair.
3. Decide how the words are related. Place the card on the note labeled with the matching relationship.
4. Choose the word from the word bank that best completes the analogy.
5. Check the key. Then record each completed analogy in its matching section on your paper.

Word Bank

bird	color	page	stingy
boring	dark	peaceful	students
busy	dribble	scratchy	teeth
cautious	full	smell	top
chew	leaves	sprint	write

Names_______________

Date_______________

Swimmers, Take Your Mark!

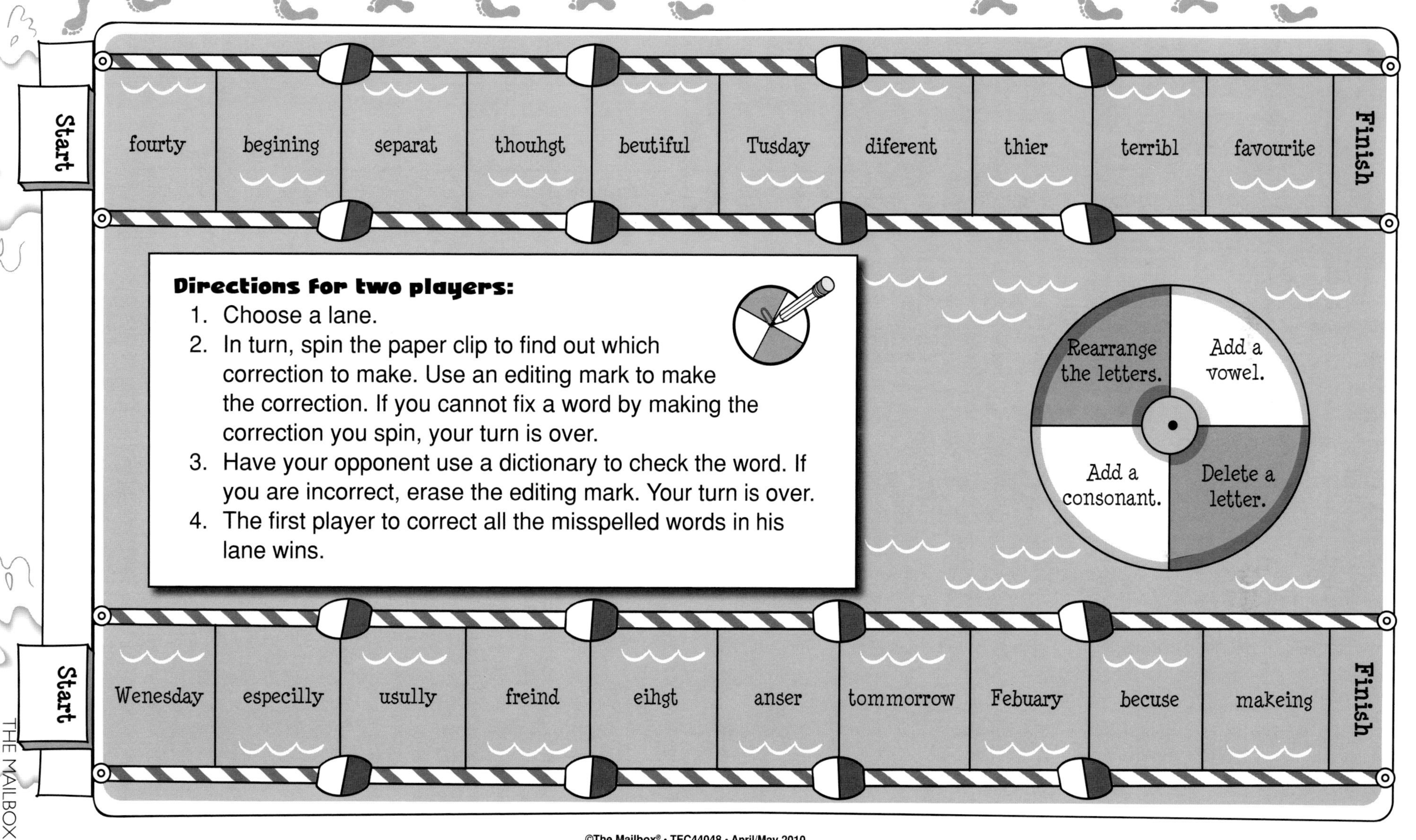

Directions for two players:

1. Choose a lane.
2. In turn, spin the paper clip to find out which correction to make. Use an editing mark to make the correction. If you cannot fix a word by making the correction you spin, your turn is over.
3. Have your opponent use a dictionary to check the word. If you are incorrect, erase the editing mark. Your turn is over.
4. The first player to correct all the misspelled words in his lane wins.

Note to the teacher: Each student pair needs a pencil, a paper clip, and a copy of the page.

Reading and Language Arts TIPS & TOOLS

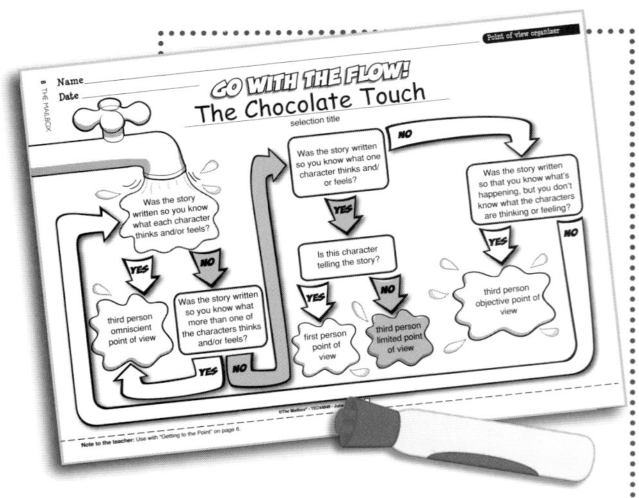

Getting to the Point
Author's point of view

Try this idea to give students a hand in analyzing point of view. Display a transparency of the flow chart from page 117. Then guide students to answer the first question about a current class reading. Shade yes or no, as appropriate, and follow the arrow to the next box, repeating until you reach the selection's point of view. Then wipe the transparency and place it near your class library as a handy reading tool. When a child is struggling to identify an author's point of view, he can simply grab the page and a wipe-off marker and follow the arrows.

See page 112 for an organizer that guides students to analyze a story's plot.

It's All in the Name
Vocabulary, research

For this exploration, list several words that were originally people's names (*eponymous words*), such as those shown. Review the words' meanings and then challenge students to guess their origins. Next, explain that each term was named for a person or is believed to have been based on a person's name. Then assign each pair of students an eponymous word and have the duo research its origin. To share their research, have the partners write a five Ws poem using the pattern shown. Then have each pair share its poem and post it on a board titled "It's All in the Names—Eponymous Words."

Isobel L. Livingstone, Rahway, NJ

Eponymous Word	Origin
America	Amerigo Vespucci, Italian explorer
Celsius	Anders Celsius, Swedish astronomer
leotard	Jules Léotard, French aerialist
sandwich	John Montagu, the fourth Earl of Sandwich

Line one: Who is the word named after?
Line two: What did he or she do?
Line three: When?
Line four: Where?
Line five: Why is the word named after this person?

Amerigo Vespucci
Explored the New World
From 1497 through 1504
Sailed along the coasts of Venezuela and Brazil
He discovered South America.

Would You Be a Mystery?

Genre

Here's a fun idea for reviewing genre features! First, lead students to brainstorm a list of genres. Then challenge each child to imagine she is a book and choose the genre in which she belongs. Next, have the child explain, in a paragraph, why her book would be in the named genre. After writing the paragraph, have each student fold a sheet of unlined paper in half and design her book's front and back covers. Finally, have the child glue her paragraph inside her book and share her work with a small group.

Melissa Jackson, Oak Ridge Intermediate, Camdenton, MO

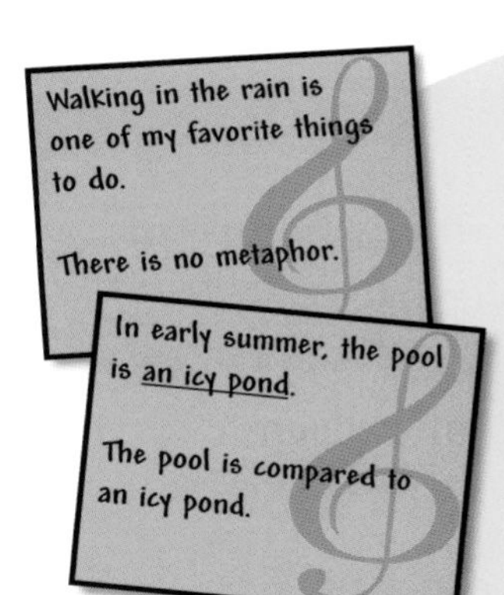

Music to My Ears

Identifying metaphor

For this partner game, have each pair of students cut apart the cards on a copy of page 118. In turn, one child draws a card and reads the first sentence to her partner. The partner decides whether the sentence contains a metaphor, identifying the metaphor if there is one. If he is correct, the partner gets the card. If he is incorrect, he returns the card to the pile. Once all the cards have been played, the partner with the most cards is declared the winner.

Laugh Lines

Using inflection

Students learn why inflection is important with this quick activity. To begin, post the opening lines of several songs or rhymes, such as those shown. Then choose one and read it in a monotone voice. Next, reread the line, emphasizing a random word. Finally, read the line with appropriate inflection and discuss the differences. Then guide each small group of students to choose an opening line and practice reading it three different ways. Have the students in each group read their line three times and explain the inflection in the best version.

Oh, do you know the muffin man?

Opening Line	Song or Rhyme
"Oh, do you know the muffin man?"	"The Muffin Man"
"A sailor went to sea, sea, sea."	"A Sailor Went to Sea, Sea, Sea"
"I'm bringing home a baby bumblebee."	"Baby Bumblebee"
"Did you ever see a lassie?"	"Did You Ever See a Lassie?"
"Do your ears hang low?"	"Do Your Ears Hang Low?"
"The itsy-bitsy spider went up the waterspout."	"The Itsy-Bitsy Spider"
"Hickory, dickory, dock, the mouse ran up the clock."	"Hickory, Dickory, Dock"
"If you're happy and you know it, clap your hands."	"If You're Happy and You Know It"
"Jack and Jill went up the hill to fetch a pail of water."	"Jack and Jill"
"Take me out to the ball game."	"Take Me Out to the Ball Game"

Colleen Dabney, Williamsburg, VA

Name ________________________________

Date ____________________

DIGGING DEEPER

Complete the organizer to analyze the selection you are reading. Then use your work to summarize the plot on another sheet of paper.

____
selection title

Who has a problem?

What is the problem?

Why is it a problem?

Describe the first attempt to solve the problem.

What happens?

Describe another attempt to solve the problem.

How is the problem finally resolved?

Check the box next to the phrase that best describes the conflict.

- ☐ person against nature
- ☐ person against person
- ☐ person against society
- ☐ person against self

Name ____________________

Date ____________________

Ready to Play

It wasn't long until the beginning of softball season. Alicia really wanted to play with the Accelerators. Everyone knew they had the best pitchers in the league. Alicia wanted to be their pitcher this season. She had played softball for four years and had really improved her pitching speed. Tryouts were coming up, and Alicia hoped she could make the team.

In the meantime, Alicia had a lot to do. She was determined to show the coach she was a great pitcher. To make sure she wouldn't get tired during the tryouts, Alicia started jogging. She jogged a mile every day.

Then she practiced pitching. She set up a net in her backyard and rounded up all the softballs she could find. There were around 50, and she made sure she pitched every single one into the net every single day. Sometimes she threw the ball as hard as she could. Sometimes she practiced placing the ball exactly where she wanted it.

Finally, tryout day arrived. Alicia woke up early and tried to eat a good breakfast, but she couldn't eat. So she went outside and practiced a few pitches before trying to eat again. Soon it was time to leave for tryouts. Alicia didn't know how the day would end. But she knew she had done her best to prepare for it.

Circle the letter of the best answer. Then answer questions 6 and 7 on another sheet of paper.

1. Which sentence best summarizes Alicia's goal?
- **A.** Alicia wants to be the strongest pitcher in the league.
- **B.** Alicia wants to be the pitcher for the Accelerators.
- **C.** Alicia wants to make sure she is in shape for the tryouts.

2. What does the author mean when she says in the fourth paragraph that Alicia couldn't eat?
- **A.** Alicia does not like to eat breakfast.
- **B.** Alicia needs to eat a light meal before tryouts.
- **C.** Alicia is too nervous to eat.

3. Who might benefit most from reading this selection?
- **A.** someone who coaches softball
- **B.** someone who is facing a challenge
- **C.** someone who likes the Accelerators

4. Which word best describes how Alicia feels about her pitching skills?
- **A.** confident
- **B.** humble
- **C.** conceited

5. What is the author's purpose for writing the selection?
- **A.** to inform
- **B.** to describe
- **C.** to entertain

6. According to the selection, what are three steps, in order, that Alicia takes to prepare for tryouts?

7. Based on the selection, how do you think this story ends?

Name ______________________________

Date ____________________

Pick ___ activities to do.
When you finish an activity, color its number.

(1) Tell whether each group of words is a noun phrase, verb phrase, or prepositional phrase. Then use each phrase in a complete sentence. • the people • around the corner • walked quickly • started reading his book • his royal highness	(2) Write ten noun phrases that describe items in your desk. Example: wadded sheet of paper 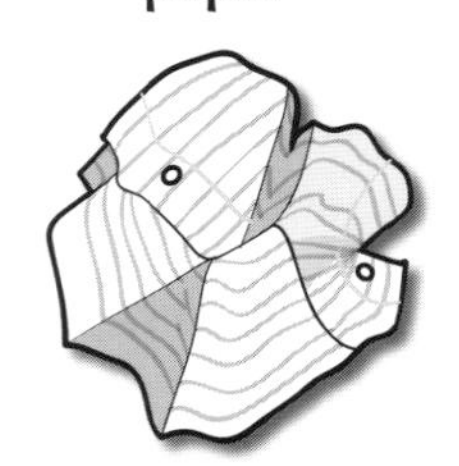	(3) Write ten verb phrases. Use a word from below in each one. Example: will start reading today dash leap plunge climb trip whisper shout read stroll hum
(4) Use different prepositions and the phrase below to write ten different prepositional phrases. the mysterious package	(5) Name the subject and predicate in each dependent clause below. Then use each clause in a sentence. • when Mom came to school • before the day ends • because I ran out • if someone picks me up	(6) Find ten examples of dependent clauses in a textbook. List the book's title, each clause, and the page on which you found each clause. 
(7) Make a poster that shows how dependent and independent clauses are the same and different. 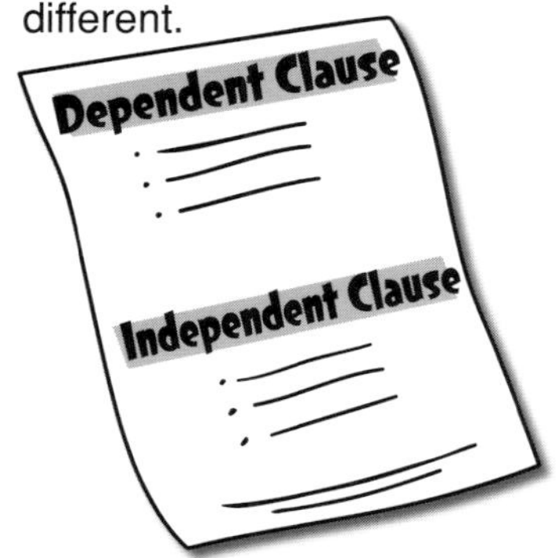	(8) Tell whether each group of words is a phrase or a clause. Then use each one in a complete sentence. —raced from the room —since you can run so fast —an inspiring role model —when my cousin called —under the stairs	(9) Write four sentences. In each sentence, include a dependent clause, a noun phrase, a verb phrase, and a prepositional phrase. Underline and label the phrases and clauses. 

Independent Practice Grid: Program the student directions on a copy of this page with the number of activities to be completed. Then copy the page for each student.

Name ______________________________

Date ____________________

Making a Splash!

Decide whether the punctuation in each sentence is correct. Circle the number in the matching column. Then use editing marks to fix the punctuation in each incorrect sentence.

	Correct	Incorrect
1. Barney! the manager of the Paddle Inn rents paddleboats, at the lake.	3,691	4,276
2. It costs $25.00, to rent a paddleboat for half an hour but it costs only, $40.00, to rent one for an hour.	9,567	3,478
3. Emily, Kayla, Marcus, and Jason pool their money, $60.00, and rent a paddleboat for one hour.	2,901	3,475
4. Jason says, "I dont need a life jacket I'm a great swimmer	17, 032	8,569
5. Barney glares at Jason and says, "Young man, if you don't wear a life jacket, you won't get on a boat."	6,397	2,983
6. Barney gives everyone a life jacket, and makes sure they strap them on correctly.	6,989	7,555
7. Then he takes them to their paddleboat it has four paddles!	8,444	9,682
8. Without thinking Marcus steps in the lake; instead of on the paddleboat.	955	1,099
9. Emily starts laughing so hard she falls in the lake too.	14,952	11,337
10. "That's why you have to wear a life jacket," Barney says as he chuckles.	5,324	4,736
11. Marcus, climbs out of the lake; and shakes the water from his hair all over Kayla.	19,766	23,789
12. Kayla squeals and ducks to get away from the water spray.	2,099	6,118
13. As she dodges the spray Kayla backs off the dock; right into the lake.	1,714	1,003
14. So far Jason is the only one who hasn't fallen in the lake so he dives in!	2,413	2,500
15. Already dripping wet, Emily, Kayla, Marcus, and Jason climb into the boat and start paddling.	1,376	1,244

The surface area of the Great Lakes is 95,000 square miles, the largest surface area of fresh water in the world.

To check your work, add the circled numbers. The sum should be 95,000.

Name ____________________

Date ____________________

Read the paragraphs. For questions 1–8, fill in the blank to complete the sentence. Draw a line to the word or words in the paragraph that support your response.

Alexis presses her ear against the door. She strains to figure out what her parents are saying, but all she can hear is the soft rumble of their voices. When she sees the knob turn, Alexis jumps back. She holds her breath as her parents walk into the room. She searches their faces and then looks into her mother's eyes. She knows the answer is yes. Her parents will finally say yes.

Noah jumps out of bed. He pulls on his lucky T-shirt and shorts. Then he digs around under his bed until he finds his glove. It's covered with dust, so he blows the dust off. Rummaging through his closet, Noah finds his cleats and squeezes his feet into them. They're a little snug, so he puts on his thinnest socks. As soon as Noah finds his bat, he'll be ready to go.

Destiny is listening to music and talking with her friends. She opens the door and walks around the corner. As soon as she turns the corner, she squeals. Her little brother, Jacob, is sitting on the floor, playing a game on her phone. Destiny grabs the phone out of Jacob's hands, glares at him, and turns around. She stomps back around the corner and slams the door.

1. Alexis feels ____________________.
2. In the other room, Alexis's parents are ____________________.
3. Alexis jumps back because ____________________.
4. Alexis thinks her parents ____________________.

5. Noah is getting ready to play ____________________.
6. Noah's glove is covered with dust because it's ____________________.
7. Noah has to squeeze his feet into his cleats because ____________________.
8. Noah's room is ____________________.

Answer questions 9–12 on another sheet of paper.

9. Where is Destiny? What makes you think that?
10. How does Destiny feel when she sees her brother? What makes you think that?
11. Why do you think Destiny doesn't say anything to her brother?
12. What do you think Destiny will do next? Why?

Name____________________

Date ____________________

GO WITH THE FLOW!

____

selection title

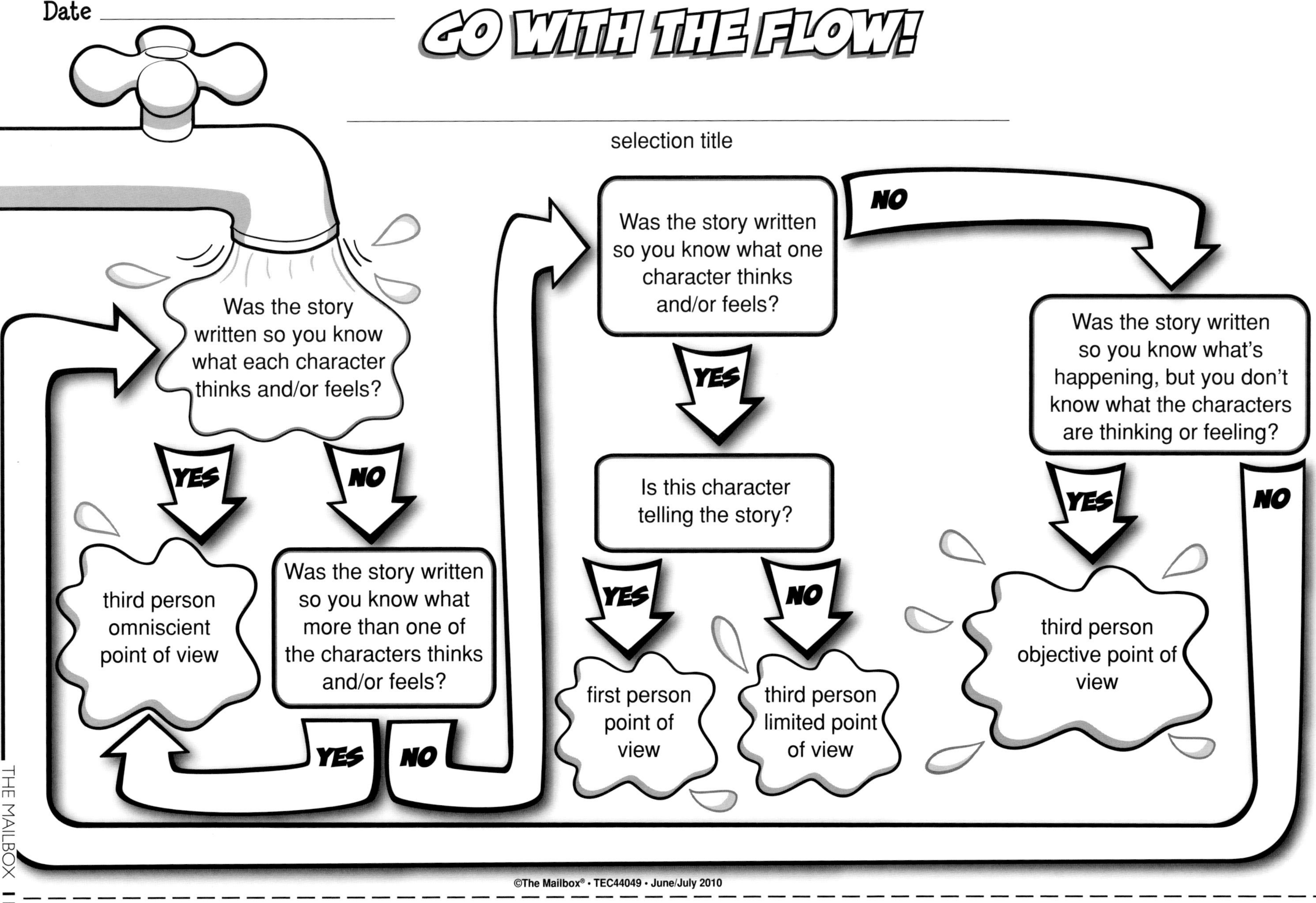

Note to the teacher: Use with "Getting to the Point" on page 110.

Game Cards

Use with "Music to My Ears" on page 111.

The dog's tail is a metronome, beating a happy rhythm.

The dog's tail is compared to a metronome.

TEC44049

Walking in the rain is one of my favorite things to do.

There is no metaphor.

TEC44049

Squirrels scamper to the bird feeder like hungry kittens to a bowl of milk.

There is no metaphor.

TEC44049

Seth's cat, a finely tuned engine, starts purring as soon as he picks it up.

The cat is compared to an engine.

TEC44049

Ants line up, crossing the sidewalk all day long.

There is no metaphor.

TEC44049

Sarah holds up her hand to block the sun, a blinding spotlight.

The sun is compared to a spotlight.

TEC44049

The bees, a milling crowd, buzz around the honeysuckle.

The bees are compared to a crowd of people.

TEC44049

Jose's family makes the long drive to the beach every summer.

There is no metaphor.

TEC44049

The sprinkler is a geyser of cold water.

The sprinkler is compared to a geyser.

TEC44049

There are only two ways to get to the park: the long way and the longer way.

There is no metaphor.

TEC44049

Katie hopes the flowers she planted will grow like weeds.

There is no metaphor.

TEC44049

The butterfly, a choosy shopper, flits from flower to flower.

The butterfly is compared to a shopper.

TEC44049

In early summer, the pool is an icy pond.

The pool is compared to an icy pond.

TEC44049

The lizard, four-legged lightning, darts under a rock.

The lizard is compared to lightning.

TEC44049

To enjoy the whole day, Mason makes sure he gets up early in the morning.

There is no metaphor.

TEC44049

As the sun sets, the sky turns dusky pink and purple.

There is no metaphor.

TEC44049

The scoop of ice cream on Kelly's cone is a slippery snowball.

The ice cream scoop is compared to a snowball.

TEC44049

When we heard the ice cream truck's music, we gathered all the change we could find.

There is no metaphor.

TEC44049

The first frozen treat of summer is an iceberg of refreshment.

The frozen treat is compared to an iceberg.

TEC44049

As Blake pedals up a steep hill, his legs are lead weights.

Blake's legs are compared to lead weights.

TEC44049

The ice cream truck is a treasure chest on wheels.

The ice cream truck is compared to a treasure chest.

TEC44049

Sierra runs barefoot through the grass, digging her toes into the plush green carpet.

The grass is compared to a carpet.

TEC44049

Watching a sparrow pick at the seed in the feeder is like watching a gardener pluck weeds.

There is no metaphor.

TEC44049

Erica is building a tree house in the backyard; it will be her own private island.

The tree house is compared to an island.

TEC44049

Seen from the building's fourth story, people on the sidewalk are scurrying mice.

People are compared to mice.

TEC44049

A Capitol Outing

A Game for Two Players

Directions:

1. Choose a path.
2. In turn, spin the spinner. Then, in the next available space on your path, write a word that includes the word root. A word can only be listed one time.
3. Your partner uses a dictionary to check the word. If the word is incorrect, erase it.
4. If you erase a word or cannot write a word, your turn is over.
5. The first player to write a correct word in each space on his or her path wins.

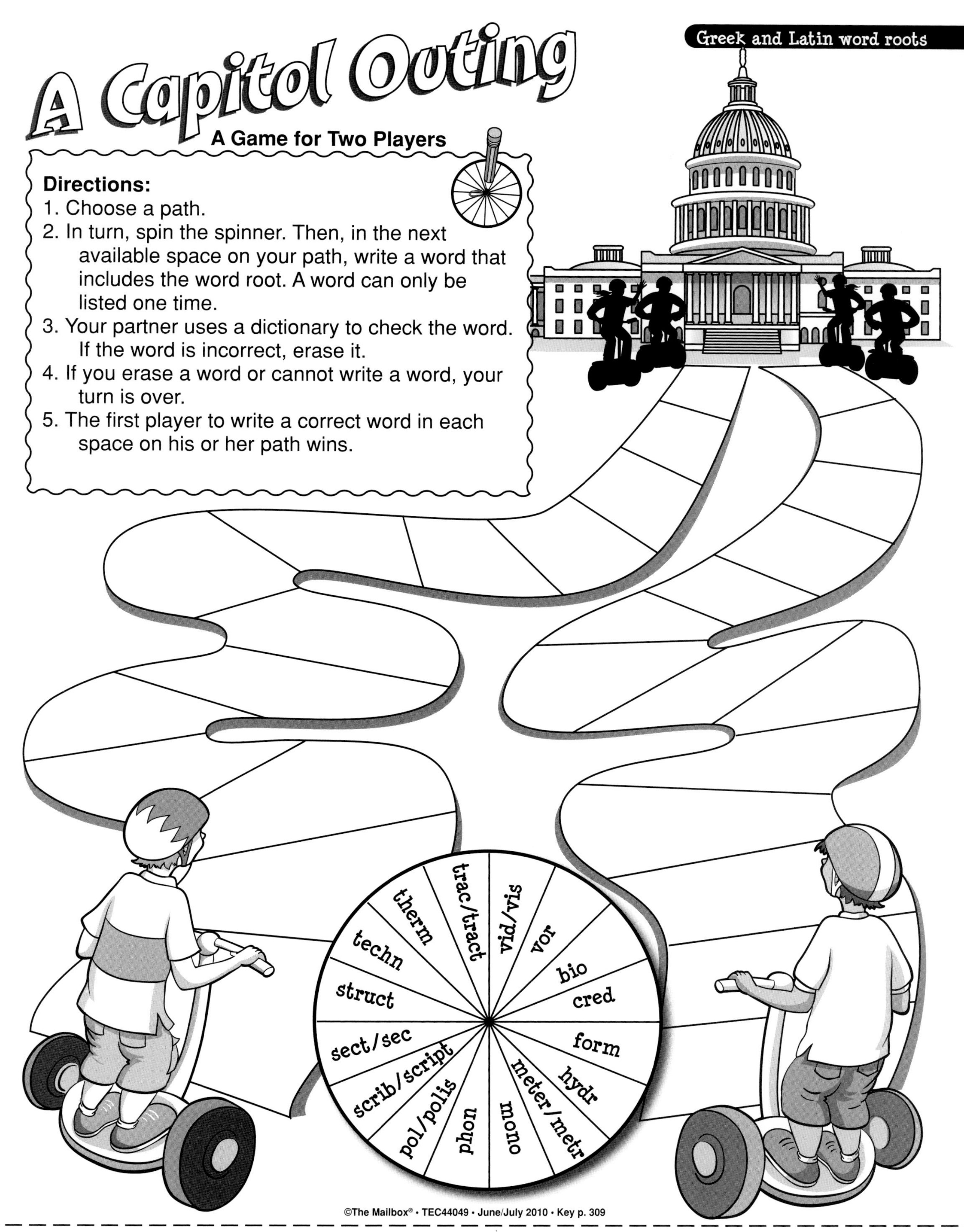

Note to the teacher: Each student pair needs a copy of the page, a paper clip, and a dictionary.

BRAIN BOOSTERS

Brain Booster 1

What sport's name, when written horizontally in this grid, forms a three-letter word in each column?

T	M	A	S	B	E
E	P	T	Y	D	E

TEC44044

Brain Booster 2

This sentence uses every letter from *A* to *Z* at least once.

The quick brown fox jumps over the lazy dog.

Write a sentence of your own that uses all 26 letters.

TEC44044

Brain Booster 3

If you write these words in alphabetical order, which one will be in the middle?

trickle tremble tried triumph trample tricky tricycle

TEC44044

Brain Booster 4

Write a pair of rhyming words for each set of clues.

a. part of a whole; something done
b. one of a kind; bill of a bird
c. dreary; stream
d. weak; slow-moving mollusk

TEC44044

Brain Booster 5

For each letter in this word, write a proper noun that begins with the letter.

artichoke

TEC44044

Brain Booster 6

Look at the boxed letters in this past U.S. president's name.

G[eor]ge
Wa[shi]ngton

Write the names of these past U.S. presidents.

a. YSS / RAN b. ALV / OOL c. OHN / NNE d. NAL / AGA

TEC44044

Brain Booster 7

Start with *COW*. C O W

Add a three-letter word that means "observe" to the end. _ _ _ _ _ _

Delete the second consonant from the left. _ _ _ _ _

Insert *H* in front of the fourth letter from the right. _ _ _ _ _ _

Switch the positions of the fourth and fifth letters from the left. _ _ _ _ _ _

Change the first vowel from the left to *E*. _ _ _ _ _ _

TEC44044

Brain Booster 8

What common expression does this nonsense sentence make if you adjust the spacing and add a missing punctuation mark?

Ifth esho efi tswe arit.

TEC44044

Note to the teacher: Give each student a copy of this page (or one card at a time) to work on during free time.

Brain Booster 1

What is the longest one-syllable word you can spell?

TEC44045

Brain Booster 2

Complete each idiom with the name of a different body part.

a. ______ the bill
b. Don't bite the ______ that feeds you.
c. keep my ______ on you
d. cost an ______ and a ______
e. ______ the line

TEC44045

Brain Booster 3

Which of these words or phrases is not on a one-dollar bill?

- Federal Reserve Note
- One Dollar
- Washington
- The Great Seal
- One Hundred Cents
- Legal Tender

TEC44045

Brain Booster 4

Unscramble the letters below to name the female that matches each male animal name.

a. gander: osego
b. drake: cdku
c. stallion: ream
d. buck: ode
e. ram: wee
f. cob: nep
g. tiercel: nfolac
h. bull: wco

TEC44045

Brain Booster 5

The answer is *kumquat.* What are all the questions you can think of that could have this answer?

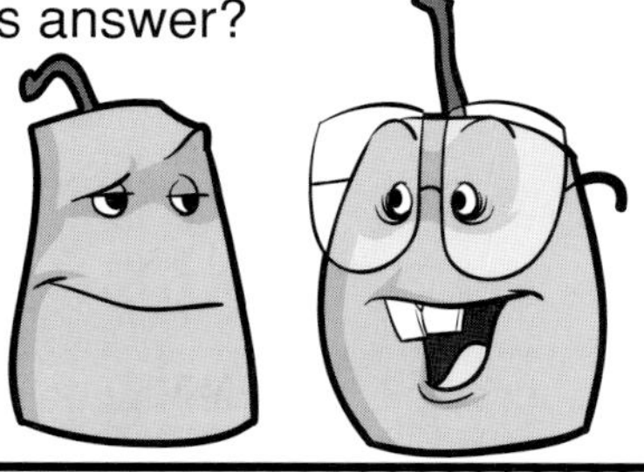

TEC44045

Brain Booster 6

For each word, name a synonym that begins with the letter *d.*

a. postpone
b. beat
c. rot
d. erase
e. bold
f. wet

TEC44045

Brain Booster 7

Which word does not belong in each set of words?

a. stripe, priest, stirrup, ripest
b. groove, runt, rut, trench
c. patch, hatch, latch, watch, batch
d. am, is, are, has, were
e. ceiling, weight, reindeer, either, perceive

TEC44045

Brain Booster 8

Find the names of eight states in the grid below. Letters must be adjacent to each other either diagonally, horizontally, or vertically.

I	Y	M	A	G
I	W	O	I	N
V	A	H	O	E
E	D	A	K	A
N	I	S	L	A

TEC44045

Note to the teacher: Give each student a copy of this page (or one card at a time) to work on during free time.

LANGUAGE ARTS

BRAIN BOOSTERS

Brain Booster 1

Avenue is a synonym for *street.* List at least five more.

TEC44046

Brain Booster 2

Fill each box with a letter to spell four five-letter words. Can you find two different ways to complete the grid?

TEC44046

Brain Booster 3

Correct the capitalization and punctuation errors in the paragraph.

christmas eve is always interesting at our house grandma insists on bringing german potato salad even though it gives my dad a rash aunt suzy brings boring store-bought cookies and uncle jim brings an empty stomach we always end up having to order chinese food for dinner

TEC44046

Brain Booster 4

Groundhog is an animal name that is a compound word. List at least five more.

TEC44046

Brain Booster 5

Write a letter from a snowman to the sun, convincing the sun not to shine.

TEC44046

Brain Booster 6

Write one word for each set of clues.

Hint: each word is pronounced in two different ways.

A. a thing you can see or touch; to express an opposite opinion
B. to say no to something; trash or useless objects
C. flawless; to make something complete or add finishing touches
D. the best accomplishment so far; to make a copy of sounds

TEC44046

Brain Booster 7

List ten words that would come between these two words in the dictionary.

movie

mummy

TEC44046

Brain Booster 8

In the acrostic shown, *bulky, important,* and *gigantic* are synonyms for the word *big.* Write acrostics in the same way, using synonyms for the words *hot* and *fast.*

Bulky	H	F
Important	O	A
Gigantic	T	S
		T

TEC44046

Note to the teacher: Give each student a copy of this page (or one card at a time) to work on during free time.

Brain Booster 1

List at least eight words that end in *dge.* Then write one sentence using as many of the words as possible.

DGE

TEC44047

Brain Booster 2

Write these names in alphabetical order starting with the first vowel in each last name.

Amelia Earhart, George Washington, Michelle Obama, Abraham Lincoln, Thomas Edison, Harriet Tubman, Bill Gates, Eleanor Roosevelt

TEC44047

Brain Booster 3

Add punctuation to make sense of this statement. Hint: use quotation marks and commas.

It was *or* he said not *and.*

TEC44047

Brain Booster 4

What adjectives can be typed using only the right-hand keys on a keyboard?

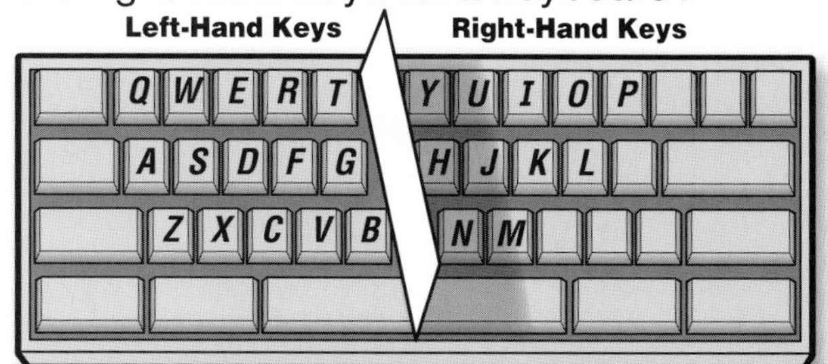

TEC44047

Brain Booster 5

Use the letters in each word shown to write three three-letter words. Use each letter only once.

A. COMMANDER: COD, MEN, RAM
B. MOUSETRAP
C. GRAPEVINE
D. ALLIGATOR

TEC44047

Brain Booster 6

The word *scuba* is an acronym that stands for **s**elf-**c**ontained **u**nderwater **b**reathing **a**pparatus. If the following words were acronyms, what could each letter stand for?

a. CAR
b. MUSIC
c. PIZZA

TEC44047

Brain Booster 7

A group of fish is called a school. Unscramble the letters to name a group of each of these animals.

a. lions
deirp

b. ants
yoclno

c. monkeys
oprto

d. whales
odp

e. deer
dhre

f. alligators
ngotinoregca

TEC44047

Brain Booster 8

Use only the letters in *shamrock* to spell a word for each clue.

a. a month
_ _ _ _ _

b. something you wear
_ _ _ _

c. a roughly built hut
_ _ _ _ _

d. money
_ _ _ _

e. swampy land
_ _ _ _ _

TEC44047

Note to the teacher: Give each student a copy of this page (or one card at a time) to work on during free time.

BRAIN BOOSTERS

Brain Booster 1

The words in each box illustrate an idiom. For example, [icing / the cake] stands for "icing on the cake." Write each idiom. Then write what each idiom means.

bend backward	the bridge water

TEC44048

Brain Booster 2

Spell at least ten prepositions using the letters below. Move from letter to letter across the connecting lines.

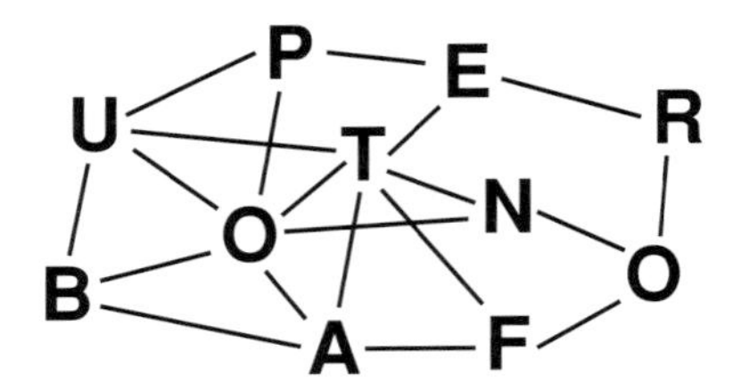

TEC44048

Brain Booster 3

For each word listed, write an antonym that begins with the letter *s.* For example, an antonym for *quick* is *slow.*

a) continue
b) noisy
c) tall
d) bland
e) uncertain

TEC44048

Brain Booster 4

List as many words as you can that break the following rule:

Use ***i*** before ***e*** except after ***c*** or when sounding like ***a*** as in *neighbor* and *weigh.*

TEC44048

Brain Booster 5

Name a city for each letter in the word *spring.* Do the same with fruits or flowers and then with animals.

SPRING

TEC44048

Brain Booster 6

Combine pairs of these words to make six different words. Use each word only once.

pat	age	kind	ridge	leg	mat
part	for	riot	end	man	mess

TEC44048

Brain Booster 7

Write the names of four kinds of trees by adding one letter to each word below and rearranging the letters. For example, add *c* to *read* and rearrange the letters to spell *cedar.*

a) pale
b) crib
c) cures
d) me

TEC44048

Brain Booster 8

Name the books and authors abbreviated below. For example, *C. W.* by E. B. W. stands for *Charlotte's Web* by E. B. White.

a) *C. a. t. C. F.* by R. D.
b) *L. H. o. t. P.* by L. I. W.
c) *W. t. W. T. A.* by M. S.
d) *T. N. K. o. t. B.* by J. P.

TEC44048

Note to the teacher: Give each student a copy of this page (or one card at a time) to work on during free time.

Brain Booster 1

Pick 15 letters of the alphabet. (Don't pick x.) For each letter, list a noun, an adjective, a verb, and an adverb that begin with that letter. Then use the words in a sentence.

Example: An angry aardvark ate annoyingly.

TEC44049

Brain Booster 2

S + S = w means Saturday + Sunday = weekend. What do each of these mean?

Ⓐ w + s + s + f = 4 s
Ⓑ WA + OR + CA = W C
Ⓒ J + J + A = s
Ⓓ TX + LA + MS + AL + FL = G C

TEC44049

Brain Booster 3

This is an unusual paragraph. Nothing is wrong with it, but it is not ordinary. Why is it odd? Think about it and add two additional thoughts.

TEC44049

Brain Booster 4

Name the word that does not belong in each set and tell why it does not belong.

A. skin, hair, eye, nose
B. Ping-Pong, baseball, soccer, tennis
C. peach, plum, apple, cherry
D. whale, shark, dolphin, manatee

TEC44049

Brain Booster 5

Make a list of ten or more words that contain the word *hot.*

TEC44049

Brain Booster 6

Find the name of a famous European city in each sentence below.

Example: Before you get **mad**, **rid** yourself of stress! (Madrid)

A. I just received a gift from Evan.
B. Please make the call on Don's cell phone.
C. For a golfer, making par is a very good score.
D. Use a number line to add negative numbers.

TEC44049

Brain Booster 7

The answer is "sunscreen." What are all the questions you can think of that have that answer?

TEC44049

Brain Booster 8

Start with *dive.* Change one letter at a time to form new words without rearranging the letters, until you spell *pool.*

d i v e
_ _ _ _
_ _ _ _
_ _ _ _
_ _ _ _
p o o l

TEC44049

Note to the teacher: Give each student a copy of this page (or one card at a time) to work on during free time.

Language Arts Activity Cards

Make a copy of the cards below. Then cut out the cards to use as center or free-time activities.

Make a copy of the cards below. Then cut out the cards to use as center or free-time activities.

Writing a poem

Do You Haiku?

Write a haiku about today's weather. Name the weather in five syllables. Describe the weather in seven syllables. Then tell how you feel about it in five syllables. Finally, draw a picture to go with your poem.

Weather in winter.
Blowing snow, howling wind, cold.
That bear is lucky.

TEC44046

Plural nouns

Pepperonis Galore!

Write the plural form of each word listed on a pepperoni slice. Then write five sentences. Use one or more of the words in each sentence.

child, person, bunch, burrito, loaf, hero, goose, anchovy, potato, baby, chief, sister-in-law

TEC44046

Combining sentences

Leaps and Bounds

There are 14 sentences in the paragraph. Rewrite it so there are only nine sentences.

As soon as Jake sees me, he takes off. If he's in a room, he runs across the room. He jogs up the stairs to catch up with me. He thunders down the stairs to catch up with me. Jake gallops across the yard when I get home from school. Then he jumps on me. Jake is my dog. He loves me. I love him. However, Jake weighs almost 150 pounds. I weigh 76 pounds. Jake weighs as much as two of me! When he jumps on me, I fall down. I fall down every time.

TEC44046

Homophones

Ho, Ho, Hoe?

For each homophone trio, write a sentence using all three words.

There are only two ways to get there, and I think you've flown too far.

- he'll, heal, heel
- Maine, main, mane
- reign, rein, rain
- sent, cent, scent
- there, their, they're

TEC44046

Language Arts Activity Cards

Make a copy of the cards below. Then cut out the cards to use as center or free-time activities.

Palindromes

It's in the Name

A palindrome reads the same forward and backward, such as *bib* or *deed.* Use the clues to write a palindrome name for each family member shown.

1. A male family member's label
2. A female family member's label
3. The baby's name begins with *A.*
4. The boy's name begins with *B.*
5. The girl's name starts with *E.*

TEC44047

Antonyms

Make Room for Me!

Add a letter to each word in column A to make an antonym for a word in column B. The letter can go anywhere in the word. Do not rearrange the letters.

A	B
mile	energetic
lay	last
act	cruel
mall	fiction
star	frown
fist	right
let	finish
kid	large

LAY

LAZY

TEC44047

Anagrams

There's a FLEA on a LEAF

An anagram is a word made by rearranging the letters in another word, such as *leaf* and *flea.* Rearrange the letters in each word below to make an anagram that is an animal's name.

tac
pea
art
sale
tab
toga
reed
fowl

TEC44047

Homophones

Have a Heart

Write a homophone pair for each set of clues.

to have eaten; number between seven and nine = ate; eight

1. permitted • with the speaking voice
2. building where the state legislature or U.S. Congress meets • uppercase letter
3. head of a school • idea or belief
4. body parts on which one stands • great act
5. single part of a whole • state of quiet
6. sent in the air with force • from the beginning to the end of

TEC44047

Make a copy of the cards below. Then cut out the cards to use as center or free-time activities.

Language Arts Activity Cards

Make a copy of the cards below. Then cut out the cards to use as center or free-time activities.

Story elements

Dive Into Storytelling!

Plan a story about the best summer vacation ever. Include each story element in your plan. Then write your story.

characters
setting
climax
plot

TEC44049

Context clues

Use the Clues

Read each sentence. Use the context clues to write a definition for each underlined word. Then check each definition with a dictionary.

1. I was ecstatic when I was named team captain; nothing could have made me happier.
2. His ailments include fever, a headache, and an upset stomach.
3. Heidi easily moves her desk because it is portable.
4. When our game resumed, I started by scoring a goal.
5. Our puppy used to be rambunctious, but now it is calm.

TEC44049

Verb tenses

Get Ready to Roll

Roll a die three times. Use each number rolled to determine a subject, a verb, and the verb's tense. Then write a sentence using the subject and verb. Write at least five interesting sentences.

Subject	Verb	Tense
1. caterpillar	1. slither	1 or 4. past
2. magician	2. devour	2 or 5. present
3. principal	3. chomp	3 or 6. future
4. sunflower	4. slurp	
5. octopus	5. sprint	
6. computer	6. collect	

TEC44049

Main idea and supporting details

GLOBAL GUIDELINES

List five details that support the following main idea. Then use the main idea and details to write a paragraph that tells how to take care of Earth.

Summer is a great time to focus on taking care of our planet.

TEC44049

WRITING

WRITE NOW!

Cubic Relationships

Comparing and contrasting

Your students will love figuring out how a cell phone and a zebra are alike with this fun compare-and-contrast activity. Give each pair of students a copy of the cubes on page 136. Instruct the partners to cut out the cubes and construct them. The first player rolls both cubes and writes three ways the two objects rolled are alike, while his partner writes three ways they are different. Then the partners share their responses. For the next round, the two players switch roles. If a combination appears more than once, have students roll again. To increase the difficulty, instruct students to write four or five similarities and differences.

Ann Fisher, Toledo, OH

Cole

A zebra and a cell phone both have a face. Both the zebra and the cell phone make noise. A zebra and a cell phone can both be found at a zoo because a zebra lives there and people carry cell phones in their pockets there.

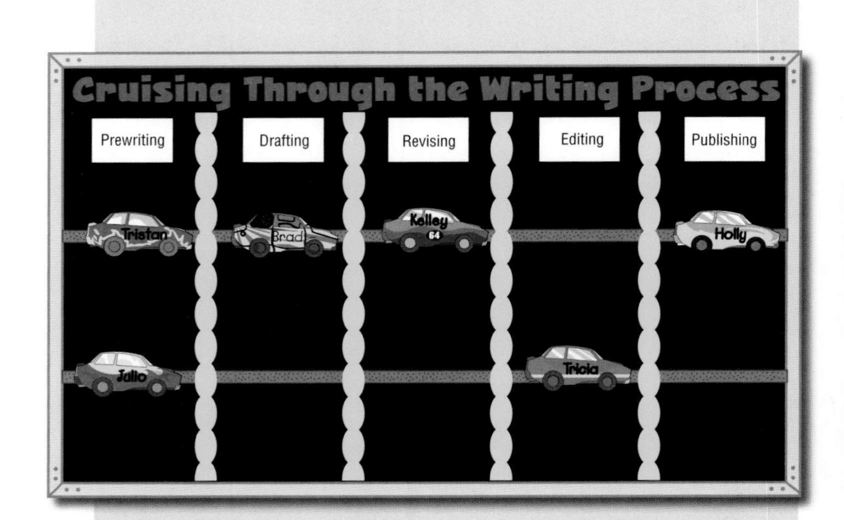

Cruising Through the Writing Process

Managing student writing

Use this display to track students' progress through the writing process and rev up their interest in writing as well! Cover a board with black paper and title it "Cruising Through the Writing Process." Use colored border to divide the board into five sections, labeled as shown. Attach Velcro fastener strips in each section. Then have each child color and personalize a copy of the racecar on page 136 and attach a small piece of Velcro fastener to the back. As the student completes each stage in the writing process, have him move his car to the next section.

Brooke Beverly, Julia Bancroft Elementary, Auburn, MA

Scrapbook Writing
Writing a descriptive paragraph

Use this back-to-school activity to spice up students' writing throughout the year. Have each child choose a writing topic from the lists shown and write a paragraph about it using descriptive vocabulary. Next, have the student paste his paragraph onto construction paper and use arts-and-crafts materials to decorate the page like a scrapbook page. To make this activity ongoing, have him write a paragraph and decorate a scrapbook page for each month. Then, in May, compile the student's monthly pages in a book to show his writing progress.

Cindy Ward, Yellow Branch Elementary, Rustburg, VA

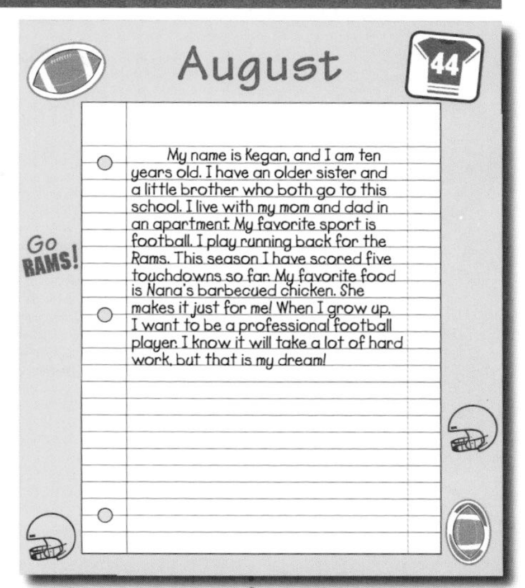

August
Tell about your summer.
What makes a good teacher?
What are some goals you would like to accomplish this school year?
Write a paragraph to introduce yourself to your new teacher.

September
How do you feel about the beginning of the school year so far?
How can you tell whether someone is a good friend?
What do you like to do during fall?
Tell about your special talent or hobby.

TED the Paragraph Man
Writing strong paragraphs

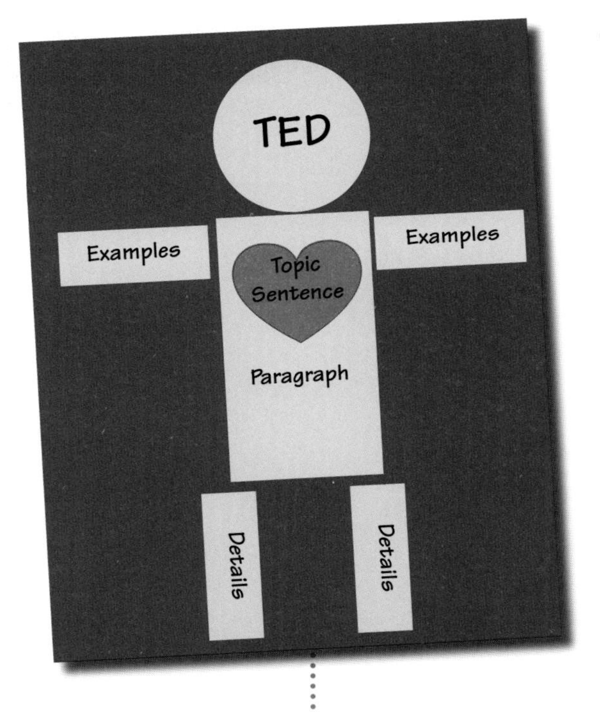

Display a fun visual to help students remember the elements of a strong paragraph. To create TED (topic sentence, examples, details) the Paragraph Man, you will need three large sheets of construction paper and two small ones. Cut a circle from one small sheet and a heart from the other. Cut two of the large sheets in half vertically. Leave the other large sheet intact. Then label and assemble TED, as shown, and introduce him to your students. Point out that the topic sentence is the heart of a paragraph. Also explain that examples and details describe the topic sentence and make a paragraph strong. Finally, have students use TED as a model to practice writing a paragraph about one of the topics shown.

Brenda B. Minor, Lillian Black Elementary, Spring Lake, NC

Topics
If you didn't know what month it was, how could you figure out the season?
What do you think is the best career? Why?
If you were on a deserted island, what one item could you not live without? Why?
What do you think it would be like to be famous? Explain.
Which would you rather do: fast-forward your life or rewind it? Why?

Name ______

Did You Hear?

1 Prompt

A store at the mall is having a game-creating contest for kids only. The winner gets a new video game system. You decide to enter the contest.

GAME STORE

2 Plan

Card Games	Board Games	Individual Games	Team Games	Video Games
What type of game will you create?	Who will play your game?	What materials will be needed to play your game?	What will be the object of your game?	What will make your game unique so it stands out from the other entries?

Come in!

3 Write

Write a clear set of instructions explaining how to play your game. Make sure the steps are sequenced correctly.

Name ____________________

Dips, Loops, and Turns

1. Cut apart the cards and sentence strips below.
2. Glue the title card and topic cards on another sheet of paper as shown.
3. Match each strip to a topic.
4. Organize the strips under each topic in a logical sequence. Then glue them in place.
5. Use your organizer to write a five-paragraph report about roller coasters.

Gravity makes the roller coaster roll to the bottom of the hill. Then the coaster's momentum carries it (or a lift pulls it) to the top of the next hill.

The history and science of roller coasters are as amazing as a ride on one.

Roller coasters move mostly by gravity and momentum since they have no engine.

Russians enjoyed one of the first roller coasters in the 1500s. They rode sleds down steep wooden slides covered in ice.

To build momentum, a train of cars is usually pulled by a chain lift to the top of a track's first hill.

The French made some changes. They built waxed slides and added wheels to the sleds. They also made a train of carts that moved along winding tracks.

People on wooden roller coasters experience bumps and up-and-down motions.

The first American roller coaster was different from the French and Russian ones. It was a train of coal cars. Riders went slowly up a Pennsylvania mountain and had a thrilling ride back down.

In contrast, people on steel roller coasters glide smoothly on tubelike tracks. They also get to experience twists, turns, and complex loops.

Roller coaster fans of the future will no doubt see the rides become higher, faster, and more complex.

The fun thing about modern roller coasters is that riders can sit, stand, or even be in a flying position.

Introduction

Roller Coaster History

Roller Coaster Science

Riding on a Roller Coaster

Dips, Loops, and Turns

Conclusion

Cube Patterns

Use with "Cubic Relationships" on page 132.

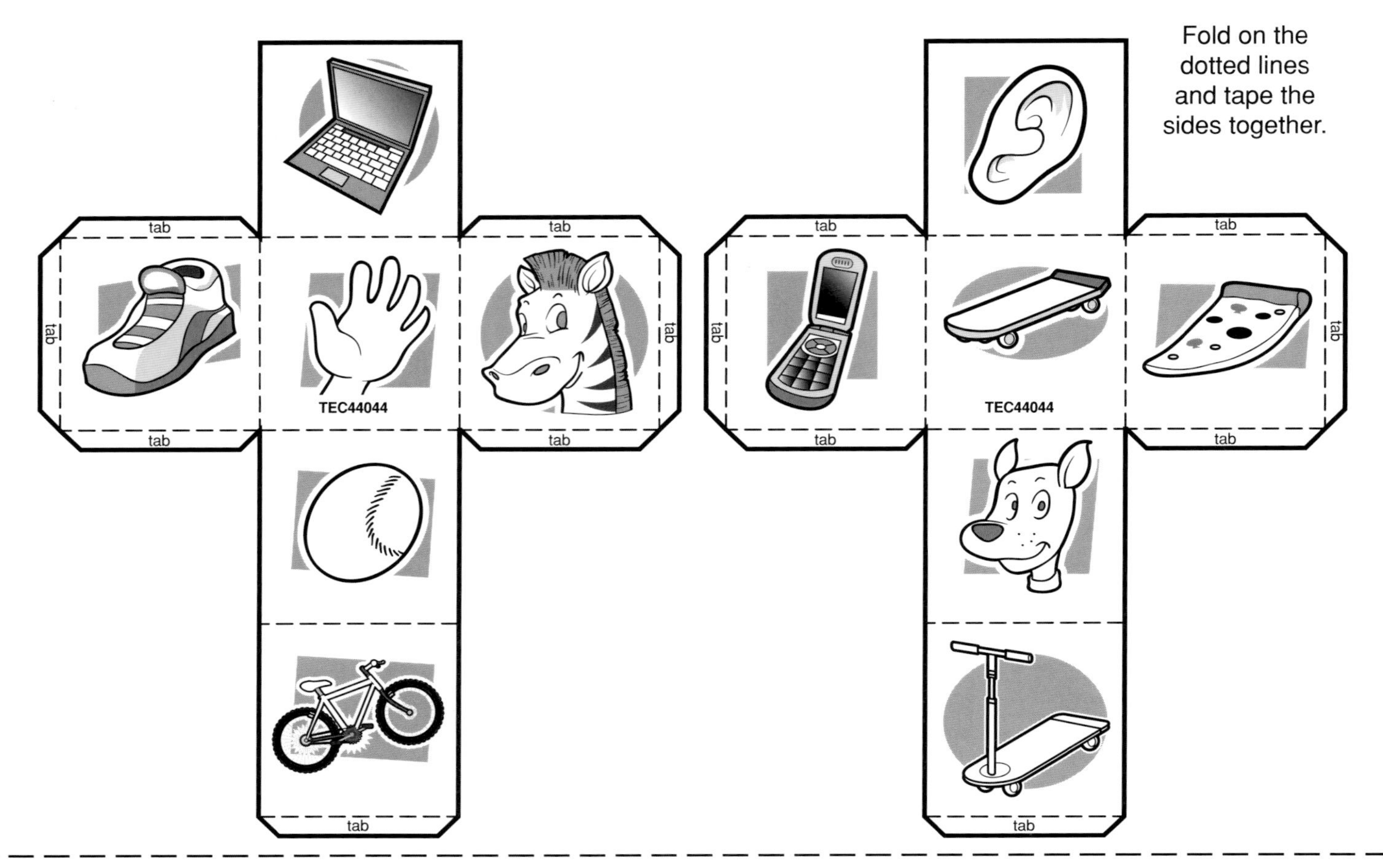

Racecar Pattern

Use with "Cruising Through the Writing Process" on page 132.

Write Now!

Sticker Code
Proofreading

Looking for a twist that will engage your students in carefully editing their writing? Try this! Create a code using mini stickers for proofreading symbols. Laminate and post the code. Then provide a supply of the matching stickers. When a student edits his or a peer's writing, he uses the stickers to identify the spots that need attention.

Kimberly Twedt, San Antonio, TX

Ms. Twedt's Proofreading Code

- Check punctuation.
- Check capitalization.
- Check spelling.
- Check grammar.
- Delete circled word(s).
- Start a new paragraph.
- Something is missing.
- I really like this part.

Evan

If I were a Super Hero, I would be Motion Man. If someone needed my help, I'd get the message on my Motion Man beeper. Then I'd get going I would not stop moving until I saved the person in trouble and made sure the bad guys were in jail.
Superman only has one weakness. It's Kryptonite. As Motion Man, I would have one weakness too. When I finishing When I finishing saving someone, I would have to rest. Since I had moved nonstop, I would have to rest for at least 15 minutes.

The One(s) Behind the Graph
Narrative writing

Here's an idea for a unique writing prompt! Collect graphs from several sources, such as math, social studies, and science textbooks or newspapers and magazines. Have each pair of students study a graph and answer the questions below about it. Next, guide the partners to pretend they are the graph makers. Then have them use their answers to the questions to draft a behind-the-scenes story about the making of the graph.

Casey Burnett, Fort Worth, TX

What is the graph's topic?
Who do you think made this graph? Describe him, her, or them.
Why do you think the person(s) made this graph?
What results do you think the graph maker(s) expected?
What is the main conclusion you can draw about the graph?
Do you think the results disappointed, excited, or confused the graph maker(s)? Why?
What do you think the graph maker(s) might want to study next?

Fact Splash
Expository writing

Help students gather the facts they need to write reports. Guide each child to list important details, facts, and terms on a copy of the web on page 141. Have the student use the web to plan and then draft her report. **To extend the use of the web,** have each student use a copy of the page to brainstorm details and ideas for narrative writing.

Kymberly Buchanan, Charles Spencer Elementary, Tifton, GA

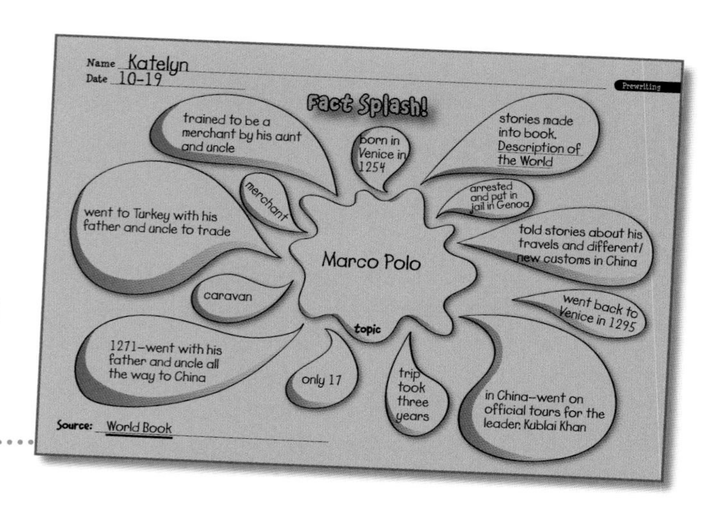

Writer's Unblock Fillers

- stress ball
- inspiring quotes about persevering
- several silly jokes or riddles
- one or two poems by Jack Prelutsky or Shel Silverstein
- interesting snapshots of students in action
- pictures cut from magazines
- excerpts from books that are class favorites
- assortment of pencils and pens
- shaped notepad

Writer's Unblock
Writing motivation

Use this simple kit to rescue students who have writer's block or think they don't know what to write. To make the kit, label a shoebox as shown. Next, fill the box with an egg timer and inspirational items such as those listed. Then place the box at your writing center. When a student gets stuck, he opens the box, sets the egg timer, and peruses the box's contents, jotting notes as inspiration strikes. When the sand in the egg timer runs out, the child returns the items to the box, replaces the lid, and gets back to writing!

Colleen Dabney, Williamsburg, VA

Big Idea Correspondence
Writing a friendly letter

Reinforce letter-writing skills and keep parents informed by having students write weekly letters home. Each Friday, discuss with students three to five big ideas or events from the week. Next, have each child draft a letter to her parents about one idea or event. Have her write the letter in her journal and then take it home and have a parent or other important adult read the letter and write a quick response. During the school year, use the journal to document student growth and parent involvement. Then, when school is out, each student can take home her journal for a great reminder of a year full of learning!

Jennifer Meizels, Chaplin Elementary, Chaplin, CT

Name ____________________

Date ____________________

Where Did He Go?

1 Prompt

You offer to take your neighbor's dog, Max, for a walk. While you're walking, Max spots a squirrel. He lunges, whipping the leash out of your hand and taking off after the squirrel. How do you get Max back?

2 Plan

What do you think as the leash whips out of your hand?

What are two things (one easy and one hard) you can do to solve this problem?

What happens when you try the easy thing and it doesn't work?

What happens when you try the hard thing and it works?

How do you feel about walking Max?

3 Write

Use your answers to the questions above to write a story about walking Max.

Name ____________________

Date ____________________

Off to a Great Start!

Read the story introductions below. For each one, write a new introduction that does a better job of grabbing the reader's attention.

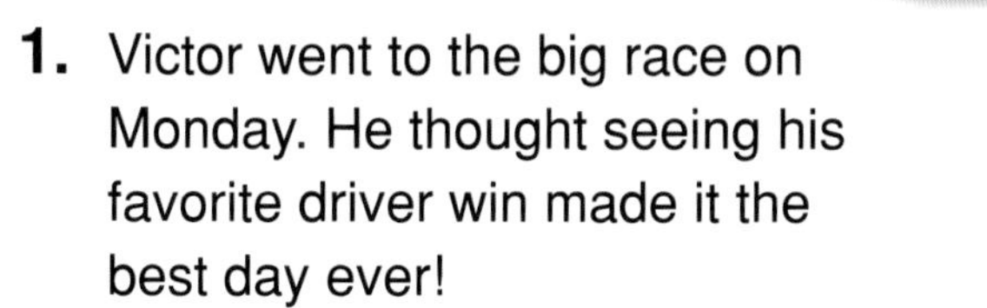

Hints

- Start with what the character says.
- Start with sounds the character hears.
- Start with what the character thinks.
- Start with an action.

1. Victor went to the big race on Monday. He thought seeing his favorite driver win made it the best day ever!

2. This is the biggest crowd Emma has ever seen. There are people everywhere she looks.

3. Ethan lost his house key.

4. Sara hopes she will win the poster contest. She spent two weeks working on her poster.

5. Tanner spent all his allowance at the gift shop. He was supposed to save some money for his sister's birthday present.

6. Kaylee wonders what is in the mysterious package.

Choose your best introduction. Now write the rest of the story.

Name ____________________

Date ____________________

Source: ____________________

Note to the teacher: Use with "Fact Splash" on page 138.

WRITE NOW!

Hot Potato Paper Pass
Peer editing

For this fast-paced editing activity, have each student collect a current piece of writing, a colored pencil, and a clipboard or book to write on. Grab a colored pencil and clipboard for yourself and sit in a circle with your students. Next, have each child pass his paper to the person on his left. Appoint the student who does not get a paper to be the timer. Then direct each child to skim the paper he was passed, mark one or two errors, and add a positive comment about the writing in a margin. After one minute, the timer claps his hands and calls, "Hot Potato Paper Pass!" Students pass their papers to the left again and repeat the activity with a new paper. Within half an hour, you get a quick look at each child's writing, and your students get some great feedback!

Lisa Kasko, Pine Bush Elementary, Schenectady, NY

A Fresh Start
Planning an expository essay

To help students focus on prewriting, display a transparent copy of the organizer on page 145. Next, introduce a familiar topic and a writing purpose (see the examples shown). Lead students to share ideas and details about the topic, filling in the organizer with important ones and eliminating those that are nonessential. Then guide each pair of students to write an essay using the plan. Have partners share their work as time allows. Follow up by guiding each child to pick a topic and use a copy of the organizer to plan an essay of her own!

Writing Topic	Writing Purpose
A polar bear would not make a good pet.	to inform
Winter is the best season of the year.	to persuade
To have a great winter vacation, try this.	to explain
Winter sports include basketball, gymnastics, swimming, and wrestling.	to inform
Winter is the worst season of the year.	to persuade
Follow these simple steps to stay warm this winter.	to explain

Name
Date
Planning an essay

Off to a Good Start

Topic: A polar bear would not make a good pet.
Purpose: to inform
Main idea:
Essay title:

INTRODUCTION:
★ Tell the reader your main idea.
★ Give the reader a reason to want to read the essay.

BODY:
★ Describe the key points that support the essay's main idea.
★ Use details to explain and support each key point.

Key point:
Details:
Key point:
Details:
Key point:
Details:

CONCLUSION:
★ Wrap up the essay.
★ Repeat the main idea in a different way.

DRY-ERASE

Flip Those Sentences!
Revising for sentence variety

Give students practice writing different kinds of sentences with this flipbook. First, guide each child to stack two sheets of paper so the bottom edges are an inch apart. Next, have him fold over the top half to make four layers, label each one as shown, and write a sentence on the top layer (see examples). Then the student flips to the next sections one at a time, rewriting the statement as a question, exclamation, and command. He repeats the steps for several more sentences and then shares his work with a small group.

Michael Foster, Kansas City, MO

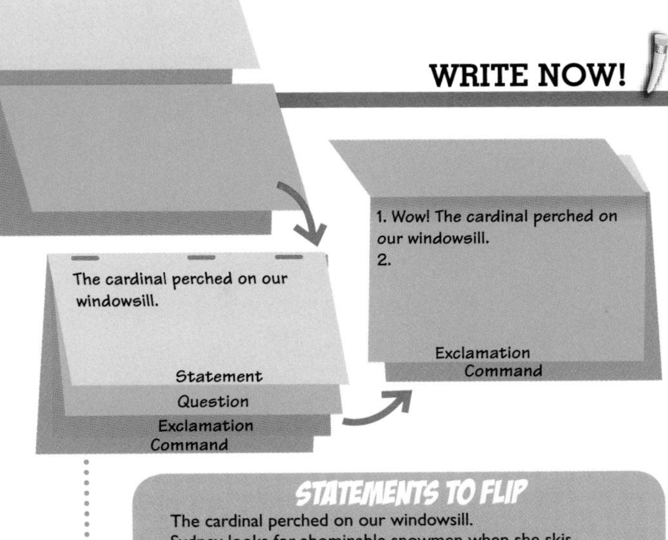

STATEMENTS TO FLIP

The cardinal perched on our windowsill.
Sydney looks for abominable snowmen when she skis.
In one week, we will be in sunny Florida.
Hot chocolate tastes better when you add extra marshmallows.
Garrett thinks it's never too cold to shoot baskets outside.
My parents make sure we don't sit too close to the fire.
My little sister, Mikayla, wrote 17 letters to Santa Claus.
School is cancelled because it snowed two feet last night.

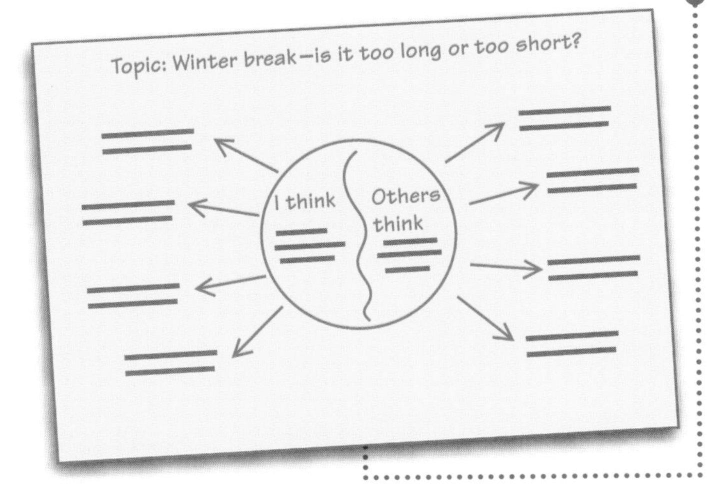

The Other Side
Persuasive writing

Use this idea to help students write winning essays. To begin, introduce a topic about which students have strong opinions. Next, have each child choose a position on the topic and draw a web as shown. Guide the student to list on one side facts and details that support her opinion. Have her list on the other side reasons someone might support the opposite position. Then lead the child to revise her facts and details as necessary to offset another point of view. Finally, have the student use her plan to write an essay sure to influence her readers.

Teri Nielsen, Tracey's Elementary, Tracys Landing, MD

The Hotter the Better
Writing process self-evaluation

After each student finishes a writing assignment, have him draw and color a chili pepper on his page to show how well he followed the writing process. For example, if the child completed each stage of the writing process, he colors a red (hot) pepper. If he struggled with one or two stages, he draws an orange (warm) pepper. If he completed only one or two stages, he draws a yellow (mild) pepper.

Julia Alarie, Williston, VT

Name ________________________________

Date ________________________________

Cats and Dogs

Everyone knows that dogs and cats are very different animals. Just how different are they? Do they have any similarities?

2 Plan

How do dogs and cats look the same?

How do dogs and cats look different?

What do dogs and cats both do?

What do cats do that dogs do not?

What do dogs do that cats do not?

3 Write

Write an essay describing dogs. Explain how dogs are different from and similar to cats.

Name ____________________

Date ____________________

Off to a Good Start

Topic: ____________________

Purpose: ____________________

Main idea: ____________________

Essay title: ____________________

INTRODUCTION: ★ Tell the reader your main idea. ★ Give the reader a reason to want to read the essay.	____________________ ____________________ ____________________ ____________________
BODY: ★ Describe the key points that support the essay's main idea. ★ Use details to explain and support each key point.	**Key point:** ____________________ **Details:** ____________________ ____________________ ____________________ **Key point:** ____________________ **Details:** ____________________ ____________________ ____________________ **Key point:** ____________________ **Details:** ____________________ ____________________ ____________________
CONCLUSION: ★ Wrap up the essay. ★ Repeat the main idea in a different way.	____________________ ____________________ ____________________

Note to the teacher: Use with "A Fresh Start" on page 142.

Write Now!

Wake Up Those Sentences!
Adding descriptive details

Here's an interactive idea for encouraging students to use vivid descriptions. To begin, read aloud one of the examples shown and ask students to say, "Wow!" if it is descriptive or to give an exaggerated yawn if it lacks details. Repeat with the rest of the sentences and then discuss with students the details that wowed them. To follow up, copy and cut apart the sentence strips on page 150. Put the strips in a bag and have each student draw one. Then challenge the child to wake up the sentence, writing his revision on the strip's flip side. As time allows, have each student share his "wow" sentence with the class.

Barclay Marcell, Chicago, IL

"Yawn" Sentences	"Wow" Sentences
Last night, Sue had a bad dream.	Sue sat up in bed, paralyzed with fear.
I am going to tell you about snakes.	What squeezes its prey and then swallows it whole?
In my report, I am going to compare frogs and toads.	It looks like a frog. It acts like a frog. Is it a frog?
Penguins are interesting creatures.	Talk about daddy day care! Did you know that a penguin dad watches over the egg while the mom goes hunting?
We went to an amusement park over spring break and had a lot of fun.	The best thing about going to an amusement park was riding the roller coaster with the steepest drop, except that I threw up on my mom after we rode it.

What a Deal
Persuasive writing

Looking for a new way for students to practice their persuasive techniques? Try this! Give each student a classified ad from a newspaper. Guide the student to write a catchy title for the ad and a paragraph about the item that makes it sound irresistible. Next, have each child work with a partner to make the item sound even more enticing. Then have each student share his ad with the class.

Carol Smallwood, Mount Pleasant, MI

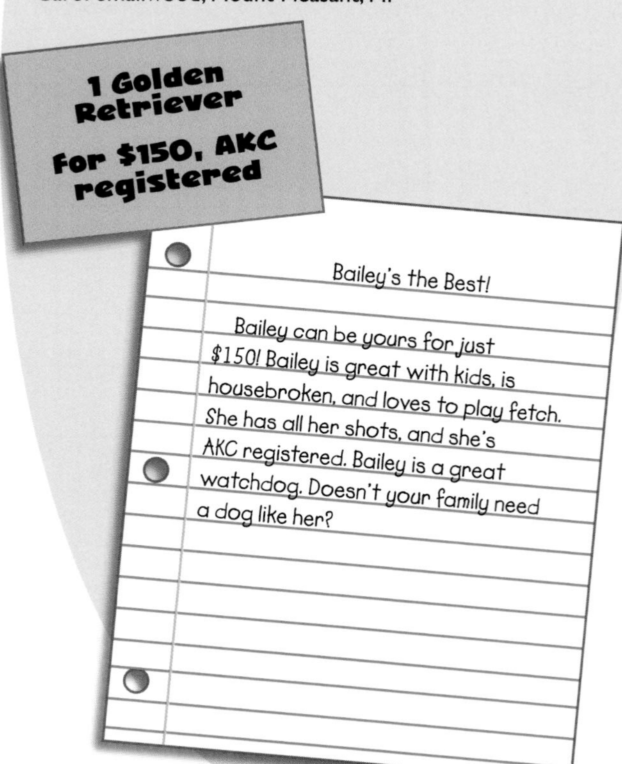

Tweet! Tweet!

Summarizing

Challenge students to condense their thoughts by having them write short notes to their classmates. Once a week, give each student two strips of colorful paper. Direct the child to summarize her day on one strip using 140 letters or fewer. Then have her trade strips with a partner and use the second strip to write a short response.

Isobel L. Livingstone, Rahway, NJ

Hannah
We just came back from playing basketball in gym. I think I'm finally perfecting my jump shot. I'll give you my autograph when I play in college one day!

Fiona
All that practice is paying off! You were on fire in the gym. I wish I were that good. Wouldn't it be cool if you did play in college? I would definitely want your autograph!

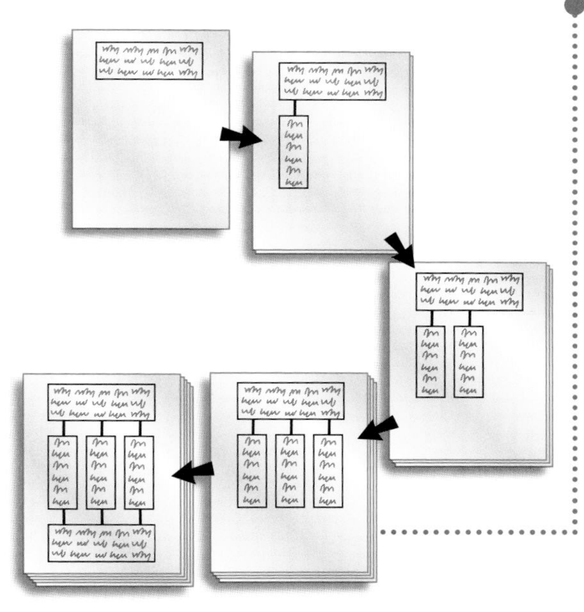

Piece by Piece

Prewriting

Take the stress out of planning a five-paragraph essay by guiding students to focus on one paragraph at a time. To prepare, gather five transparencies and a permanent marker. On the first sheet, draw a box for the introductory paragraph. Next, place the second sheet on top of the first one and add a box for the second paragraph. Then set the third sheet on top of the first two and add a third box. Repeat for sheets four and five.

To use the organizer, grab a wipe off marker. Introduce a writing topic, display the first transparency, and lead students to brainstorm details for the first paragraph as you record their ideas in the box. Next, add the second sheet and guide students to plan that paragraph. Continue adding sheets and having students plan each paragraph. Then have each student use the plan to write an essay. Finally, clean off the sheets and keep them handy for easy reuse.

Janie R. Hardison, Arapahoe Charter School, Arapahoe, NC

Take Note!

Notetaking

Guide each student to identify important details and to take notes in an outline format with these simple tips. Then have the child use his outline as a handy study guide or to write a report.

adapted from an idea by Amanda Campbell, Finley Elementary, Finley, TN

Topic: ______
A. Important idea: ______
 1. Supporting detail: ______
 2. Supporting detail: ______
 3. Supporting detail: ______
B. Important idea: ______
 1. Supporting detail: ______
 2. Supporting detail: ______
 3. Supporting detail: ______

Noteworthy Tips

- You do not need to write complete sentences.
- Use your own words.
- List important facts.
- Be brief.

Name ______________________________

Date ______________________

Introducing...

1 Prompt

Imagine that your favorite celebrity is coming to your school and you've been asked to introduce him or her. What will you say about the celebrity to let everyone know he or she is terrific?

2 Plan

Who is the celebrity?

What adjectives can you use to describe him or her?

What are his or her major accomplishments?

What strong verbs can you use to describe what he or she has done?

How has the celebrity influenced you?

3 Write

Write a speech to introduce the celebrity. Let your emotions and personality show in what you write.

Name ______________________________

Date ______________________

Twists and Turns

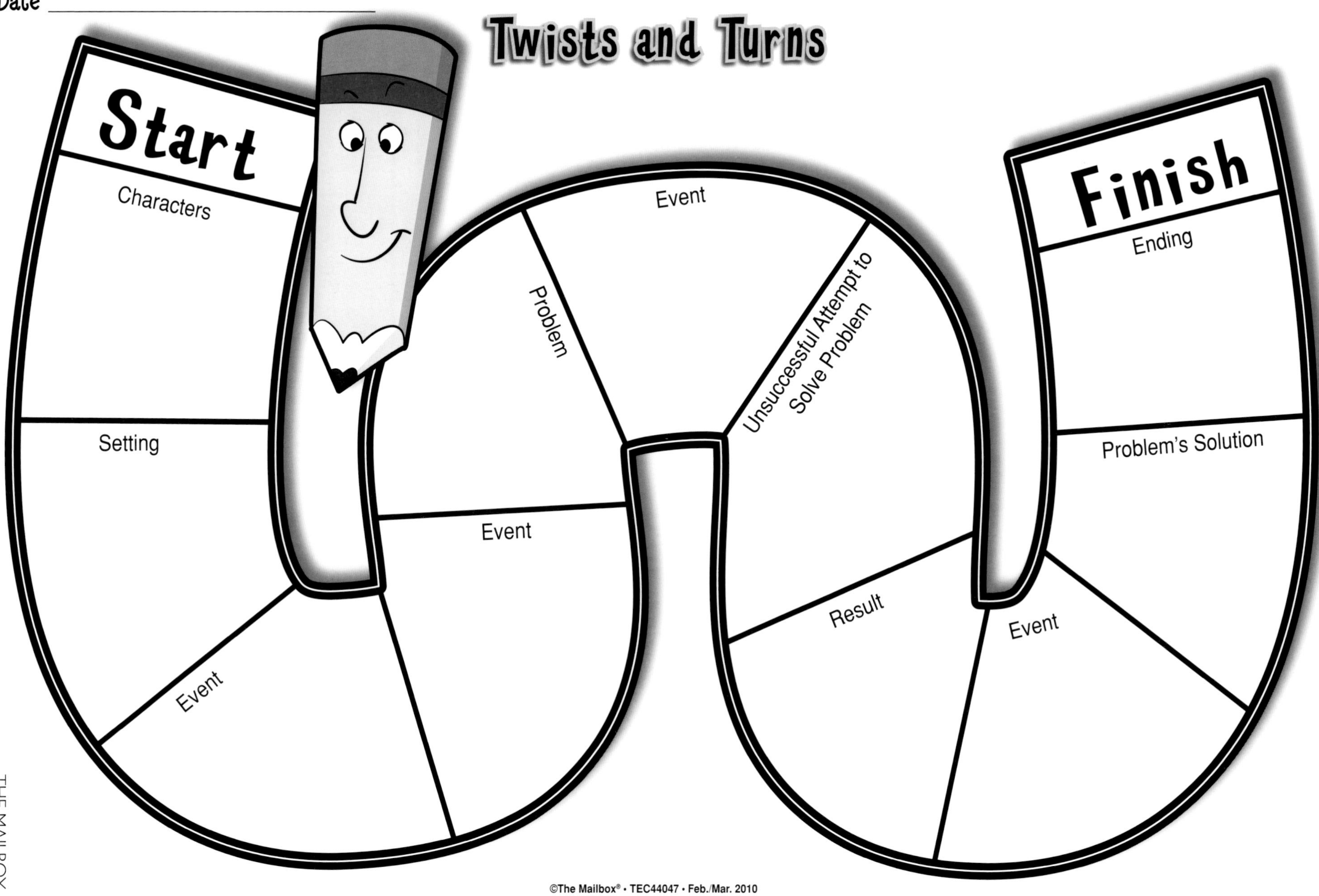

Note to the teacher: Have each student use a copy of the organizer to plan a narrative essay.

Sentence Strips

Use with “Wake Up Those Sentences!” on page 146.

It is dark outside. TEC44047	Maggie drinks her hot chocolate. TEC44047
The pizza is good. TEC44047	I finished my homework. TEC44047
Her father is walking by the window. TEC44047	This oatmeal tastes bad. TEC44047
I am going to tell you all about the solar system. TEC44047	Today is a snow day. TEC44047
It is the first day of school. TEC44047	I knew I was in trouble. TEC44047
The dog runs outside. TEC44047	I am going to teach you how to play soccer. TEC44047
It looks like rain. TEC44047	My favorite animal is a horse. TEC44047
I had fun at my friend’s house. TEC44047	The weather is nice. TEC44047
In my report, I am going to compare dogs and cats. TEC44047	Mark is eating a sandwich. TEC44047
The girl walks into the store. TEC44047	The sun came up. TEC44047

WRITE NOW!

Assembly Required

Varying sentence structure

Want your students to write sentences that are more than ordinary? Have each pair of students cut apart the words on strip 1 from a copy of page 155. Guide the partners to use some of or all the words to create a sentence, record it on a separate sheet of paper, and then share their work. Next, have each pair cut apart the words on strip 2 and arrange the words twice to create two different sentences, recording each one. Discuss students' work and repeat with strip 3. Then have the partners cut apart the two boxes at the bottom of the page and each take one box. Have each student follow the instructions to practice writing sentences that are not run-of-the-mill!

Shawna Miller, Wellington Elementary, Flower Mound, TX

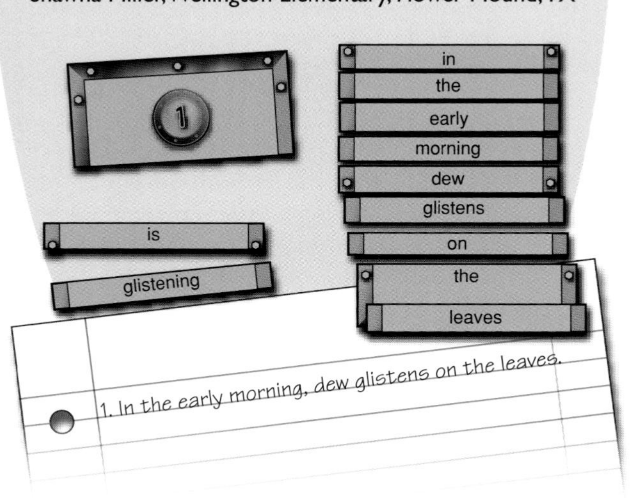

Flowering Facts

Research

To help students organize their research, try this! First, have each child fold a sheet of unlined paper in half. In each section, guide the student to draw a circle and then add several large petals, a stem, and two leaves. Next, have the child flip the paper and draw two more flowers. Direct the child to label each flower's center with a subtopic such as those shown. As each student researches her topic, she jots notes in the petals of the appropriate flowers and records each resource on a leaf.

adapted from an idea by Farrah P. Milby, Weddington Hills Elementary, Concord, NC

Cryptic Clues
Descriptive writing

For this idea, have each student choose a familiar activity or event, such as one of those shown. Next, guide the child to brainstorm important, interesting, and sensory details about the event. Then have each student draft a paragraph that describes the activity but doesn't name it. Follow up by having the child read his paragraph aloud, challenging classmates to name the mystery topic.

Rebecca Juneau, Highland Elementary, Lake Stevens, WA

Familiar Events and Activities

- birthday party
- eating lunch at school
- riding the school bus
- recess
- P.E. class
- doing homework
- tooth-brushing
- visiting the dentist
- first day of school
- last day of school
- performing in a program or play
- riding a bike or skateboard

Shapely Verse
Concrete poetry

With these simple steps, each student can write a unique concrete poem. Have each child choose an interesting animal or object and brainstorm words, phrases, and sentences that describe it. Next, have the student make a simple line drawing of the subject. Then, using a fine-tip marker or pen, the child writes her brainstormed ideas inside the shape or writes the words, phrases, and sentences along the lines. When she finishes, the student gently erases her pencil lines. Finally, each child posts her work on a board titled "Shaping Up With Concrete Poetry."

Precision Editing
Using specific nouns and adjectives

Here's a nifty peer-editing activity! To begin, have each pair of students trade rough drafts. Next, guide each student to highlight the nouns on her partner's paper and circle the adjectives. Then have the child rate each highlighted noun according to the scale shown. After that, have the duo brainstorm specific noun and adjective alternatives for each noun rated 3 or 4. Follow up by having each student use the brainstormed ideas to revise her work.

Kristin Lane, Marietta, GA

Rate A Noun

1 = specific and does not need an adjective
2 = has an effective adjective
3 = needs to be specific
4 = needs an effective adjective

Madam Mingo's Adventure

It was summer (1) and Madam Mingo (1) was on a ship (3) looking for an island (4) that had treasure (4). Madam Mingo (1) searched and searched.

Then she saw a (sea) serpent (2) and it tried to climb onto (Madam Mingo's) ship (2). The serpent (4) was too (big) and it tipped the ship (4) over. Madam Mingo (1) would have to swim for it.

Before she knew it th... (4)

Name ____

Date ______________________________

Mouthwatering!

1 Prompt Imagine your best friend has never heard of your favorite food. You'd like to share the food with your friend.

2 Plan

What does your food look like?

How does your food smell?

What is the texture of your food?

What sounds do you hear while the food is being prepared? What sounds do you hear while you eat it?

How does your food taste?

3 Write Use your answers to the questions above to describe your favorite food. Include details that will make your friend eager to try it!

Name____________________

Date____________________

SHOW, DON'T TELL!

Write an email message about each subject. Use descriptive words and phrases to make each message vivid.

To:	Sun E. Day
Subject:	Warm Day
Message:	

To:	What A. Meal
Subject:	Noisy Family Dinner
Message:	

To:	Scare D. Pants
Subject:	I'm Frightened!
Message:	

To:	Nif T. Gift
Subject:	New Birthday Present
Message:	

To:	Run E. Nose
Subject:	I'm Sick
Message:	

Sentence Strips

Use with "Assembly Required" on page 151.

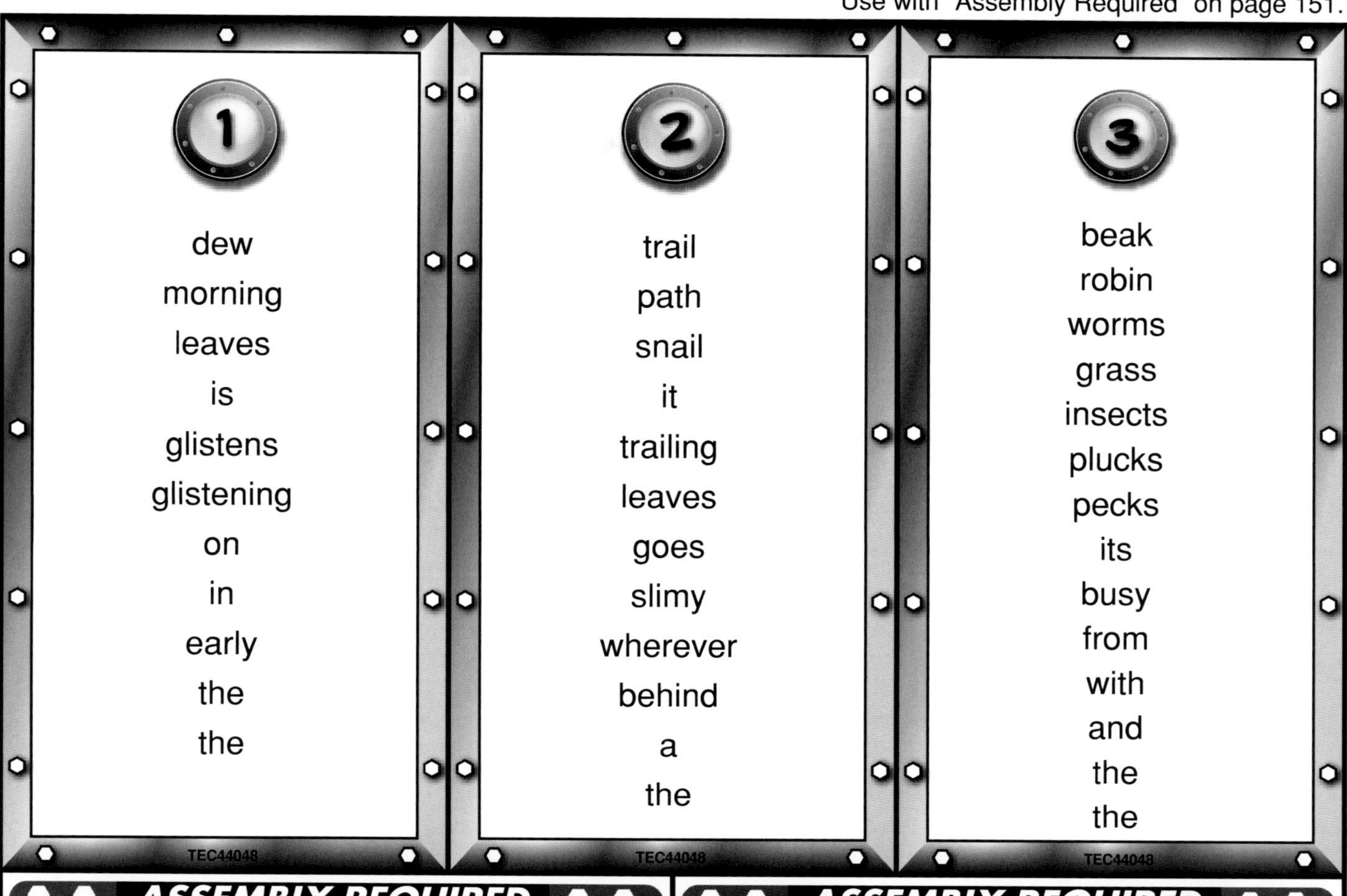

ASSEMBLY REQUIRED

Steps:

1. Cut apart the words in box A.
2. Use some of or all the words to create a sentence. Record it on another sheet of paper.
3. Rearrange the words two more times to create two more sentences. Record each one.
4. Repeat Steps 1–3 with the words in box B.

ASSEMBLY REQUIRED

Steps:

1. Cut apart the words in box A.
2. Use some of or all the words to create a sentence. Record it on another sheet of paper.
3. Rearrange the words two more times to create two more sentences. Record each one.
4. Repeat Steps 1–3 with the words in box B.

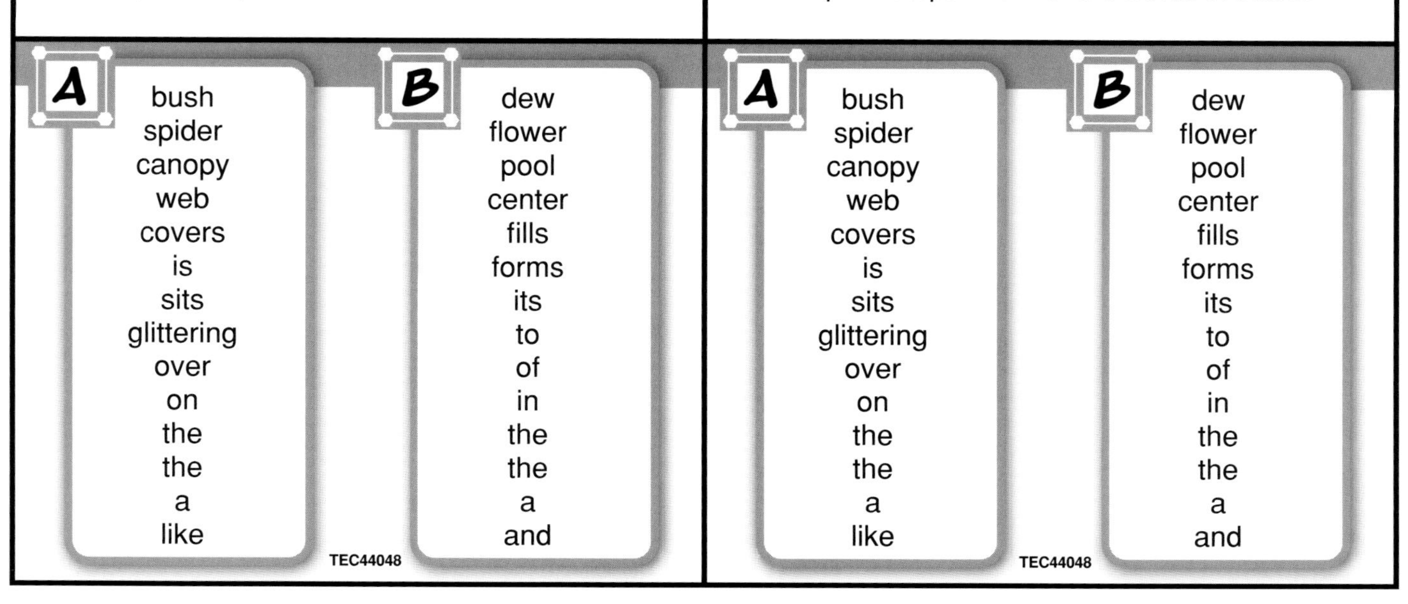

WRITE NOW!

Just the "Write" Words

Word choice

Use catalog descriptions to inspire students to collect words and phrases that will make a difference in their writing! To begin, have each student fold down the top two inches of a sheet of construction paper. Next, have her fold the bottom edge up to the top fold and then trim the top corners to make a trunk shape. Then have the child personalize the trunk, open it, and make a chart inside as shown. Guide each child to skim a catalog. When she finds a specific noun, strong verb, precise adjective, or clever phrase, she records it on her chart. Then she keeps her treasury of terms handy as a ready resource any time she's writing.

Litsa Jackson, Dyersburg, TN

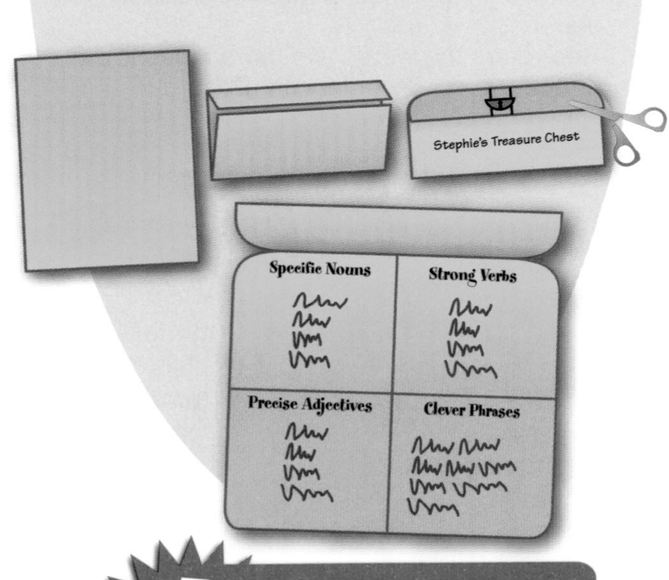

Help students use transition words with the organizer on page 158!

Important People

Biography reports

Begin this biography project by reading aloud *The Important Book* by Margaret Wise Brown. Next, assign each student an important person to research. Then have him label several index cards with descriptive categories such as those shown. Guide the child to find facts and details about his subject for each category. When he writes his report, have him introduce each category with a sentence that mimics Margaret Wise Brown's introductions in the book *("The important thing about…")*. If desired, bind students' work in a class book titled "Important People."

adapted from an idea by Jodi Lind, La Crosse, WI

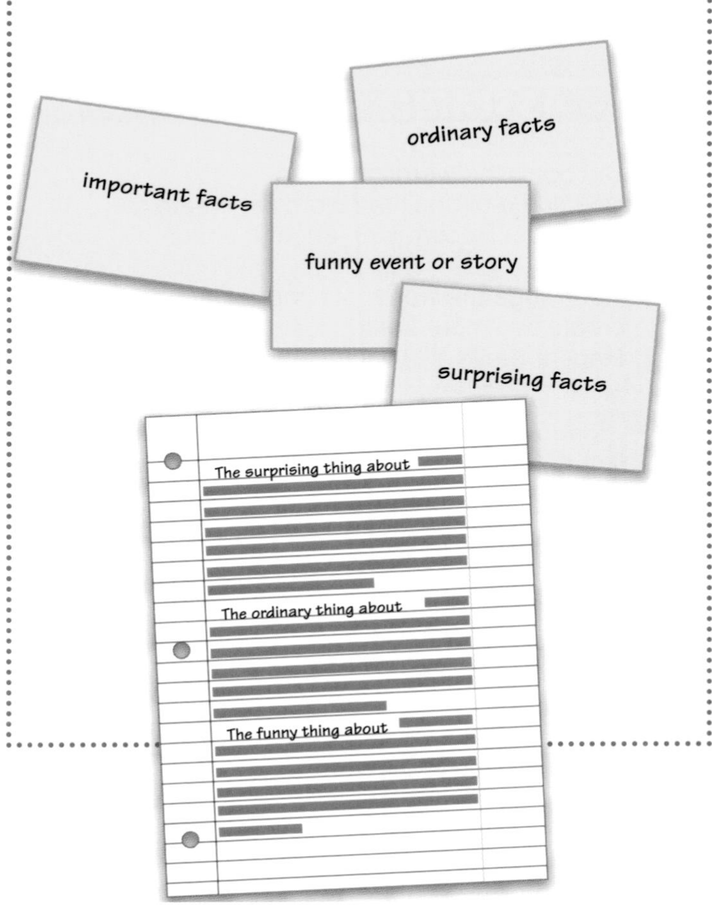

Bibliography Rotation
Citing sources

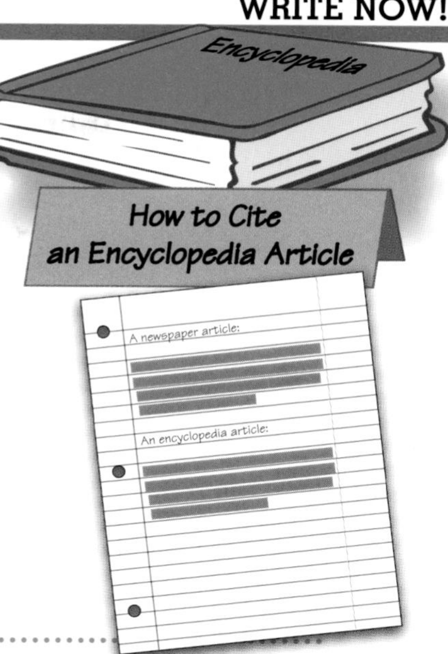

Are your students using resources they don't know how to cite? Show them what to do with these simple learning centers. At each center, place several examples of one type of resource and post the directions for citing that type of source. Then divide students into small groups and assign each group a different center. At the center, each child takes a resource. She chooses a quote from the source and records it on a sheet of lined paper. Next, the student uses the guide to cite the source. As the groups finish, they rotate to the other centers. After visiting all the centers, each child tapes her bibliography guide inside her writing folder or journal for easy referencing.

Nancy Welch, Abigail Adams Intermediate, Weymouth, MA

Statements to Defend or Oppose
- School should be held during night instead of daytime hours.
- All the months of the year should have the same number of days.
- There should be a water park in every neighborhood.
- Skateboarding should be a school sport.
- The cafeteria should serve food at the mall.
- We should take a field trip to the moon.
- We should begin school every day by doing 25 jumping jacks.
- The best way to eat a slice of pizza is with a knife and fork.
- Baby carrots should never be dipped in creamy dressing.
- The best place to take your family on vacation is the desert.

In My Opinion
Writing a persuasive letter

To introduce this idea, read aloud the statements shown and have each student choose one to defend or oppose. Next, guide the child to draft a letter about the topic that will convince classmates to agree with him. After drafting his letter, the student cuts apart the checklists on a copy of page 160 and uses the "I Am the Judge!" list to evaluate his work and guide his revisions. Then the child reads his final letter to a partner who fills out the "You Are the Judge!" checklist as he reads.

Teri Nielsen, Tracey's Elementary, Tracys Landing, MD

Bright Futures
Narrative writing

For this activity, challenge each student to set a goal she would like to achieve within ten years. Next, have her record the goal on a copy of page 159 and fill out the organizer to plan and then write a narrative that describes the day she achieves her goal. To publish her work, the child folds her final draft to make an envelope as shown. Then she tapes the envelope shut and addresses it to herself with a note to open the envelope in ten years to see whether she's achieved her goal.

Name ____________________

Date ____________________

On Tour

1 Prompt

Your mother has invited her best friend's daughter to spend the weekend with your family. She does not live in your town. It's your job to keep her entertained all day Saturday. What will you do?

2 Plan

To begin,

Next,

Then

After that,

When

Finally,

3 Write

Write a note to your mom that explains what you will do, where you will be, and what help you will need from her.

Name______________________________

Date______________________

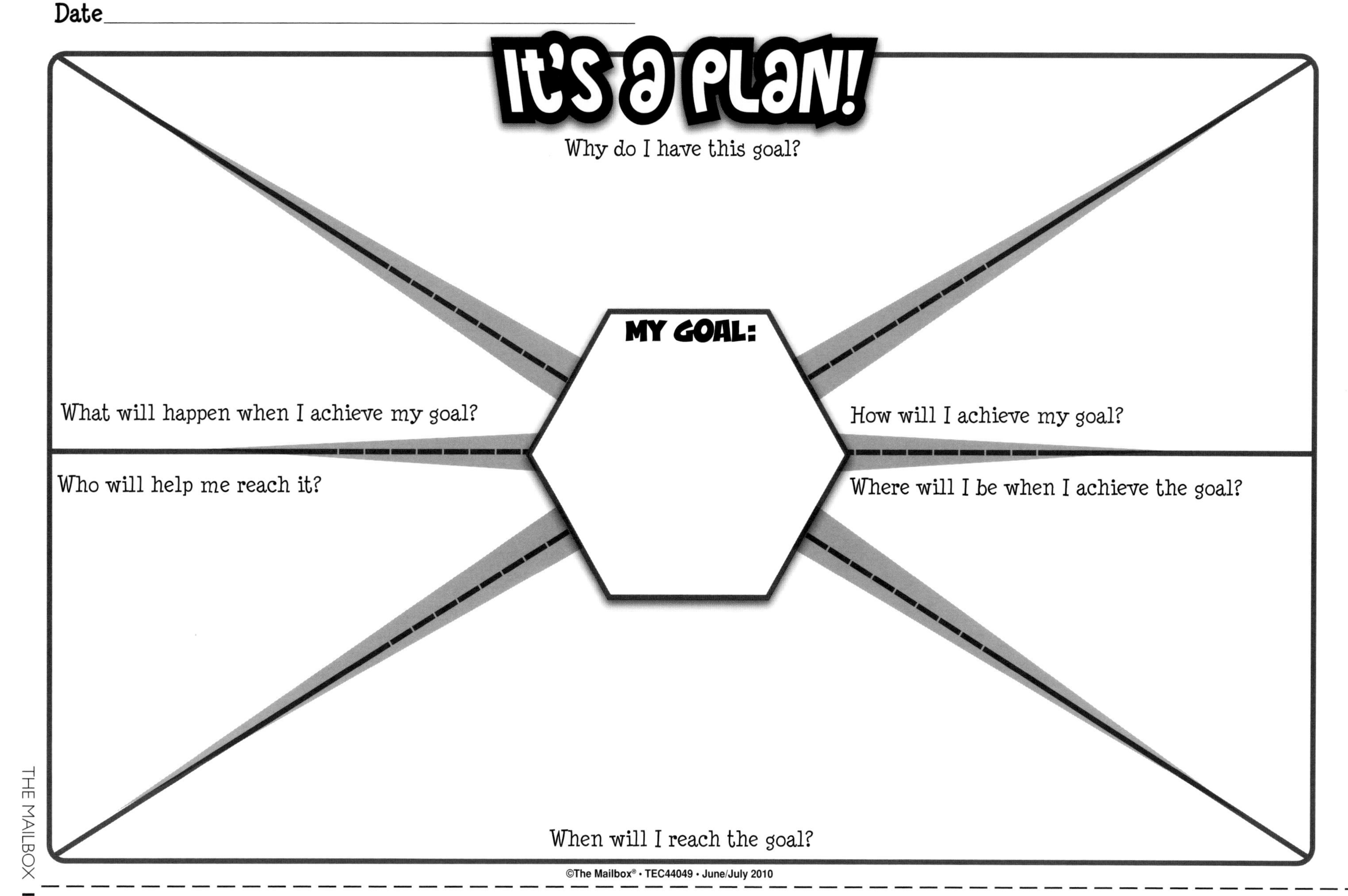

Note to the teacher: Use with "Bright Futures" on page 157.

Name ____________________ **Persuasive writing**

Date ____________________

I AM THE JUDGE!

At the beginning of the letter, my opinion is ___.

- ☐ clearly stated and strong
- ☐ not very strong
- ☐ not very clear

My first key point ___.

- ☐ clearly supports my opinion
- ☐ sort of supports my opinion
- ☐ doesn't support my opinion

There are ___ that support and explain my first key point.

- ☐ two good examples
- ☐ not two good examples

The second key point ___.

- ☐ clearly supports my opinion
- ☐ sort of supports my opinion
- ☐ doesn't support my opinion

There are ___ that support and explain my second key point.

- ☐ two good examples
- ☐ not two good examples

My opinion is ___ in the closing argument.

- ☐ clearly restated
- ☐ hard to find

Both of the key points are ___ in the closing argument.

- ☐ clearly restated
- ☐ not clearly restated

What's the Verdict?

- ☐ My argument is convincing.
- ☐ My argument is not yet convincing.

Name ____________________ **Persuasive writing**

Date ____________________

Author ____________________

YOU ARE THE JUDGE!

At the beginning of the letter, the writer's opinion is ___.

- ☐ clearly stated and strong
- ☐ not very strong
- ☐ not very clear

The writer's first key point ___.

- ☐ clearly supports the writer's opinion
- ☐ sort of supports the writer's opinion
- ☐ doesn't support the writer's opinion

There are ___ that support and explain the writer's first key point.

- ☐ two good examples
- ☐ not two good examples

The second key point ___.

- ☐ clearly supports the writer's opinion
- ☐ sort of supports the writer's opinion
- ☐ doesn't support the writer's opinion

There are ___ that support and explain the writer's second key point.

- ☐ two good examples
- ☐ not two good examples

The writer's opinion is ___ in the closing argument.

- ☐ clearly restated
- ☐ hard to find

Both of the key points are ___ in the closing argument.

- ☐ clearly restated
- ☐ not clearly restated

What's the Verdict?

- ☐ I'm convinced. I agree!
- ☐ I'm not convinced. I disagree.

 Note to the teacher: Use with "In My Opinion" on page 157.

Writing Prompts

Name

August	September
☐ What is the best part of a new school year? Explain.	☐ Labor Day is the first Monday in September. Write a letter to a worker in your family describing your plans to make this person's day relaxing and fun.
☐ How is getting ready for a new school year like riding a roller coaster?	☐ Do you think it's important to make your bed every day? Why or why not?
☐ August is National Inventors' Month. Describe a contraption you'd like to have to help you do your homework.	☐ Describe the perfect school day.
☐ Francis Scott Key was born August 1, 1779. After a noisy War of 1812 battle, he wrote a poem that later became "The Star-Spangled Banner." Can you work well with noise around you? Explain.	☐ What is your favorite cartoon character? Why?
☐ S'mores are fun treats to eat around a campfire. What foods would you want to eat if you were camping out? Why?	☐ List seven positive qualities that someone who works with people who are blind, deaf, or unable to walk should have.
☐ List all the household chores you'd be willing to do to earn a banana split.	☐ What are three easy ways you can help your family save money this week? What are three ways you can spend more time together?
☐ Which would you prefer: lots of toys and no friends or lots of friends and no toys? Explain.	☐ Which would you rather be: a newspaper or a menu in a fancy restaurant? Why?
☐ You've just found out that your principal is moving into the house next to yours. How does this make you feel?	☐ A safety pin is a handy thing to have around. List ten uses for this helpful item.
☐ If you could travel to any country in the world, which one would you visit? Why?	☐ Describe five things you love about this time of year when summer ends and fall begins.
☐ On August 28, 1963, Dr. Martin Luther King Jr. gave his famous "I have a dream" speech in Washington, DC. Describe a dream you have for the future.	☐ Leaves change color in the fall. How do you feel when you notice that you are changing in some way? Why?

Note to the teacher: Have each student staple a copy of this page in his writing journal. Or cut copies in half and distribute only one month's prompts at a time to students. When a student uses a prompt, he checks it off in the box.

Writing Prompts

Name

October	November
☐ It's Vegetarian Month. What is your favorite meatless food? Draw a picture of it and then describe it.	☐ What would you like to ask or tell the president of the United States? Write an email to him and share your thoughts.
☐ President Theodore Roosevelt once told a group of children, "Keep your eyes on the stars but remember to keep your feet on the ground." What do you think he meant? What can you do to follow his advice?	☐ In 2008, the average salary for an NFL player was $1,850,000. Do you think pro football players are paid too much? Explain.
☐ Do you like baseball? Why or why not?	☐ It's Peanut Butter Lovers' Month! What is the strangest peanut butter sandwich you think you could eat? Describe it.
☐ October is National Go on a Field Trip Month. If you could take your class anywhere in your state, where would you go? What could you and your class learn on this trip?	☐ List seven things you cannot do without.
☐ What do you think is the hardest thing about being in this grade? What do you think is the easiest thing? What do you think is the best thing? Explain.	☐ The first Sesame Street episode premiered on November 10, 1969. Do you think it's good for young children to watch TV? Explain.
☐ On October 24, 1901, Annie Taylor rode over Niagara Falls. She was the first person to go over the falls in a barrel and survive. What do you think her ride was like? Write a story about it.	☐ Design a float for a Veterans Day parade. Tell how the float will honor veterans.
☐ Design a uniform you would like to wear to school. Then write a letter to your district school board. Persuade the board to make this your school's new uniform.	☐ Do you think you are too old to watch cartoons? Why or why not?
☐ If you were a superhero, who would you be? What would you do? Explain.	☐ What would a pilgrim think of Thanksgiving today? Pretend that a pilgrim appears at your house for Thanksgiving. Write a story about what happens.
☐ Make a Difference Day reminds us to try to make our world better. List ten or more things you and your class can do to make a difference.	☐ Black Friday is the Friday after Thanksgiving. Why do you think it's called Black Friday? Do you want to go shopping on Black Friday? Why or why not?
☐ Which would you rather do: find your way through a corn maze or tour a haunted house? Explain.	☐ If you need to travel 400 miles, would you rather ride in a car, on a train, or in an airplane? Explain.

Note to the teacher: Have each student staple a copy of this page in his writing journal. Or cut copies in half and distribute only one month's prompts at a time to students. When a student uses a prompt, he checks it off in the box.

Writing Prompts

Name

December	January
☐ Rudolph is famous for his shiny red nose. Describe a unique quality you have.	☐ Imagine you are the host of a new trivia game show. Write ten questions you would ask to stump the contestants.
☐ It's traditional to do things for others during the eight nights of Hanukkah. Make a list of kind things you can do for others on each of those eight days.	☐ Choose one main goal you would like to reach this year. Make a list of strategies to help you achieve your goal.
☐ Imagine you wake up one morning to find that you are a snowman. What happened?	☐ What is your favorite winter smell? Describe the scent without naming it.
☐ Write a song similar to *The Twelve Days of Christmas* about what you would like to receive each day.	☐ Imagine the sun and a snowman could talk to each other. Write a conversation between the two of them.
☐ Imagine you have won $1,000,000. What would you buy for your best friend? Why?	☐ Your best friend wants to sled down a dangerous hill. Persuade him or her not to do it.
☐ Using each of your senses, describe the perfect breakfast.	☐ If you were president, what would you change about our country? Explain.
☐ Invent a new winter sport. How will it be played? Where will it be played? What equipment will players need?	☐ Describe the perfect snow day.
☐ The Nobel Peace Prize is awarded this month. The award goes to the person who has done the best work toward world peace. Name a person you think is peaceful. Tell why he or she is peaceful.	☐ You are skiing in the mountains when you hear the rumble of an avalanche. Using sequencing words, tell what happens next.
☐ Make up your own holiday to celebrate a special event or person in your life. Name the holiday. Write a letter persuading your teacher to celebrate the holiday.	☐ The days are shorter in the winter. List ten ways your life is affected by fewer hours of daylight.
☐ If all the calendars disappeared, what might you do to keep track of the date and important events? Explain.	☐ Imagine you are an icicle and the weather is slowly beginning to get warmer. Describe your thoughts and feelings.

Note to the teacher: Have each student staple a copy of this page in his writing journal. Or cut copies in half and distribute only one month's prompts at a time to students. When a student uses a prompt, he checks its box.

February Writing Prompts

Name

- [ ] Frederick Douglass, born February 7, 1817, was a leading African American spokesman who helped with the Underground Railroad. What do you know about the Underground Railroad? What would you like to know about it?
- [ ] If you came across a six-foot-wide snowball, what would you do with it?
- [ ] Describe your favorite Valentine's Day treat. Why is it your favorite?
- [ ] Compose an email to the president. In it, persuade him to invite your class to visit the White House.
- [ ] What is the quickest way to get from school to your home? Explain.
- [ ] February is American Heart Month. List ten or more things you can do to keep your heart healthy.
- [ ] What advice would you give an alien about riding a school bus for the first time? Write a letter to the alien to share your suggestions.
- [ ] What does this quote from Abraham Lincoln tell you about him? "I am never easy now, when I am handling a thought, till I have bounded it north and bounded it south and bounded it east and bounded it west."
- [ ] National Pancake Week starts February 21. Plan a pancake party. Describe the party's games, snacks, and favors.
- [ ] If your teacher won a million dollars, what do you think she or he would buy first? Why?

March Writing Prompts

Name

- [ ] Which genre do you most like to read? Write a paragraph to persuade everyone in your class to read the same genre.
- [ ] If you were magically beamed to a tropical island, what would you do there?
- [ ] Leprechauns are known for playing silly pranks on people. If you were a leprechaun for a day, what would you do?
- [ ] What is your favorite board game? Why do you like it? With whom do you most like to play it?
- [ ] March is Humorists Are Artists Month. Who is the funniest person you know? What makes him or her comical?
- [ ] The first American woman to travel in space was Sally Ride. What would be the most exciting part of being in space? Why?
- [ ] Which of your possessions might someday be sold in an antiques store? How will you keep it safe until then?
- [ ] On March 20, spring officially starts. Does it seem like spring right now? Why or why not?
- [ ] How many times do you think you could jump rope in a row? What would be the hardest part of jumping rope that many times? What would be the easiest?
- [ ] In honor of National Cleaning Week (March 21–27), write a letter to thank the custodian or custodians for keeping your school clean.

Note to the teacher: Have each student staple a copy of this page in his writing journal. Or cut copies in half and distribute only one month's prompts at a time to students. When a student uses a prompt, he checks its box.

Name

April Writing Prompts

- ☐ April is National Poetry Month. Think of five adjectives that begin with the same letter. Use them to write a descriptive poem.
- ☐ It's time for spring cleaning! Write directions telling how to clean your bedroom. Add a warning about something that might be lurking under your bed.
- ☐ Write about an hour you wish you could go back and change. What would you do differently, do over, or erase?
- ☐ April is National Humor Month. Write a detailed paragraph that begins, "The hardest I ever laughed was…"
- ☐ Use your five senses to describe your favorite spring activity. Be sure to include the sights, sounds, and smells you look forward to every year.
- ☐ You are a news reporter. Your photographer is out sick. Describe your town's new water park so your readers can picture it.
- ☐ It's Physical Wellness Month. Write a commercial urging students to get physically fit.
- ☐ Imagine you could spend $1,000 to create the perfect room. Describe the room.
- ☐ Your family is planning a vacation. Would you rather go surfing in Hawaii or white-water rafting on the Colorado River? Why?
- ☐ Where would you go if you went on a daylong hike? Who would you go with? What would you take? Write about the hike.

Name

May Writing Prompts

- ☐ If a person were described as being "all bark and no bite," what do you think this person would be like?
- ☐ How is the month of May different from the month of June? How are they the same?
- ☐ May is National Moving Month. Write a letter persuading your parents to let you move to a different room in your home.
- ☐ Imagine you are given a bike from 1985. What would you do with it? Why?
- ☐ While on a road trip, you notice a blank billboard. Plan a billboard ad that will persuade others to save gas.
- ☐ It's Older Americans Month. Which older American would you choose to spend the day with? Why?
- ☐ You find a strange nest in your garden. What is in the nest? What happens after you discover it?
- ☐ It's Personal History Month. For what would you like to be remembered in 100 years? Explain.
- ☐ If you could take your mother, grandmother, or another important woman on a special trip for Mother's Day, where would you take her? Why?
- ☐ Everyone knows flowers are supposed to bloom in spring. Write a letter to a shy blossom convincing it to bloom.

Note to the teacher: Have each student staple a copy of this page in his writing journal. Or cut copies in half and distribute only one month's prompts at a time to students. When a student uses a prompt, he checks its box.

Name

June Writing Prompts

- ☐ Some people say that letter-writing is a lost art. Do you agree? Why or why not?
- ☐ What would happen on a perfect summer day? Write a story about it.
- ☐ Which would you rather enter—a hot dog–eating contest or a pie-eating contest? Explain.
- ☐ Would you rather plant a flower garden or a vegetable garden? Describe the garden you would plant.
- ☐ Would you rather be a fly on the wall or an ant at a picnic? What would you see, hear, and do?
- ☐ Father's Day is celebrated this month. Name the top ten qualities of a great dad.
- ☐ Imagine you and a friend are riding bikes. Your friend takes off her helmet and says, "It's too hot to wear a helmet today." Write a speech that will convince her to wear her helmet.
- ☐ Name the cartoon character that is most like you. Explain.
- ☐ Suppose you win a free hot-air balloon ride. The cash value of the ticket is $210.00. Would you take the ride or the cash? Explain.
- ☐ June is National Dairy Month. Create a new flavor of ice cream. Give it a fun name and then describe it.

Name

July Writing Prompts

- ☐ What would be the best summer job for someone your age? What would you have to do?
- ☐ Nadia Comaneci earned the first perfect gymnastics score in the 1976 Summer Olympics. What do you do that would earn a perfect score? Explain.
- ☐ List eight or more ways a person can show patriotism for his or her country.
- ☐ Imagine that you and your class camp out at your school over the weekend. What happens?
- ☐ The Tour de France, a three-week-long bicycle race, takes place every July. Would you rather watch the race or be in it? Explain.
- ☐ Name one part of your school that you would like to change. Write a letter to persuade the principal to make the improvement.
- ☐ Would you rather swim in a river, a lake, a pool, or an ocean? Why?
- ☐ Suppose you find a diamond ring while walking home. Write a story about it.
- ☐ What would you do if you suddenly became rich and famous?
- ☐ Imagine that you are stranded on a tropical island. Your only way of reaching help is to put a message in a bottle. What would you write?

Note to the teacher: Have each student staple a copy of this page in his writing journal. Or cut copies in half and distribute only one month's prompts at a time to students. When a student uses a prompt, he checks its box.

Math

Place Value Mansions

Using base ten blocks

To practice place value in a creative way, give a supply of base ten blocks (flats, rods, and cubes) to each group of four or five students. Direct the group to use some or all of its manipulatives to construct a home. When the structures are finished, have the groups rotate among the homes to determine each mansion's value. To check students' answers, have each group dismantle its structure into groups of flats, rods, and cubes.

Leigh Anne Newsom, Cedar Road Elementary, Chesapeake, VA

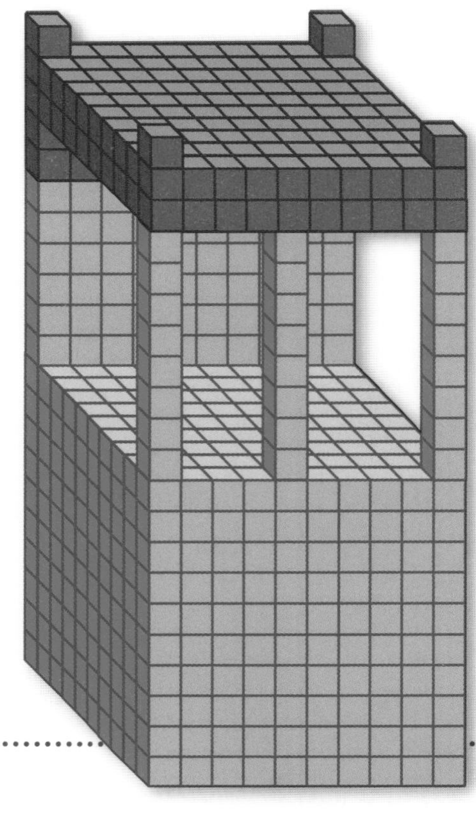

Dueling Numbers

Reading and comparing whole numbers

Five million, six hundred thirty-two thousand, four hundred seventy-three.

Begin this fun partner activity by having each pair of students shuffle and stack facedown a deck of playing cards from which the aces, tens, and face cards have been removed. For round one, each partner turns one card faceup and reads his number aloud. The player with the greater number keeps his card, and the other player returns his card to the bottom of the stack. If the cards match, players repeat the round. For round two, each player turns two cards faceup, sets them next to each other, and reads the resulting two-digit number aloud. The player with the greater number chooses one card to keep. All other cards are returned to the bottom of the stack. For each successive round, players turn over one more card than the previous round to form a number that has one more digit than before. The player with more cards at the end of the seventh round wins.

Shawna Bonnin, Webster Elementary, Mesa, AZ

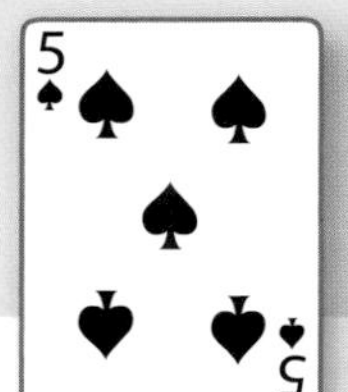

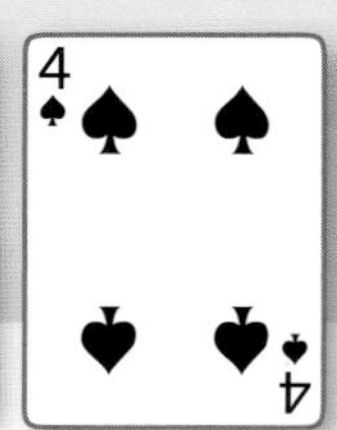

Number Sharks

Number sense

Assess students' understanding of number sense by having each child complete a copy of page 172 as directed. Periodically repeat the activity to monitor students' understanding of place value, number forms, and computation.

Peggy Biedermann, Seven Bar Elementary, Albuquerque, NM

Name Devin
Date September 9

Number sense

Number Shark

1. Cut out the number cards below. Shuffle the cards and stack them facedown.
2. Draw nine cards and arrange them in the chart to make the largest number you can.
3. Glue the cards to the chart.
4. Complete the page as directed.

7	7	6	,	5	4	2	,	2	1	0
Millions				Thousands				Ones		

A. Write your number in standard form. 776,542,210
B. Write your number in expanded form. 700,000,000 + 70,000,000 + 6,000,000 + 500,000 + 40,000 + 2,000 + 200 + 10 + 0
C. Write your number in word form. seven hundred seventy-six million, five hundred forty-two thousand, two hundred ten
D. Which digit is in the ten millions place? 7
E. Which digit is in the hundred thousands place? 5
F. What number is 500 more than your number? 776,542,710
G. What number is 500 less than your number? 776,541,710
H. What number is twice your number? 1,553,084,420
I. What number is 999 more than your number? 776,543,209
J. What number is 999 less than your number? 776,541,211

Ready to Roll!

Multiplication, addition

Liven up computation practice for small groups or the whole class with colorful 12-sided dice! Choose a game variation below. Instruct the first child who answers correctly to record a tally mark on her paper. Continue until one player has ten tallies.

- **Two dice of the same color:** Find the product of the numbers rolled.
- **Three dice (two of the same color, one of a different color):** Find the sum of the numbers on the same-colored dice. Then multiply the sum by the number on the different-colored die.
- **Four dice (two of each color):** Find the sum of the numbers on each pair of same-colored dice. Then multiply one sum by the other.

Cristie Hetrick-Bennett, Hawthorne, CA

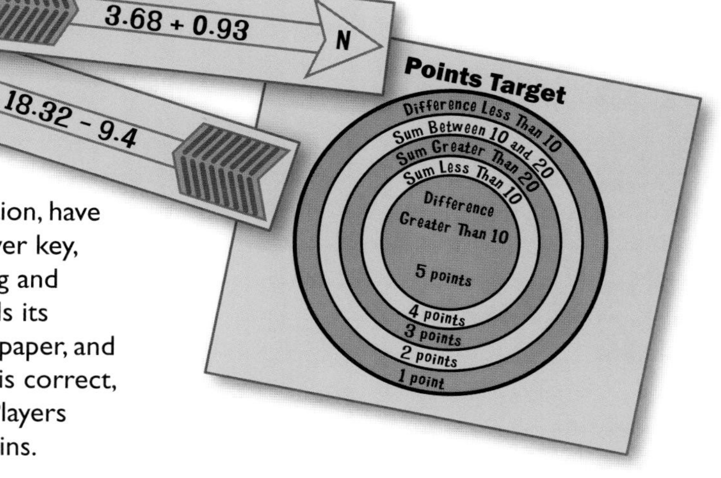

Right on Target!

Reading, adding, and subtracting decimals

For a game that hits the mark with decimal computation, have each pair of students cut apart the game cards, answer key, and points target from a copy of page 173. After shuffling and stacking the game cards, Player 1 selects a card and reads its problem to Player 2. Player 2 solves the problem on his paper, and Player 1 uses the key to check his answer. If the answer is correct, Player 2 uses the points target to determine his score. Players then switch roles. The first player to earn eight points wins.

Jennifer Otter, Oak Ridge, NC

Name ____________________

Brick by Brick

Round the numbers in each row as directed.
Find each estimated sum or difference.
Cross off the matching answer on the stack of bricks.
Four numbers will not be crossed off.

6,000	670	100,000	1,190,000
1,360	1,460	50,000	45,000
500	15,900	780,000	400,000
60	12,800	121,000	1,000,000
9,500	600,000	1,300	8,500
598,000	500,000	70	12,000

nearest ten	1. 87 − 28	2. 476 + 23	3. 695 − 32	4. 716 + 644
nearest hundred	5. 9,418 + 111	6. 11,644 + 4,251	7. 22,873 − 14,352	8. 17,234 − 4,429
nearest thousand	9. 8,667 + 3,489	10. 600,083 − 1,956	11. 61,832 + 58,539	12. 21,947 − 16,499
nearest ten thousand	13. 161,789 − 58,618	14. 841,650 − 787,004	15. 652,941 + 128,653	16. 405,601 + 783,999
nearest hundred thousand	17. 789,055 − 364,988	18. 161,718 + 253,545	19. 887,868 + 131,415	20. 807,050 − 166,227

 Key p. 310

Name ____________________

Reading and interpreting a double-bar graph

Hand Me the Mic!

Study the graph. Then answer the questions.

Contestants: Carli  Charlie

1. Which contestant talked longer about pet peeves? ____________________
2. Which topic did the contestants talk about for the same amount of time? ____________________
____
3. Which topic did Carli talk about most? ____________________
   Which topic did Charlie talk about most? ____________________
4. Charlie talked half as much as Carli about two topics. Which topics are they? ____________________
____
5. Which contestant talked twice as long as the other about bubble gum? ____________________
6. How much longer would Carli need to talk about TV commercials to equal Charlie's time?
____
7. What is the average time each contestant talked about TV commercials? ____________________
8. Who won the contest by talking for more total minutes: Carli or Charlie? ____________________
   By how many minutes did the contestant win? ____________________

Name ______________________________

Date ______________________

Number Shark

1. Cut out the number cards below. Shuffle the cards and stack them facedown.
2. Draw nine cards and arrange them in the chart to make the largest number you can.
3. Glue the cards to the chart.
4. Complete the page as directed.

			,				,			
	Millions		,		Thousands		,		Ones	

A. Write your number in standard form. ______________________________

B. Write your number in expanded form. ______________________________

____

C. Write your number in word form. ______________________________

____

____

D. Which digit is in the ten millions place? ______________________________

E. Which digit is in the hundred thousands place? ______________________________

F. What number is 500 more than your number? ______________________________

G. What number is 500 less than your number? ______________________________

H. What number is twice your number? ______________________________

I. What number is 999 more than your number? ______________________________

J. What number is 999 less than your number? ______________________________

0	0	1	1	2	2	3	3	4	4
5	5	6	6	7	7	8	8	9	9

 Note to the teacher: Use with "Number Sharks" on page 169.

Game Cards, Answer Key, and Points Target

Use with "Right on Target!" on page 169.

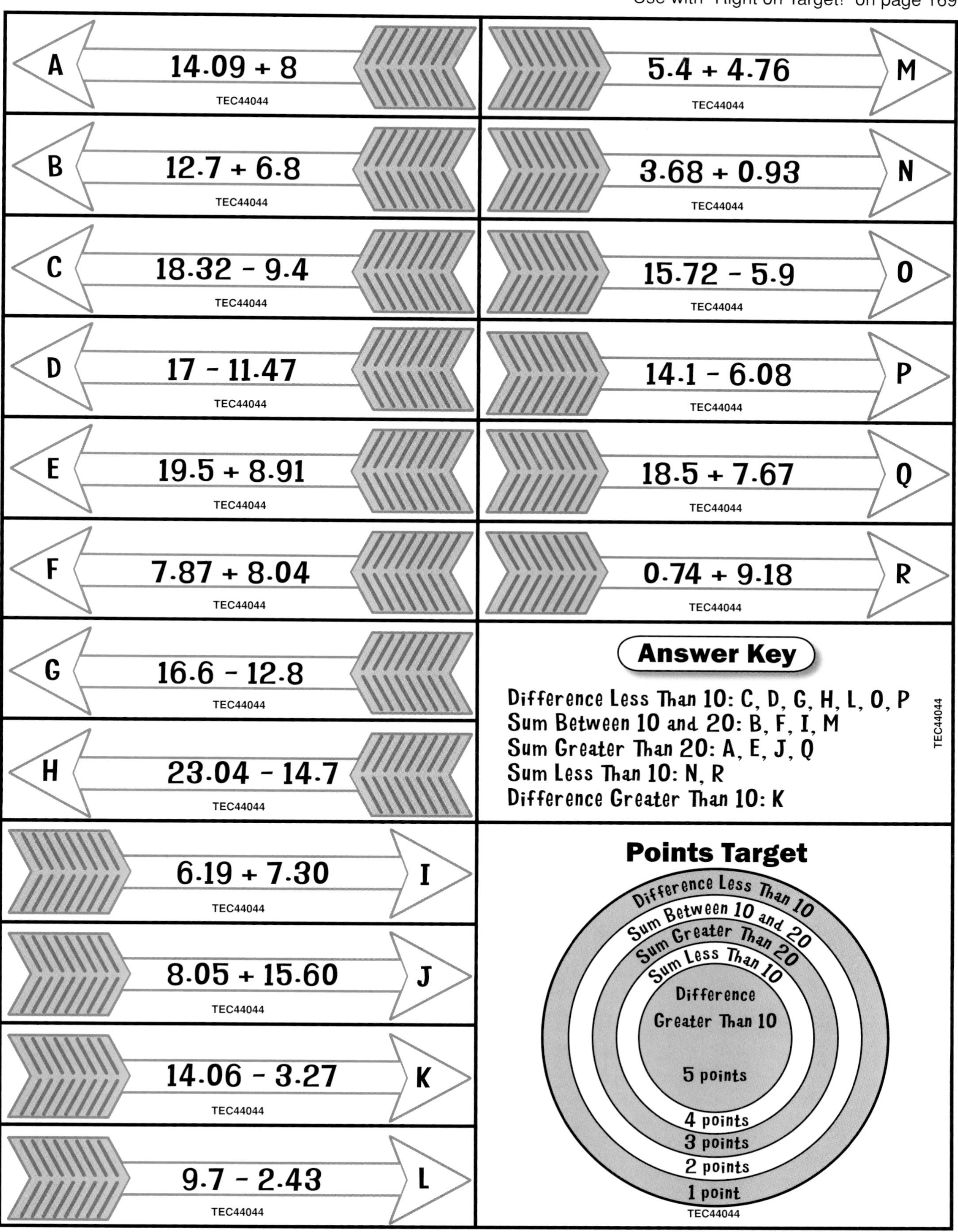

Game Cards and Answer Key

Use with "Painters' Challenge" on page 175. Copy and mount on construction paper the game mat on page 175 and the cards and answer key below. If desired, laminate the pages before cutting the cards apart.

8 ounces TEC44044	2 cups TEC44044	2 pints TEC44044	4 quarts TEC44044
8 quarts TEC44044	4 cups TEC44044	8 cups TEC44044	16 cups TEC44044
32 cups TEC44044	16 ounces TEC44044	4 ounces TEC44044	8 pints TEC44044
$\frac{1}{2}$ pint TEC44044	$\frac{1}{2}$ quart TEC44044	$\frac{1}{4}$ gallon TEC44044	4 pints TEC44044

Answer Key for "Painters' Challenge"

Measurement	Equivalent Measurement(s)
$\frac{1}{2}$ cup	4 ounces
1 cup	8 ounces or $\frac{1}{2}$ pint
1 pint	16 ounces, 2 cups, or $\frac{1}{2}$ quart
1 quart	32 ounces, 4 cups, 2 pints, or $\frac{1}{4}$ gallon
$\frac{1}{2}$ gallon	64 ounces, 8 cups, 4 pints, or 2 quarts
1 gallon	128 ounces, 16 cups, 8 pints, or 4 quarts
2 gallons	256 ounces, 32 cups, 16 pints, or 8 quarts

TEC44044

Painters' Challenge

Directions for two players:

1. Shuffle the cards and stack them facedown.
2. Choose a ladder.
3. When it's your turn, draw one card and find its equivalent measurement on your ladder.
4. Have your opponent use the key to check your answer. If your answer is correct, use your card to cover the matching space on your ladder. If your answer is incorrect, your turn is over and you return the card to the bottom of the stack.
5. If you draw a card for a capacity that is already covered, return the card to the bottom of the stack and draw again.
6. The first player to cover three spaces in a row on his ladder wins.

Names ____________________

Hit That Note!

A Game for Two Players

Directions:

1. Select a crayon or colored pencil in a color different than your partner's.
2. Roll two dice. Match the number on the first die to a singer below. Round the number on that person's card using the rule that matches the second die's number.
3. Color a music note with the matching answer. If the answer is on a note that is already colored, your turn is over.
4. When all the notes are colored or time is up, count the number of horizontal, vertical, and diagonal runs in your color. Use the points chart to determine your score.
5. The player with the higher score wins.

1,985,410	1,500,000	1,730,000	2,000,000	1,700,000	2,516,350
1,500,000	2,000,000	1,498,640	2,412,000	1,725,200	1,990,000
1,000,000	1,530,000	2,000,000	1,531,700	2,400,000	1,498,600
2,410,000	2,411,980	2,520,000	1,500,000	2,516,000	3,000,000
1,985,400	2,000,000	1,532,000	2,500,000	1,725,000	1,499,000
1,531,680	2,516,400	1,985,000	1,725,150	2,412,000	2,000,000

① 1,498,637

② 2,516,354

③ 1,725,154

④ 1,985,409

⑤ 2,411,983

⑥ 1,531,677

Rounding Rules

Roll of 1 = nearest ten
Roll of 2 = nearest thousand
Roll of 3 = nearest hundred thousand
Roll of 4 = nearest hundred
Roll of 5 = nearest million
Roll of 6 = nearest ten thousand

Points Chart

Each run of four = 1 point
Each run of five = 3 points
Each run of six = 5 points

Note to the teacher: Each student pair needs a copy of the page, two different-colored crayons or pencils, and a pair of dice.

MATH TIPS + TOOLS

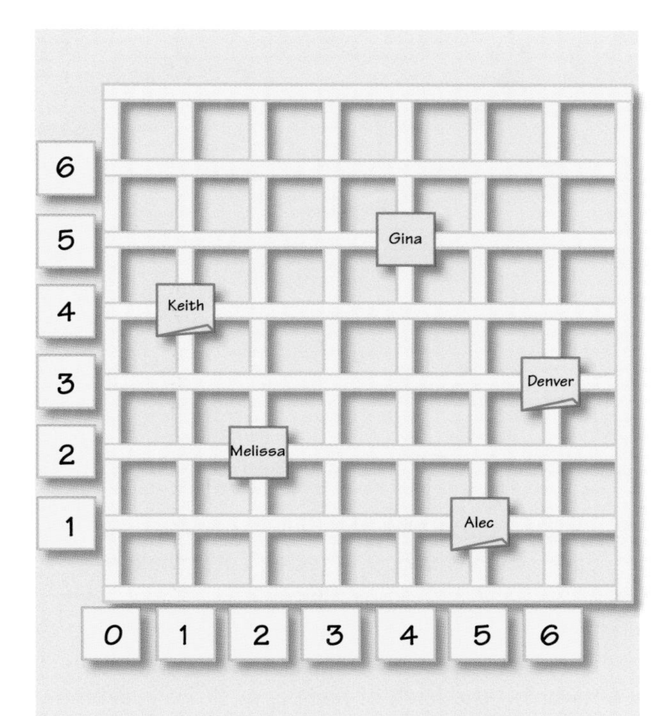

A Giant Grid

Coordinate graphing

Bring graphing to life by turning your classroom floor into a large coordinate grid. In advance, make a copy of your class list for each student. Then attach masking tape to form a grid on your floor and label each *x*-axis and *y*-axis value with a sticky note as shown. Next, write each student's name on a separate sticky note and randomly plot the note on the grid. Have each student look at the floor grid and then write a coordinate pair beside each name on his class list. For additional review, move students' names to new locations on the grid.

Carrie Sindoni, Wilson Elementary, Manchester, NH

Where's the Answer?

Number and operations mixed review

To prepare this whole-class game, choose 16 problems. Draw and label four columns on the board as shown. Then divide your class into four groups. Randomly write each problem's answer in one of the four columns until each column contains four answers. Next, assign each group a numbered column. Then read a problem aloud and have the groups work together to solve it. The team whose column contains the correct answer sends a member to the board to circle it. The first team that circles all the answers in its column wins.

Jennifer Otter, Oak Ridge, NC

Group 1	Group 2	Group 3	Group 4
24	(8)	9	12
150	108	92	56
81	40	18	250
72	16	7	64

How many factors does twenty-four have?

Inching Along

Measurement, fractions

Here's a hands-on activity for helping students recognize the fractions of an inch. First, give each student a copy of an inchworm pattern from page 181. Explain that the pattern shows the ruler markings for one inch but is not drawn to scale. Then have each student label the first mark "0" and the last mark "1." Next, the child folds his worm in half, opens it, and labels the fold "½." Then he folds the worm into fourths and labels the new folds "¼" and "¾." The child continues folding his worm until he can label eighths and sixteenths. Finally, he compares his inchworm ruler with the markings on an actual ruler.

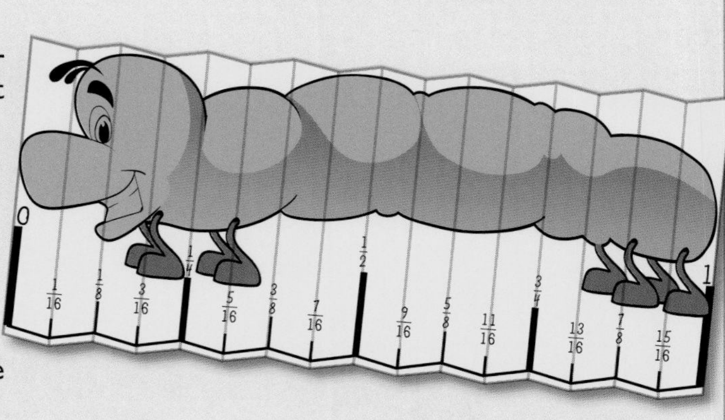

Jennifer Otter, Oak Ridge, NC

A Is for Algebra

Algebraic equations

Liven up your math lesson with this alliterative idea! To begin, have each student choose a letter. Then challenge her to write an algebraic equation using the letter. Next, have her write and illustrate an alliterative story problem based on the equation. Finally, have each student solve her problem and write the answer on the back of her paper. If desired, bind students' pages into a class book titled "*A Is for Algebra.*"

Haley Wolgamot, Altavista Elementary, Altavista, VA

Times Table Tic-Tac-Toe

Multiplication review

Put a spin on this traditional game by playing with multiplication facts instead of Xs and Os. First, have each student draw a tic-tac-toe grid and program the boxes with different facts from a designated set. To play, call out a product from the set (without giving the equation). If a student has the matching fact on his grid, he draws an X in the box. Next, announce another product, continuing until a student gets three in a row horizontally, vertically, or diagonally. Have that student announce the facts he's marked. If they match the products you called, the student wins. If not, the student erases the incorrect Xs and play continues. To play another round, have students draw new grids with the same facts, different facts, or division facts.

9 x 3 = 27	6 x 8 = 48	7 x 6 = 42
6 x 9 = 54	7 x 4 = 28	9 x 5 = 45
7 x 8 = 56	9 x 12 = 108	8 x 9 = 72

Patty Boniti, St. Joseph the Worker Grade School, Weirton, WV

Name ______________________________ Date ______________________________

Tournament Time

Round each factor to the nearest hundred or ten and estimate the product. Then lightly color each box that has the correct estimate to find out which place the team won in the tournament.

Problem	Rounded			
1. 143 x 34	100 x 30	3,000	1,300	4,000
2. 158 x 58		2,600	12,000	1,200
3. 115 x 15		1,000	21,000	2,000
4. 162 x 44		10,000	8,000	42,000
5. 189 x 71		14,000	27,000	140,000
6. 235 x 65		12,000	14,000	1,400
7. 348 x 73		37,000	28,000	21,000
8. 454 x 54		20,000	25,000	2,000
9. 563 x 47		3,000	24,000	30,000
10. 772 x 55		86,000	48,000	40,000
11. 226 x 39		2,400	8,000	80,000
12. 719 x 85		63,000	56,000	6,300

Bonus Box: Solve the problems without rounding. Then compare your answers with your estimates.

1ST

3RD

Name ______________________

Date ______________

LIBRARY MIX-UP

Draw each book on its matching shelf. Color each book after it has been used.
Hint: One book does not belong on a shelf.

Bonus Box: On the back of this page, write an equivalent decimal for each shelf label.

Inchworm Patterns

Use with "Inching Along" on page 178.

MATH TIPS + TOOLS

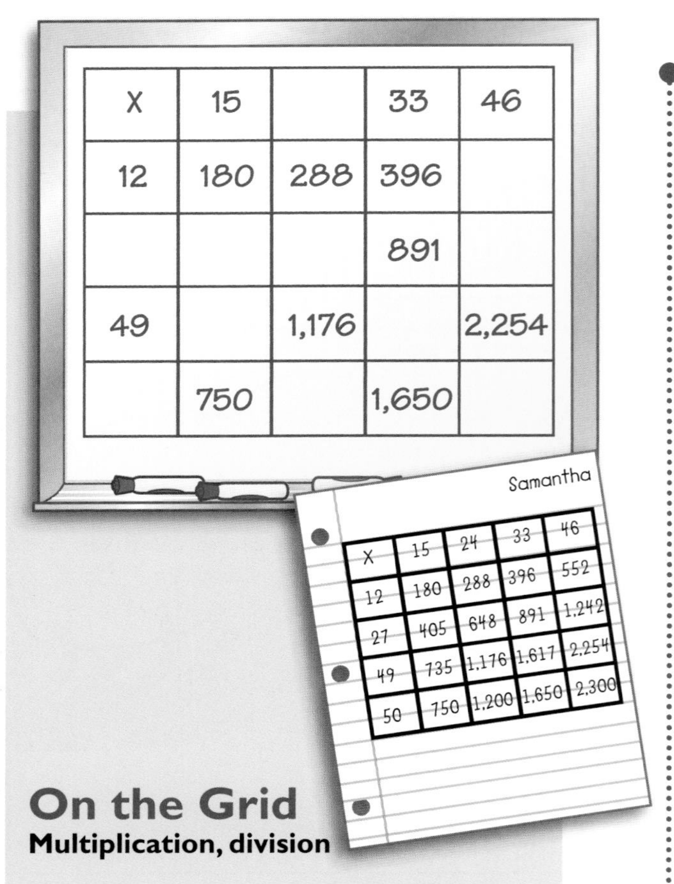

On the Grid
Multiplication, division

This activity gives students plenty of computation practice. Just draw on the board a partially filled-in grid similar to the one shown. Then have each child copy the grid on her paper and start dividing and multiplying to fill it in! If desired, have each student check her work using a calculator. **To vary the activity,** program the boxes with one-digit numbers, decimals, or fractions.

Ann E. Fisher, Toledo, OH

UPC Comparisons
Comparing decimals

Here's a small-group game that's simple to set up! Just clip 16 or more UPC codes from any kind of packaging. Glue each code onto an index card and add a zero and a decimal point as shown. Place the cards in a stack. To play, each student draws and shows one card. The players determine the card with the highest value. The player with that card collects the other students' cards, and the group plays another round. After four rounds, the player with the most cards is declared the winner. Then students shuffle the cards and play again as time allows.

Colleen Dabney, Williamsburg, VA

Stately Fractions

Writing and simplifying fractions

With this portable center, students build fraction concepts using a map of the United States. To set it up, place in an envelope a political map of the United States along with a copy of the cards and answer key from page 186. A student draws a card, reads the question, and uses information from the map to find the answer. Then he jots the card's number on his paper and records his answer (in simplest form) before drawing another card. When time is up, the child checks the key. He tallies one point for each correct answer and adds up his score.

Colleen Dabney, Williamsburg, VA

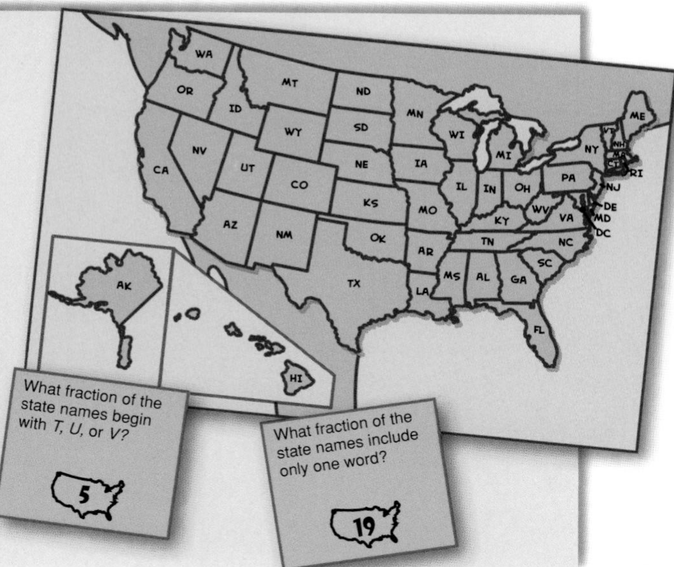

Do the Two-Step!

Problem solving

Guide students to spot the hidden questions in two-step problems with this simple tip! When a child reads a two-step question, have her draw two foot shapes next to the problem or on scrap paper. Next, the student copies the problem's question in one shape. Then she figures out the "missing" question, writes it in the other shape, calculates the answer, and records it. Finally, the child uses her answer to the hidden question to solve the problem's stated question.

Vickie Robertson, Whittier, CA

Measure Twice!

Standard and metric measurement

To play this partner game, students must make precise measurements. Each pair of students cuts apart the grid and object strips from a copy of page 187. Next, one partner draws a strip and measures the object's length to the nearest eighth of an inch or tenth of a centimeter. He finds the matching measurement on the grid, lists the strip's number, and initials the small box. (The standard and metric measurements of each item are listed in separate spaces.) Then the child returns the strip to the bottom of the pile and his partner takes a turn. If a student draws a strip that has already been measured both ways, he loses his turn. When time's up, the partner who initialed the most boxes wins.

Jennifer Otter, Oak Ridge, NC

Name ______________________________ **Congruent figures**

Date ____________________

Climbing Up?

Color each climbing hold using the clues below.

1. Find three hexagons. If they are all congruent, color them red; if not, color them green.
2. Find three right triangles. If they are all congruent, color them blue; if not, color them green.
3. Find five parallelograms. If they are all congruent, color them orange; if not, color them yellow.
4. Find three acute triangles. If they are all congruent, color them pink; if not, color them brown.
5. Find two obtuse triangles. If they are congruent, color them gray; if not, color them orange.
6. Find three trapezoids. If they are all congruent, color them purple; if not, color them red.
7. Find four rectangles. If they are all congruent, color them yellow; if not, color them blue.
8. Find four pentagons. If they are all congruent, color them green; if not, color them brown.

Circle true or false.

9. Some of the rectangles are congruent. **True** **False**
10. All the trapezoids are congruent. **True** **False**
11. None of the parallelograms are congruent. **True** **False**
12. None of the acute triangles are congruent. **True** **False**
13. Some of the pentagons are congruent. **True** **False**
14. Some of the obtuse triangles are congruent. **True** **False**
15. Some of the right triangles are congruent. **True** **False**

Name ______________________

Date ______________________

Ancient Meets Modern

Add or subtract. Write each answer in its simplest form.

$\frac{5}{24} + \frac{13}{24} =$ 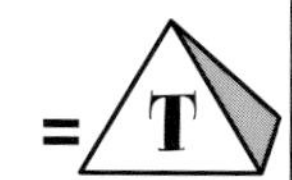 = T	$\frac{17}{18} - \frac{11}{18} =$ = A	$\frac{2}{9} + \frac{2}{3} =$ = S
$\frac{7}{12} - \frac{5}{12} =$  = P	$\frac{7}{20} + \frac{9}{20} =$ = F	$\frac{2}{3} - \frac{2}{7} =$ = R
$\frac{1}{4} + \frac{3}{5} =$  = H	$\frac{15}{16} - \frac{9}{16} =$ = B	$\frac{3}{14} + \frac{5}{14} =$ = Y
$\frac{8}{15} - \frac{1}{3} =$  = M	$\frac{3}{10} + \frac{4}{15} =$ = G	$\frac{7}{10} - \frac{1}{4} =$ = I
$\frac{3}{8} + \frac{1}{4} =$ = O	$\frac{9}{10} - \frac{5}{6} =$ = D	$\frac{2}{6} + \frac{1}{5} =$ 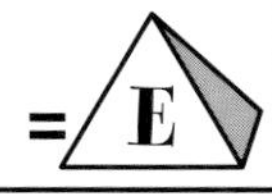 = E

To complete the sentence below, write each letter from above on its matching numbered line or lines below.

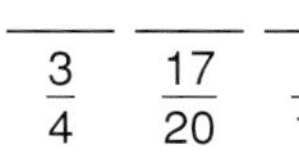

$\frac{3}{4}$ $\frac{17}{20}$ $\frac{8}{15}$ $\frac{3}{8}$ $\frac{1}{3}$ $\frac{8}{9}$ $\frac{8}{15}$ $\frac{5}{8}$ $\frac{4}{5}$ $\frac{3}{4}$ $\frac{17}{20}$ $\frac{8}{15}$

$\frac{17}{30}$ $\frac{8}{21}$ $\frac{8}{15}$ $\frac{1}{3}$ $\frac{3}{4}$ $\frac{1}{6}$ $\frac{4}{7}$ $\frac{8}{21}$ $\frac{1}{3}$ $\frac{1}{5}$ $\frac{9}{20}$ $\frac{1}{15}$

in Egypt is as large as a parking lot for ten jumbo jets.

Fraction Cards

Use with "Stately Fractions" on page 183.

What fraction of the state names begin with *N?*

1

TEC44046

What fraction of the state names begin with *N* or *M?*

2

TEC44046

What fraction of the states border Canada?

3

TEC44046

What fraction of the states border Mexico?

4

TEC44046

What fraction of the state names begin with *T, U,* or *V?*

5

TEC44046

What fraction of the states touch the banks of the Mississippi River?

6

TEC44046

What fraction of the states are on the Atlantic coast?

7

TEC44046

What fraction of the states are on the Pacific coast?

8

TEC44046

What fraction of the state names begin with *B, E, J,* or *K?*

9

TEC44046

What fraction of the states are on the Gulf of Mexico coast?

10

TEC44046

What fraction of the states have *New, North,* or *South* in their names?

11

TEC44046

What fraction of the states are completely east of the Mississippi River?

12

TEC44046

What fraction of the states are completely west of the Mississippi River?

13

TEC44046

What fraction of the states have area both east and west of the Mississippi River?

14

TEC44046

What fraction of the states are not on the Atlantic, Pacific, or Gulf of Mexico coasts?

15

TEC44046

What fraction of the state names include two words?

16

TEC44046

What fraction of the states share a border with another country?

17

TEC44046

What fraction of the Great Lakes touch the state of Michigan?

18

TEC44046

What fraction of the state names include only one word?

19

TEC44046

What fraction of the state names have seven or fewer letters in their names?

20

TEC44046

Answer Key for "Stately Fractions"

1. $\frac{4}{25}$
2. $\frac{8}{25}$
3. $\frac{13}{50}$
4. $\frac{2}{25}$
5. $\frac{1}{10}$
6. $\frac{1}{5}$
7. $\frac{7}{25}$
8. $\frac{1}{10}$
9. $\frac{1}{25}$
10. $\frac{1}{10}$
11. $\frac{4}{25}$
12. $\frac{13}{25}$
13. $\frac{11}{25}$
14. $\frac{1}{25}$
15. $\frac{3}{25}$
16. $\frac{1}{5}$
17. $\frac{17}{50}$
18. $\frac{4}{5}$
19. $\frac{4}{5}$
20. $\frac{2}{5}$

TEC44046

Measurements Grid and Object Strips

Use with "Measure Twice!" on page 183.

$5\frac{1}{2}$ in. # ________ Initial here.	13.3 cm # ________ Initial here.	6.7 cm # ________ Initial here.	$2\frac{5}{8}$ in. # ________ Initial here.	5.4 cm # ________ Initial here.
9.3 cm # ________ Initial here.	$2\frac{1}{4}$ in. # ________ Initial here.	5.7 cm # ________ Initial here.	4.8 cm # ________ Initial here.	$\frac{7}{8}$ in. # ________ Initial here.
2.2 cm # ________ Initial here.	$3\frac{5}{8}$ in. # ________ Initial here.	$2\frac{1}{8}$ in. # ________ Initial here.	8.6 cm # ________ Initial here.	$5\frac{1}{4}$ in. # ________ Initial here.
$3\frac{3}{8}$ in. # ________ Initial here.	11.1 cm # ________ Initial here.	$1\frac{7}{8}$ in. # ________ Initial here.	13.9 cm # ________ Initial here.	$4\frac{3}{8}$ in. # ________ Initial here.

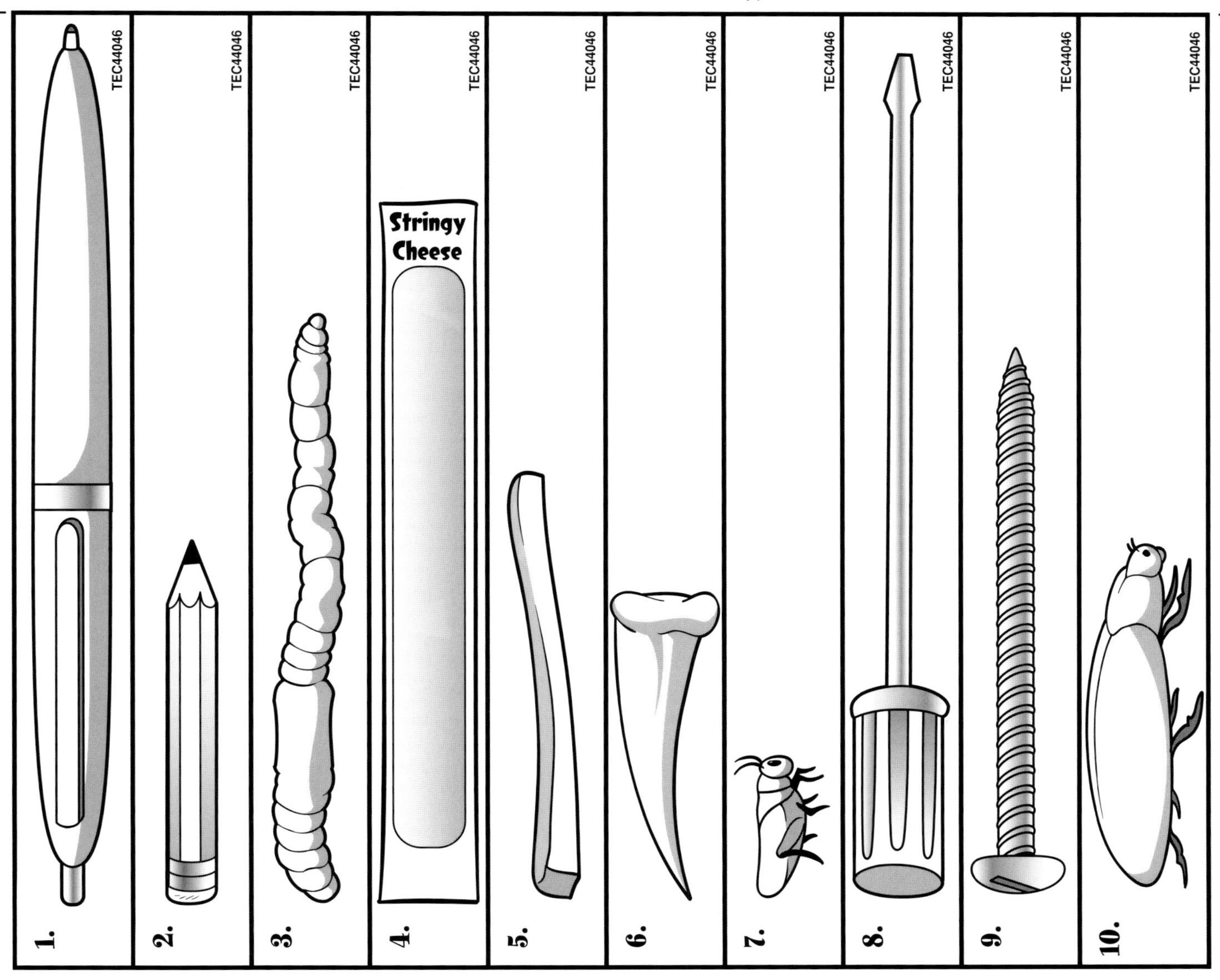

Names ____________________

Date ____________________

MOVIN' ON!

A Game for Two Pioneers

PIONEER 1
438
58.24
283.92
681.59
73.92
119.84
207.90
1,660.75
23.04
87.36
532.35
163.80

Directions:

1. Choose a trail.
2. In turn, multiply a decimal by a whole number from the wheels. Show your work on a separate sheet of paper.
3. If the product is on your trail, color its space.
4. The first pioneer to color each space on his or her trail wins!

4.62 18.25 3.64 11.83 7.49 0.96

24 16 45 91

PIONEER 2
189.28
87.36
110.88
292
420.42
179.76
821.25
15.36
331.24
43.20
1,076.53
337.05

Note to the teacher: Each student pair needs a copy of the page. Each player needs a crayon or colored pencil and a sheet of paper on which to show his work.

MATH TIPS + TOOLS

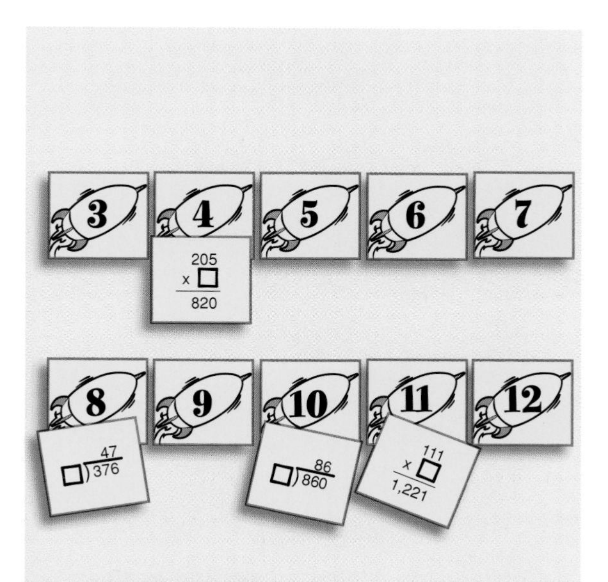

Blast Off!

Mixed-review game

Students accelerate their mental math skills with this fast-paced partner game. To play, have each student in a pair cut apart a copy of the cards on page 194. Next, have each student line up the number cards, as shown, and stack the equation cards. To play, both partners say, "Three, two, one, blast off!" and turn over their top cards. Next, each player solves her problem and puts her card on the number card that matches her answer. She draws the next card and continues in the same way until she solves ten problems. The first player to finish says, "Splash-down!" Then the partners check the key to make sure their matches are correct. Each player earns one point for each of her correct matches. Then each partner shuffles her cards, and the pair plays again. The first player to reach a predetermined number of points wins the game.

Amy Hashberger, Greenville, SC

All in a Day

Elapsed time

Use this hands-on idea to help students visualize the passage of time. Each student divides a sentence strip into 24 one-inch sections. The child writes *midnight* at one end of the strip and labels the sections in one-hour increments, as shown. Next, the student draws sketches in the sections to show what he does each hour. Then he tapes the strip's ends together to create a loop. The student keeps the strip as a handy resource for calculating elapsed time.

Lynn Austin, Midstreams Elementary, Bricktown, NJ

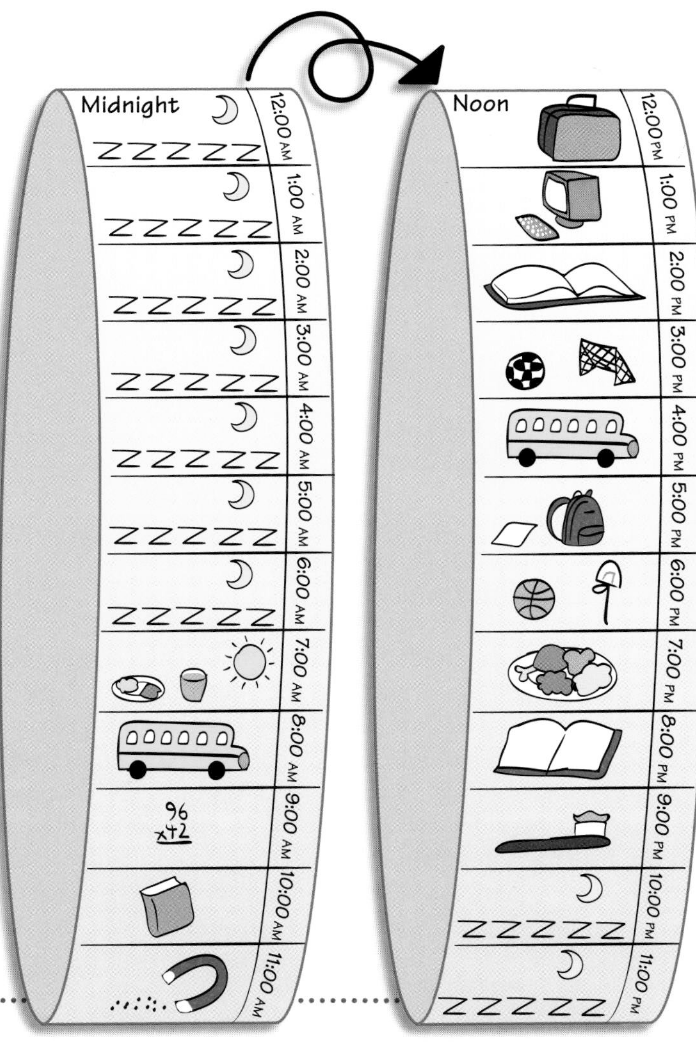

Domino Dynamos

Common denominators

For this partner game, have each student spread ten dominoes facedown. To play, each child turns over one domino and names the fraction shown. The first player to identify the lowest common denominator for the two fractions keeps both dominoes. Play continues as time allows or until one player wins all the dominoes.

Jill Reed, Lewis and Clark Elementary, Lewistown, MT

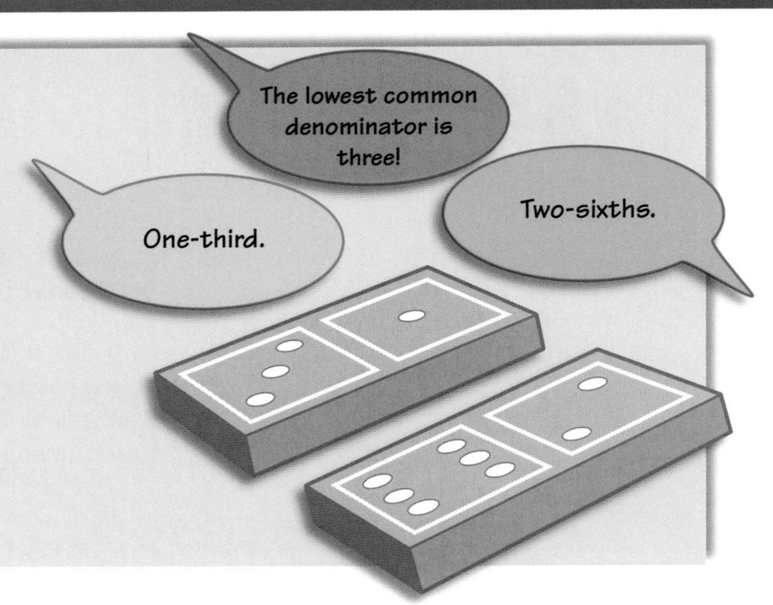

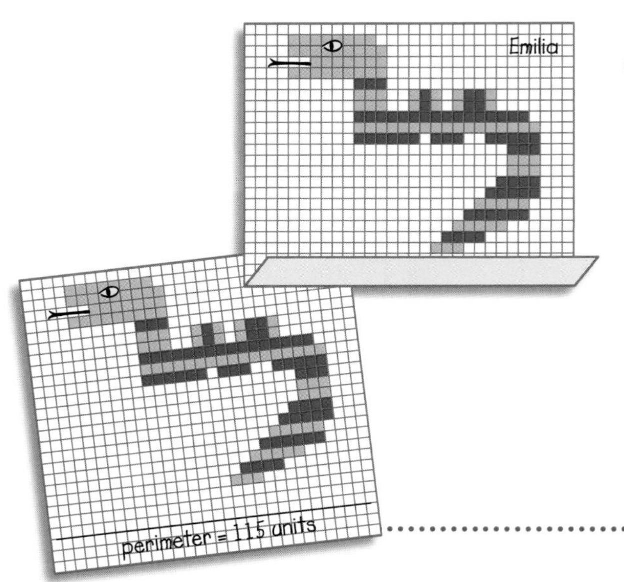

All the Way Around

Perimeter

Here's a fun idea for reinforcing perimeter skills while encouraging students to use their imaginations. To begin, have each student draw a fantasy pet on a sheet of grid paper. Next, guide the child to calculate the pet's perimeter, record it at the bottom of the page, and fold her paper to cover the answer. Then have each student trade her paper with a partner, calculate the perimeter of her partner's pet, and unfold the page to check her answer. Extend the activity by having each child calculate her pet's area too.

Teresa Vilfer-Snyder, Fredericktown, OH

Show Me the Money!

Fraction and decimal relationships

To prepare this guided small-group activity, collect 100 pennies and a hundred chart for each student. Begin the activity by having each student draw and label a four-column table as shown. Then have the child place 100 pennies on the hundred chart and fill in the rows of his table for that number of pennies. Next, direct the student to remove ten pennies from his chart and fill in the table for 90 pennies. Repeat with different amounts, having the student model each amount with pennies and fill in the table each time.

Rachel Pepe, River Place Elementary, Austin, TX

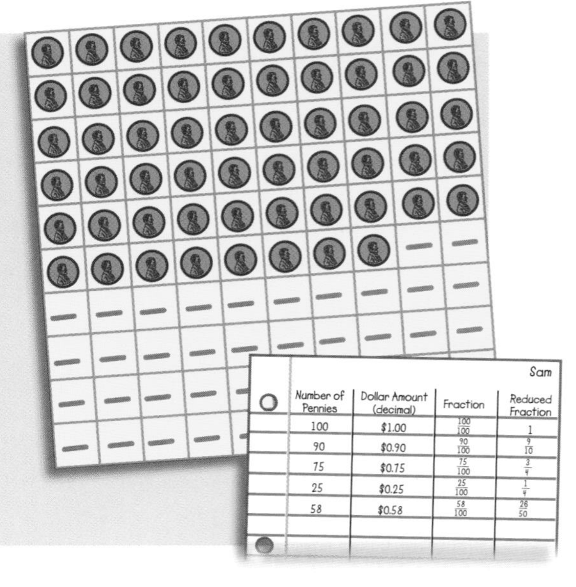

Sam

Number of Pennies	Dollar Amount (decimal)	Fraction	Reduced Fraction
100	$1.00	$\frac{100}{100}$	1
90	$0.90	$\frac{90}{100}$	$\frac{9}{10}$
75	$0.75	$\frac{75}{100}$	$\frac{3}{4}$
25	$0.25	$\frac{25}{100}$	$\frac{1}{4}$
58	$0.58	$\frac{58}{100}$	$\frac{26}{50}$

Name ____________________________________

Date ______________________

Pick ___ activities to do.
When you finish an activity, color its number.

1 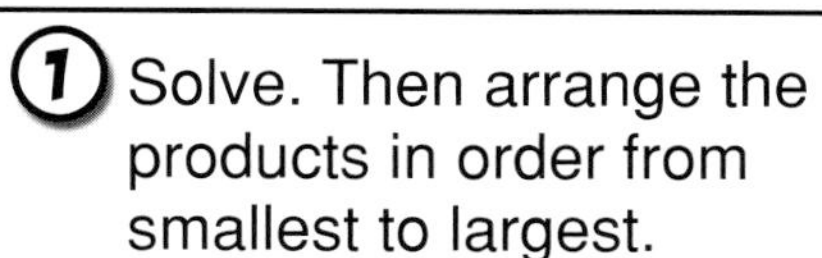
Solve. Then arrange the products in order from smallest to largest.

A. 597 x 81 = y

B. 829 x 64 = y

C. 605 x 77 = y

D. 242 x 16 = y

E. 107 x 38 = y

2 For each clue below, write and solve a different multiplication problem.

A. The product is less than 11,000.

B. The product is greater than 25,000.

C. The product is greater than 11,000 but less than 25,000.

3 Estimate the product of each problem by rounding the first factor to the nearest hundred and the second factor to the nearest ten. Then solve each problem.

A. 941 x 82 = x

B. 359 x 67 = x

C. 413 x 94 = x

D. 526 x 33 = x

4 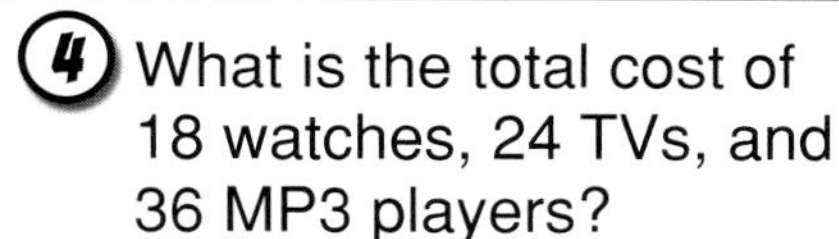
What is the total cost of 18 watches, 24 TVs, and 36 MP3 players?

5 Multiply each of the following by the number of students in your class:

A. your area code

B. the first three digits of your phone number

C. the last four digits of your phone number

D. your school's zip code

6 Estimate the product of each problem by rounding the first factor to the nearest thousand and the second factor to the nearest ten. Then solve each problem.

A. 2,365 x 31 = n

B. 3,128 x 64 = n

C. 7,947 x 48 = n

7 At J. Q. Adams School, 1,263 students have accepted a five-day reading challenge. Each student will read 15 pages a day. How many pages altogether will they read in one day? In three days? In five days?

8 Write five multiplication problems. For each problem, choose a number from the cylinder and a number from the sphere. Then solve each problem.

Cylinder: 35, 62, 81, 55, 74, 93

Sphere: 1,983, 3,745, 6,128, 5,261, 7,129

9 Multiply the four-digit number in each row by the two-digit number in each column.

4	5	6	7
2	3	8	9

4,567
x 42

Independent Practice Grid: Program the student directions on a copy of this page with the number of activities to be completed. Then copy the page for each student.

Name ______________________

Date ______________________

Dinner Is Served!

In the boxes, write the symbols for the operations needed to solve each problem. Then solve the problem on another sheet of paper.

Step 1 Step 2

☐ ☐ 1. Three of the zoo's elephants eat 125 pounds of hay each day. The other elephant eats 150 pounds of hay a day. How many pounds of hay do all the elephants eat in one day? ____________

☐ ☐ 2. The young tiger eats $13\frac{1}{2}$ pounds of meat every day. The older tiger eats five pounds less than that. How many pounds of meat altogether do the tigers eat in a day? ____________

☐ ☐ 3. One beluga whale eats 80 pounds of clams, herring, and squid each day. The staff has 140 pounds of clams, 315 pounds of herring, and 105 pounds of squid. How many days will this food last? ____________

☐ ☐ 4. The gorilla needs 70 pounds of food a day. It has already eaten $7\frac{1}{4}$ pounds of leaves, $3\frac{1}{4}$ pounds of berries, 9 pounds of vegetables, and $18\frac{1}{2}$ pounds of fruit. How many more pounds of food should it have? ____________

☐ ☐ 5. One of the giraffes eats 86 pounds of hay, grain, and fruit a day. Two of the giraffes eat 73 pounds each. Three of the giraffes each eat 64 pounds a day, and the biggest giraffe eats 122 pounds every day. What is the average amount of food each giraffe eats in one day? ____________

☐ ☐ 6. The panda pair equally shares 80 pounds of bamboo a day. How many pounds of bamboo will one panda eat in four days? ____________

☐ ☐ 7. Each gray wolf eats 4 pounds of meat a day. There are 7 gray wolves at the zoo. How many pounds of meat will the zoo need to feed the wolves for one year? ____________

☐ ☐ 8. Use the grocery list shown. How much will the zoo's groceries cost this week? ____________

Zoo Weekly Grocery List

apples, 80 pounds ($2 per pound)
bananas, 50 pounds ($1 per pound)
carrots, 10 pounds ($1 per pound)
spinach, 4 pounds ($3 per pound)
yams, 25 pounds ($1 per pound)
meat, 280 pounds ($4 per pound)
eggs, 5 dozen ($2 per dozen)

Name ______________________________
Date ____________________

Antarctic Antics

Use the graphs to answer each question.

Penguin Dives

pirouette	cannonball	pike	belly flop
	X		
	X		
	X		X
	X		X
X	X		X
X	X		X
X	X	X	X
X	X	X	X

TYPE

Number of Dives per Penguin for Three Days

1	1, 9
2	0, 5, 6, 7
3	4, 5, 8
4	0, 2, 5, 5, 8, 9
5	0, 1, 3, 6, 9

1. How did most of the penguins get into the water?

   ____

2. How were the penguins least likely to get into the water?

   ____

3. Which two dives did the penguins use most?

   ____

4. In three days, how many penguins dove fewer than 25 times? ____________

5. How many penguins dove 25 or more times? ____________

6. How many penguins dove 45 times? ____________

7. How many dives altogether did the penguins make in three days? ____________

8. How many penguins were diving?

   ____

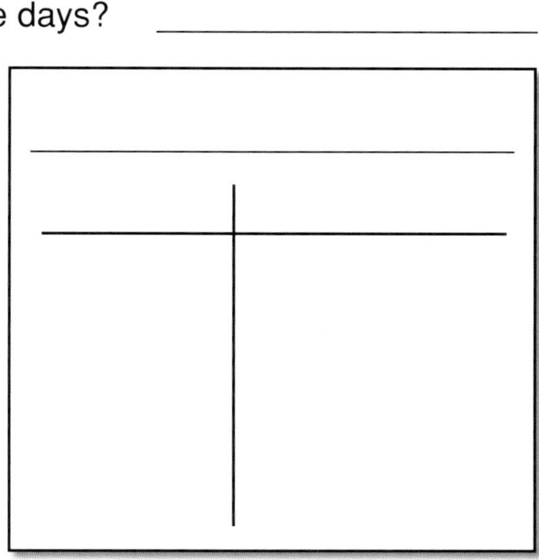

9. Draw a stem-and-leaf plot that shows the following data:
   Number of Dives Per Penguin for One Day:
   22, 8, 11, 24, 9, 20, 15, 22, 3, 16, 21, 11,
   20, 6, 14, 8, 13, 16, 7, 12, 6

10. How many penguins dove 15 or more times in one day?

    ____

Number and Equation Cards

Use with "Blast Off!" on page 189.

3 TEC44047	4 TEC44047	5 TEC44047	6 TEC44047	7 TEC44047
8 TEC44047	9 TEC44047	10 TEC44047	11 TEC44047	12 TEC44047
308 x □ 2,156 TEC44047	65 □)715 TEC44047	78 □)390 TEC44047	18 x □ 108 TEC44047	97 □)582 TEC44047
38 □)456 TEC44047	215 x □ 645 TEC44047	67 x □ 603 TEC44047	47 □)376 TEC44047	1,356 x □ 13,560 TEC44047
205 x □ 820 TEC44047	175 x □ 1,400 TEC44047	81 □)567 TEC44047	432 x □ 5,184 TEC44047	59 □)236 TEC44047
86 □)860 TEC44047	41 □)369 TEC44047	111 x □ 1,221 TEC44047	121 □)363 TEC44047	789 x □ 3,945 TEC44047

Answer Key for "Blast Off!"

3. 215 x □ = 645; 363 ÷ □ = 121
4. 205 x □ = 820; 236 ÷ □ = 59
5. 789 x □ = 3,945; 390 ÷ □ = 78
6. 18 x □ = 108; 582 ÷ □ = 97
7. 308 x □ = 2,156; 567 ÷ □ = 81
8. 175 x □ = 1,400; 376 ÷ □ = 47
9. 67 x □ = 603; 369 ÷ □ = 41
10. 1,356 x □ = 13,560; 860 ÷ □ = 86
11. 111 x □ = 1,221; 715 ÷ □ = 65
12. 432 x □ = 5,184; 456 ÷ □ = 38

TEC44047

Problem Strips

Use with "Hold On!" on page 196. Copy and mount the strips from this page and the center mat from page 196 on sturdy paper. Laminate the strips and center mat, if desired. Then cut on the dotted lines on the center mat and cut out the strips.

$n = \frac{1}{7}$

10. $\frac{1}{3} \times \frac{3}{7} = n$

$n = \frac{2}{25}$

9. $\frac{4}{5} \times \frac{1}{10} = n$

$n = \frac{9}{35}$

8. $\frac{3}{5} \times \frac{3}{7} = n$

$n = \frac{1}{12}$

7. $\frac{1}{8} \times \frac{2}{3} = n$

$n = 1\frac{1}{6}$

6. $9\frac{11}{12} - 8\frac{3}{4} = n$

$n = 7\frac{3}{10}$

5. $7\frac{4}{5} - \frac{1}{2} = n$

$n = 10\frac{1}{4}$

4. $10\frac{1}{2} - \frac{1}{4} = n$

$n = 12\frac{5}{24}$

3. $6\frac{3}{8} + 5\frac{5}{6} = n$

$n = 5\frac{37}{40}$

2. $5\frac{4}{5} + \frac{1}{8} = n$

$n = 2\frac{7}{8}$

1. $2\frac{1}{4} + \frac{5}{8} = n$

Pull.

TEC44047

$p = \frac{7}{20}$

10. $\frac{2}{5} \times \frac{7}{8} = p$

$p = \frac{1}{9}$

9. $\frac{1}{7} \times \frac{7}{9} = p$

$p = \frac{3}{28}$

8. $\frac{2}{7} \times \frac{3}{8} = p$

$p = \frac{1}{4}$

7. $\frac{2}{5} \times \frac{5}{8} = p$

$p = 7\frac{1}{5}$

6. $11\frac{8}{15} - 4\frac{1}{3} = p$

$p = 8\frac{7}{40}$

5. $8\frac{4}{5} - \frac{5}{8} = p$

$p = 4\frac{2}{9}$

4. $4\frac{5}{9} - \frac{1}{3} = p$

$p = 17\frac{1}{20}$

3. $7\frac{3}{10} + 9\frac{3}{4} = p$

$p = 2\frac{11}{14}$

2. $2\frac{1}{2} + \frac{2}{7} = p$

$p = 6\frac{17}{24}$

1. $6\frac{3}{8} + \frac{1}{3} = p$

Pull.

TEC44047

HOLD ON!

DIRECTIONS:

1. Thread a strip through the slots. Slide the strip until problem 1 shows.
2. Solve the problem on another sheet of paper. Show your answer in simplest form.
3. Pull the strip down to check your answer.
4. Repeat Steps 2 and 3 for each problem on the strip.
5. If you have time, thread the other strip through the slots and solve the problems.

Names ______________________

Dates ______________________

A ROUGH RIDE

A Game for Two Players

DIRECTIONS:

1. Fold the answer key behind the page. Choose a crayon or colored pencil that is a different color than your partner's.
2. In turn, choose a fraction from the alien's ship. Find an asteroid with the matching decimal or percent. Have your partner check the key. If the match is correct, color the asteroid. If it is not correct, your turn is over.
3. Play until all the asteroids have been colored. The player with more colored asteroids wins.

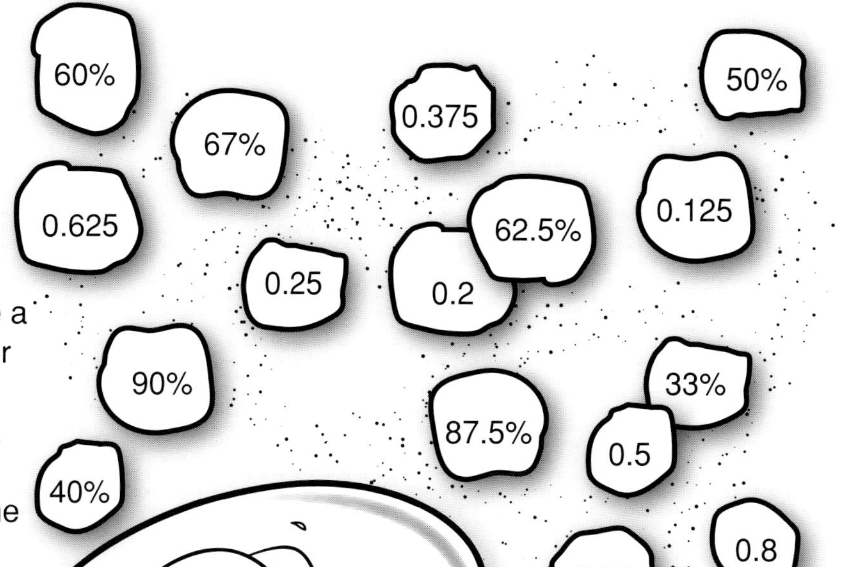

ANSWER KEY FOR "A ROUGH RIDE"

$\frac{1}{10}$ = 0.1, 10%

$\frac{1}{8}$ = 0.125, 12.5%

$\frac{1}{5}$ = 0.2, 20%

$\frac{1}{4}$ = 0.25, 25%

$\frac{3}{10}$ = 0.3, 30%

$\frac{1}{3}$ = 0.33, 33%

$\frac{3}{8}$ = 0.375, 37.5%

$\frac{2}{5}$ = 0.4, 40%

$\frac{1}{2}$ = 0.5, 50%

$\frac{3}{5}$ = 0.6, 60%

$\frac{5}{8}$ = 0.625, 62.5%

$\frac{2}{3}$ = 0.67, 67%

$\frac{7}{10}$ = 0.7, 70%

$\frac{3}{4}$ = 0.75, 75%

$\frac{4}{5}$ = 0.8, 80%

$\frac{7}{8}$ = 0.875, 87.5%

$\frac{9}{10}$ = 0.9, 90%

MATH TIPS + TOOLS

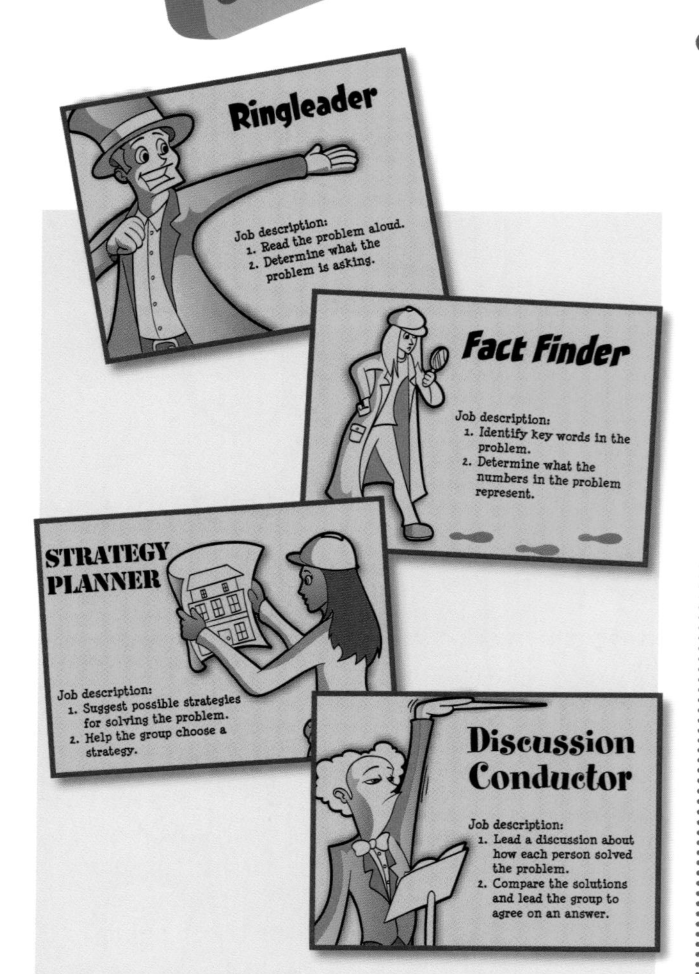

Math Circles

Problem solving

Want to build students' problem-solving skills? Copy and cut apart the cards from page 205 for each group of four students. Next, introduce the roles on the cards and give each group member a different card. Then assign a multistep problem and guide each group's ringleader, fact finder, and strategy planner to help the group analyze the problem. After that, each student solves the problem. Then the discussion conductor leads the group members to compare and check their answers.

Becky Faulkner, Trinity Presbyterian School, Montgomery, AL

Division Dash

Division

To play this partner game, have each pair of students remove the tens and face cards from a deck of playing cards. Then guide the duo to follow the steps below.

Dianna Stavros, Mills Park Elementary, Cary, NC

Directions:

1. Deal five cards to each player.
2. Use your cards to make a division problem with a three-digit dividend and a two-digit divisor.
3. Solve your problem.
4. Trade papers with your partner and check each other's work. If a problem is correct, you earn the number of points in your quotient (excluding the remainder). If a problem is not correct, you don't earn any points.
5. Play for five rounds. The player with the higher total wins.

Adapt this game for students at any level by changing the number of digits in the dividends and the divisors.

Your Opinion Counts!
Mean, median, and mode

Here's a lesson on statistics that students are sure to love! First, guide each small group of students to create a survey question and record it on a sheet of construction paper folded as shown. Next, have the group label four disposable cups with three possible responses and "other." Then allow students to read the groups' survey questions and respond by placing small paper clips in the appropriate cups. After everyone answers all the questions, have each group collect its cups; calculate the mean, median, and mode; and present the results.

Terry Healy, Marlatt Elementary, Manhattan, KS

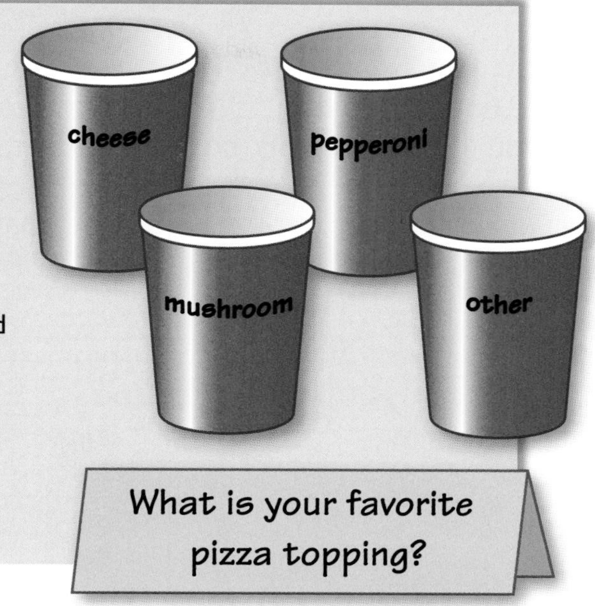

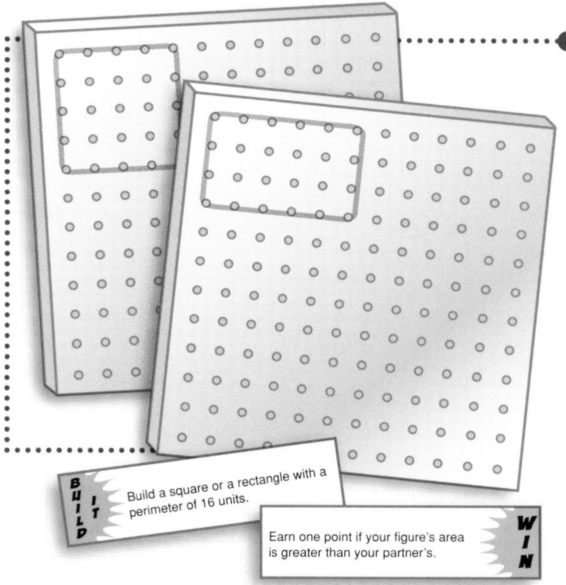

Build It!
Area and perimeter

Use this partner game to review area and perimeter. Give each student pair two Geoboards, rubber bands, and a copy of the cards from page 206. Have the duo cut apart the cards, separate the Build It and Win cards, and stack each pile facedown. In turn, one student draws a Build It card. Each player makes a figure that has the given perimeter on his Geoboard and then determines the figure's area. Next, one student draws a Win card, and the players evaluate their area measurements as guided on the card. If neither shape's area matches the Win card's description, neither player earns a point. Play continues until one student earns ten points.

Jennifer Otter, Oak Ridge, NC

Memory Boosters
Reviewing math concepts

Looking for a fun way to help students review important topics before standardized tests? Try this! List key math terms on paper strips. Put the strips in a bag and have each child draw one. Then guide the student to create on a large sheet of construction paper a poster with interesting facts and hints about her topic. Have each student present her poster to the class and then post it on a board titled "Remember This!"

Kim Williamson, C. Roy Carmichael Elementary, Portola, CA

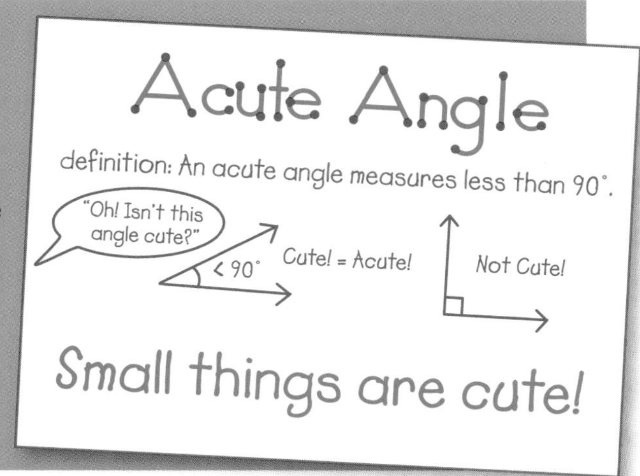

Name ______________________________

Date ____________________

Stretch!

Pick ___ activities to do.
When you finish an activity, color its number.

1 Find the missing measurements.

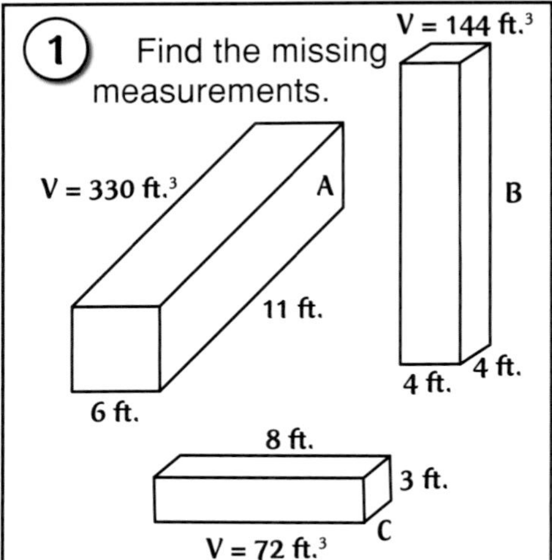

2 Name the box that holds the most. Show your work.

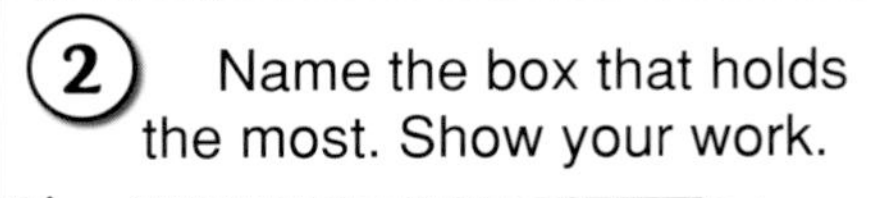

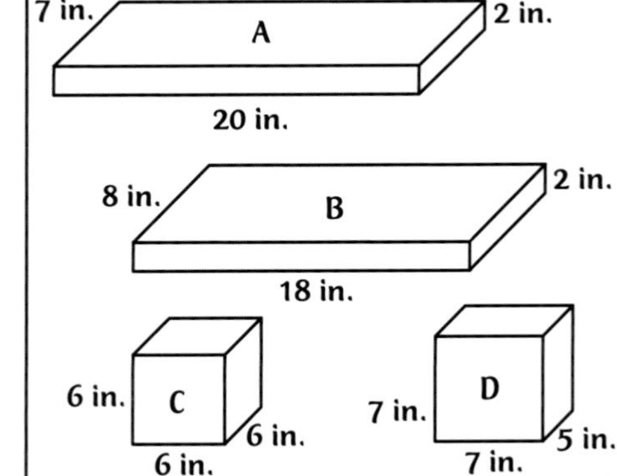

3 Find a tissue box, box of crayons, or another box in your room. Measure its length, width, and height. Calculate its volume. Repeat with another container.

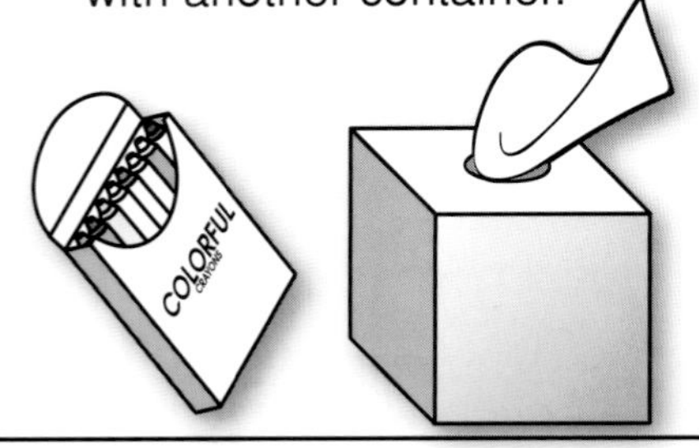

4 Predict how this box's volume will change if the length, width, and height are each increased by 1 cm. Check your prediction. Then predict the change in volume if the measurements are decreased by 1cm. Check your prediction.

5 cm
10 cm
3 cm

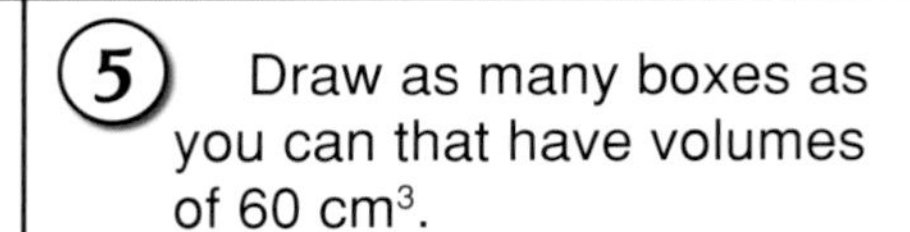

5 Draw as many boxes as you can that have volumes of 60 cm³.

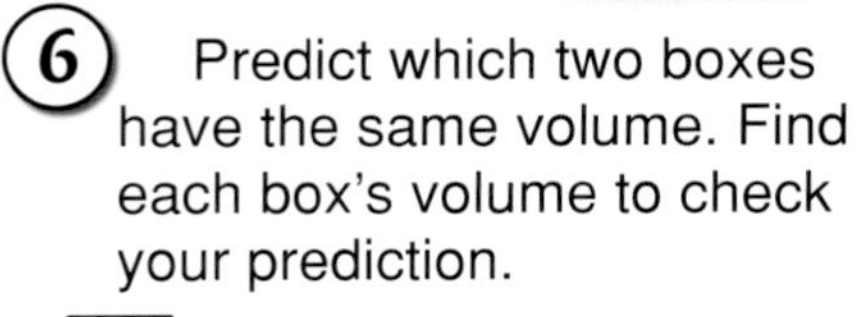

6 Predict which two boxes have the same volume. Find each box's volume to check your prediction.

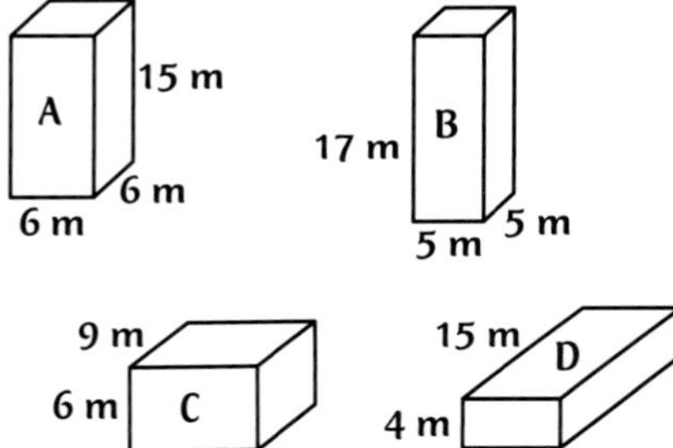

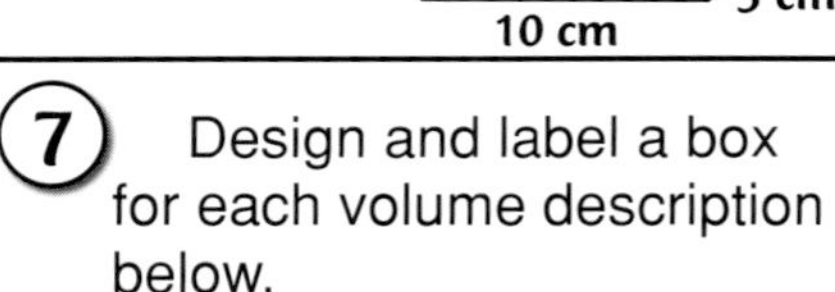

7 Design and label a box for each volume description below.

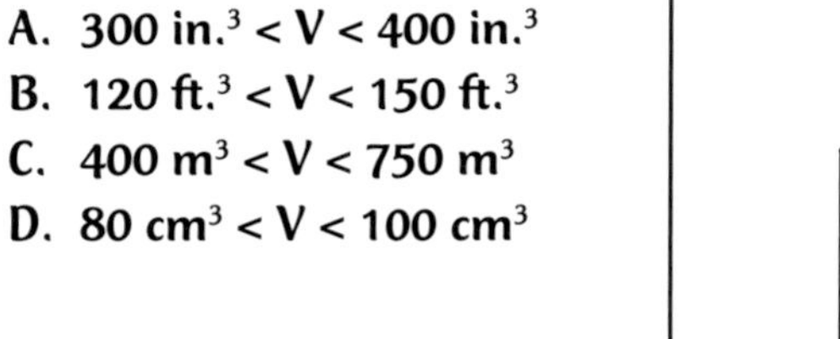

A. 300 in.³ < V < 400 in.³
B. 120 ft.³ < V < 150 ft.³
C. 400 m³ < V < 750 m³
D. 80 cm³ < V < 100 cm³

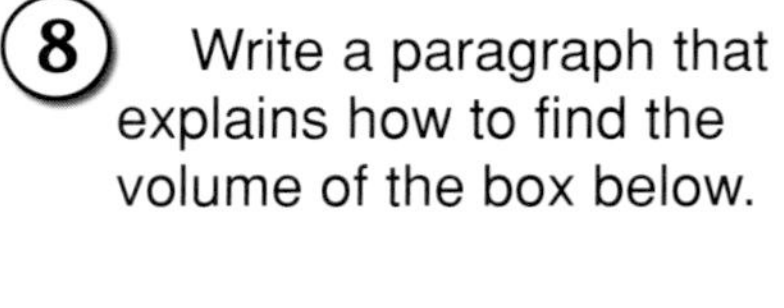

8 Write a paragraph that explains how to find the volume of the box below.

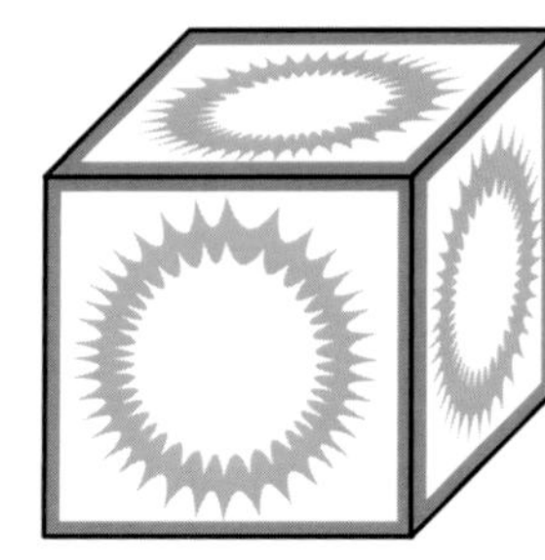

9 What is the combined volume of the boxes below?

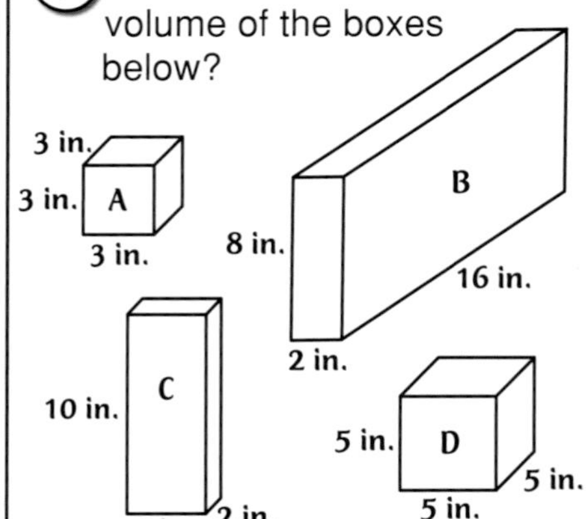

Independent Practice Grid: Program the student directions with the number of activities to be completed. Then copy the page for each student.

Names ______________________________

Date ______________________

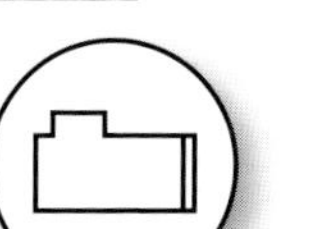

SHAPER CAPER

A Game for Two Players

Directions:

1. Choose a crayon or colored pencil in a color different from your partner's.
2. Roll a die. Use the code to find a box with the matching transformation of a figure shown above.
3. Lightly color the box with the matching answer. If the answer is already colored, your turn is over.
4. When all the boxes are colored or time is up, count the boxes in your color. The player with more colored boxes wins.

Transformation Code

Roll of 1 = translation or slide

Roll of 2 = reflection or flip

Roll of 3 = 90° rotation or turn

Roll of 4 = 180° rotation or turn

Roll of 5 = 270° rotation or turn

Roll of 6 = 360° rotation or full turn

Note to the teacher: Each student pair needs a copy of the page, two different-colored crayons or pencils, and a die.

Name ______________________ **Algebraic expressions**

Date ______________________

Ready, Set, LEAP!

Cut apart the cards below. Then glue each one beside its matching expression. Hint: Z = Zach's frog.

1. $Z + 3$

2. $\frac{Z}{4}$

3. $2Z$

4. $3Z$

5. $Z - 4$

6. $Z + 1$

7. $Z - 7$

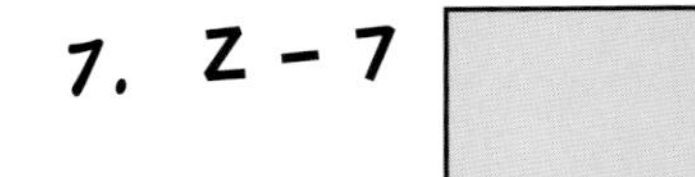

8. $Z - 3$

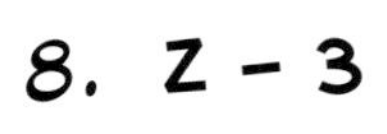

9. $Z + 4$

10. $Z + 6$

11. $\frac{Z}{2}$

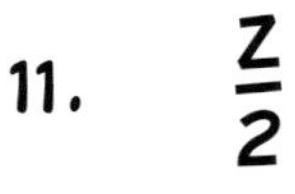

12. $Z - 2$

Bonus Box: Zach's frog jumped 16 inches. On another page, evaluate each expression.

A. Myrah's frog jumped twice as far as Zach's frog.	**B.** Brandon's frog jumped seven inches short of Zach's frog's jump.	**C.** Trevor's frog jumped six inches farther than Zach's frog.
D. Ansley's frog jumped half the distance of Zach's frog.	**E.** Gena's frog jumped three inches beyond the jump of Zach's frog.	**F.** Kapri's frog landed two inches behind Zach's frog.
G. Jack's frog jumped four inches farther than Zach's.	**H.** Zach's frog landed four inches ahead of Hunter's frog.	**I.** McKenzie's frog's jump was three inches shorter than Zach's frog.
J. Miguel's frog jumped one-fourth the distance of Zach's frog.	**K.** Alex's frog jumped three times as far as Zach's frog.	**L.** Destiny's frog jumped one inch farther than Zach's frog.

Name ______________________________

Date ______________

LINE DANCE

Read each clue. Then write the integer on the blank.

B	H	D	O	G	E	W	U	M	I	P	K	S	F	Y	L	N	C	A	V	T	J	Q
−11	(−10)	−9	−8	−7	−6	−5	−4	−3	−2	−1	0	1	2	3	4	5	6	7	8	9	10	11

1. __−10__ ten degrees below zero
2. ______ eight feet above sea level
3. ______ loss of six yards
4. ______ withdrawal of three dollars
5. ______ one degree above zero
6. ______ stepping up two stairs
7. ______ deposit of seven dollars
8. ______ loss of five pounds
9. ______ gain of six yards
10. ______ three feet above sea level
11. ______ decrease of four
12. ______ increase of nine
13. ______ temperature drop of eight degrees
14. ______ gain of four pounds
15. ______ walking down eleven stairs
16. ______ one degree below zero

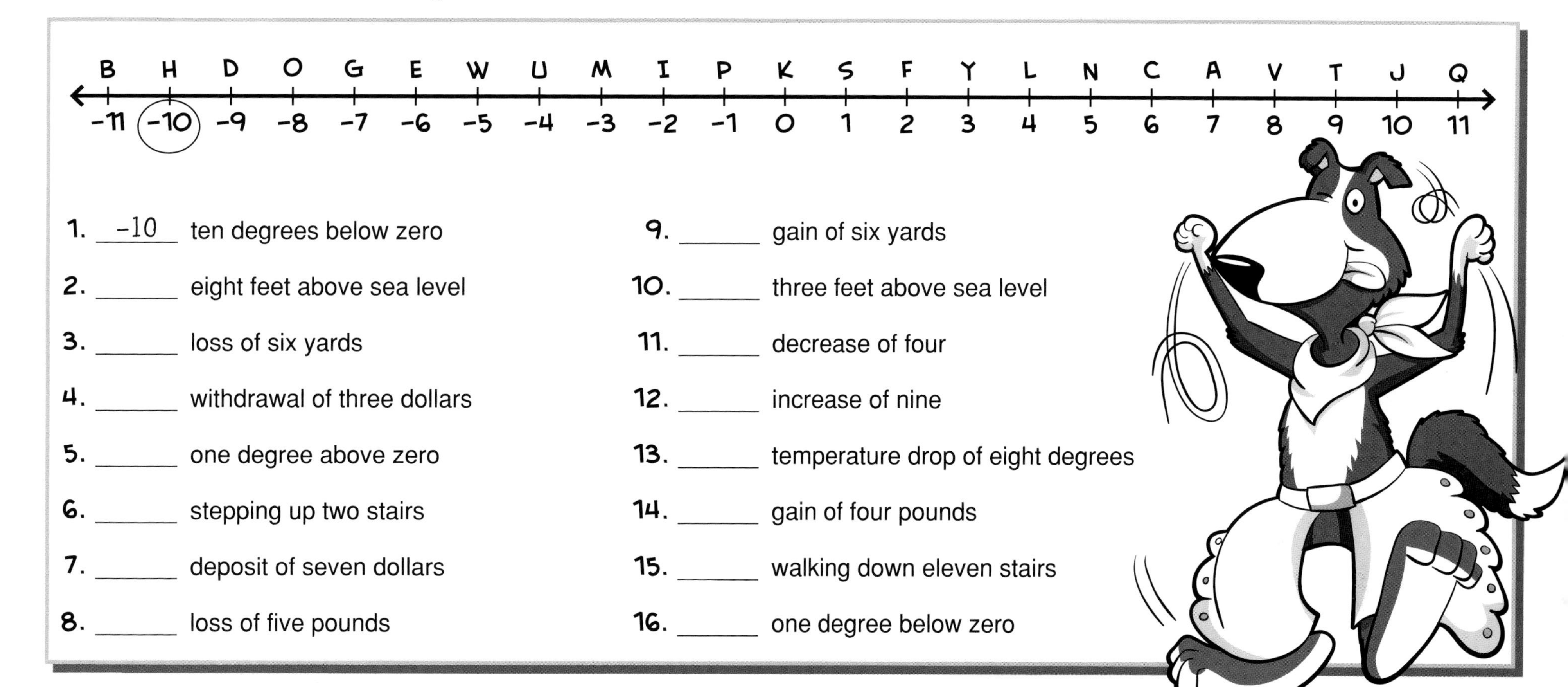

Why aren't dogs good dancers?

To find out, circle each problem's answer on the number line. Then write its letter on the matching numbered line or lines below.

__ __ __ __ __ __ __   __ H __ __   H __ __ __   __ __ __   __ __ __ __   __ __ __ __!

15 3 9 7 11 5 3   12 1 3 10   1 7 2 3   12 8 13   14 3 6 12   6 3 3 12

Name ______________________________

Date ______________________

Multiplying fractions

PIANO PROBLEMS

Multiply. Simplify your answer. Then shade the box with the correct answer.
Follow the path to find out which animal is hiding in the piano.

Problem	Work			
1. $\frac{4}{5} \times 15$	$\frac{4}{5} \times \frac{15}{1} = \frac{60}{5} = 12$	12	10	18
2. $\frac{3}{5} \times \frac{2}{3}$		$\frac{1}{3}$	$\frac{2}{5}$	$\frac{5}{6}$
3. $\frac{1}{3} \times \frac{3}{10}$		$\frac{9}{10}$	$\frac{2}{30}$	$\frac{1}{10}$
4. $\frac{3}{4} \times 8$		$5\frac{3}{4}$	2	6
5. $\frac{7}{9} \times \frac{3}{4}$		$\frac{7}{4}$	$\frac{7}{12}$	$\frac{5}{12}$
6. $30 \times \frac{3}{5}$		16	18	12
7. $\frac{5}{8} \times \frac{3}{10}$		$\frac{3}{16}$	$\frac{5}{16}$	$\frac{5}{20}$
8. $\frac{5}{12} \times \frac{6}{7}$		$\frac{5}{14}$	$\frac{4}{7}$	$\frac{5}{7}$
9. $\frac{5}{6} \times 12$		8	10	9
10. $\frac{1}{12} \times \frac{6}{11}$		$\frac{1}{11}$	$\frac{3}{22}$	$\frac{1}{22}$
11. $\frac{3}{8} \times \frac{2}{9}$		$\frac{3}{20}$	$\frac{1}{12}$	3
12. $9 \times \frac{2}{3}$		$\frac{1}{6}$	6	5
13. $\frac{2}{5} \times 10$		4	$\frac{6}{20}$	6
14. $\frac{6}{7} \times \frac{3}{4}$		$\frac{9}{14}$	$\frac{9}{21}$	$\frac{3}{38}$
15. $\frac{3}{6} \times \frac{4}{7}$		$\frac{1}{3}$	$\frac{2}{7}$	$\frac{4}{7}$

Use with "Math Circles" on page 198.

Game Cards

Use with "Build It!" on page 199.

BUILD IT	WIN
Build a square or a rectangle with a perimeter of 20 units. TEC44048	Earn one point if your figure's area is greater than your partner's. TEC44048
Build a square or a rectangle with a perimeter of 16 units. TEC44048	Earn one point if your figure's area is greater than your partner's. TEC44048
Build a square or a rectangle with a perimeter of 26 units. TEC44048	Earn one point if your figure's area is greater than your partner's. TEC44048
Build a square or a rectangle with a perimeter of 32 units. TEC44048	Earn one point if your figure's area is smaller than your partner's. TEC44048
Build a square or a rectangle with a perimeter of 12 units. TEC44048	Earn one point if your figure's area is smaller than your partner's. TEC44048
Build a square or a rectangle with a perimeter of 22 units. TEC44048	Earn one point if your figure's area is smaller than your partner's. TEC44048
Build a square or a rectangle with a perimeter of 36 units. TEC44048	Earn one point if your figure's area is less than its perimeter. TEC44048
Build a square or a rectangle with a perimeter of 24 units. TEC44048	Earn one point if your figure's area is less than its perimeter. TEC44048
Build a square or a rectangle with a perimeter of 40 units. TEC44048	Earn two points if your figure's area is greater than its perimeter. TEC44048
Build a square or a rectangle with a perimeter of 28 units. TEC44048	Earn two points if your figure's area is greater than its perimeter. TEC44048

What's in the Bag?

Geometry

Give students practice visualizing solid figures with this whole-class game. Before class, place several solid figures—such as rectangular prisms, pyramids, and cones—in separate paper bags. Jot each figure's name on the bottom of its bag. Next, divide the class into two teams. Then guide students to follow the directions shown.

Melissa Bryan, Pear Tree Point School, Darien, CT

To play:

1. A player from Team 1 reaches into a bag without looking. He feels the object inside, trying to determine the number and shape of its faces, edges, and vertices.
2. After ten seconds, the student goes to the board and draws the object he felt.
3. The player's teammates use the drawing to help them name the object in the bag. If they are correct, they earn one point and the object is displayed.
4. If the team does not guess correctly, Team 2 gets a chance to name the object and earn the point. If Team 2 does not guess correctly, the object is revealed and both teams work together to identify its components.
5. Play continues until all the objects have been revealed. The team with more points wins the game.

Just a Hint

Measurement

Help students make conversions between large and small units of measure with this handy booklet of hints. Have each child cut apart the pages from a copy of page 213, stack the pages in order, and staple them together as shown. Then guide the student to cut along the dotted lines on the cover and first page. To use her booklet, the student opens the cover flap of the appropriate measurement system, identifies the conversion she needs, and lifts that flap to reveal the hint.

Angel David, Paradise Elementary, Ball, LA

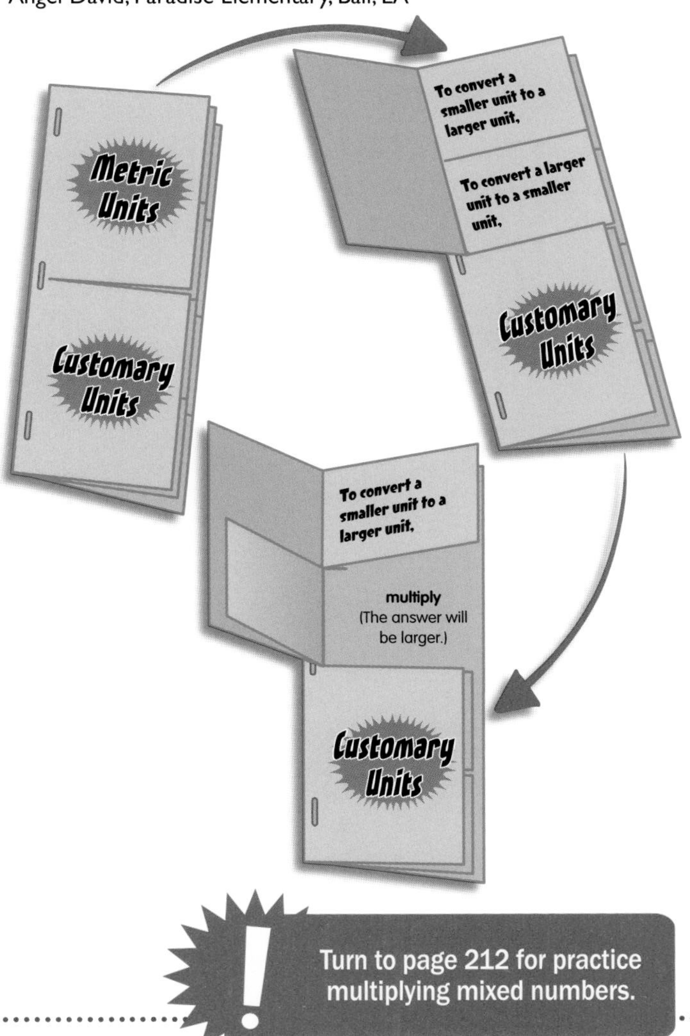

Turn to page 212 for practice multiplying mixed numbers.

Pasta Parentheses
Order of operations

Here's a hands-on activity that helps students figure out which part of an equation to solve first. Give each child a copy of page 214 and two pieces of uncooked elbow macaroni. Guide the student to use the macaroni as temporary parentheses to help him mark which part of each equation was solved first. Once he identifies the operation, he removes the noodles, draws the parentheses on the equation, and moves on to the next problem.

Bonnie Gaynor, Franklin, NJ

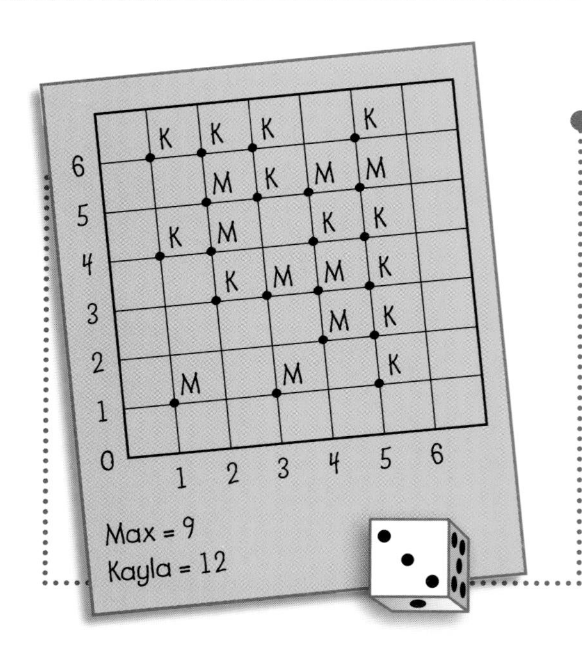

A Battle of Initials
Ordered pairs

For this fun partner game, give each pair of students a die and a sheet of grid paper. Next, have the duo draw and label *x*- and *y*-axes as shown. In turn, one partner rolls the die to determine an *x*-coordinate. She rolls again to find a *y*-coordinate. Then the child records the ordered pair on another sheet of paper, plots the point on the grid, and labels the point with her initial. If a student rolls the coordinates for a point that has already been plotted, her turn is over. The player who plots more points in a set amount of time wins.

Brooke Beverly, Dudley Elementary, Dudley, MA

"A-maze-ing" Addition
Adding fractions

Put a spin on fraction computation with this idea. To begin, draw on the board columns of fractions as shown. Then explain that this is a maze and the goal is to draw a line from one side of the maze to the other. However, you can only draw a line between two fractions whose sum is greater than one. Guide students to solve the maze. Then challenge each pair of students to create its own fraction maze and exchange papers with another duo.

Ann Fisher, Toledo, OH

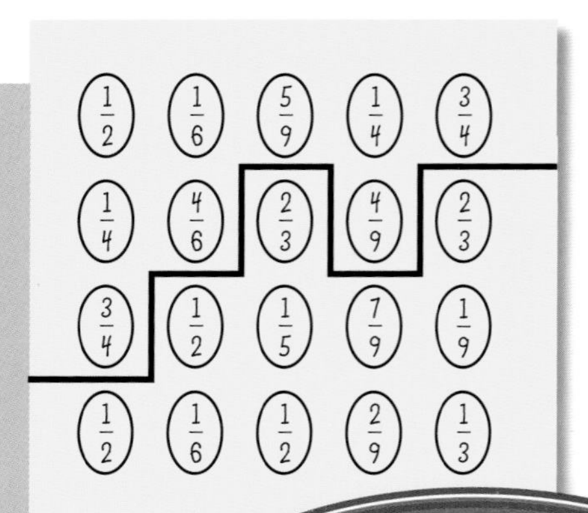

Editor's Tip:
This activity is easy to adapt for any computation skill—just create a rule for drawing a line between whole numbers, fractions, mixed numbers, or decimals!

Name ____ **Division**

Date ______________________________

Now That's Talent!

Pick ______ activities to do.
When you finish an activity, color its number.

1 Use the digits to write five division problems. Then solve each one.

2 6
5 8

2 Solve the division problem shown. Then write and solve four more problems by replacing each digit with the next consecutive number.

$6\overline{)341}$

(Hint: $7\overline{)452}$ comes next.)

3 Copy each problem. Then label the quotient, dividend, and divisor in each one.

A. $\begin{array}{r} 49 \\ 4\overline{)196} \end{array}$ B. $\frac{165}{5} = 33$

C. $474 \div 6 = 79$

D. 448 divided by 7 is 64.

4 Explain how you can tell whether each problem shown will have a remainder before you divide. Solve to check your answers.

A. $2\overline{)564}$ B. $5\overline{)376}$

C. $10\overline{)643}$ D. $3\overline{)612}$

5 Solve each problem. Then check your answers using inverse operations.

A. $5\overline{)728}$ B. $3\overline{)693}$

C. $12\overline{)432}$ D. $54\overline{)609}$

6 Solve. Then arrange the quotients in order from largest to smallest.

A. $5\overline{)360}$ B. $9\overline{)738}$

C. $74\overline{)962}$ D. $24\overline{)648}$

7 Fill in the missing digits to make the remainders as large as possible. Solve.

A. $7\overline{)28\square}$

B. $8\overline{)9\square1}$

C. $11\overline{)5\square3}$

D. $13\overline{)24\square}$

8 If you divide each number below by 16, which problems will have remainders? Divide to check your predictions.

789 928

256 857

9 Write and solve ten division problems (three digits divided by two digits) using only multiples of 10 (numbers that end with a zero).

Example:

$\begin{array}{r} 8 \\ 30\overline{)240} \end{array}$

Independent Practice Grid: Program the student directions on a copy of this page with the number of activities to be completed. Then copy the page for each student.

Name ______________________________
Date ______________________________

Pack and Ship

We'll Get It There Faster!

Calculate the base perimeter, base area, and total volume for each box below. Show your work on another sheet of paper. Then write the letter of each box on the bin with the matching description. Hint: some boxes will fit in more than one bin.

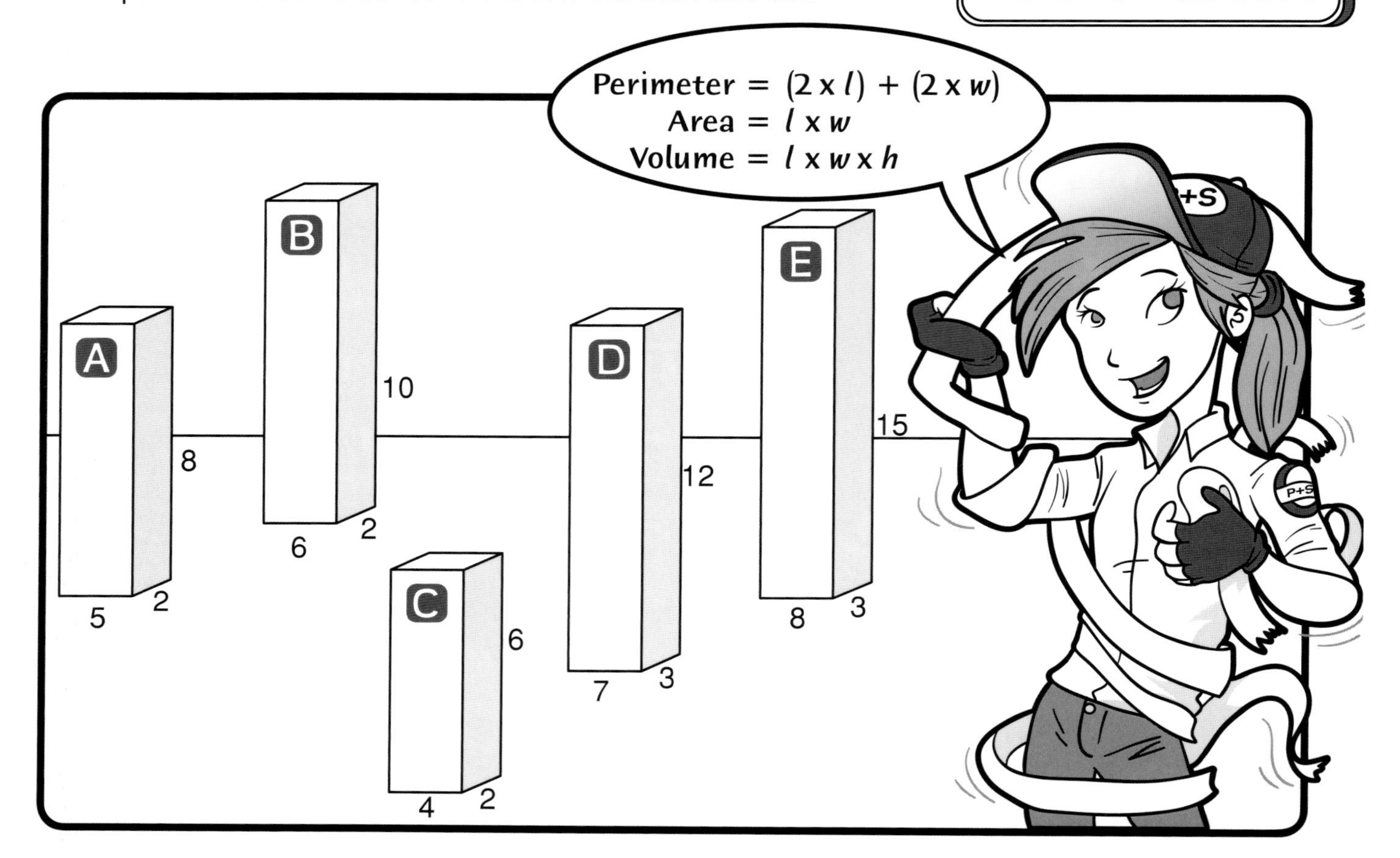

1. ______
2. ______
3. ______

Boxes with a base area greater than 11 square inches

1. ______
2. ______
3. ______

Boxes with a base perimeter less than 20 inches

1. ______
2. ______
3. ______

Boxes with a volume between 100 and 400 cubic inches

Name ______________________________

Date ______________________________

And the Winner Is...

Solve each equation. Then write the solution in the third column to find out which cat wins the most ribbons.

Cat	Problem	Number of Ribbons
TIGER	$4t + 3 = 15$ $4t = 15 - 3$ $4t = 12$	$t = 3$
CASH	$c(3 + 6) - 11 = 70$	
CALLIE	$15 + 9 + 3 + c = 41$	
PATCH	$90 \div p = 3 \times 3$	
FLUFFY	$(45 \div 3) - f = 13$	
TOBY	$t \times (3 \times 2) = 30$	
OLIVER	$8 + (4 \times 3) - (24 \div 2) = o$	
BUTTERSCOTCH	$19 - (16 \div 4) - 11 = b$	
BOOTS	$24 \div 3 - 7 = b$	
PRINCESS	$46 - p = 3 \times 11$	
SIMBA	$2(6 \times 2) - (26 - 9) = s$	
SMOKY	$48 \div 6 + (3 \times 4) - s = 5$	
MIDNIGHT	$3m - (9 \div 3) + 5 = 20$	
SOPHIE	$2 \times 2 \times 2s = 96$	
CASPER	$33 + 2c = 55$	

Name ______________________________

Date ______________________________

She Shoots! She Scores!

Multiply. Show your work on another sheet of paper. Write the answer in each box and color according to the code. Then connect the red and blue boxes to show the path to the goal.

Color Code

between 2 and 3 = yellow
between 3 and 4 = blue
between 4 and 5 = green
between 5 and 6 = red

Start

1. $1\frac{1}{3} \times 2\frac{1}{2} =$
2. $2 \times 2\frac{1}{8} =$
3. $1\frac{1}{3} \times 4 =$
4. $4 \times 1\frac{3}{8} =$
5. $1\frac{3}{5} \times 1\frac{2}{3} =$
6. $2 \times 1\frac{7}{8} =$
7. $1\frac{1}{2} \times 2\frac{1}{3} =$
8. $1\frac{1}{5} \times 4\frac{1}{2} =$
9. $3\frac{3}{5} \times 1\frac{1}{6} =$
10. $2\frac{1}{3} \times 1\frac{1}{4} =$
11. $2 \times 2\frac{3}{4} =$
12. $1\frac{2}{3} \times 2\frac{1}{4} =$
13. $4 \times 1\frac{2}{5} =$

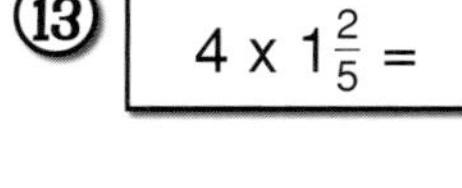

14. $3\frac{1}{8} \times 1\frac{1}{3} =$
15. $1\frac{5}{8} \times 1\frac{3}{5} =$
16. $\frac{3}{4} \times 4\frac{1}{6} =$
17. $3\frac{1}{8} \times 1\frac{1}{5} =$
18. $6\frac{4}{7} \times \frac{7}{8} =$

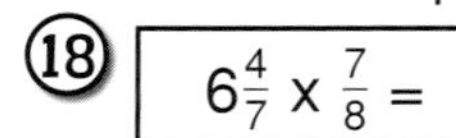

Finish

Conversion Booklet

Use with "Just a Hint" on page 207.

cover

Metric Units

Customary Units

TEC44049

Staple. (page 1)

Staple.

Staple.

To convert a smaller unit to a larger unit,

To convert a larger unit to a smaller unit,

To convert a smaller unit to a larger unit,

To convert a larger unit to a smaller unit,

Staple. (page 2)

Staple.

Staple.

divide.
(The answer will be smaller.)

multiply.
(The answer will be larger.)

divide.
(The answer will be smaller.)

multiply.
(The answer will be larger.)

Name ______________________

Date ______________________

Oodles of Noodles

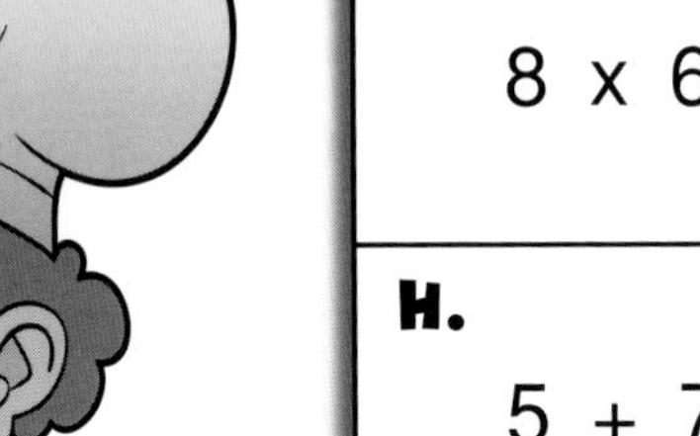
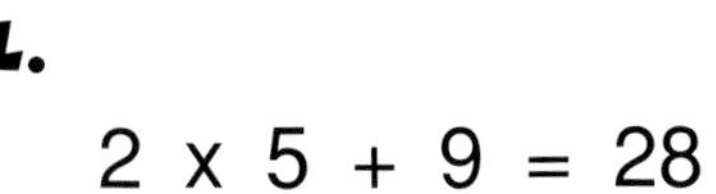
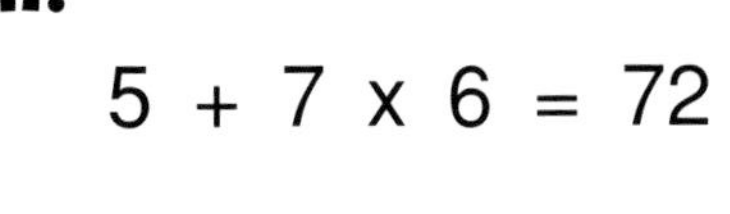

Insert parentheses to make each statement true.

A. 14 ÷ 2 + 5 = 2	**B.** 10 – 3 x 4 = 28	**C.** 16 – 4 + 9 = 3	**D.** 14 – 7 + 5 = 2
E. 12 – 4 ÷ 2 = 4			**F.** 8 x 6 + 4 = 80
G. 3 x 6 – 2 = 12			**H.** 5 + 7 x 6 = 72
I. 4 + 2 x 6 = 36			**J.** 72 ÷ 6 + 3 = 8
K. 14 – 6 ÷ 2 = 4			**L.** 2 x 5 + 9 = 28
M. 9 + 2 x 5 = 55	**N.** 24 ÷ 15 – 9 = 4	**O.** 7 x 12 – 6 = 42	**P.** 50 – 26 ÷ 3 = 8

Note to self: not so many noodles next time.

Note to the teacher: Use with "Pasta Parentheses" on page 208.

Game Cards and Answer Key

Use with "'Geome-tree'" on page 216. Copy and mount on construction paper the game mat on page 216 and the cards and answer key below. If desired, laminate the pages before cutting the cards apart. Students will need two different colors of game markers.

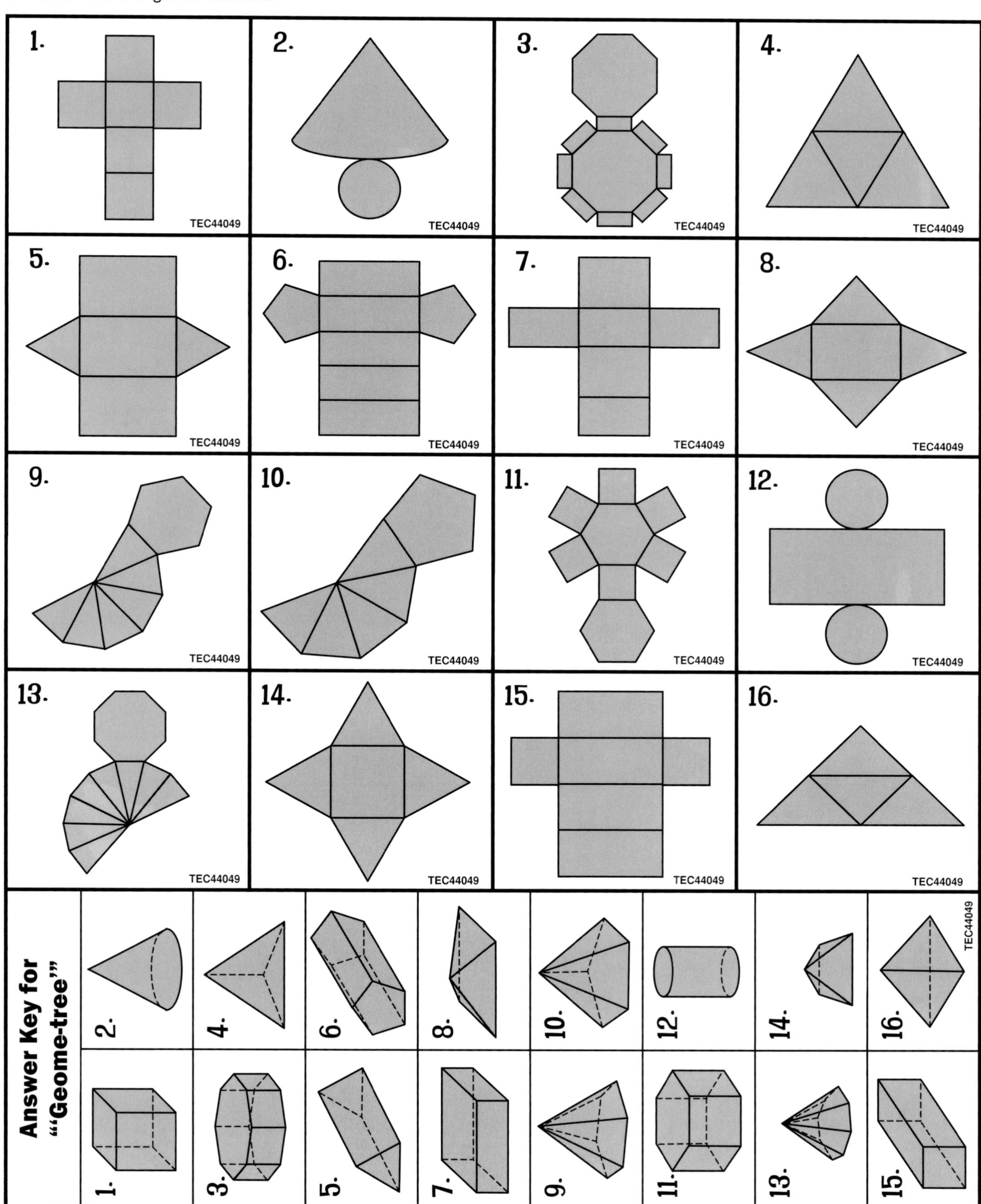

"Geome-tree"

Directions for two players:

1. Shuffle the cards and stack them facedown.
2. When it's your turn, draw one card, look at the net, and point to the matching solid figure on the tree.
3. Have your opponent use the key to check your answer. If your answer is correct, put a marker on top of the matching solid figure. If your answer is incorrect, your turn is over. Return the card to the bottom of the stack.
4. The first player to cover eight solid figures wins.

Names ______________________________
Date ______________________________

SLIP AND SLIDE!

A GAME FOR TWO PLAYERS

Directions:

1. Choose a crayon or colored pencil that is a different color than your partner's.
2. In turn, multiply a decimal from the washing machine by a number from the laundry basket. Show your work on a separate sheet of paper.
3. Color the soap bubble with the matching answer. If your answer has already been colored, your turn is over.
4. Play for a set amount of time or until all the soap bubbles have been colored. The player with more colored bubbles wins.

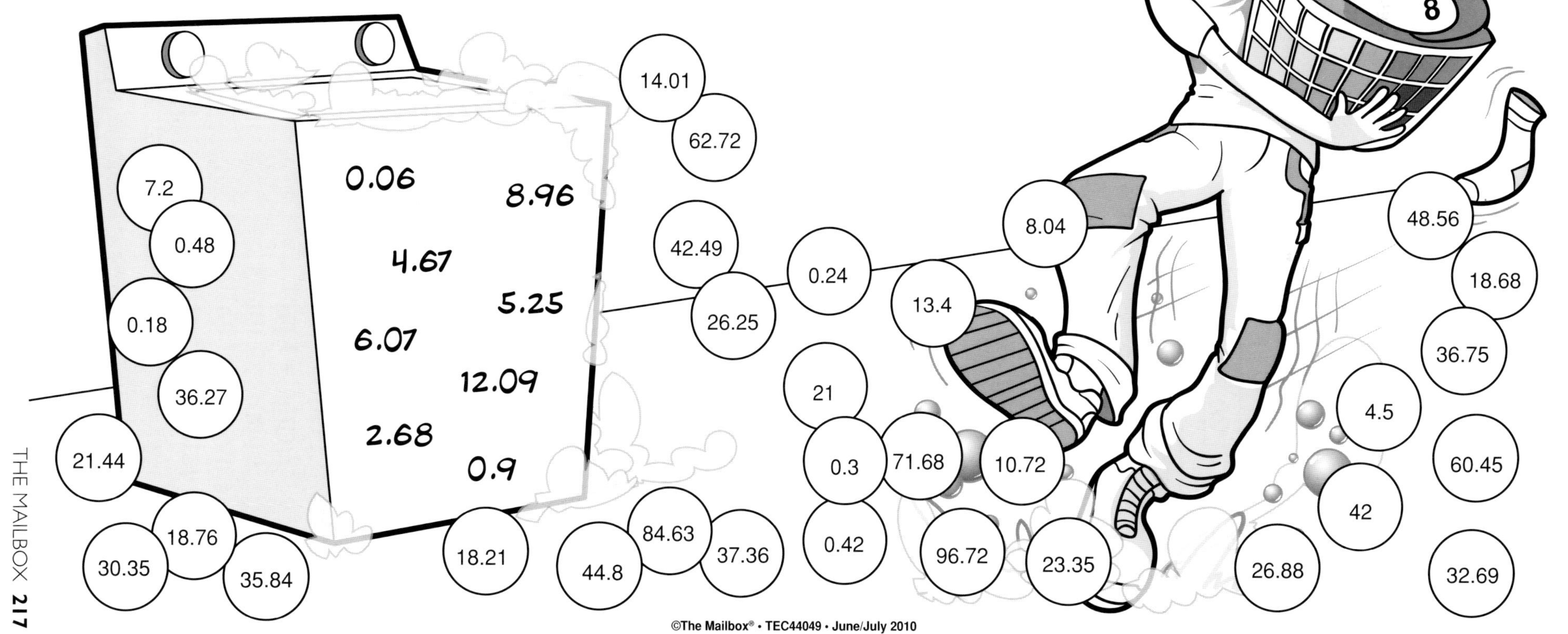

MATH

MIND BUILDERS

MIND BUILDER 1

Use the arrows to find the path of this grid's number pattern. What is the pattern? What number does each letter represent?

6	12	10	16
32	A	36	14
B	40	C	D
28	E	24	18

TEC44044

MIND BUILDER 2

When Jim is 50, he will be twice as old as his son Daniel. If Daniel is now 22, how old is Jim?

TEC44044

MIND BUILDER 3

These math sentences are all true.

$$A + B = 13$$
$$A + B + C = 18$$
$$A - B = 1$$

Which of these are true?

a. $C = 5$ b. $B = 10$ c. A or B = 7

TEC44044

MIND BUILDER 4

You have 15 coins (all nickels and dimes) that total $1.05. How many of each type of coin do you have?

TEC44044

MIND BUILDER 5

This addition problem uses each digit from 1 to 9 exactly once. Write two more addition problems that follow this pattern. Use only three-digit numbers. What do you notice about each problem's sum?

$$\begin{array}{r} 273 \\ +\,645 \\ \hline 918 \end{array}$$

TEC44044

MIND BUILDER 6

If today is Tuesday, what day came after the day before yesterday?

TEC44044

MIND BUILDER 7

How many tablespoons are in two gallons?

1 cup = 16 tablespoons
2 cups = 1 pint
2 pints = 1 quart
4 quarts = 1 gallon
2 gallons = _?_ tablespoons

TEC44044

MIND BUILDER 8

Draw how you could arrange these four dominoes to represent two multiplication facts.

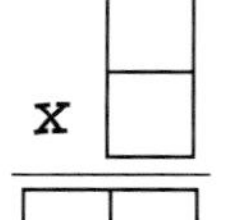
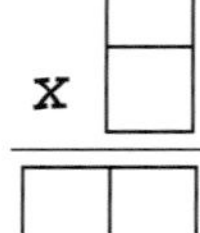

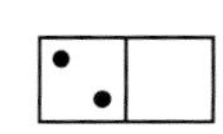
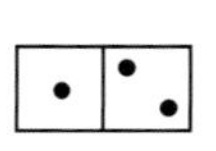
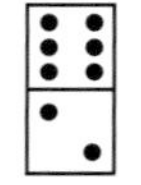

TEC44044

Note to the teacher: Give each student a copy of this page (or one card at a time) to work on during free time. Have the student solve the problems on a separate sheet of paper.

MIND BUILDERS

MIND BUILDER 1

A wagon wheel has 12 spaces between spokes. How many spokes does the wheel have: 10, 11, 12, or 14?

TEC44045

MIND BUILDER 2

What is the number described by all the clues below?

- The number is not less than 20.
- The number is not greater than 40.
- The number is not divisible by 2, 3, or 7.
- The number is not a prime number.
- The sum of the number's digits is not 8.

TEC44045

MIND BUILDER 3

Farmer Fiona raises cows and chickens. In all, her animals have 20 heads and 70 legs. How many cows and how many chickens does she have?

TEC44045

MIND BUILDER 4

Jill has 24 coins in her pocket. How much money does she have?

- $\frac{1}{2}$ are nickels
- $\frac{1}{4}$ are quarters
- $\frac{1}{6}$ are dimes
- $\frac{1}{12}$ are pennies

TEC44045

MIND BUILDER 5

What comes next?

STONE = 12345
NEST = 4512
SON = 134
TO = ________

TEC44045

MIND BUILDER 6

Arrange the digits 1, 3, 5, and 7 in the boxes to get the largest product possible.

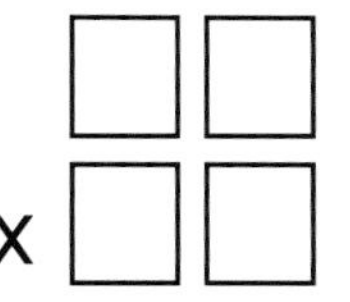

TEC44045

MIND BUILDER 7

What do these numbers have in common?

715 67 1462 328

TEC44045

MIND BUILDER 8

Replace each number with its roman numeral. What words do they spell?

a. 50 1 500 = _____
b. 1,000 9 = _____
c. 500 1 1,000 = _____
d. 50 4 1 500 = _____

TEC44045

Note to the teacher: Give each student a copy of this page (or one card at a time) to work on during free time. Have the student solve the problems on a separate sheet of paper.

MATH

MIND BUILDERS

MIND BUILDER 1

What is two more than twice the difference between 78 and 13?

What is four less than half the difference between 95 and 19?

What is three times the sum of 12, 15, 26, and 42?

? ? ?

TEC44046

MIND BUILDER 2

The product of the reciprocal of two of the numbers below is 3. Which two numbers?

$\frac{1}{2}$ $\frac{1}{3}$ $\frac{2}{3}$ 3

TEC44046

MIND BUILDER 3

If you know the perimeter of a rectangle, can you calculate its area? Explain.

P = 23

TEC44046

MIND BUILDER 4

You can change a problem by changing its operations and the parentheses. Find at least three more answers by changing the operations and parentheses.

$4 + (8 \times 5) - 6 = 38$

$4 \times 8 - (5 + 6) = 21$

TEC44046

MIND BUILDER 5

On the planet Murko, coins have the values shown.

= 1¢  = 5¢ = 10¢

What is the value of 6 pennies, 3 nickels, and 5 dimes on the planet Murko?

What is the value of 2 pennies, 7 nickels, and 3 dimes on the planet Murko?

What is the value of 10 pennies, 9 nickels, and 6 dimes on the planet Murko?

TEC44046

MIND BUILDER 6

Find values for x and y where $x = 2y$ and both numbers are less than 9.

$x = ?$

$y = ?$

TEC44046

MIND BUILDER 7

An even composite number can be written as the sum of two prime numbers. Write 40, 66, and 94 as the sum of two prime numbers.

$20 = 13 + 7$

TEC44046

MIND BUILDER 8

The average temperature for the first five days in January was 0°F. What was the temperature on January 5?

January					
Day	1	2	3	4	5
Temp.	2°F	10°F	1°F	3°F	?

TEC44046

Note to the teacher: Give each student a copy of this page (or one card at a time) to work on during free time. Have the student solve the problems on a separate sheet of paper.

MIND BUILDERS

MIND BUILDER 1

Arrange these three chicken coops to make a coop for the loose chicken. Don't add any extra lines or let any chickens out.

TEC44047

MIND BUILDER 2

The following equation makes five 3s equal 13: $(3 \times 3) + 3 + \frac{3}{3} = 13$
Now make

a. five 4s equal 13.

b. five 6s equal 9.

c. five 7s equal 8.

TEC44047

MIND BUILDER 3

Draw the grid. Then arrange these numbers on the grid so that the sum of each row, column, and diagonal totals $1\frac{7}{8}$.

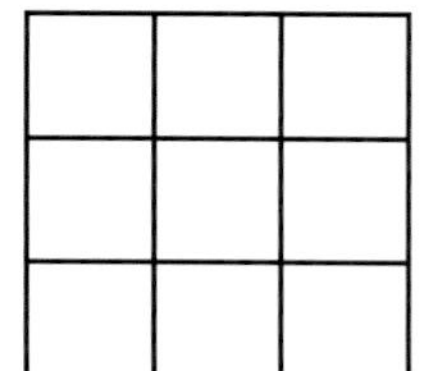

$\frac{3}{8}$ $\frac{1}{8}$ $\frac{1}{2}$ $\frac{7}{8}$ $\frac{5}{8}$ $\frac{1}{4}$ $\frac{3}{4}$

1 $1\frac{1}{8}$

TEC44047

MIND BUILDER 4

Show two ways you can make a dollar using

a. 6 coins

b. 8 coins

c. 12 coins

TEC44047

MIND BUILDER 5

At 11:17 PM, the power goes off for $1\frac{1}{2}$ hours. It comes back on for ten minutes. Then it goes off again for 40 minutes. What time is it when the power comes back on?

TEC44047

MIND BUILDER 6

Each letter stands for a different digit from 0 to 9. If $E = 9$, find two ways to solve the addition problem. Hint: not all the numbers will be used.

```
   EAT
+ MORE
------
  FOOD
```

TEC44047

MIND BUILDER 7

If odd numbers are lemons and even numbers are bananas, which fruit is the answer for each problem?

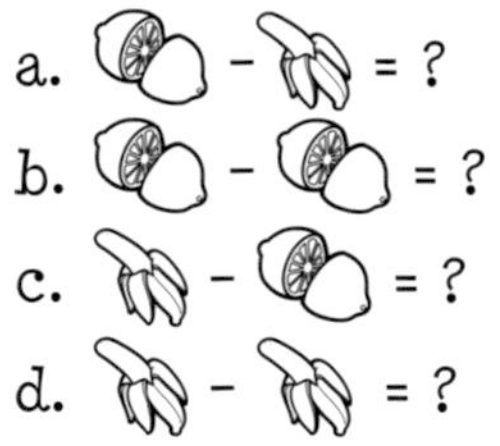

a. − = ?

b. − = ?

c. − = ?

d. − = ?

TEC44047

MIND BUILDER 8

Blaze ran 8 furlongs in 130 seconds. Dandy ran 2 miles in 4 minutes. Which horse ran faster? (Hint: 1 furlong = 220 yards; 1 mile = 1,760 yards)

TEC44047

Note to the teacher: Give each student a copy of this page (or one card at a time) to work on during free time. Have the student solve the problems on a separate sheet of paper.

MATH MIND BUILDERS

MIND BUILDER 1

The mass of a nickel is 5 grams. Estimate the mass of a penny, a dime, a quarter, and a dollar bill. Explain.

TEC44048

MIND BUILDER 2

These are mirror reflections of three clocks. One of the clocks is fast, one is slow, and one is correct. What time is it?

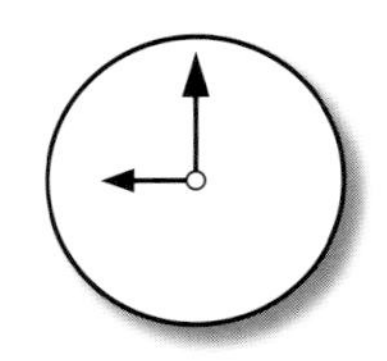
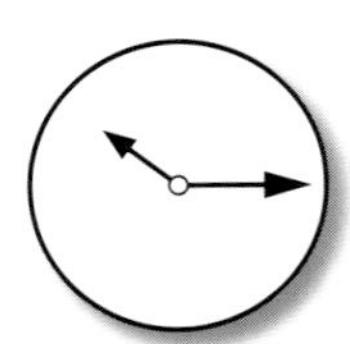
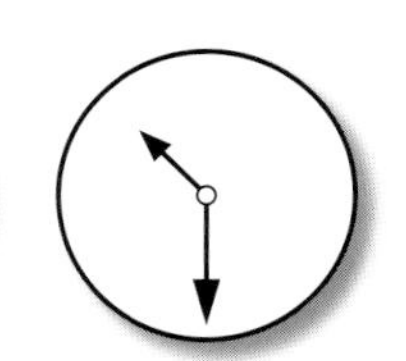

TEC44048

MIND BUILDER 3

A robin says to a woodpecker, "If you give me one of your worms, I will have twice as many as you."

The woodpecker replies, "If you give me one of your worms, we'll have the same number."

How many worms does each bird have?

TEC44048

MIND BUILDER 4

Solve these problems.

A. 37 x 3 B. 37 x 6 C. 37 x 9

Add the missing factor to complete each problem below.

D. 37 x n = 444 E. 37 x n = 555
F. 37 x n = 777 G. 37 x n = 999

TEC44048

MIND BUILDER 5

Start at any number; then follow any path and perform each operation as you go. Use each number and symbol exactly one time. What is the greatest answer you can get?

5, 1, x, +, 20, 10, ÷

TEC44048

MIND BUILDER 6

How many diamonds are in the figure below?

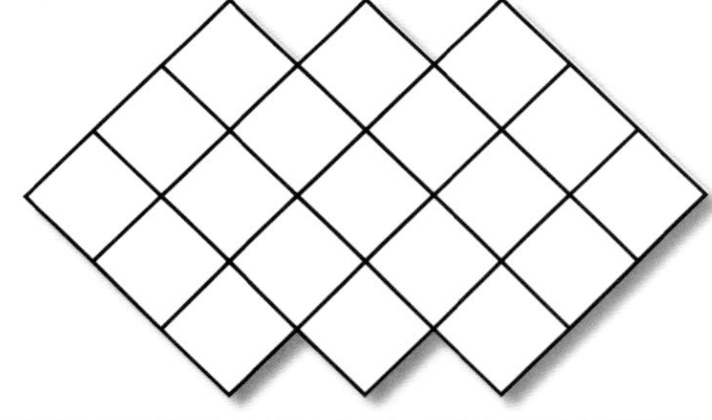

TEC44048

MIND BUILDER 7

Suckers cost 30¢. Two jawbreakers cost 25¢. Five jelly beans cost 10¢. You can spend exactly $2.00, and you buy four suckers and four jawbreakers. How many jelly beans can you buy? Name two more combinations of candies that equal exactly $2.00.

TEC44048

MIND BUILDER 8

Which statements are false?

A. 7.14 cm = 71.4 mm
B. 904 m = 0.904 mm
C. 895 km = 895,000 m
D. 2.34 m = 234 cm
E. 50 mm = 0.5 cm

TEC44048

Note to the teacher: Give each student a copy of this page (or one card at a time) to work on during free time. Have the student solve the problems on a separate sheet of paper.

MIND BUILDER 1

One batch of brownies makes 20 servings. It calls for 2 eggs. How many eggs are needed to make enough brownies for 30 servings? 50 servings?

TEC44049

MIND BUILDER 2

Draw and label three different triangles that each have an area of 18 square inches.

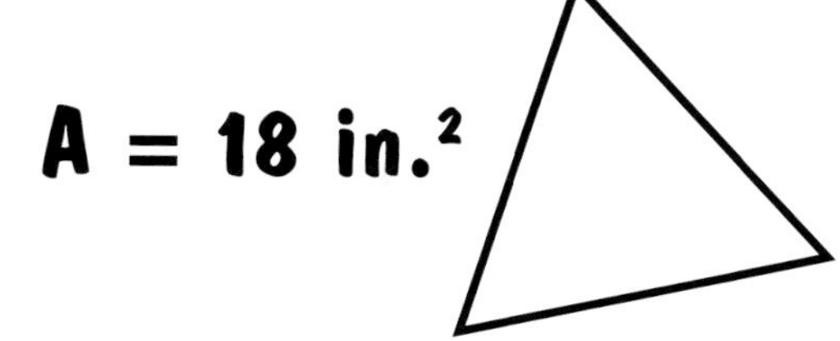

TEC44049

MIND BUILDER 3

Complete the equation below with two fractions so that each fraction has a different denominator.

$$\frac{5}{12} + ? + ? = 1$$

TEC44049

MIND BUILDER 4

Jayden is rolling two dice. Describe two events that are *certain* to happen. Describe two events that are *impossible.*

TEC44049

MIND BUILDER 5

Which list includes the most numbers?

A: multiples of 3 that are less than 40
B: multiples of 6 that are less than 100
C: multiples of 9 that are less than 130

TEC44049

MIND BUILDER 6

An inchworm travels one inch an hour from 9:00 AM until noon. It covers three-fourths of an inch each hour from noon until 5:00 PM and one-fourth of an inch an hour from 5:00 PM until midnight. It rests until 9:00 AM and then repeats the pattern again. What is the total distance the worm travels in one week?

TEC44049

MIND BUILDER 7

A is a two-digit number. The sum of its digits is 12. *A* plus 12 is divisible by 20. What is *A?*

TEC44049

MIND BUILDER 8

Move two pencils to make the equation true.

TEC44049

MATH MIND BUILDERS

Note to the teacher: Give each student a copy of this page (or one card at a time) to work on during free time. Have the student solve the problems on a separate sheet of paper.

Math Activity Cards

Copy and cut out the cards to use as center or free-time activities.

Estimating products

How Many?

Use the numbers to write eight different multiplication problems. Estimate the product for each problem. Then solve. Compare your estimates and answers.

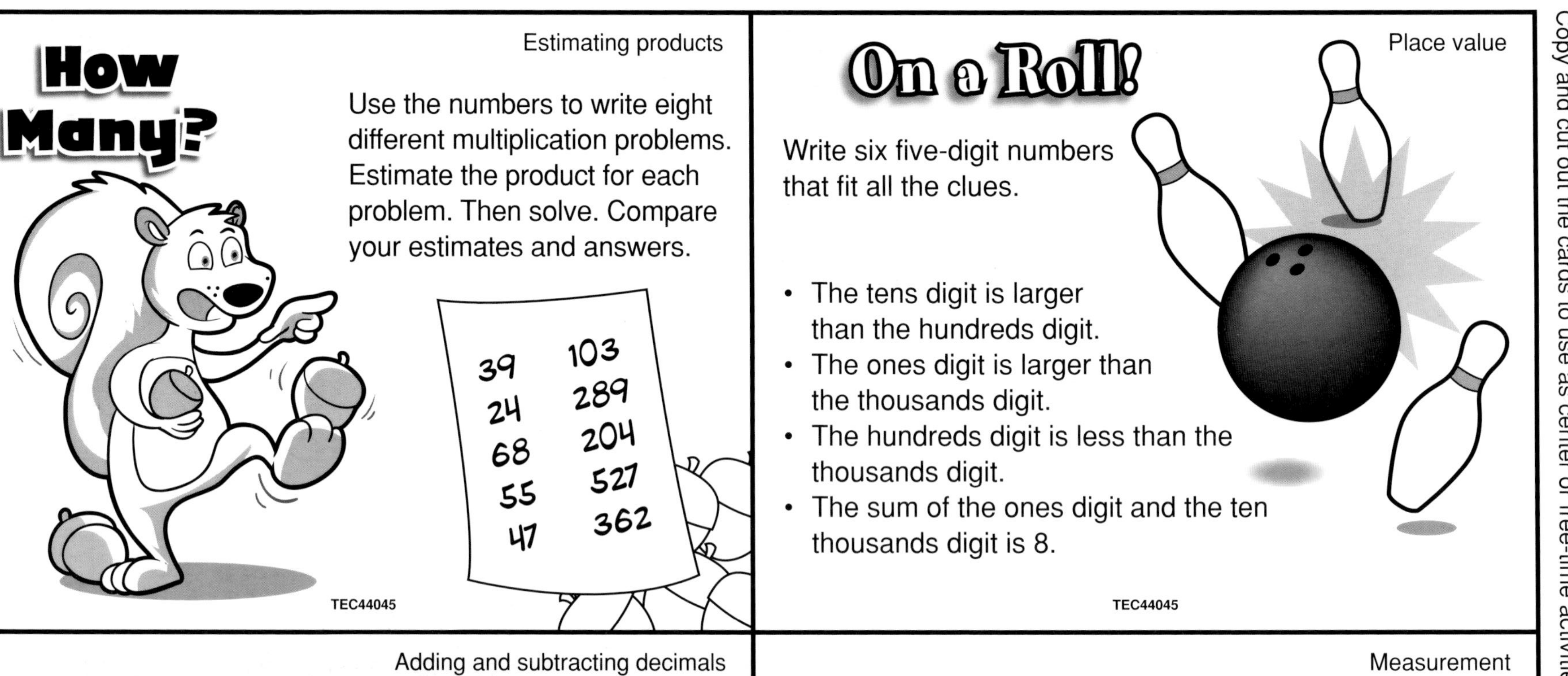

TEC44045

Place value

On a Roll!

Write six five-digit numbers that fit all the clues.

- The tens digit is larger than the hundreds digit.
- The ones digit is larger than the thousands digit.
- The hundreds digit is less than the thousands digit.
- The sum of the ones digit and the ten thousands digit is 8.

TEC44045

Adding and subtracting decimals

Are We There Yet?

Use mixed decimals to write ten problems: five addition and five subtraction. Solve each problem.

Then use the code to label each answer.

For example: 11.6 + 8.4 = 20

Answer	Symbol
The sum is a whole number.	
The difference is a whole number.	
The sum is a mixed decimal.	
The difference is a mixed decimal.	

TEC44045

Measurement

Glow-in-the-Dark

Draw ten pumpkins. Then label each pumpkin with a different inequality using feet, inches, and yards.

TEC44045

Copy and cut out the cards to use as center or free-time activities.

Math Activity Cards

Copy and cut out the cards to use as center or free-time activities.

Copy and cut out the cards to use as center or free-time activities.

Decimal operations

DIFFERENT STROKES

Write a problem to match each sum, difference, and product below.

Sum	Difference	Product
59.18	125.6	5.76
6.7	11.4	133.5
45.03	37.09	42.08

TEC44048

Lines

Just Down the Street

Write ten statements about the streets on the map shown. Use words such as *parallel, perpendicular,* and *intersecting.*

TEC44048

Capacity

WET YOUR WHISTLE?

Write about how you might use water in each amount named below.

1 cup
1 pint
1 quart
1 gallon
1 milliliter
1 liter

TEC44048

Variables

MIX IT UP!

For each equation shown, change the value of x three times. Then solve each equation.

Example: $(5 \cdot x) + 7$

$x = 2$	$x = 5$	$x = 12$
$(5 \cdot 2) + 7 = 17$	$(5 \cdot 5) + 7 = 32$	$(5 \cdot 12) + 7 = 67$

1. $(8 + x) \cdot 12$

2. $\frac{x}{6} \cdot 3$

3. $4x + 87$

4. $\frac{x}{5} + 123$

5. $9x + 17$

TEC44048

Math Activity Cards

Copy and cut out the cards to use as center or free-time activities.

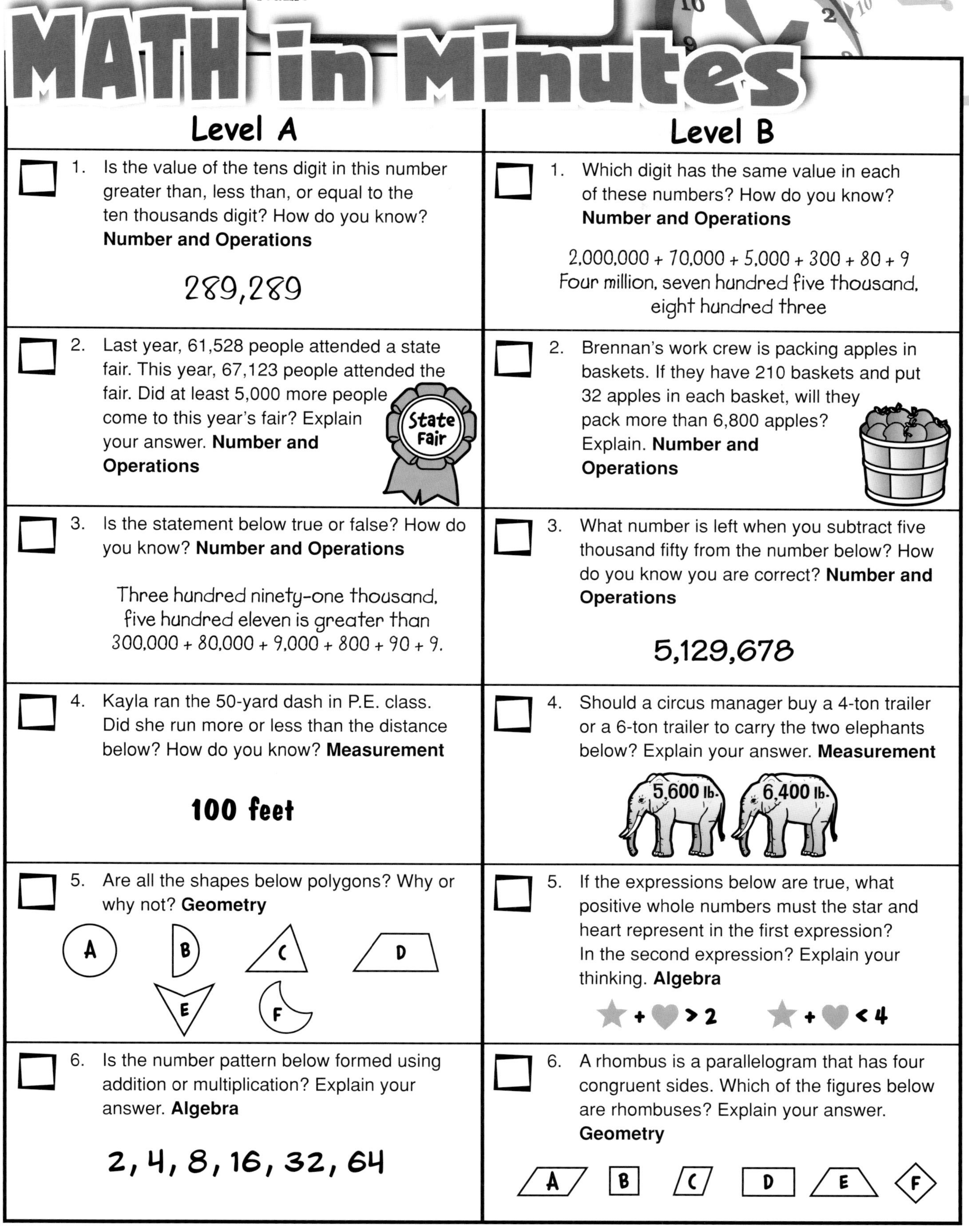

Name

MATH in Minutes

Level A

☐ 1. Is the value of the tens digit in this number greater than, less than, or equal to the ten thousands digit? How do you know? **Number and Operations**

289,289

☐ 2. Last year, 61,528 people attended a state fair. This year, 67,123 people attended the fair. Did at least 5,000 more people come to this year's fair? Explain your answer. **Number and Operations**

State Fair

☐ 3. Is the statement below true or false? How do you know? **Number and Operations**

Three hundred ninety-one thousand, five hundred eleven is greater than 300,000 + 80,000 + 9,000 + 800 + 90 + 9.

☐ 4. Kayla ran the 50-yard dash in P.E. class. Did she run more or less than the distance below? How do you know? **Measurement**

100 feet

☐ 5. Are all the shapes below polygons? Why or why not? **Geometry**

A B C D E F

☐ 6. Is the number pattern below formed using addition or multiplication? Explain your answer. **Algebra**

2, 4, 8, 16, 32, 64

Level B

☐ 1. Which digit has the same value in each of these numbers? How do you know? **Number and Operations**

2,000,000 + 70,000 + 5,000 + 300 + 80 + 9
Four million, seven hundred five thousand, eight hundred three

☐ 2. Brennan's work crew is packing apples in baskets. If they have 210 baskets and put 32 apples in each basket, will they pack more than 6,800 apples? Explain. **Number and Operations**

☐ 3. What number is left when you subtract five thousand fifty from the number below? How do you know you are correct? **Number and Operations**

5,129,678

☐ 4. Should a circus manager buy a 4-ton trailer or a 6-ton trailer to carry the two elephants below? Explain your answer. **Measurement**

5,600 lb. 6,400 lb.

☐ 5. If the expressions below are true, what positive whole numbers must the star and heart represent in the first expression? In the second expression? Explain your thinking. **Algebra**

$\star + \heartsuit > 2$ $\star + \heartsuit < 4$

☐ 6. A rhombus is a parallelogram that has four congruent sides. Which of the figures below are rhombuses? Explain your answer. **Geometry**

A B C D E F

Note to the teacher: Photocopy the entire page, one level, or selected problems to distribute to students. When a student solves a problem, he checks its box.

Name

MATH in Minutes

Level A	Level B
1. The cafeteria chef fixed bag lunches for a field trip. He made $\frac{1}{3}$ of the sandwiches with peanut butter and jelly, $\frac{1}{4}$ with ham, and the rest with turkey. Did more than half of the students get turkey? How do you know? **Number and Operations**	1. Students at Lewis School are selling tickets to the talent show for $5 each. They have collected $1,965. Have the students sold more than or less than 390 tickets? How do you know? **Number and Operations** ADMIT ONE
2. The school record for running the mile was 6 minutes and 42 seconds. Callie ran 15 hundredths of a second faster than the record. What was Callie's time? How did you find your answer? **Number and Operations** 6:42.00	2. Troy mailed 125 letters. Together, a stamp and envelope cost $0.48. Troy's mom gave him $50. Did he need to use some of his own money to buy supplies? Explain how you know. **Number and Operations** 44¢
3. Brady's dad reset the car odometer to zero before leaving for vacation. Halfway through the trip, the odometer read 148 miles. About how many total miles was the trip? Explain your answer. **Number and Operations** 148.0	3. Arrange the digits 2, 3, 6, and 7 so the tenths digit is twice the hundredths digit, three times the tens digit, and one less than the ones digit. How do you know you're correct? **Number and Operations** ___ ___ . ___ ___
4. Tell whether the following statement is true or false: The perimeter of a square is always greater than the area. Explain your answer. **Geometry**	4. Use the circle graph to estimate the percentage of students who prefer each ice cream flavor. Explain your answers. **Data Analysis and Probability** strawberry, chocolate, vanilla, rocky road
5. Based on the line plot's data, about how many crackers should you expect to find in a box? How do you know? **Data Analysis and Probability** Line plot: 53: X X; 54: X X X X; 55: X X X; 56: X; 57: X X X; 58: X. Number of crackers in a box	5. In the rectangle ABCD, which sides are parallel and which are perpendicular? How do you know? **Geometry** A B D C
6. How many centigram weights are needed to balance five one-gram weights? How did you find your answer? **Measurement**	6. Explain what is wrong with this recipe. **Measurement** 2 quarts lemonade; 8 quarts fruit punch; 2 quarts cranberry juice; 4 quarts ginger ale; Makes 3 gallons.

Note to the teacher: Copy the entire page, one level, or selected problems to distribute. When a student solves a problem, he checks its box.

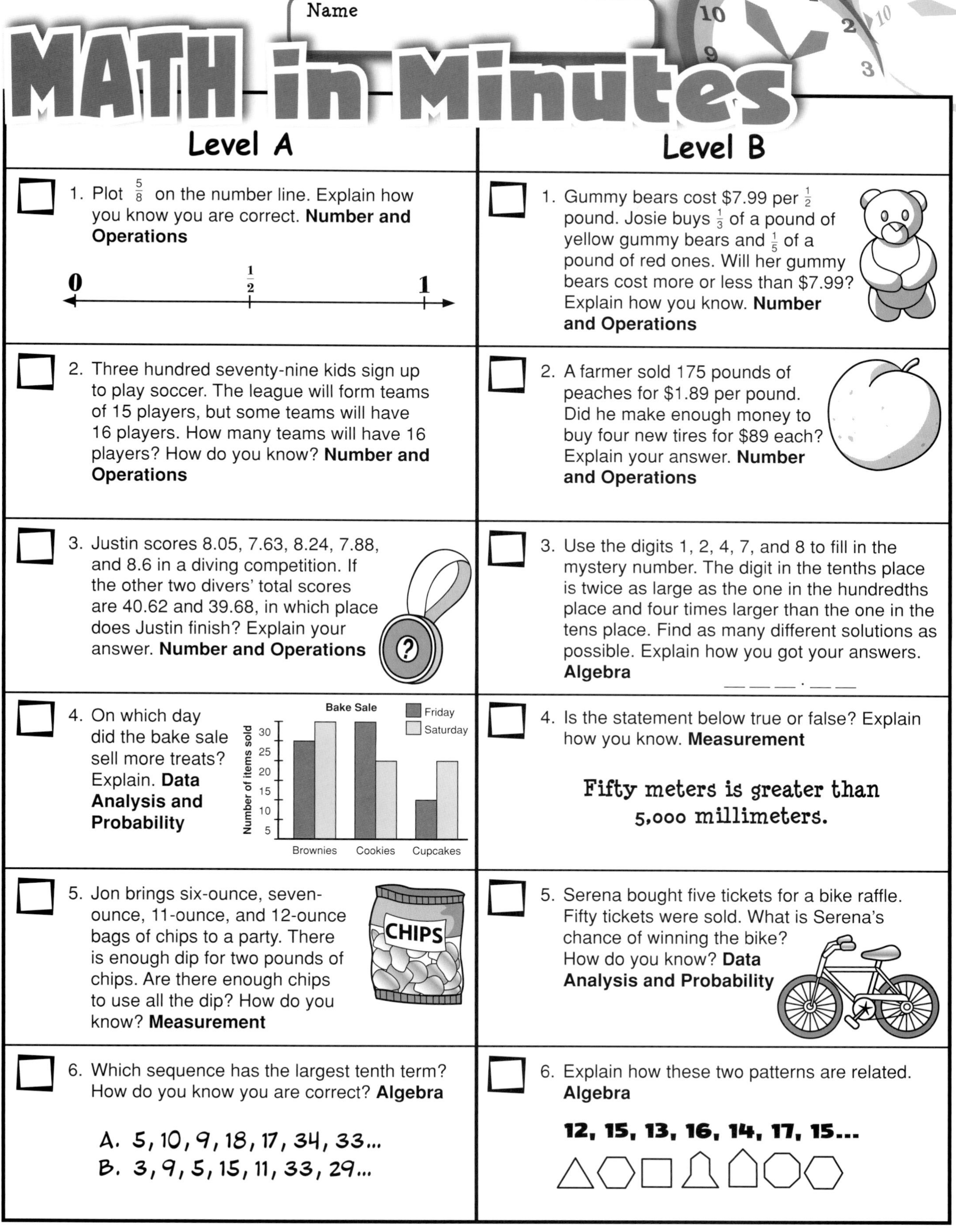

Name

MATH in Minutes

Level A

☐ 1. Plot $\frac{5}{8}$ on the number line. Explain how you know you are correct. **Number and Operations**

☐ 2. Three hundred seventy-nine kids sign up to play soccer. The league will form teams of 15 players, but some teams will have 16 players. How many teams will have 16 players? How do you know? **Number and Operations**

☐ 3. Justin scores 8.05, 7.63, 8.24, 7.88, and 8.6 in a diving competition. If the other two divers' total scores are 40.62 and 39.68, in which place does Justin finish? Explain your answer. **Number and Operations**

☐ 4. On which day did the bake sale sell more treats? Explain. **Data Analysis and Probability**

☐ 5. Jon brings six-ounce, seven-ounce, 11-ounce, and 12-ounce bags of chips to a party. There is enough dip for two pounds of chips. Are there enough chips to use all the dip? How do you know? **Measurement**

☐ 6. Which sequence has the largest tenth term? How do you know you are correct? **Algebra**

A. 5, 10, 9, 18, 17, 34, 33...
B. 3, 9, 5, 15, 11, 33, 29...

Level B

☐ 1. Gummy bears cost $7.99 per $\frac{1}{2}$ pound. Josie buys $\frac{1}{3}$ of a pound of yellow gummy bears and $\frac{1}{5}$ of a pound of red ones. Will her gummy bears cost more or less than $7.99? Explain how you know. **Number and Operations**

☐ 2. A farmer sold 175 pounds of peaches for $1.89 per pound. Did he make enough money to buy four new tires for $89 each? Explain your answer. **Number and Operations**

☐ 3. Use the digits 1, 2, 4, 7, and 8 to fill in the mystery number. The digit in the tenths place is twice as large as the one in the hundredths place and four times larger than the one in the tens place. Find as many different solutions as possible. Explain how you got your answers. **Algebra**

__ __ __ . __ __

☐ 4. Is the statement below true or false? Explain how you know. **Measurement**

Fifty meters is greater than 5,000 millimeters.

☐ 5. Serena bought five tickets for a bike raffle. Fifty tickets were sold. What is Serena's chance of winning the bike? How do you know? **Data Analysis and Probability**

☐ 6. Explain how these two patterns are related. **Algebra**

12, 15, 13, 16, 14, 17, 15...

Note to the teacher: Photocopy the entire page, one level, or selected problems to distribute to students. When a student solves a problem, he checks its box. If desired, display a transparency of the page and have students solve the problems on their own papers.

MATH IN MINUTES MATH IN MINUTES

Name ______

Level A

Number and Operations

1. Justin says the greatest common factor of 18 and 36 is 6. Mike says the greatest common factor is 9. Who is correct? Explain.

? ? ? ? ?

Number and Operations

2. Is the mean larger or smaller than the median of the number set below? Tell how you know.

23, 15, 20, 12, 27, 20, 13, 22

Number and Operations

3. Mia has saved $35 to buy an MP3 player. She sees a $50 player that is discounted 40%. Can Mia buy the MP3 player? Why or why not?

40% OFF

Measurement

4. Tyler and Jonathan are measuring the length of the hallway. They measure 22.5 meters. How many centimeters long is the hallway? Explain your answer.

1 2 3 4 5 6 7 8 9 10

Geometry

5. Which figure has the largest area: a square with a perimeter of 40 units or a rectangle with a perimeter of three times the length and half the width of the square? How do you know?

Data Analysis and Probability

6. If you want to get an even number, would it be better to use a die or the spinner shown? Explain your choice.

1 1 2 2 3 3

Name ______

Level B

Number and Operations

1. Alex wants to buy a skateboard. Which board is the least expensive? How do you know?

$80 40% OFF

$70 35% OFF

Number and Operations

2. Sydney's recipe makes a dozen cookies. The recipe calls for $\frac{3}{4}$ cup chopped nuts. If she wants to make $\frac{1}{4}$ of the cookie recipe, how many nuts will Sydney need? How did you find your answer?

Number and Operations

3. Hannah buys nails and bolts at the store. Which amounts could be her total cost? Explain how you found your answer.

$0.30 $0.31 $0.50

$0.07 each $0.03 each

Measurement

4. A large book weighs as much as the milk and cookies combined. How many kilograms does the book weigh? Tell how you know.

MILK 2,800 g 200,000 mg

Geometry

5. Complete the inequality below with <, >, or =. Explain your answer.

largest obtuse angle − largest acute angle	◯	smallest obtuse angle − smallest acute angle

Data Analysis and Probability

6. The high temperature is expected to reach 38°F. The low temperature will be –6°F. By how many degrees will the temperature change that day? Explain how you found your answer.

Note to the teacher: Copy the entire page, one level, or selected problems to distribute to students. When a student solves a problem, he checks its box. If desired, display a transparency of the page and have students solve the problems on their own papers.

MATH IN MINUTES MATH IN MINUTES

Level A

Name ______________________

NUMBER AND OPERATIONS

1 Ms. Johnson's 36 students often work in teams. How many different teams of equal size can she make? List all the possibilities. How did you find your answer?

TEAM 1

NUMBER AND OPERATIONS

2 Marcus can trim three bushes in 12 minutes. He needs to trim 25 bushes in two hours. Will he finish in time? How do you know?

NUMBER AND OPERATIONS

3 The drama club put on two plays and collected cans of food for the food bank. The club collected 1,534 cans at the first performance and twice as many at the second. Did the club beat last year's collection of 4,330 cans? Explain.

MEASUREMENT

4 Molly wants to make a gallon of lemonade. She found a one-quart pitcher, a pint jar, and a two-quart pitcher. Can Molly make a gallon of lemonade using these containers? Explain.

ALGEBRA

5 Bruno eats twice as much dog food as Spot and three times as much as Fifi. If Spot eats three ounces of food, how much do Bruno and Fifi eat? How do you know?

DATA ANALYSIS AND PROBABILITY

6 Each student earns a prize for selling at least 15 candy bars. There are 15 prizes. Based on this plot's data, are there enough prizes? Explain.

		X		X	
X	X	X		X	
X	X	X	X	X	X
X	X	X	X	X	X
5	10	15	20	25	30

Number of candy bars sold

Level B

Name ______________________

NUMBER AND OPERATIONS

1 Of our class, $\frac{2}{5}$ are signed up to take chorus next year, and $\frac{3}{7}$ are signed up for band. Are more students signed up for chorus or band? How do you know?

NUMBER AND OPERATIONS

2 For which set or sets of numbers below are the mode and range the same? Explain your answer.

A. 1, 2, 2, 6, 6, 2, 7
B. 4, 6, 4, 4, 9, 8
C. 5, 3, 5, 0, 2, 5, 4

NUMBER AND OPERATIONS

3 Three out of every five cows in the herd are black. The rest are brown. Are there more than 20 brown cows in the 45-cow herd? Explain.

GEOMETRY

4 Find the missing length, height, width, and volume measures for this cube. How did you find your answers?

$20 \text{ cm}^3 < \text{Volume} < 30 \text{ cm}^3$

DATA ANALYSIS AND PROBABILITY

5 Based on the plot shown, how many more children (12 years old and younger) than teenagers bought ice cream? Than adults? Than adults and teenagers combined? Explain.

Ages of Ice Cream Customers

Stem	Leaves
0	4 5 6 6 7 8 8 8 9 9 9 9
1	0 0 1 1 1 2 2 3 3 4 4 5 6 6 7
2	1 2 5
3	0 1 6 8

DATA ANALYSIS AND PROBABILITY

6 Each car in Cameron's model train is five inches long. Will all 30 cars fit on three yards of track? How do you know?

Note to the teacher: Photocopy the entire page, one level, or selected problems to distribute to students. When a student solves a problem, he shades its box. If desired, display a transparency of the page and have students solve the problems on their own papers.

MATH IN MINUTES MATH IN MINUTES

Level A

Name ______________________

NUMBER AND OPERATIONS

1. Which operations would you use to solve this problem? Explain.

Alex ate $\frac{1}{2}$ of the pizza, and Micah ate $\frac{1}{3}$ of the pizza. How much pizza is left?

NUMBER AND OPERATIONS

2. Seventy-five percent of the students in Gena's class have dogs. If 18 students have dogs, how many students are in Gena's class? How do you know?

NUMBER AND OPERATIONS

3. Which of these is larger? Explain.

the greatest common factor of 20 and 15

or

the least common multiple of 20 and 15

MEASUREMENT

4. Put these measurements in order from least to greatest. How do you know your answer is correct?

5 gallons
88 cups
10 quarts
5 pints

ALGEBRA

5. In which equations do you think n will have the same value? Why? Solve each equation.

A. $6 \times n = 48$
B. $n - 2 = 5$
C. $17 + n = 23$
D. $n \times 5 = 35$
E. $n \div 1 = 7$

GEOMETRY

6. Are all perpendicular lines also intersecting lines? Are all intersecting lines also perpendicular lines? Explain.

Level B

Name ______________________

NUMBER AND OPERATIONS

1. Last month, Kelly's family used 921.8 kilowatt hours of electricity. This month, they used 871.9 kilowatt hours. Is the following statement true? Explain.

Kelly's family used 50 fewer kilowatt hours of electricity this month than last month.

NUMBER AND OPERATIONS

2. Order the numbers from greatest to least. Tell how you know you are correct.

5.5 5.05 5.105 5.1
5.150 5.505 5.51

NUMBER AND OPERATIONS

3. Complete the Venn diagram.

multiples of $2 < 30$ | multiples of $5 < 30$

ALGEBRA

4. Find all the values for x that make both statements true. How do you know you have all the solutions?

$$(x+3)-8>0$$
$$(x+3)-8<10$$

MEASUREMENT

5. Which measures are equal? How can you be sure?

$2\frac{1}{2}$ gallons
48 cups
20 pints
8 quarts
320 fluid ounces

GEOMETRY

6. Draw a polygon that matches each description. How do you know your drawings are correct?

A. has no parallel sides
B. has one pair of parallel sides
C. has two pairs of parallel sides
D. has no perpendicular sides
E. has no parallel lines and one perpendicular angle

Note to the teacher: Copy the entire page, one level, or selected problems to distribute to students. When a student solves a problem, he checks its box. If desired, display a transparency of the page and have students solve the problems on their own papers.

Science

Sort It Out
Classifying vertebrates

Provide each student with a copy of the cards on page 237 and a large sheet of construction paper. Have the student cut out the cards and sort them into five categories as shown. Then have her arrange each classification's cards in numerical order to reveal the name of an animal. After she glues the cards in place, have her draw a picture of the mystery animal (or another animal belonging to that classification) under each column.

adapted from an idea by Elizabeth Spohn, Butler Catholic School, Butler, PA

Sweet Rocks
Igneous rocks

To make rock-solid examples of igneous rocks, have parents donate chocolate ice cream and Magic Shell ice cream topping. Have each student use a spoon to shape a serving of ice cream to look like a volcano. Then pour Magic Shell topping on top of the volcano, pretending it is lava. Have the student watch as the topping cools and hardens into an edible example of igneous rock. As the student eats his treat, have him write an explanation of how igneous rocks form.

Brittney Byers, Tucker Memorial Elementary, Ponchatoula, LA

Fabulous Friction
Force, experiment

For each small group of students, fill a small plastic basket with classroom items. Make sure each basket is identical; then give each child a recording sheet similar to the one shown. Have each student take a turn hooking a spring scale to the front of his group's basket, pulling it along the classroom floor, and recording on his sheet in grams or ounces the amount of force needed to pull it. If desired, have him use a calculator to convert the measurement to newtons. Once all group members have had a turn, repeat the process on three different surfaces, such as a sidewalk, tabletop, or grassy area. Afterward, discuss the experiment's results and friction's role in the amount of force needed.

Rebecca Dupuy, Vincent Settlement Elementary, Sulphur, LA

Name Turon
Date Sept. 17
Force

Fabulous Friction

Surface	Measurement (ounces or grams)	Newtons (1 newton = 3.59 oz. or 101.97 g)
carpet	4 oz.	4 ÷ 3.59 = 1.11 newtons
desktop	1.5 oz.	1.5 ÷ 3.59 = 0.42 newtons
tile floor	3 oz.	3 ÷ 3.59 = 0.84 newtons
concrete	7 oz.	7 ÷ 3.59 = 1.95 newtons

Vertebrate Cards

Use with "Sort It Out" on page 236.

1. P	1. C	1. T
1.	1. G	2. MAMMALS I 2. BIRDS E
2. FISH A	2. AMPHIBIANS	2. REPTILES U
3. all are cold-blooded R	3. all are cold-blooded T	3. most are cold-blooded T
3. all are warm-blooded R	3. all are warm-blooded L	4. all have dry, scaly skin T
4. all have feathers and wings I	4. most have scales and fins F	4. all have true hair A
4. most have smooth skin O	5. most females lay eggs A	5. all hatch from eggs I
5. all females lay eggs C	5. most females give birth to live young F	5. some females lay eggs and some give birth to live young L
6. all use gills to breathe S	6. all use lungs and gills to breathe at some point in life D	6. all use lungs to breathe F
6. all use lungs to breathe A	6. all use lungs to breathe E	7. all feed mother's milk to young E
7. all have many hollow bones N	7. most never leave water H	7. usually live part of life in water and part on land S TEC44044

Product Testers

Scientific method

Reviewing the scientific method has never been so fun! To begin, remind students that the flavors of different kinds of gum last different lengths of time. Next, lead students to generate a testable question about gum flavor. Then divide students into small groups and give each group a timer. Give each child in the group a piece of a different kind of gum and have her follow the steps on a copy of page 239. Guide the students in the group to compare their results and then draw a conclusion about which gum has the longest-lasting flavor.

Becky Juneau, Highland Elementary, Lake Stevens, WA

Weather Watch

Weather patterns

	Josh				
	City	Forecast High Temperature	Forecast Low Temperature	Chance of Precipitation	Probable Precipitation Form
	Stickney	60°	36°	40%	mist, rain

To help students practice drawing weather conclusions, have each child make a chart labeled as shown. Next, announce the day's predicted high and low temperatures and chance for precipitation. Have each child record the information on his chart, decide which form of precipitation is most likely, and note his prediction. Repeat for several locations across the state, country, or world, and then have students share their work in small groups. For a great sponge activity, read different cities' weather data during transitions to and from other classes, challenging students to make precipitation forecasts as they line up.

Jennifer Hoff, Edison Elementary, Stickney, IL

WANTED

LION

Lions are big cats that live on the African plains. They are carnivores that are important to the grassland food chain.

Lions will eat nearly any meat, but when they eat herbivores like springboks, they are doing their job in the food chain.

If lions didn't eat grassland herbivores, the herbivores' populations might grow too large. There wouldn't be enough grass for all the herbivores, and many might starve. Then the habitat would be out of balance.

Reward: Healthy Savannah Habitat

Noah and Julia

Most Wanted

Food chains

Here's a great idea for reinforcing food chain concepts. Guide each pair of students to choose a food chain and identify its parts. Then the partners pretend one part of the chain is missing. They create a wanted poster about the missing producer, herbivore, carnivore, omnivore, scavenger, or decomposer. On their poster, the partners include a sketch and description of the missing part, its role in the food chain, a warning about the chain's future without the part, and a reward for the part's safe return. The pair tears the edges of the poster to give it an antique look and posts it on a board titled "Wanted: Balanced Food Chains."

Nancy Alley, Columbus, OH

Name ______________________________

Date ____________________

Savor the Flavor!

Item to be tested:

piece of ______________________ gum
gum's name

Steps:

1. Write the name of your gum above. Write your question below.
2. Tell what you know about the flavors of different kinds of gum. Then make a hypothesis about your group's results.
3. Start chewing your gum. After one minute, use the flavor scale to rate the gum's flavor. Then list words that describe the gum's flavor.
4. Repeat Step 3 for a total of six minutes, rating and describing the flavor each minute.
5. Compare your results with each member of your group. Then draw a conclusion about which gum's flavor lasts the longest.

Testable Question ______________________________

What I Know ______________________________

My Hypothesis ______________________________

Data and Observations

Flavor Rank ☐ — 1 minute	Flavor Rank ☐ — 2 minutes	Flavor Rank ☐ — 3 minutes
Flavor Rank ☐ — 4 minutes	Flavor Rank ☐ — 5 minutes	Flavor Rank ☐ — 6 minutes

Flavor Scale

- **10 (packed with flavor)**
- **5 (has some flavor)**
- **0 (has no flavor)**

Conclusion ______________________________

Note to the teacher: Use with "Product Testers" on page 238.

Simply Science

Lifestyles of the Cuddly and the Creepy

Habitat research

Here's a project that capitalizes on the popularity of TV shows about how favorite celebrities live. To begin, have each student choose an animal and research details about its habitat. After the child finds out where and how the critter lives, guide her to prepare a detailed tour of its habitat that mimics a television tour of a celebrity home. Then have the student use pictures, props, and a dramatic voice to share her research.

Heidi Teichert-Divizio, Covington Elementary, Oak Lawn, IL

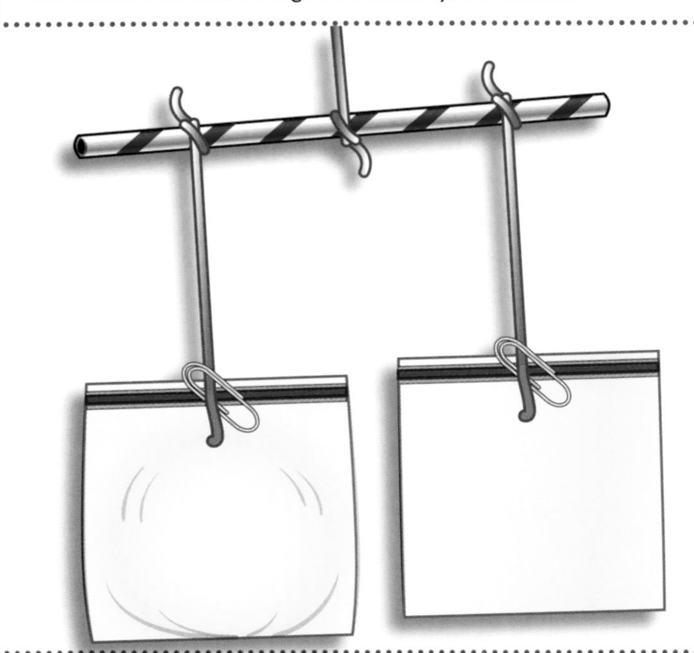

A Balancing Act

Properties of matter, weight of air

Help students observe the properties of gas with this quick exploration. To begin, give each pair of students a copy of page 241 and the materials listed. Guide each pair through the steps. Then discuss students' findings. *(The bag filled with air weighs more than the empty bag because gases have weight. Air does not have a specific shape or volume, so it takes on the bag's shape.)* To follow up, lead students to make predictions and then research the properties of other gases, such as helium or hydrogen.

Valerie Wood Smith, Morgantown, PA

On the Move!

Simple machines

Want your students to be on the lookout for simple machines? Try this! Have each child fold a sheet of paper in half three times and then cut apart each section. Next, guide the student to label seven of the pieces with the types of simple machines, including combinations. Then have him staple the pieces together to make a booklet, using the blank piece as the cover. Direct each student to draw or describe in his booklet two or more examples of each type of simple machine. Then have each student share his work with a small group.

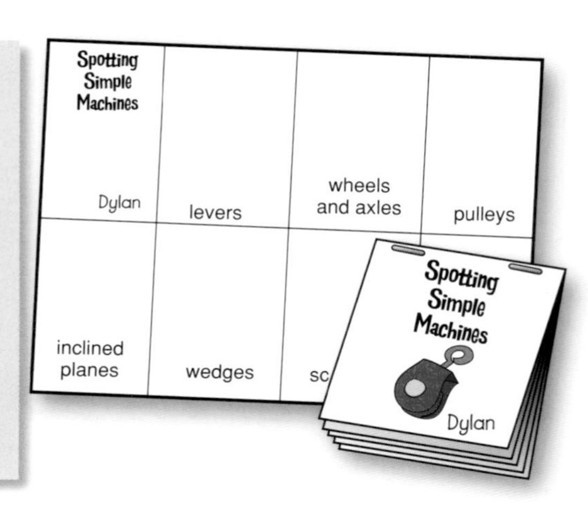

Names ______________________________

Date ________________

A Balancing Act

Materials for each pair of students:
2 straws (not bendable)
three 12-inch lengths of yarn
2 resealable sandwich-size plastic bags
2 same-size paper clips
tape

Steps:

1. Tie one length of yarn around the middle of a straw. Tape the other end of the yarn to the edge of a desk or table. Adjust the yarn to make the straw level, or balanced.
2. Tie one length of yarn to each of the straw's ends to create a balance scale. Then make sure the straw is still level.
3. Clip a bag to one side of the balance. Close the other bag around the remaining straw. Then, holding the bag closed around the straw, blow air into the bag. Press the bag closed as you draw out the straw, keeping the bag full of air. What do you think will happen when you clip the bag filled with air to the other side of the balance?

   Our prediction: ______________________________

4. Clip the inflated bag to the empty side of the balance.
5. What happens? Draw and describe the results.
6. Based on your experiment, describe the properties of air.

Note to the teacher: Use with "A Balancing Act" on page 240.

Pocket Review

Vocabulary

Use this interactive display to reinforce science vocabulary. Post several library pockets on a board titled "Vital Vocab." Then, during each unit of study, guide students to define the vocabulary words. Make a card for each word, writing the class's definition at the bottom of the card as shown. Slide each card in a pocket and have students visit the board regularly to review the words. As you explore other science topics, simply add new cards.

Stacie Jordan, Wichita, KS

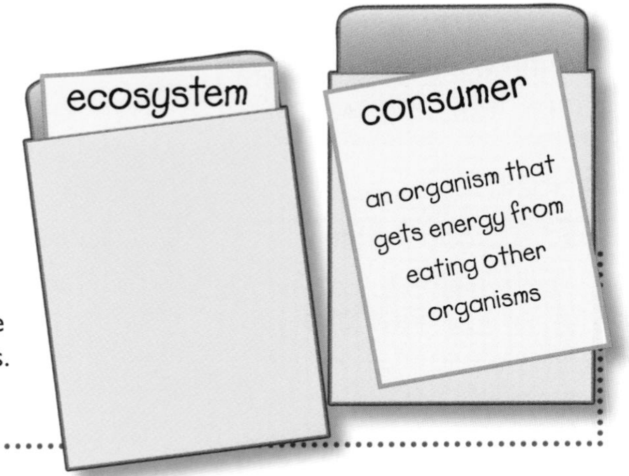

Can You Find Me?

Animal adaptations

For this creative activity, give each student a copy of an animal card and a magnifying glass pattern from page 243. Then guide the child to research his animal's camouflaging features and color the animal card appropriately. Next, have the student glue his picture onto a sheet of white construction paper and draw a scene around the animal to show where it might hide. After that, have the student cut out the magnifying glass, remove the middle, and glue the magnifying glass atop the animal as shown. Finally, post students' work on a board titled "Camouflage Helps Keep Us Safe!"

Leigh Anne Newsom, Cedar Road Elementary, Chesapeake, VA

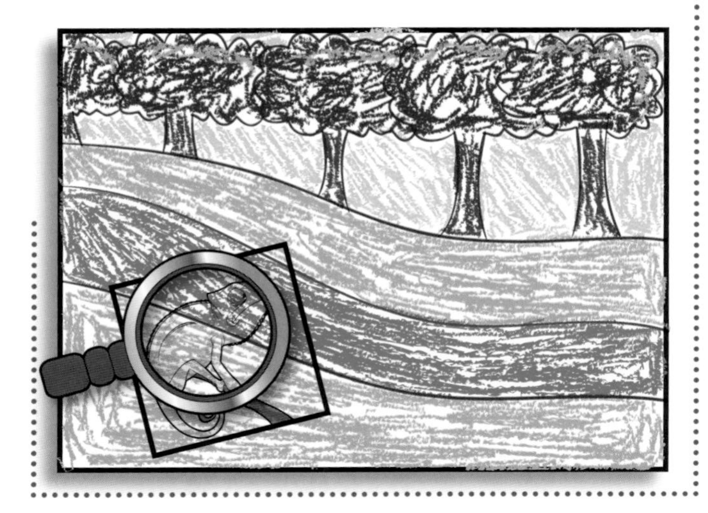

Rockin' Science Tune

Comets

To introduce this musical activity, sing the first three verses of "The Twelve Facts About Comets" shown. Next, guide each pair of students to research comets and write the song's remaining nine verses. Then have each duo share its song with the class.

Brooke Beverly, Dudley Elementary, Dudley, MA

The Twelve Facts About Comets
(sung to the tune of "The Twelve Days of Christmas")

On the first day I saw it,
The comet said to me,
"I leave a trail of debris."

On the second day I saw it,
The comet said to me,
"I'm ice and rock,
And I leave a trail of debris."

On the third day I saw it,
The comet said to me,
"I orbit the sun,
I'm ice and rock,
And I leave a trail of debris."

Animal Cards and Magnifying Glass Patterns

Use with "Can You Find Me?" on page 242.

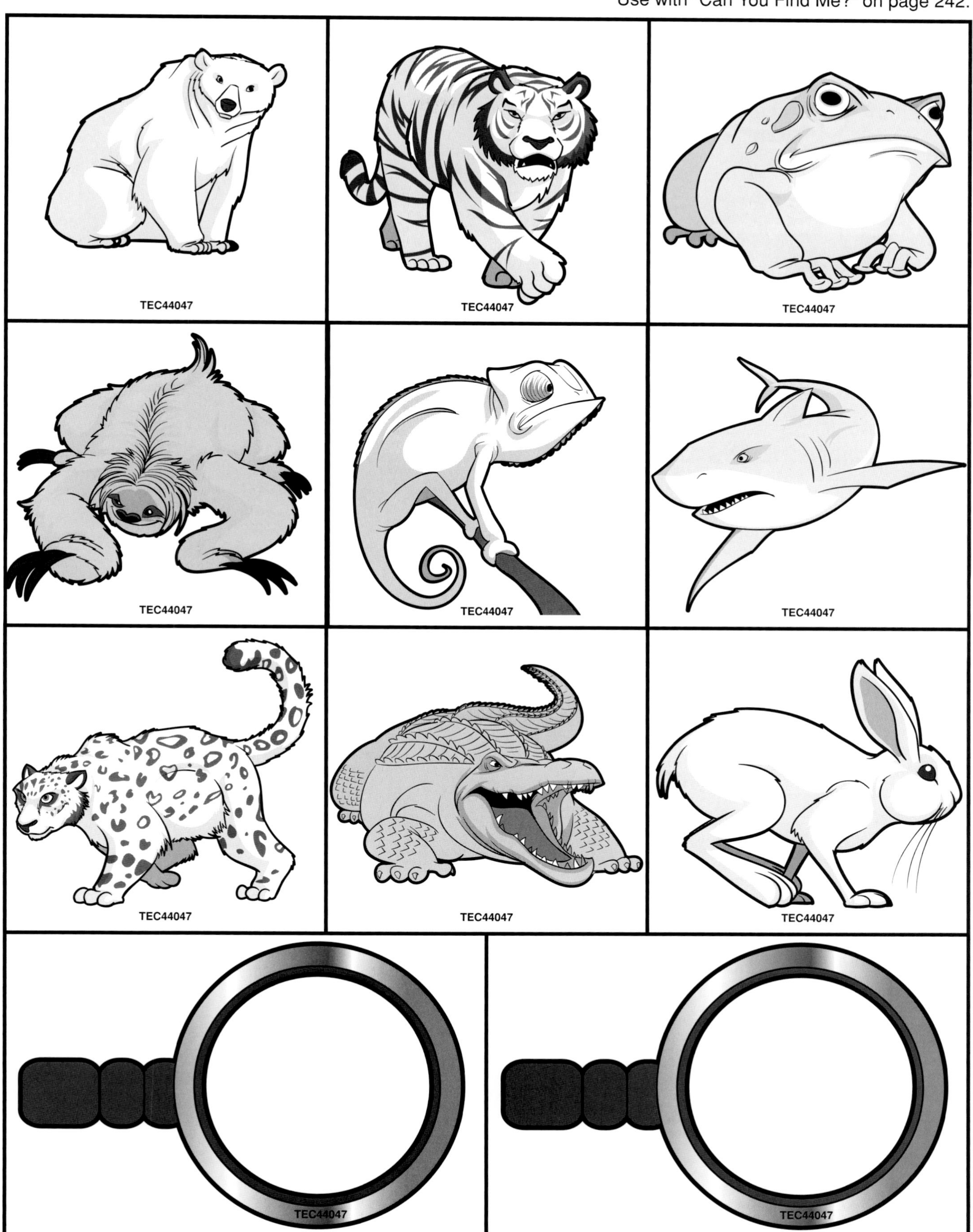

All in the Family

Classifying living things

This twist on the game of Concentration gives students practice distinguishing between vertebrate and invertebrate animal groups. First, have each pair of students cut apart the animal cards on a copy of page 245 and spread the cards facedown. Then have the partners take turns flipping two cards, looking for a match between the animal and its classification. Once all the matches have been made, the player with the most cards wins.

adapted from an idea by Lindsey Weeks, West Elementary, Kings Mountain, NC

Why not use what you've already got? SOLAR ENERGY!

Forms of Energy

- mechanical
- heat
- electric
- chemical
- solar

I'm the Best!

Forms of energy

For a motivating research project, have each student choose a form of energy. Next, guide the child to pretend she is the energy form and write a speech to convince listeners she is the most important type of energy. Then have the student create a slogan that advertises her energy form and present it along with her speech. If desired, allow students to vote for the most convincing speech.

Cynthia Holcomb, San Angelo, TX

Lunar Model

Solar system

To begin this activity, explain that the average distance between the earth and the moon is 382,500 kilometers. Next, hold up a basketball and a tennis ball as representations of the earth and moon. *(The scale is 1 cm = 531.5 km.)* Then guide each small group of students to figure out how far apart the basketball and tennis ball should be to correspond to the actual distance between the earth and the moon. Have the group record its prediction and reasoning, and set aside time for each group to share its work. Then head to the gym or playground and have a student hold the basketball. Carrying the tennis ball, walk 7.2 meters from the basketball to represent the actual distance. Follow up by having each group compare its prediction with the actual distance.

Animal Cards

Use with “All in the Family” on page 244.

1 **butterfly** TEC44048	**2** **newt** TEC44048	**3** **snail** TEC44048	**4** **shrimp** TEC44048	**5** **alligator** TEC44048
6 **lizard** TEC44048	**7** **beetle** TEC44048	**8** **snake** TEC44048	**9** **clam** TEC44048	**10** **toad** TEC44048
11 **squid** TEC44048	**12** **centipede** TEC44048	**13** **salamander** TEC44048	**14** **frog** TEC44048	**15** **oyster** TEC44048
16 **scorpion** TEC44048	**17** **turtle** TEC44048	**Vertebrate** **reptile** (cold-blooded; dry, scaly skin) TEC44048	**Vertebrate** **reptile** (cold-blooded; dry, scaly skin) TEC44048	**Vertebrate** **reptile** (cold-blooded; dry, scaly skin) TEC44048
Vertebrate **reptile** (cold-blooded; dry, scaly skin) TEC44048	**Vertebrate** **amphibian** (moist skin, no scales) TEC44048	**Vertebrate** **amphibian** (moist skin, no scales) TEC44048	**Vertebrate** **amphibian** (moist skin, no scales) TEC44048	**Vertebrate** **amphibian** (moist skin, no scales) TEC44048
WILD CARD (Matches anything!) TEC44048	**Invertebrate** **arthropod** (jointed legs, bodies have 2 or more parts) TEC44048	**Invertebrate** **arthropod** (jointed legs, bodies have 2 or more parts) TEC44048	**Invertebrate** **arthropod** (jointed legs, bodies have 2 or more parts) TEC44048	**Invertebrate** **arthropod** (jointed legs, bodies have 2 or more parts) TEC44048
Invertebrate **arthropod** (jointed legs, bodies have 2 or more parts) TEC44048	**Invertebrate** **mollusk** (soft-bodied, usually has outer skeleton) TEC44048	**Invertebrate** **mollusk** (soft-bodied, usually has outer skeleton) TEC44048	**Invertebrate** **mollusk** (soft-bodied, usually has outer skeleton) TEC44048	**Invertebrate** **mollusk** (soft-bodied, usually has outer skeleton) TEC44048

Answer Key for “All in the Family”

1. arthropod
2. amphibian
3. mollusk
4. arthropod
5. reptile
6. reptile
7. arthropod
8. reptile
9. mollusk
10. amphibian
11. mollusk
12. arthropod
13. amphibian
14. amphibian
15. mollusk
16. arthropod
17. reptile

TEC44048

Unfair Science Fair

General science

Wish you could squeeze in a few more science lessons during the last few weeks of school? Try this! List several grade-level topics on the board. Then challenge each pair of students to choose one, study it, and create a science fair–like display to convince you that the topic did not get fair exposure this year. Explain that each display should include a model or an experiment and a poster or brochure that touts the topic's important facts and details. Follow up by having students rearrange their desks to display their work in an "It's unfair!" science fair. Then have the partners turn on their persuasive charm and present their work!

Katie Kolowski, Bolin School, East Peoria, IL

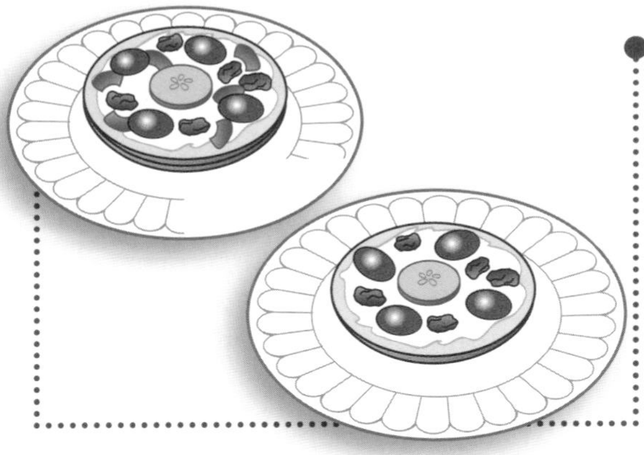

Tasty Exploration

Plant and animal cells

For this edible exercise in examining cell structure, give each pair of students a copy of page 247 and the supplies listed. Next, guide the partners through the steps to build animal and plant cell models. Then have students compare and contrast the cells' features before making a snack of their tasty models.

adapted from an idea by Joanne Sowell, Futral Road Elementary, Griffin, GA

Planetary Products

Solar system

Here's a nifty idea for finding out what students have learned about the solar system! Recruit students to design party supplies that will be appealing to children and will teach them about the solar system. Have each student design a cup, a napkin, two different-size plates, and a party balloon that each includes three important facts about the solar system. For the cup, each student draws his design on a half sheet of paper, rolls the paper into a cylinder, and tapes the edges together. The child folds a sheet of paper in fourths to represent a napkin and trims unlined paper for the plate and balloon designs. As time allows, have each child share his work and give the class a sales pitch about his party ware!

Dawn Murray, Freehold, NJ

Names ____________________

Date ____________________

A TASTY EXPLORATION

Materials for each pair of students:
2 small pita pockets
2 tbsp. softened cream cheese
2 cucumber slices
8 cherry or grape tomatoes
10 raisins
6 celery slices
2 paper plates
plastic knife

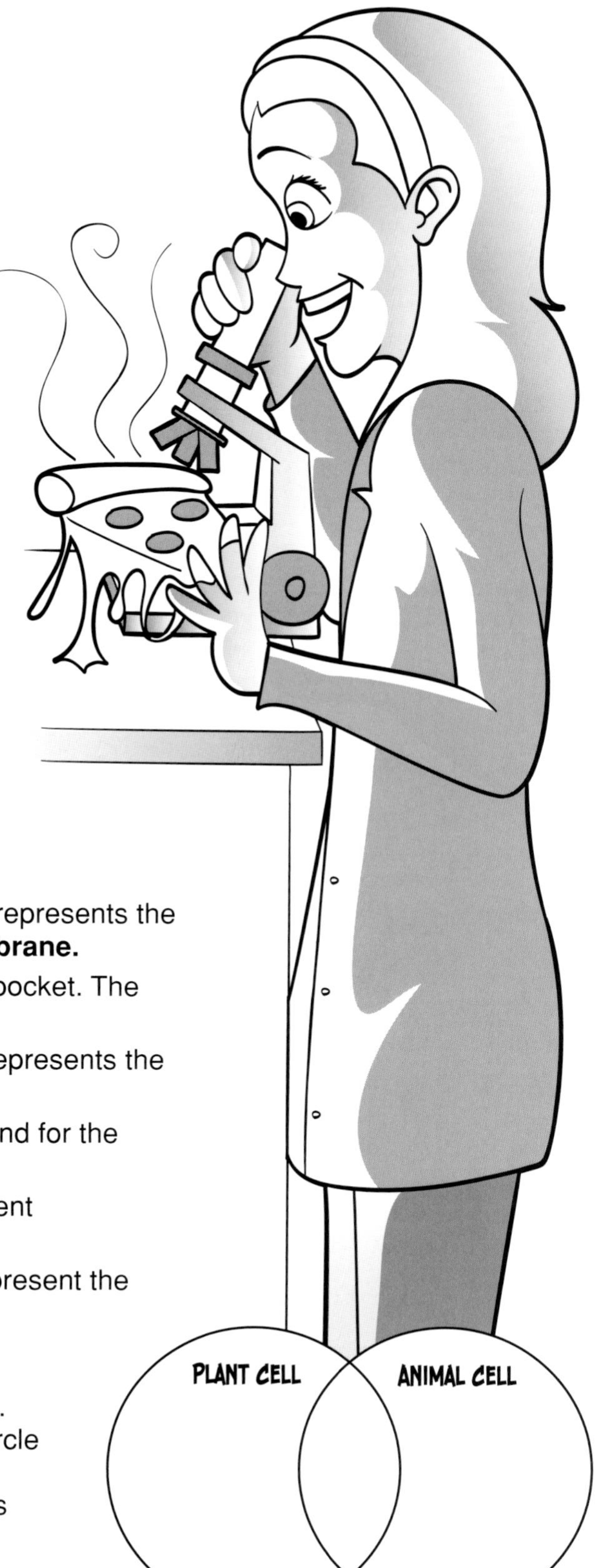

A. STEPS TO MAKE AN ANIMAL CELL MODEL

1. Cut away the bottom layer of a pita pocket and set it aside. Place the top layer on a plate. This represents the **cell membrane.**
2. Spread one tablespoon of cream cheese on the pocket. The cream cheese represents the **cytoplasm.**
3. Place one cucumber slice near the center. This represents the **nucleus.**
4. Put four tomatoes around the nucleus. These stand for the cell's **vacuoles.**
5. Scatter five raisins around the cell. These represent **mitochondria.**

B. STEPS TO MAKE A PLANT CELL MODEL

1. Place a pita pocket on a plate. The bottom layer represents the **cell wall**. The top layer represents the **cell membrane.**
2. Spread one tablespoon of cream cheese on the pocket. The cream cheese represents the **cytoplasm.**
3. Place one cucumber slice near the center. This represents the **nucleus.**
4. Put four tomatoes around the nucleus. These stand for the cell's **vacuoles.**
5. Scatter five raisins around the cell. These represent **mitochondria.**
6. Place the celery slices around the cell. These represent the cell's **chloroplasts.**

C. COMPARE AND CONTRAST

1. On another sheet of paper, draw a Venn diagram. Label the left circle "Plant Cell." Label the right circle "Animal Cell."
2. Fill in the diagram with details about how the cells are alike and how they are different.

Note to the teacher: Use with "Tasty Exploration" on page 246.

Name ____________________

Date ____________________

Super Storms

An average hurricane lasts from three to 14 days and may travel from 3,000 to 4,000 miles.

Hurricanes are strong, swirling storms that form over warm seas and then move westward. Florida has been hit by more hurricanes than any other U.S. state. Texas is second, and Louisiana is third.

A hurricane's life is divided into four parts. It begins as a **tropical disturbance.** This is when rain clouds form. The next stage is a **tropical depression.** It begins when winds start to blow in a circular pattern around a low-pressure area. The third stage is a **tropical storm.** It begins when winds exceed 38 miles per hour. Once winds exceed 74 miles per hour, the storm becomes a **hurricane.**

Not all hurricanes are the same strength. A Category I hurricane is the weakest. The strongest is a Category 5, which can cause great destruction. Hurricane Katrina was a Category 5 hurricane. When this storm hit the Gulf Coast of the United States in 2005, it caused severe damage and killed many people.

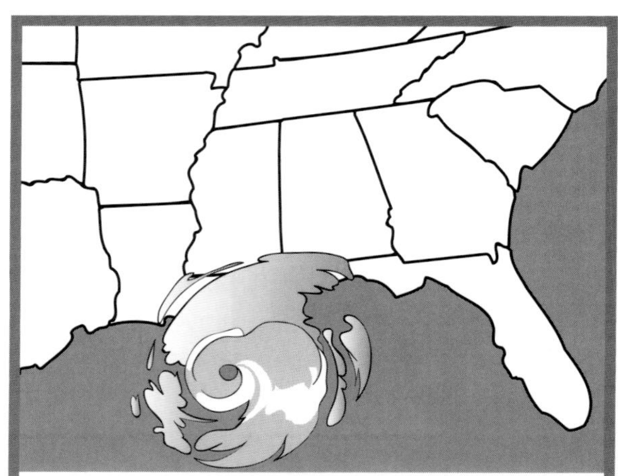

Aerial View of Hurricane Katrina Hitting the Gulf Coast

A *hurricane watch* means that conditions are right for a hurricane to hit within 36 hours.

A *hurricane warning* means that a hurricane could strike an area in 24 hours or less.

1. Where do hurricanes form? ____________________
   In which direction do they move? ____________________
2. What happens during each part of a hurricane's life?
   a. tropical disturbance: ____________________
   b. tropical depression: ____________________
   c. tropical storm: ____________________
   d. hurricane: ____________________
3. What is the difference between a hurricane watch and a hurricane warning? ____________________
4. How is a Category 5 hurricane different from a Category 1 hurricane? ____________________
5. Why do you think Florida gets hits by hurricanes so often? ____________________

Name ____

Date __________________________

The Heat Under Your Feet

The upper ten feet of most of the earth's crust ranges between 50 and 60 degrees Fahrenheit. Temperatures in the earth's core are hotter than the sun's surface.

Have you ever been to Yellowstone National Park and watched Old Faithful erupt? Old Faithful is a *geyser*. Geysers are similar to volcanoes, but they spew out hot water and steam instead of melted rock. Geysers form deep below the earth's surface where water seeps into channels through cracks in the earth's crust. The deeper the water goes, the more it is heated.

Geysers are a form of geothermal energy. Scientists are learning how to use steam and hot water from deep within the earth to heat buildings and make electricity. People who heat their homes with this form of energy help our environment stay clean.

Geothermal energy is renewable. That means we will not run out of it. Heat within the earth is produced constantly, and water that erupts from geysers is gained back when it rains. Geothermal energy can be used by people around the world.

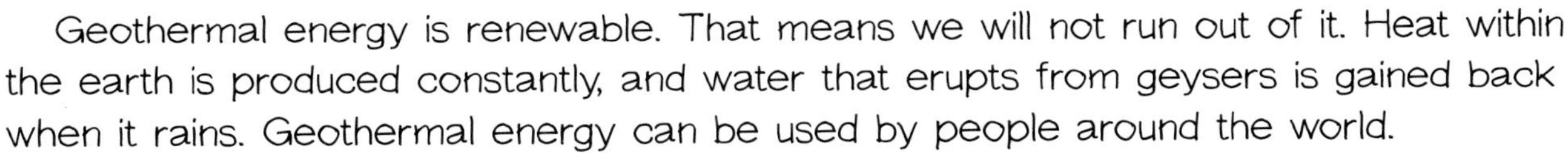

Write a word from the word bank to complete each sentence. Some words will not be used.

1. Geothermal energy is ____________________.
2. Old Faithful is a ____________________.
3. Temperatures closer to the earth's ____________________ are ____________________ than they are at the surface.
4. Hot water ____________________ from geysers.
5. Renewable energy is energy that ____________________ be replaced.
6. People around the ____________________ can use geothermal energy.
7. Scientists can use ____________________ and hot water to make ____________________ and to heat ____________________.

Word Bank

steam
can
buildings
hotter
electricity
core
cannot
nonrenewable
United States
erupts
geyser
atmosphere
world
colder
volcano
renewable

Bonus Box: Geothermal energy is a clean, underused form of power. How can people around the world use it more? Write your answer on the back of this page.

Name ______________________________ **Animal adaptations**

Date ________________

Tusk, Tusk!

To get out of the water, a walrus digs its tusks into the ice. Then it pulls its heavy body up.

What does it take to survive in the bitter cold of the Arctic? (In the winter, Arctic temperatures can drop to −27°C.) For a walrus, it takes a lot of blubber to survive. An adult walrus may weigh up to 1,400 kilograms.

The walrus is the only seal that has tusks. Its tusks are actually canine teeth. A walrus's tusks may grow almost a meter long. Using its strong tusks, a walrus can break holes in the ice from underwater. Tusks also come in handy if a walrus needs to protect itself or its territory.

The walrus has flat flippers for feet. The flippers make the walrus a good swimmer. With its sensitive, bristly whiskers, a walrus can find clams on the dark ocean floor. When it isn't eating or searching for food, a walrus often rests on floating sea ice. Because the ice floats, a walrus can find food in many places away from the shore.

As temperatures rise, there is less sea ice for walruses to rest on. Scientists wonder what will happen if more walruses begin resting on land. Will there be enough food for the walruses? Will walruses be safe? Scientists are tracking walruses to see where they go and what they do.

Write "Yes" or "No" to answer each question. Then give a reason for your answer.

1. If a polar bear attacked a walrus, could the walrus defend itself? ☐

   ____

2. In the arctic food chain, is a walrus a producer? ☐

   ____

3. Is there a reason that a walrus's feet are flat flippers? ☐

   ____

4. Is it more important for a walrus to have a lot of blubber than for it to have strong tusks? ☐

   ____

5. Is it possible that warmer temperatures will affect walrus survival? ☐

   ____

 Note to the teacher: See the answer key for Fahrenheit and standard–measurement equivalencies.

Name ____

Date ____________________

Solid as a Rock!

You will probably use 2,000,000 pounds of rocks and minerals in your lifetime.

We see rocks and minerals every day. We drive on them, build with them, clean with them, and even eat them! Minerals and igneous, sedimentary, and metamorphic rocks are part of our lives every day.

The minerals copper, silver, gold, palladium, and platinum make up about 25% of a cell phone. Asbestos, another mineral, is used to make cloth and yarn fireproof. Halite is used in our food. It's also used to make soap and to deice highways.

Igneous rocks–such as pumice, granite, and basalt–form when magma cools. Pumice can be used to rub dry skin off our elbows. Granite is used to make monuments that last. Basalt is used in brake pads to add friction.

How do we use rock that forms in layers? Limestone is a sedimentary rock. We use limestone when we use chalk. Did you know it's in toothpaste, lipstick, and ink too? There is even limestone in tires, mag wheels, and hair mousse.

How do we use the metamorphic rocks that are formed by heat and/or pressure? Marble, which was once limestone, is often used for statues. It is soft and easy to carve. Quartzite is often used in jewelry instead of green, purple, and pink jade.

Circle the best answer. Then explain your choice.

1. We know (halite, pumice, marble) as salt. ____________________

2. Asbestos is a(n) (igneous rock, mineral, sedimentary rock). ____________________

3. Marble is a metamorphic rock that (time, cooling, heat and pressure) formed from limestone. ____________________

4. Igneous rocks form (in layers, when magma cools, quickly). ____________________

5. (Pumice, Quartzite, Limestone) is a widely used sedimentary rock. ____________________

Name ______________________________

Date ____________________

The Glacial Glide

Around 75 percent of the world's freshwater is frozen in glaciers!

A glacier forms as layers of snow build up. The weight of the snow packs together the bottom layers and forms ice. Over many years, the snow and ice accumulate. Most glaciers are at least 30.48 meters, or 100 feet, thick and cover 100,000 square meters or more. The ice and snow form a mass so great that it moves, or flows, downhill.

As it flows, a glacier reshapes the land. It wears away, or erodes, the rock and soil under it. The icy mass picks up large rocks and carries them downhill. Rocks, dirt, and even trees get pushed ahead or out of the way of the glacier. Along its path, a glacier deposits bits and pieces of the matter it has picked up. Nothing is the same after a glacier passes by!

Glacial Landforms

A boulder like this is called a **glacial erratic.** It was picked up by a glacier and then dropped in a field far away.

A U-shaped valley, or **glacial trough,** is formed by a glacier as it wears away the land.

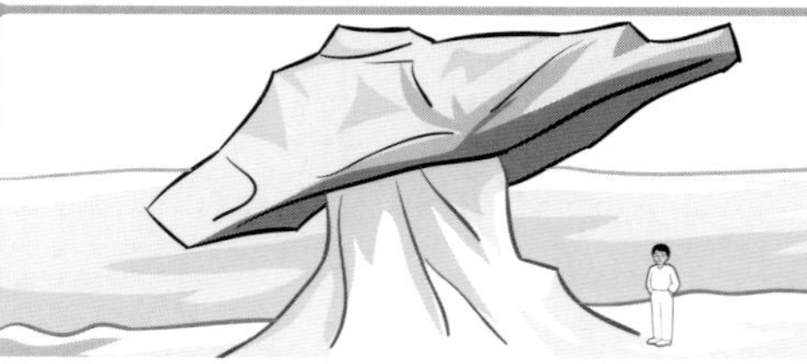

A **glacier table** is a rock sitting on an ice platform. As a glacier melts and evaporates, the column under the rock stays frozen.

1. How are glaciers formed? ______________________

____

____

2. A football field's area is about 5,851.79 square meters. About how many football fields would fit on a glacier with an area of 100,000 square meters?

____

3. Describe what happens when a glacier flows downhill.

____

____

4. Something that is *erratic* wanders around. How do you think the *glacial erratic* got its name?

____

____

5. The world's fastest moving glacier moved an average of 112 meters a day. Do you think the glacier was moving fast enough that people could see it move? Why or why not?

____

____

Name ______________________________
Date ______________________

Seeing the Invisible

Black holes are not really holes at all!

Black holes are the darkest spots in the universe. Would you believe that a black hole can begin as a gigantic shining star? Once that huge star uses all its fuel, it dies out. Then the star collapses inward because of the pull of its own gravity. This creates a black hole. The gravity of a black hole is so strong that it swallows everything that gets close to it. Any matter that falls into the black hole disappears from sight. Even light cannot escape from a black hole. This is why we cannot see a black hole.

So how do scientists know black holes exist? Dust, gases, and stars that are pulled toward a black hole become very hot. Scientists use instruments that detect this heat to locate a black hole. They also use the Hubble Space Telescope to find black holes. Gases near the black hole get pulled and swirl down to the black hole. This is like water swirling down a bathtub drain. Instruments on the telescope measure the speed of the swirling gases. Then scientists identify the black hole.

There is much more to learn about black holes. Most astronomers believe that millions of them lurk inside our galaxy.

Answer the questions. For questions 1–5, use the colors in parentheses to underline the text evidence above.

1. Why does a black hole trap everything near it? (green) ______________________________
2. What can escape from a black hole? (yellow) ______________________________
3. Why do scientists measure the heat given off by falling dust, gases, and stars? (blue) __________
4. How do gases near a black hole act? (orange) ______________________________
5. What is one way the Hubble Space Telescope helps scientists? (purple) ______________
6. Do you think our sun will ever turn into a black hole? Why or why not? ______________

Name ______________________________

Date ______________

Ants! Ants! Too Many to Count!

Some soldier ants use their blunt, plug-shaped heads to keep enemies out of the nest by blocking the tunnels with their heads!

Scientists think there are over 20,000 different species of ants. Ants can be found just about anywhere there is land, unless it's really cold. Ants live in colonies and can be grouped by how they live.

Army ants prey on insects and spiders. For some, their main food is other ants. Army ants live in huge colonies. One colony of army ants may include millions of ants. These ants don't build long-lasting nests. They make nests that are just temporary.

Harvester ants build mound-shaped nests and collect seeds. They store the seeds in their nests. Storing the seeds means these ants will always have food. They chew up the insides of the seeds. Then they make a paste called *ant bread,* which they feed each other.

Dairying ants treat insects almost like dairy cows. Insect pests, such as aphids, suck juice from plants. Then they release sugary liquid called *honeydew.* The ants live on the protein and nutrients in the liquid. To get the honeydew, dairying ants protect the pests.

Fungus-growing ants grow fungi inside their nests. The fungus provides food for the ants. To fertilize the fungi, the ants gather seeds, parts of flowers, and leaves. They take care of their gardens by weeding out unwanted fungi.

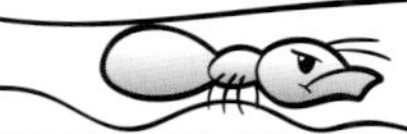

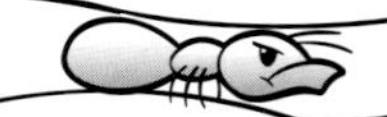

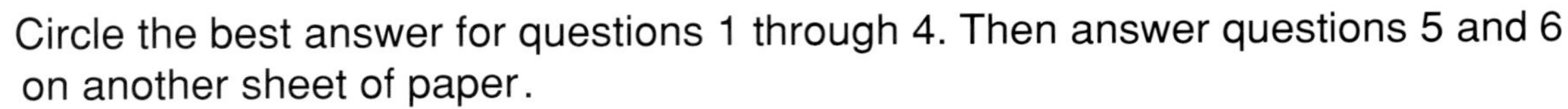

Circle the best answer for questions 1 through 4. Then answer questions 5 and 6 on another sheet of paper.

1. How are the ants in this selection grouped?
   A. by their locations
   B. by their lifestyles
   C. by the sizes of their colonies

2. Why are aphids important to dairying ants?
   A. The ants eat the aphids.
   B. Aphids eat farmers' crops.
   C. Aphids make honeydew.

3. What is the author's purpose for writing this article?
   A. to persuade you that ants are important
   B. to share information about ants
   C. to tell interesting stories about ants

4. What is the meaning of the following sentence from the second paragraph?
   "They make nests that are just temporary."
   A. The ants don't stay in one nest for very long.
   B. The ants move into the nest of another colony.
   C. The ants build nests that are not very strong.

5. Based on the information in the selection, how do you think **carpenter ants** might be different from **fungus-growing ants?**

6. Why do you think **dairying ants** cause problems for farmers?

Name ____________________

Date ____________________

The "Eyes" Have It!

A giant squid's eyes can be bigger than basketballs!

The giant squid is one of the world's most mysterious animals. It lives in a deep-sea habitat. Most of what is known about giant squids has been learned by studying their bodies when they wash up on beaches or get tangled in fishing nets. The largest giant squid carcass that's been retrieved so far was 59 feet long and weighed almost a ton! (That's as long as a power pole and as heavy as a bull.)

Scientists believe giant squids may live in all the world's oceans. The giant squid lives at depths of 1,000 to 3,000 feet. There is no light this deep. To adapt to the darkness, the giant squid has big eyes—*really* big eyes. Each eye is ten inches in diameter. With its large eyes, the giant squid can spot prey in the deep, dark water.

Another deep-sea adaptation is in the giant squid's flesh. It is partly made of a substance lighter than water. This makes it possible for the squid to hover in the deepest part of the ocean.

It's very rare for anyone to see a living giant squid. In fact, the first pictures of a live giant squid weren't taken until 2004. Researchers from Japan took those first pictures. A live giant squid wasn't seen again until 2006.

Shade the circle next to the best answer.

1. The giant squid is mysterious because _____.
   - Ⓐ it is huge
   - Ⓑ it has giant, round eyes
   - Ⓒ it is hard to study

2. According to the selection, what is a carcass?
   - Ⓐ sea creature
   - Ⓑ dead body
   - Ⓒ part of a squid

3. Which trait helps the giant squid survive in its deep-sea habitat?
   - Ⓐ its large eyes
   - Ⓑ its length
   - Ⓒ its massive weight

4. What is the most important idea of the selection?
   - Ⓐ The giant squid always stays in the deepest part of the ocean.
   - Ⓑ The giant squid's eyes and flesh help it adapt to deep-sea life.
   - Ⓒ The giant squid has bigger eyes than any other animal.

5. On another sheet of paper, write a summary of the selection. Include three important details from the selection.

Bonus Box: Research ways a giant squid moves through the water. On another sheet of paper, draw diagrams with captions and labels that show how a giant squid can move through the water.

Name ____________________

Date ____________________

Flash! Boom!

An average lightning flash is five times hotter than the surface of the sun!

Lightning and thunder have always been a puzzling force. Ancient Greeks believed lightning was the god Zeus's weapon. When the Norse heard thunder, they thought the god Thor was throwing a hammer at his enemies. We know now that lightning begins when a cloud becomes electrically charged. The electric charges then flow inside the cloud, to the air, or to another cloud. Thunder is the sound the lightning causes when it travels through the air.

The lightning that occurs most often is intracloud lightning, flowing within a cloud. Yet the lightning we see most often flows from a cloud to the ground. Those flashes we see are named by their features.

When a flash has branches, it is called forked lightning. A flash of lightning that forms an uneven line is streak lightning.

In the summer, people often see what is called heat lightning. They see the lightning but don't hear thunder. There really is thunder. It's just that the lightning is so far away that the people can't hear the thunder.

Ball lightning is a glowing ball that floats in the air. This fiery ball may be as big as a basketball. Ball lightning has been seen inside houses, barns, and even airplanes!

Write a word from the word bank to complete each sentence. Some words will not be used.

1. The ancient Greeks believed ____________________ caused lightning.
2. The most ____________________ lightning occurs within a cloud.
3. ____________________ seems not to have thunder.
4. Lightning is caused by flowing electric ____________________.
5. Lightning ____________________ begins in a cloud.
6. Lightning flashes are named according to their ____________________.
7. The Norse thought thunder was the god Thor throwing a ____________________.
8. With forked lightning, the flash has ____________________.
9. ____________________ can be as big as a basketball.
10. We generally see lightning that flows from a ____________________ to the ground.

Word Bank
- always
- strikes
- Heat lightning
- hammer
- cloud
- Streak lightning
- branches
- common
- features
- charges
- Zeus
- Ball lightning
- sometimes

Bonus Box: Draw diagrams to illustrate each lightning feature described above.

Social Studies

EXPLORING Social Studies

1. This mystery location is north of the equator.
2. This mystery location is east of the prime meridian.
3. This mystery location is between 20°N and 40°N.
4. This mystery location is landlocked.
5. This mystery location is east of Iran and west of Pakistan.

Map Mysteries
Geography

Use this daily warm-up activity to review map skills. On five index cards, write clues about a mystery location (one clue per card). Begin with a general clue on the first card and then make each additional clue increasingly more specific, as shown. On Monday, read the first clue aloud. Then affix the card in a randomly chosen location on a world map and give students time to guess the mystery location. Repeat this process each day. On Friday, read the last clue and allow students to guess. Then reveal the mystery location.

Christy Flynn, Olla-Standard Elementary, Olla, LA

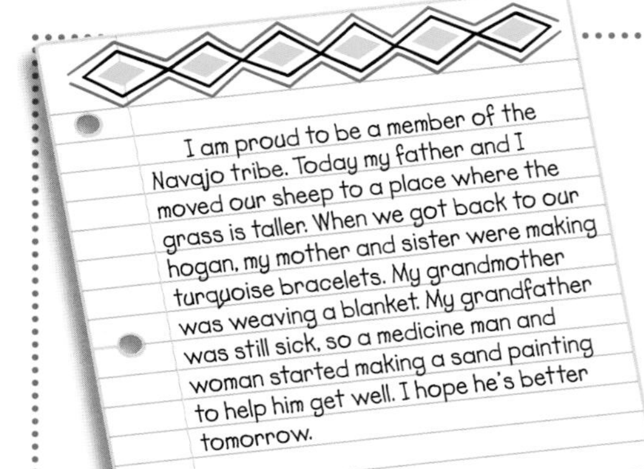

A Day in the Tribe
Native Americans

To help your students better understand the Native American tribe you are studying, have each child imagine he is a member of that tribe hundreds of years in the past. Instruct him to write a diary entry about a day in his life. Require the entry to include cultural information such as the tribe's daily living practices, food, and customs. After students share their entries with the class, compile the writings into a class book. If desired, repeat the activity with different tribes. Then have students use the class books to compare and contrast the different tribes.

Crissie Stephens, Kelly Edwards Elementary, Williston, SC

Explorers Beware!
Exploration, research

Add a fun twist to a study of famous explorers by throwing pirates into the mix! Give each student a copy of page 259. Have her follow its instructions to write a brief report about an explorer of her choice, including a labeled map of his voyages. When students are finished, have them share their work with the class.

Karen Slattery, Dundas, Ontario, Canada

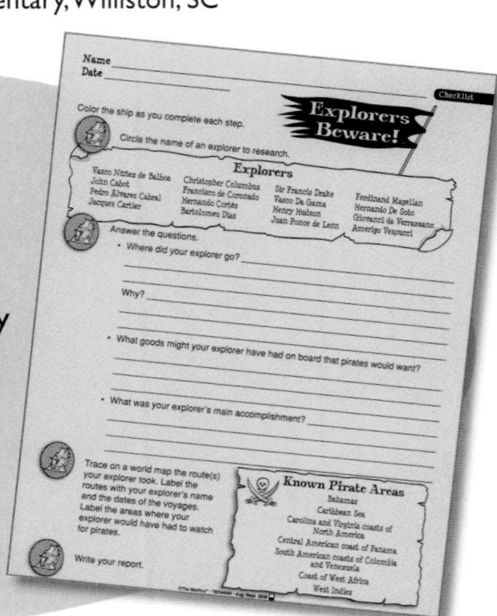
Name
Date

Checklist

Explorers Beware!

Color the ship as you complete each step.

Circle the name of an explorer to research.

Explorers

Vasco Núñez de Balboa, John Cabot, Pedro Álvares Cabral, Jacques Cartier, Christopher Columbus, Francisco de Coronado, Hernando Cortés, Bartolomeu Dias, Sir Francis Drake, Vasco Da Gama, Henry Hudson, Juan Ponce de León, Ferdinand Magellan, Hernando De Soto, Giovanni da Verrazano, Amerigo Vespucci

Answer the questions.
- Where did your explorer go?

  Why?
- What goods might your explorer have had on board that pirates would want?
- What was your explorer's main accomplishment?

Trace on a world map the route(s) your explorer took. Label the routes with your explorer's name and the dates of the voyages. Label the areas where your explorer would have had to watch for pirates.

Known Pirate Areas
Bahamas
Caribbean Sea
Carolina and Virginia coasts of North America
Central American coast of Panama
South American coasts of Colombia and Venezuela
Coast of West Africa
West Indies

Write your report.

Name ____________________

Date ____________________

Checklist

Explorers Beware!

Color the ship as you complete each step.

Circle the name of an explorer to research.

Explorers

Vasco Núñez de Balboa	Christopher Columbus	Sir Francis Drake	Ferdinand Magellan
John Cabot	Francisco de Coronado	Vasco Da Gama	Hernando De Soto
Pedro Álvares Cabral	Hernando Cortés	Henry Hudson	Giovanni da Verrazzano
Jacques Cartier	Bartolomeu Dias	Juan Ponce de León	Amerigo Vespucci

Answer the questions.

- Where did your explorer go? ____________________

  Why? ____________________

- What goods might your explorer have had on board that pirates would want?

  ____

- What was your explorer's main accomplishment? ____________________

Trace on a world map the route(s) your explorer took. Label the routes with your explorer's name and the dates of the voyages. Label the areas where your explorer would have had to watch for pirates.

Known Pirate Areas

Bahamas

Caribbean Sea

Carolina and Virginia coasts of North America

Central American coast of Panama

South American coasts of Colombia and Venezuela

Coast of West Africa

West Indies

Write your report.

Note to the teacher: Use with "Explorers Beware!" on page 258.

EXPLORING Social Studies

Up-to-Date Flash Cards

Current events

For an activity that helps students keep up with what's going on in the world around them, try this! Have each pair of students choose an illustrated article from a current newspaper or magazine. Guide the duo to read the article and answer the five questions shown. Next, have the partners cut out the article's photo, glue it onto construction paper to make a card, and list their answers on the back. After students share their work, put the cards in a handy basket or bag. Then, for a quick sponge activity, draw a card, show the photo, and quiz students about what's going on!

Marsha Erskine, Madison, NC

- Who is it about?
- What happened?
- Where did it happen?
- When did it happen?
- Why is it important?

Is It a Deal?

Economics, supply and demand

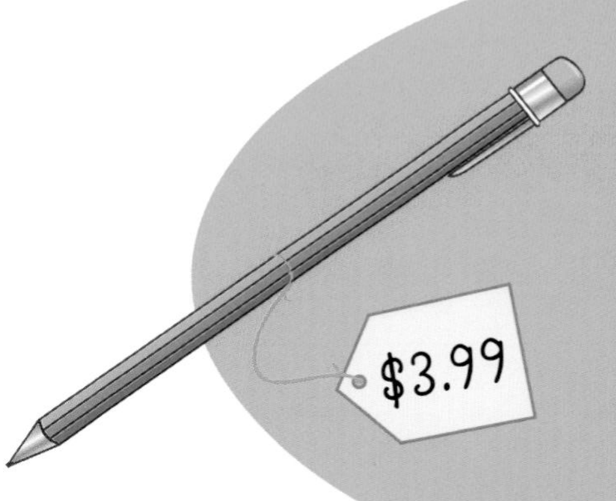

Here's an activity that gets students exploring the roles of supply and demand on product pricing. To begin, have each child choose one object from her desk. Next, lead the student to pretend she is going to sell the item. Have her label the object with a fair price and display the priced object on her desk. Then have each child silently walk around the room and observe other students' items and prices. Next, guide each student to read the statements at the top of a copy of page 261 and then complete the page. Follow up with a class discussion to help students relate the experience to the everyday world.

Follow the Team!

Using map scale to determine distance

Capitalize on students' interest in sports with this simple-to-set-up center! Choose a professional sports team for the class to track. Provide a U.S. map and a copy of the team's schedule. Then have each pair of students use the map's scale to calculate the distance from your school to the team's home stadium. Direct the partners to set up a recording sheet as shown and calculate the distance they would have to travel to attend each game this season. **To extend the activity,** have students determine each city's longitude and latitude.

William
Anna

Our Team: Carolina Panthers, Charlotte, NC

Date	Opponent	Game Location	Travel Distance
10-11	Washington	Charlotte, NC	150 miles
10-18	Tampa Bay	Tampa, FL	650 miles
10-25	Buffalo	Charlotte, NC	150 miles
11-1	Arizona	Phoenix, AZ	2,000 miles

Kim Minafo, Apex, NC

Name ______________________________

Date ______________

What Makes It a Deal?

If the supply of a product...
- stays the same and the demand increases, then the price will go up.
- stays the same and the demand decreases, then the price will go down.
- decreases and the demand stays the same, then the price will go up.
- increases and the demand stays the same, then the price will go down.

12 doz. Mechanical Pencils
12 doz. Mechanical Pencils

Answer the questions.

1. What item did you choose? ______________________
   What price did you give it? ______________________
2. What object did you see the most? ______________________
   Do you think this object is in high demand? __________ Explain. ______________________
   ____
   ____
3. What object did you see the least? ______________________
   Do you think this object is in high demand? __________ Explain. ______________________
   ____
   ____
4. Do you think your object is in high demand? __________ Why or why not? ______________
   ____
   ____
5. Think about your price. Would you raise it, lower it, or leave it the same? ______________
   Why? ____
   ____
6. If you could choose a different object from your desk, would you? __________ Why or why not?
   ____
   ____
7. Name an item that is easy to find right now but will be hard to find in about one month.
   ______________________ Why will the item be hard to find in a month?
   ____
   Will it be worth more or less then? __________ Explain. ______________________
   ____

Note to the teacher: Use with "Is It a Deal?" on page 260.

EXPLORING Social Studies

Fit for the Job

Government, analyzing a chart

Help students explore the executive, legislative, and judicial branches of government with a transparent copy of the chart on page 263. Lead students to analyze the chart using questions such as those shown. Then have each student choose one position from the chart and explain why she will someday be perfect for that job.

- Why do you think there are different age requirements?
- Do you think the requirement that a president be 35 is too young, too old, or just right? Explain.
- How are the requirements for the Senate and the House of Representatives different?

Simone Lepine, Fayetteville, NY

A Day in the Life

American history

Help students get a glimpse into the life of a Continental soldier. To begin, post the list of food rations a soldier was supposed to get each day. Next, explain that supply wagons had a hard time getting to or catching up with marching soldiers, so a lot of the rations spoiled. Soldiers often had to make do with fire cake and water. *(When all they had was flour, Continental soldiers mixed it with water and baked the dough on rocks in the fire, making hard, often burned bread they called fire cake.)*

Then have each child use the supplies and steps listed to make a fire cake. While the fire cakes cook, have each student write a letter to her parents as if she were a Continental soldier, describing her rations and making a prediction about her feast of fire cake and water. *(The fire cake will be hard and crusty on the outside and may be doughy in the middle.)*

adapted from an idea by Terri Myers, Dalton, GA

A Continental Soldier's Daily Rations

one pound beef
one pint milk
one ounce butter
one pound bread or flour
a little molasses

Supplies for each student: cup, ½ cup flour, ⅛ teaspoon salt, craft stick, 4" x 4" foil square, and access to water

Directions:

1. In a cup, mix the flour and salt.
2. Stir in water, a little at a time, to make thick dough.
3. Pat the dough into a biscuit shape on your foil square. Write your initials on the foil and put it on a cookie sheet.
4. Bake at 450° for 30 minutes.

Place Race

Geography, using cardinal and intermediate directions

For this activity, display a state or U.S. map. Next, have a student volunteer stand in front of the map, facing the class. Silently point to a city or geographic feature on the map, write its name on a strip of paper, and fold the strip. Then challenge the volunteer to guess the mystery location. After each guess, have students use actions such as those shown to give the volunteer directional clues. When the child locates the site, display the strip to confirm his guess and repeat as time allows.

Marsha Erskine, Madison, NC

Direction	Actions
north	Raise your left hand.
northeast	Fold your arms.
east	Hold both arms straight out.
southeast	Put both hands behind your head.
south	Touch the tip of your chin.
southwest	Touch your nose.
west	Stretch both legs straight out.
northwest	Touch the top of your head.

Fit for the Job

Branch		Minimum Age Requirement	Citizenship Requirement	Residency Requirement	Elected, Appointed, or Selected	Term Length	Term Limit	Number of People in the Position
Executive Branch	President	35	natural-born citizen	at least 14 years in the United States	elected	four years	two terms	one
	Vice President	35	natural-born citizen	at least 14 years in the United States	selected by presidential candidate	four years	none	one
	Cabinet	none	none	none	chosen by the sitting president	usually as long as the president is in office	none	15
Legislative Branch	Senate	30	citizen for at least nine years	keep a legal residence in the state being represented	elected	six years	none	100
	House of Representatives	25	citizen for at least seven years	legal resident of state being represented	elected	two years	none	435
Judicial Branch	Supreme Court	none	none	none	nominated by the president and approved by the Senate	until retirement	not applicable	nine

Note to the teacher: Use with "Fit for the Job" on page 262.

EXPLORING Social Studies

One Head—Seven Hats

Government, roles of the president

For this idea, divide students into seven small groups. Assign each group one of the U.S. president's basic roles. (See the list.) Next, have the group research the responsibilities that come with that part of the job. Then guide the group to make a construction paper cutout of a hat. Have the team summarize the president's duties on the cutout, share its work, and then post the hat on a board titled "How Many Hats Does the President Wear?"

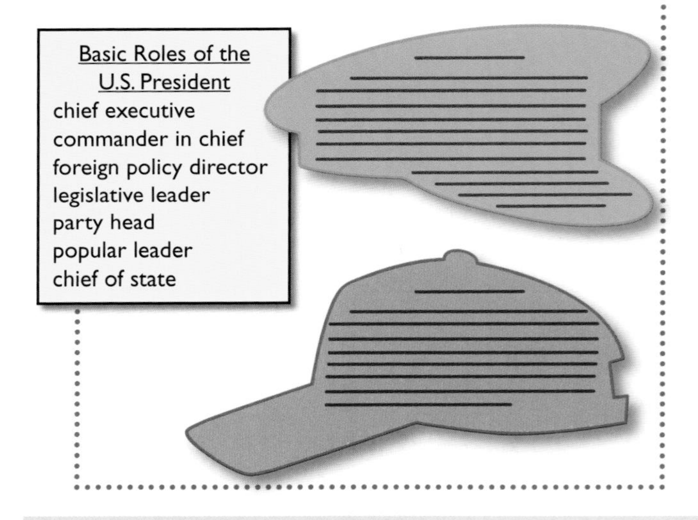

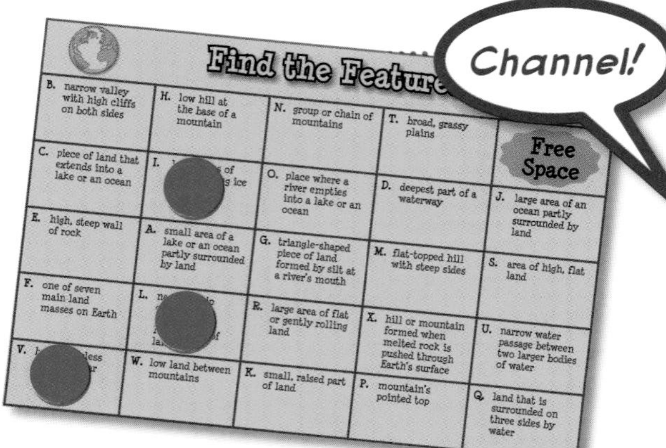

Feature Find

Geography, physical features

This twist on the game of bingo gives students practice identifying the United States' natural features. To play, have each child cut out the grid and cards on a copy of page 265 and glue the cards on the grid in random order. Next, give each student several game markers and call out the name of a physical feature (found on page 313). Guide the child to identify the matching definition and put a marker on it. Continue until a student covers five spaces in a row. Award a small prize to the winner; then have students clear their grids and play again.

Project Podcast

Research

To build enthusiasm for state, region, or country research, have students share their results in faux podcasts! After each small group researches its topic, guide the group to use its notes to write a script that includes music and sound effects. Next, have the students practice reading the script, helping each other speak slowly and clearly. When the group is ready, have students record their work using a tape recorder or a classroom computer. Have each group listen to and assess its podcast before presenting it to the class.

Rabecca Hart, Pine Forge Elementary and Earl Elementary, Boyertown, PA

Natural Feature Grid and Cards

Use with "Feature Find" on page 264.

Find the Feature!

		TEC44047		

A. small area of a lake or an ocean partly surrounded by land	**B.** narrow valley with high cliffs on both sides	**C.** piece of land that extends into a lake or an ocean	**D.** deepest part of a waterway	**E.** high, steep wall of rock
F. one of seven main land masses on Earth	**G.** triangle-shaped piece of land formed by silt at a river's mouth	**H.** low hill at the base of a mountain	**I.** large mass of slow-moving ice	**J.** large area of an ocean partly surrounded by land
K. small, raised part of land	**L.** narrow strip of land that connects two larger areas of land	**M.** flat-topped hill with steep sides	**N.** group or chain of mountains	**O.** place where a river empties into a lake or an ocean
P. mountain's pointed top	**Q.** land that is surrounded on three sides by water	**R.** large area of flat or gently rolling land	**S.** area of high, flat land	**T.** broad, grassy plains
U. narrow water passage between two larger bodies of water	**V.** broad, treeless plain in polar region	**W.** low land between mountains	**X.** hill or mountain formed when melted rock is pushed through Earth's surface	**Free Space**

EXPLORING Social Studies

1. Which ocean is closest to this state?
2. In which region is this state located?
3. What is this state's capital?
4. What is an important natural feature in this state?
5. Which states border this state?

1. The Atlantic Ocean is closest to this state.
2. The state is located in the southeast region.
3. Raleigh is the state's capital.
4. The state's shores are very treacherous.
5. Virginia, Tennessee, and South Carolina border this state.

North Carolina

Clued In

Geography

Here's a center game for partners that your early finishers prepare for you! To begin, post the questions shown and have each student choose a different state. Next, guide each child to write her state's name at the bottom of an index card and answer each question in a sentence without naming the state. Then collect the cards and put them at a center along with a U.S. map and the directions shown. If your students are studying your state, have each student research a different county within your state. Or put a global focus on the activity and have students make cards about different countries.

Directions for two players:

1. In turn, draw a card.
2. Read aloud each of the card's sentence clues one at a time. After each clue, your partner guesses the name of the mystery state.
3. If your partner is correct, award him five points plus one point for each unread clue. If he is not correct, repeat Steps 2 and 3.
4. The player with more points when time is up wins.

adapted from an idea by Janis Harless, Wilkesboro Elementary, Wilkesboro, NC

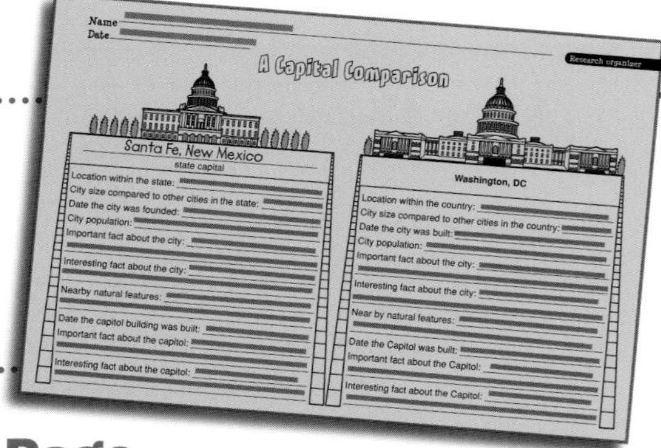

Name
Date

A Capital Comparison

Research organizer

Santa Fe, New Mexico
state capital

Location within the state:
City size compared to other cities in the state:
Date the city was founded:
City population:
Important fact about the city:
Interesting fact about the city:
Nearby natural features:
Date the capitol building was built:
Important fact about the capitol:
Interesting fact about the capitol:

Washington, DC

Location within the country:
City size compared to other cities in the country:
Date the city was built:
City population:
Important fact about the city:
Interesting fact about the city:
Near by natural features:
Date the Capitol was built:
Important fact about the Capitol:
Interesting fact about the Capitol:

A Capital Comparison

Government, geography

For this idea, have each child research your state capital and Washington, DC, taking notes as guided on a copy of page 267. Then have each child summarize the capitals' similarities and differences in a five-paragraph essay.

My Page

History

What might George Washington's social-networking homepage have looked like? Challenge each student to design a fictional homepage to share his research about an important historic figure. To begin, the child creates the homepage frame and adds the subject's profile, including his or her biographical data and a picture. Next, the student writes a blog entry about an important historic event from the subject's point of view. Then the child lists four important people in the subject's life and adds thumbnail pictures of each one. Finally, the child adds messages and comments about the blog topic between the subject and his or her friends.

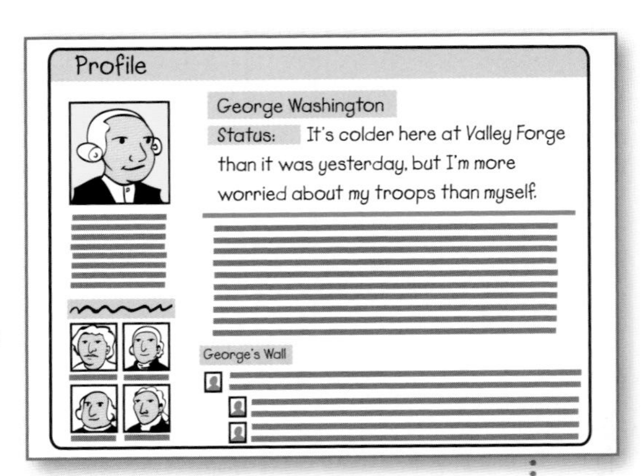

Terry Healy, Marlatt Elementary, Manhattan, KS

Name ____________________
Date ____________________

A Capital Comparison

____
state capital

Location within the state: ____________________
City size compared to other cities in the state: ____________________
Date the city was founded: ____________________
City population: ____________________
Important fact about the city: ____________________
____
Interesting fact about the city: ____________________
____
Nearby natural features: ____________________
____
Date the capitol building was built: ____________________
Important fact about the capitol: ____________________
____
Interesting fact about the capitol: ____________________
____

Washington, DC

Location within the country: ____________________
City size compared to other cities in the country: ____________________
Date the city was founded: ____________________
City population: ____________________
Important fact about the city: ____________________
____
Interesting fact about the city: ____________________
____
Nearby natural features: ____________________
____
Date the Capitol was built: ____________________
Important fact about the Capitol: ____________________
____
Interesting fact about the Capitol: ____________________
____

Note to the teacher: Use with “A Capital Comparison” on page 266.

EXPLORING Social Studies

Pin the Name on the State

U.S. geography

To prepare this anytime activity, post a laminated map of the United States that shows state outlines without names. Next, write each state's name on a paper strip and put the strips in a bag. Then have a student draw a strip, read the state's name aloud, locate the state on the map, and tape the strip in place. Repeat with several students and then check each strip's placement against a labeled U.S. map. Award a point to the class for each correctly named state. When the class earns a set number of points, celebrate with a class reward. After each session, peel the strips off the map and return them to the bag so they'll be ready for the next round!

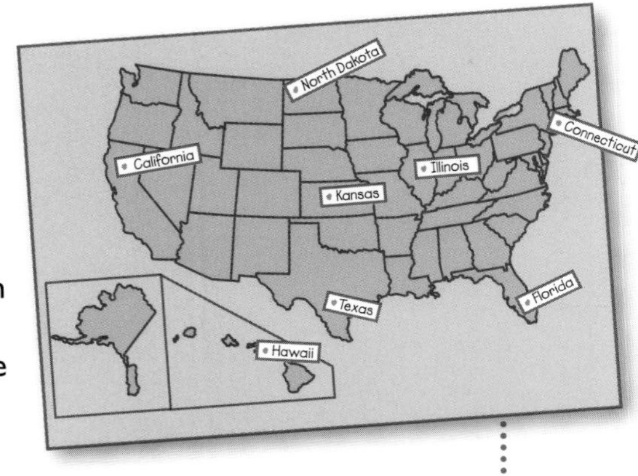

Karyn Karr, Cleveland School, Cedar Rapids, IA

Storyboard Learning

Government, legislation

Help students learn how a bill becomes a law by capitalizing on their love for comics. First, have each child draw a character named A. Bill on a sheet of unlined paper. Next, have the student research the steps through which a bill becomes a law. Then have the child fold a sheet of unlined paper in half three times and then unfold it to make eight sections. In each section, the student draws his character acting out one phase of the process. If desired, post students' work on a board titled "The Adventures of A. Bill on the Way to Becoming A. Law."

Teresa Vilfer-Snyder, Fredericktown Intermediate, Fredericktown, OH

Civil War Search

History

With this center, students go on a scavenger hunt to find facts about the Civil War. Make a copy of page 269 for every two students and provide access to materials such as a social studies text, encyclopedias, or nonfiction books about the Civil War. A pair of students searches the resources to name each item on the checklist. The partners record each fact and cite the resource they used. For every correct fact, the pair earns a point. Present the duo that earns the most points with a small reward.

adapted from an idea by Juli Engel, Flint, TX

Names ______
Date ______

Civil War

Civil War Scavenger Hunt

Shade the box next to each fact you find.
Then record the fact and your resource.

1. a slave who, after living in a free territory for four years, sued for his freedom ______ Source: ______
2. the name for a state that did not allow slavery ______ Source: ______
3. Speaker of the House in 1820 ______ Source: ______
4. the abolitionist who tried to lead a revolt at Harper's Ferry in 1859 ______ Source: ______
5. the man elected President of the United States in 1860 ______ Source: ______
6. to break away from the rest of the country ______ Source: ______
7. the first state that broke away from the rest of the country ______ Source: ______
8. the man chosen to be president of the Confederate States of America ______ Source: ______
9. Virginia, Arkansas, Tennessee, and North Carolina joined this ______ Source: ______
10. a war fought between regions of one nation ______ Source: ______
11. the first real battle of the Civil War fought July 21, 1861 ______ Source: ______
12. the Union General ______ Source: ______
13. the Confederate General ______ Source: ______
14. President Lincoln's official announcement that ended slavery in the Confederate states in 1862 ______ Source: ______
15. woman who went into Virginia battlefields to treat wounded soldiers ______ Source: ______
16. In 1865, General Grant accepted this from General Lee ______ Source: ______

Names ______________________________

Date ______________________________

CIVIL WAR SCAVENGER HUNT

Shade the box next to each fact you find.
Then record the fact and your resource.

1. a slave who, after living in a free territory for four years, sued for his freedom
   ______________________ Source: ______________________
2. the name for a state that did not allow slavery
   ______________________ Source: ______________________
3. Speaker of the House in 1820
   ______________________ Source: ______________________
4. the abolitionist who tried to lead a revolt at Harper's Ferry in 1859
   ______________________ Source: ______________________
5. the man elected President of the United States in 1860
   ______________________ Source: ______________________
6. to break away from the rest of the country
   ______________________ Source: ______________________
7. the first state that broke away from the rest of the country
   ______________________ Source: ______________________
8. Virginia, Arkansas, Tennessee, and North Carolina were among the states that joined this
   ______________________ Source: ______________________
9. the man chosen to be president of the Confederate States of America
   ______________________ Source: ______________________
10. a war fought between regions of one nation
    ______________________ Source: ______________________
11. the first real battle of the Civil War, fought July 21, 1861
    ______________________ Source: ______________________
12. the Union general who later became president
    ______________________ Source: ______________________
13. the Confederate general whose surrender led to the end of the Civil War
    ______________________ Source: ______________________
14. President Lincoln's official announcement to end slavery in the Confederate states
    ______________________ Source: ______________________
15. woman who went into Virginia battlefields to treat wounded soldiers
    ______________________ Source: ______________________
16. in 1865, General Grant accepted this from General Lee
    ______________________ Source: ______________________

Note to the teacher: Use with "Civil War Search" on page 268.

Name ______________________________

Date ____________________

A Noble Explorer

Juan Ponce de León, the Spanish explorer famous for discovering Florida, was trained to be a knight.

Legends say Ponce de León found Florida when he was looking for the Fountain of Youth. The idea of finding magic water probably was not what inspired Ponce de León. He wanted to find and settle new lands.

Juan Ponce de León was born around 1460. He became a page when he was young. As a page, Ponce de León was taught to read and write. He learned to value duty and honor. Ponce de León was trained to use weapons, ride horses, and hunt. He was prepared to become a knight and join the Spanish fight with the Moors.

When the Spanish defeated the Moors, Ponce de León sailed west. He set sail to help claim new land for Spain. Ponce de León landed on the island of Hispaniola in 1502. He led Spanish forces against the native people there. Then he helped settle part of the island. In 1508, Ponce de León explored the island of San Juan, which we know as Puerto Rico. He tried to find an island called Bimini in 1513, and that was when he found Florida.

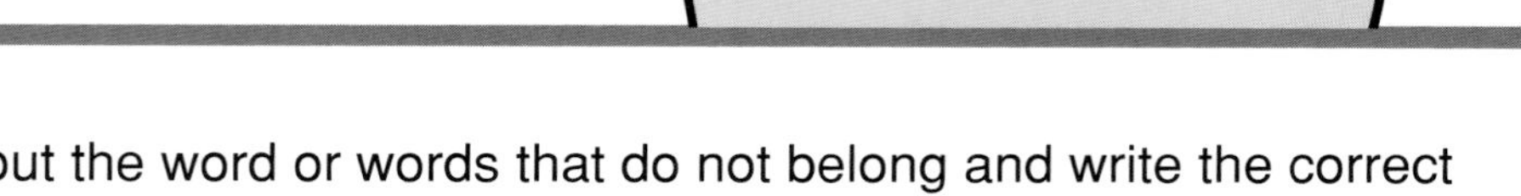

Make each sentence true. Cross out the word or words that do not belong and write the correct word or words above it.

1. Ponce de León was trained to be an explorer.
2. As a page, Ponce de León learned the value of youth and honor.
3. People used to think Ponce de León found a Fountain of Youth.
4. In his training to become a knight, Ponce de León learned to sail.
5. Ponce de León first landed on the island of Puerto Rico.
6. Ponce de León conquered Hispaniola in 1502.
7. Ponce de León is most famous for discovering the Fountain of Youth.
8. Ponce de León found Florida when he was looking for an island called Hispaniola.

Name ____________________

Sailing Across the Prairie

What was the greatest danger a pioneer faced? Would you guess it had to do with falling out of the wagon? Many of the people who were hurt or killed on the trip out west were run over by wagons.

From 1812 to 1866, about 500,000 *emigrants,* or pioneers, headed west. Most emigrants were families who were moving to California, Oregon, or Utah. Some were looking for land they could call their own. Others hoped to find opportunities they could not find in crowded cities. For pioneers, starting a new life would be worth the 2,000 mile trek. They loaded farm wagons with their clothes, some furniture, supplies, and tools to start new lives. To protect their goods, emigrants tied canvas covers over their wagons. Then they hitched their wagons to teams of mules or oxen, and they moved out.

The pioneers were heading into the frontier; there would not be many places where they could buy supplies or get help. They had to be prepared. The trip would take from four to six months.

Many emigrants joined wagon trains, groups of 50 to 100 wagons that traveled together. The wagon trains were led by scouts who knew the way. Making the trip with a group of other families provided friendship, safety, and help on the trail. As the covered wagons crossed the prairie, their billowing covers made the wagons look like ships sailing across the prairie. Before long, the wagons were nicknamed prairie schooners after the sailing ships that carried cargo.

Draw a line to match each sentence starter with the rest of its sentence.

1. When they joined a wagon train,	land they could call their own.
2. Another name for a pioneer	is an emigrant.
3. A wagon train's scout showed	pulled the covered wagons.
4. Many emigrants headed west to find	meant pioneers had to pack everything they would need.
5. Teams of oxen or mules	the emigrants where to go.
6. Traveling with a wagon train for up to six months	emigrants found friendship and support.

Bonus Box: Pioneer families often painted mottos or decorations on their wagon covers. If you and your family were pioneers, what might you paint on your cover? Draw a covered wagon to show your family's design.

Name ______________________________

Date ______________________

STANDING TALL

On average, 25 people visit the Washington Monument every five minutes!

The Washington Monument was built to honor George Washington's military leadership. In 1833, a group of people started raising money to build the monument. This group was called the Washington National Monument Society. The society chose a unique design. The monument was to be made in the shape of an obelisk like those in Egypt. This obelisk, though, would be much bigger.

On July 4, 1848, the building began. The cornerstone was laid using a trowel George Washington had used. He had used the trowel to lay the cornerstone of the U.S. Capitol.

Six years after it had started, construction of the Washington Monument stalled. The society ran out of money. Then the Civil War began. The monument stood unfinished, looking like a broken chimney. After the war, Congress voted to finish the project. On December 6, 1884, the Washington Monument was at long last complete.

Today, the Washington Monument is one of the most popular sites in Washington, DC. Visitors can ride an elevator to a viewing level near the top. From there, visitors can see for more than 30 miles.

MONUMENTAL FACTS

- An obelisk is a tall column with four sides and a pyramid-shaped top.
- The Washington Monument is 555 feet 5⅛ inches tall. At the base, each side is 55 feet 1½ inches long.
- Near the 150-foot level, the color changes. That's about how tall the monument was when construction stalled.
- Until 1888, visitors had to climb 897 stairs to get to the viewing level.
- An aluminum cap protects the monument's tip.

Shade the circle next to the best answer for questions 1–5. Then answer question 6 on another sheet of paper.

1. Which statement best fits the selection?
   - Ⓐ Construction of the Washington Monument was smooth.
   - Ⓑ Construction of the Washington Monument was discontinuous.
   - Ⓒ Construction of the Washington Monument was slow.
2. Why was the Washington Monument built?
   - Ⓐ to honor George Washington's presidency
   - Ⓑ as a tribute to the capitol city
   - Ⓒ to honor George Washington's military leadership
3. How many years elapsed between the laying of the cornerstone and the monument's completion?
   Ⓐ 36 years Ⓑ 35 years Ⓒ 48 years
4. According to the selection, which of the following is a reason construction stalled?
   - Ⓐ The top needed an aluminum cap for protection.
   - Ⓑ An elevator had to be built.
   - Ⓒ The society ran out of money.
5. In the sentence below, what does the word *cap* mean?
   An aluminum cap protects the monument's tip.
   - Ⓐ natural cover or top
   - Ⓑ something that protects a tip or end
   - Ⓒ container holding an explosive charge
6. Why do you think the Washington Monument is one of the most popular sites in Washington, DC? List three facts from the selection in your response.

Name ____

Date ______________________

THE FIRST ONE

In 1865, most people thought the transcontinental railroad would be the only railroad that would ever cross the continent.

The United States was expanding in the mid-1800s. People were moving west. To get there, they had to travel by wagon or by boat. There were no highways. Railroads went as far west as St. Louis, Missouri. Goods had to be shipped around the tip of South America to reach California.

Then, in 1862, Congress passed the Pacific Railroad Act. With this act, two railroad companies were hired to connect the east and west. They would build the first railroad to cross North America.

The Central Pacific Company started laying railroad track in Sacramento, California. They began in 1863. They followed the forty-second parallel, or 42° north latitude, moving east.

Two years later, the Union Pacific Company started laying the other half of the track. This company began in Omaha, Nebraska. Their track also followed the forty-second parallel, but they moved west.

Thousands of immigrants from China and Europe worked on the railroad. They worked with former Civil War soldiers, laying track at a record pace. The two tracks met in Promontory, Utah, on May 10, 1869. The United States had built the world's first transcontinental railroad.

KEY
—— transcontinental railroad
- - - - boat route

Shade the circle next to the best answer for questions 1–5.

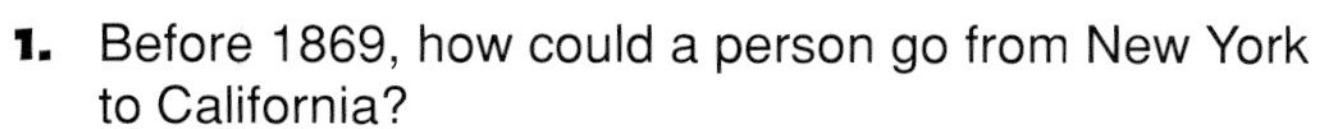

1. Before 1869, how could a person go from New York to California?
Ⓐ by wagon or train
Ⓑ by train
Ⓒ by wagon or boat

2. Which railroad company laid track moving from west to east?
Ⓐ Union Pacific Company
Ⓑ Central Pacific Company

3. Based on the selection, which inference can be made about the forty-second parallel?
Ⓐ It was the shortest, easiest path across the country.
Ⓑ It was halfway across the country.
Ⓒ It was a straight line between Omaha and Sacramento.

4. What is the meaning of the word *parallel* in the third paragraph?
Ⓐ having the same elements
Ⓑ line of latitude
Ⓒ to match

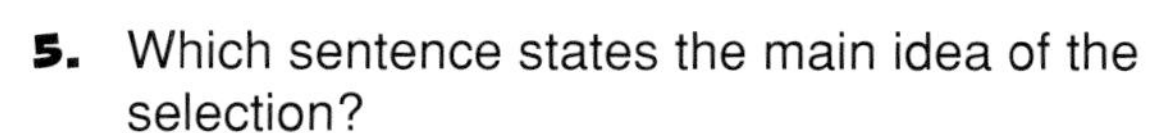

5. Which sentence states the main idea of the selection?
Ⓐ The United States was expanding in the mid-1800s.
Ⓑ The United States had built the world's first transcontinental railroad.
Ⓒ Then, in 1862, Congress passed the Pacific Railroad Act.

Answer questions 6-8 on another sheet of paper.

6. Why was the transcontinental railroad built? List two facts from the selection in your response.

7. Why do you think so many immigrants and former Civil War soldiers worked on the railroad?

8. The Panama Canal was completed in 1914. This waterway connected the Atlantic and Pacific oceans. How do you think the Panama Canal affected railroad travel across the United States?

Name ____________________

Date ____________________

An American Symbol

You can climb all the way to the Statue of Liberty's crown (522 steps), but the temperature inside can be up to 20° hotter than it is outside!

The Statue of Liberty was a gift from the people of France. It was a gift of friendship. The statue, titled *Liberty Enlightening the World,* was also a tribute to democratic government. The United States had just survived a civil war. It had proved that democracy could work. The statue was built to honor that achievement too.

The Statue of Liberty was designed by Frederic-Auguste Bartholdi. He modeled the statue's face after his mother's. The statue weighs 225 tons. Its copper "skin" is just $\frac{3}{32}$-inch thick. (That's about as thick as two pennies stacked together.) Its metal support frame was designed by Alexandre Gustave Eiffel. He also designed the Eiffel Tower.

Aunt Liberty, as the statue has been called, stands 151 feet 1 inch tall. The statue holds a tablet that is stamped with the date of the Declaration of Independence. The links of a broken chain at Aunt Liberty's feet represent freedom from slavery and *tyranny,* or unjust rule.

The Statue of Liberty has become a symbol of the United States. It stands for freedom for people throughout the world.

Unscramble the following important words from the selection. Then underline each one in the selection.

1. USATET _ _ _ _ _ _
2. EALTBT _ _ _ _ (_) _
3. TYBLREI _ _ _ (_) _ _ _
4. LOBMYS _ _ _ _ (_) _
5. SPEDFIIRNH (_) _ _ _ _ _ _ _ _ _
6. MOCDYCRAE _ _ (_) _ _ _ _ _ _
7. SDNEIDEG (_) _ _ _ _ _ _ _
8. ORCPEP _ _ _ _ _ _
9. BEUTTRI _ (_) _ _ _ _ _
10. YYNNART _ _ _ _ _ _ _

Rearrange the circled letters to name the quality for which the Statue of Liberty stands.

_ _ _ _ _ _ _

Bonus Box: Write each word's definition on another sheet of paper.

What Works for You?

What Works For You?

Classroom Routines and Procedures

To eliminate **pencil sharpening** in the middle of class, I place two cups, labeled as shown, near the pencil sharpener. When a student's pencil becomes dull, he puts it in the "To Be Sharpened" cup and takes a fresh pencil from the "Sharpened" cup. At the end of the day, I have a student Pencil Monitor sharpen the dull pencils and place them in the "Sharpened" cup. Our pencils are ready for the next day, and there are fewer classroom interruptions.

Vicky Fioravante, PS 16, Staten Island, NY

To get our day started, I use a **morning routine** called Shake, Rattle, and Roll. First, students "shake" out their bookbags and turn in any notes, library books, and homework assignments. For the "rattle" part, they sharpen their pencils for the day, use the bathroom, and get water. Finally, my students "roll" by starting on their morning work. I hang a poster in my classroom to remind students of this morning routine!

Robyn Gallagher, Richneck Elementary, Newport News, VA

All I do is count clothespins to take **lunch and attendance** counts! I write each student's name on a wooden clothespin. Then I write "Parking Lot" on one sentence strip, as shown, and laminate it along with three other strips. I tape the strips over the edge of an unused desk and use a wipe-off marker to label the blank strips with the day's lunch options. When a student arrives in the morning, she takes her clip out of the "Parking Lot" and places it on the correct lunch strip. After all students have arrived, I tally my lunch count and look at the "Parking Lot" to see who is absent.

Carrie L. Greene
Oakfield-Alabama Elementary
Oakfield, NY

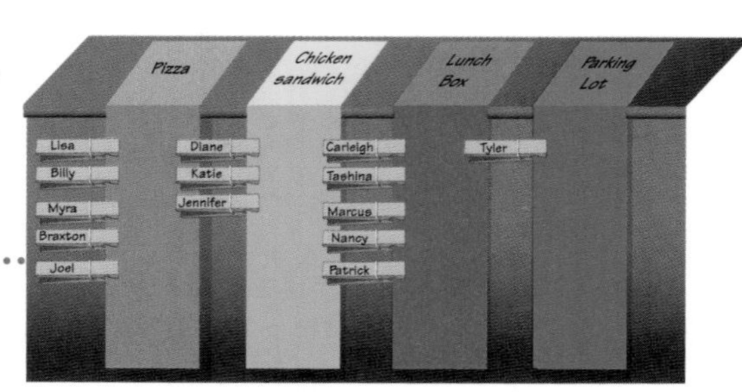

To keep my **hall passes** from being lost or germ infested, I use badges (patterns on page 277) that hang from my students' necks. I write my name and room number on the back of each badge, laminate it, and punch a hole in the top corners. Then I thread each hole with yarn and tie a knot at the end to create a necklace. These handy badges are sturdier and easier to see than handheld ones.

Anna Windsor, Arcola Elementary, Arcola, IN

For a list of fun classroom jobs, see page 278.

Hall Pass Patterns

Use with the last idea on page 276. To give students access to another location, fill in the blank on the sixth badge.

HELP WANTED!

Job	Description
Reporter	Carries notes to and from enrichment classes (gym, art, etc.)
Billboard Manager	Erases, cleans, and readies the board for the next day
Calendar Keeper	Keeps the class calendar up to date
Mail Carrier	Returns graded papers to students
Chef	Announces the day's lunch choices, and conducts and delivers the lunch count
Substitute Teacher	Collects and organizes missed assignments for absent students
Secretary	Records homework and notes from classroom meetings on the board
Broadcaster	Turns classroom television on and off
Travel Agent	Announces classroom activities and enrichment classes for the day
Electrician	Turns the classroom lights on and off
Cowpoke	Rounds up classmates at the end of recess
Gardener	Keeps classroom plants watered
Book Advertiser	Introduces new classroom books
Goalie	Transports and collects all class recess equipment
Veterinarian	Feeds classroom pets and cleans their habitats
Runner	Takes notes and messages to their destinations
Distributor	Passes out class materials to students
Librarian	Maintains the classroom library and checkout procedures
Census Taker	Conducts morning attendance and takes it to the office if necessary
Disc Jockey	Turns the CD player or radio on and off
Bird Feeder	Stocks the bird feeder and notifies the teacher when more birdseed is needed
Cleanup Crew	Two students who oversee the afternoon classroom cleanup
Operator	Answers the classroom telephone with appropriate manners
Tour Guide	Leads the class line to and from destinations
Pencil Patrol	Sharpens dull pencils at the end of the day
Tech Squad	Manages the computer station and shuts down the computers at the end of the day
Lunchroom Managers	Two students who wash lunchroom tables and sweep the floor
Human Resources Manager	Introduces new students or visitors to the class

Note to the teacher: Use this list as a guide when assigning classroom jobs.

What Works For You?

Building a Sense of Community

Let's reach for the stars!

To help my students **set common goals,** I guide them to create a class motto. Once students agree on the motto, I have each small group make a banner or poster for the classroom. Then I make strips with the motto and add one to each assignment, skill sheet, or newsletter before copying. That way our motto is printed on all the papers I give students and send home to parents!

Julia Alarie, Williston, VT

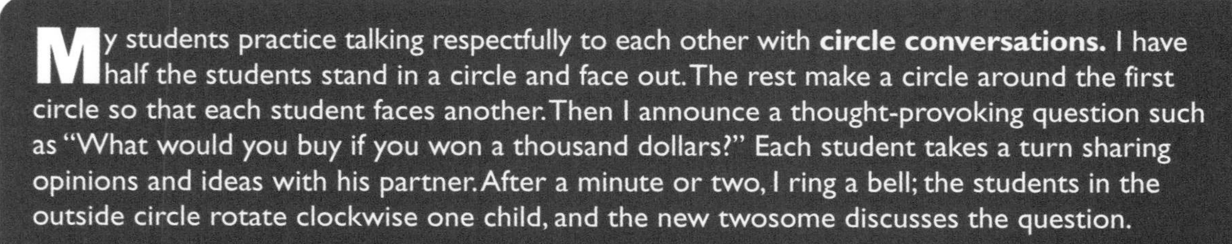

My students practice talking respectfully to each other with **circle conversations.** I have half the students stand in a circle and face out. The rest make a circle around the first circle so that each student faces another. Then I announce a thought-provoking question such as "What would you buy if you won a thousand dollars?" Each student takes a turn sharing opinions and ideas with his partner. After a minute or two, I ring a bell; the students in the outside circle rotate clockwise one child, and the new twosome discusses the question.

Richard McCoy, Laquey, MO

My students like to catch each other **succeeding in the classroom!** I keep a supply of fun tickets handy. Whenever a student notices another child's academic, behavioral, or interpersonal success, he fills out a ticket (see page 280) and drops it in a jar. At the end of the week, I pass out each ticket with a well-deserved pat on the back.

Catch Other People Succeeding!

On October 14, 2009,
date

I witnessed Caleb
classmate's name

helping Laura practice her spelling words.

Brendan
your name

C.O.P.S.

Kaitlin Tallman, O'Malley Elementary, Anchorage, AK

For a simple **class motivator,** I use a chain of large colored paper clips. Each time a student, a pair of students, a small group, or the class as a whole displays great behavior, I point it out. Then I add a paper clip to the chain. When the chain reaches the floor, we celebrate with a class reward, such as five extra minutes of recess or a popcorn party.

Marie E. Cecchini, West Dundee, IL

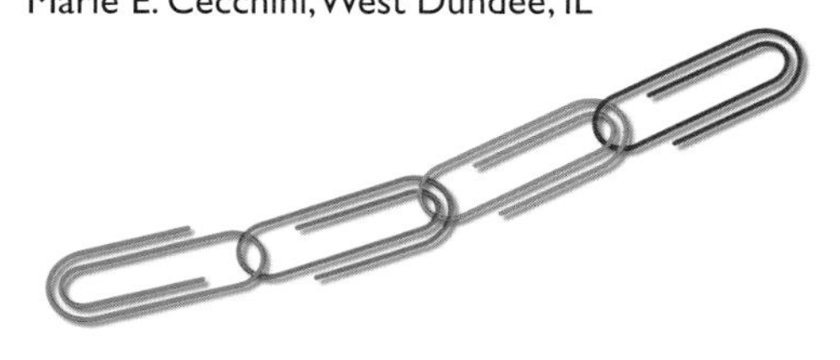

To remind students to listen to each other when they're working together, use a copy of the reminder cards on page 281.

Ticket Patterns

Use with the third idea on page 279.

Catch Other People Succeeding!

On ______________________________,
date

I witnessed ______________________
classmate's name

____

____

____

____

____

____
your name

C.O.P.S.

TEC44045

Catch Other People Succeeding!

On ______________________________,
date

I witnessed ______________________
classmate's name

____

____

____

____

____

____
your name

C.O.P.S.

TEC44045

Catch Other People Succeeding!

On ______________________________,
date

I witnessed ______________________
classmate's name

____

____

____

____

____

____
your name

C.O.P.S.

TEC44045

Catch Other People Succeeding!

On ______________________________,
date

I witnessed ______________________
classmate's name

____

____

____

____

____

____
your name

C.O.P.S.

TEC44045

Catch Other People Succeeding!

On ______________________________,
date

I witnessed ______________________
classmate's name

____

____

____

____

____

____
your name

C.O.P.S.

TEC44045

Catch Other People Succeeding!

On ______________________________,
date

I witnessed ______________________
classmate's name

____

____

____

____

____

____
your name

C.O.P.S.

TEC44045

Catch Other People Succeeding!

On ______________________________,
date

I witnessed ______________________
classmate's name

____

____

____

____

____

____
your name

C.O.P.S.

TEC44045

Catch Other People Succeeding!

On ______________________________,
date

I witnessed ______________________
classmate's name

____

____

____

____

____

____
your name

C.O.P.S.

TEC44045

Catch Other People Succeeding!

On ______________________________,
date

I witnessed ______________________
classmate's name

____

____

____

____

____

____
your name

C.O.P.S.

TEC44045

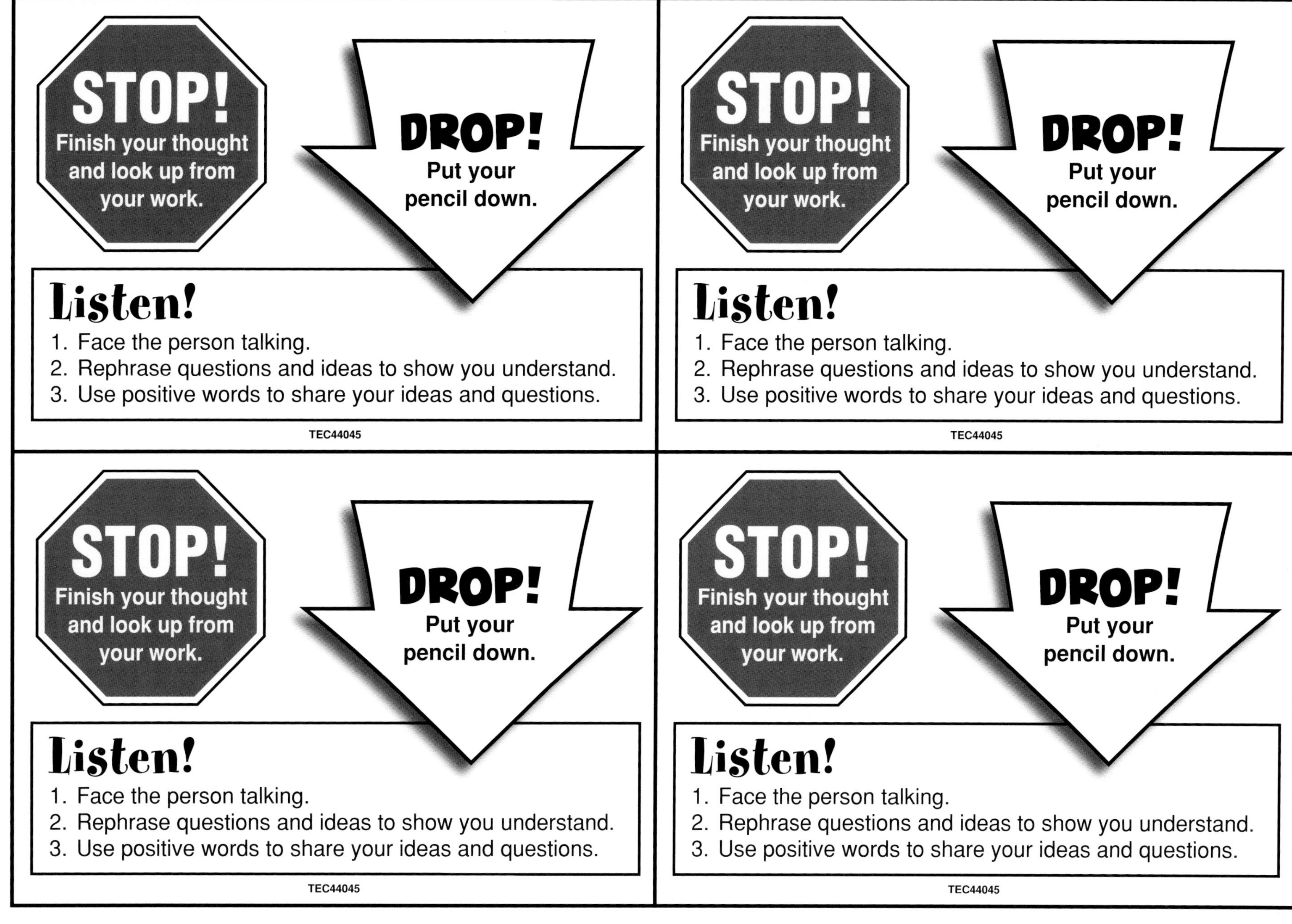

Note to the teacher: Encourage students to listen to and work respectfully with each other. Review the listening process above and have each child glue a copy of the reminder inside the cover of his journal.

What Works For You?

Maximizing Classroom Space

Check out the fun pocket labels for your catch-up wall on page 283.

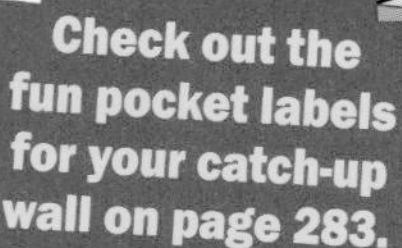

Instead of using shelf space for baskets or cubbies, I use an inexpensive vinyl shoe bag to keep track of students' unfinished work. I use magnetic clips to stick the bag to a metal door, label each pocket with a student's name, and title it "The Catch-Up Wall." Throughout the day, unfinished assignments go in students' pockets. Each student knows he is responsible for taking any work in his pocket home that night and bringing it back finished in the morning.

Virginia Zeletski, Whispering Pines Elementary, Boca Raton, FL

I tape charts and posters that I use regularly to my pull-down projector screen. When I don't need the visual aids, I just roll them up with the screen. The information is there when I need it and gone when I don't!

Lisa Borge, North Caldwell Schools, North Caldwell, NJ

To expand limited shelf space in my classroom, I use an inexpensive undershelf basket from the hardware store. The basket slides easily over any shelf and provides extra space for papers or books.

Dawn Unger, Arnett C. Lines Elementary, Barrington, IL

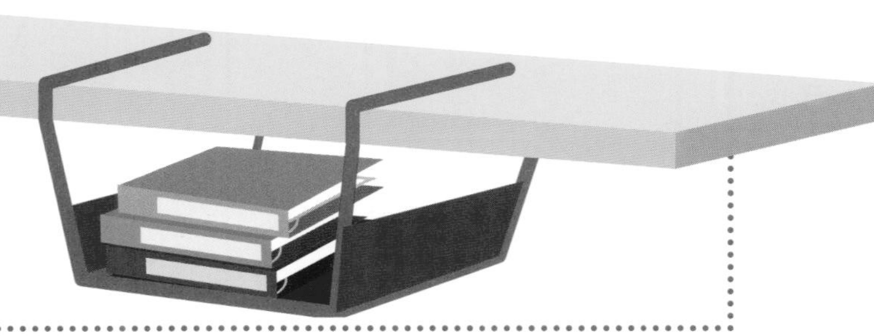

I post laminated posters on my whiteboard using magnetic strips. This allows me to easily arrange the posters and change them in a snap! When I teach a lesson in another classroom, I simply grab the posters I need and some magnetic strips, and I'm ready to teach!

Samantha Call
Father Anglim Academy
Fort Myers, FL

Motivate students to keep your classroom neat and tidy with the Clutter Buster Awards on page 284.

Pocket Labels

Use with the first idea on page 282.

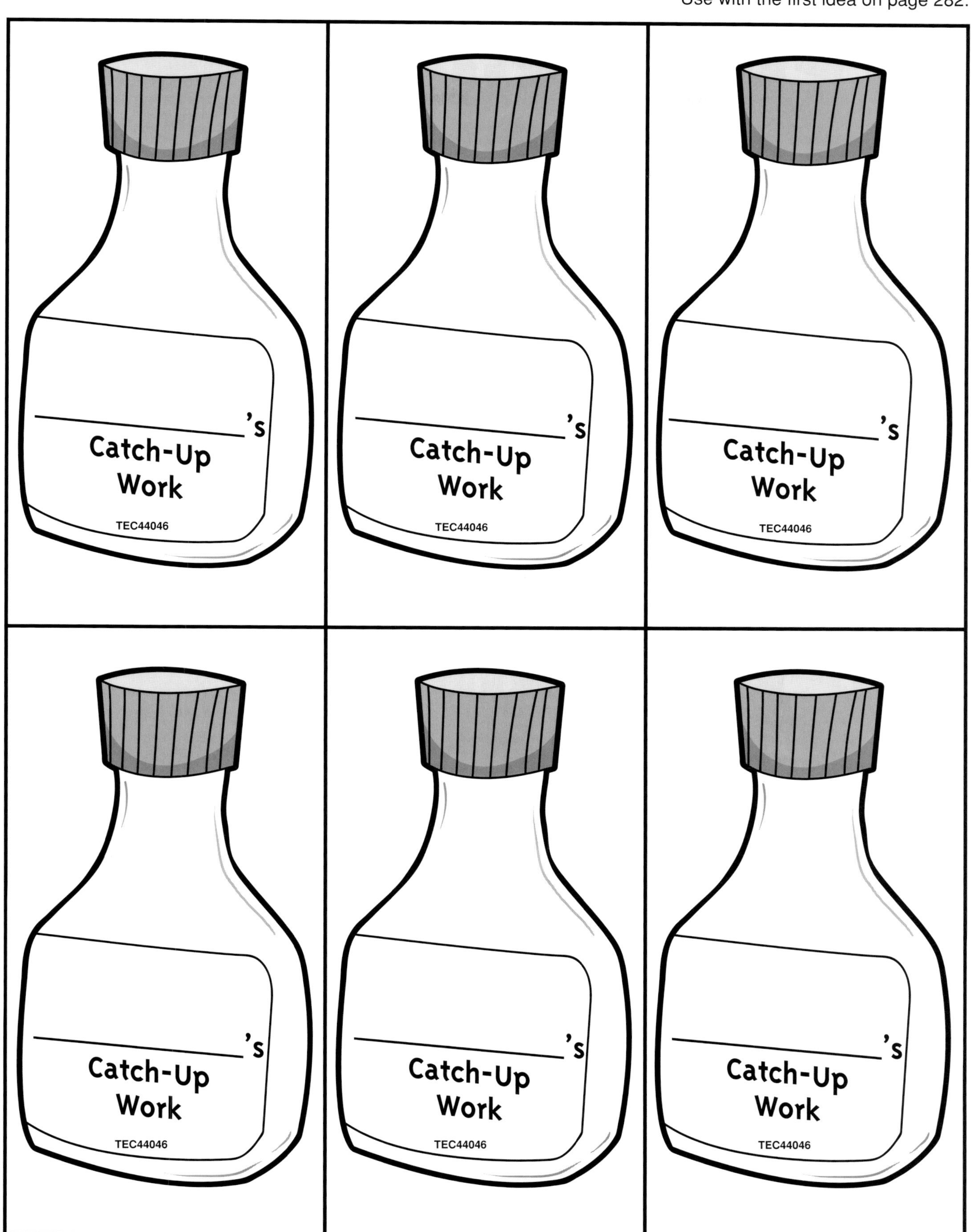

Award Patterns

Present awards to students who keep their desks or work spaces tidy.

Management Tips & Timesavers

Management Tips and Timesavers

VIP of the Day

For an easy alternative to a weekly helper job chart, designate a **personal assistant** each day. Explain that this student becomes the line leader, messenger, paper passer, etc. At the end of the day, announce the next day's helper by writing that child's name on a special wipe-off poster. Once every student has been the VIP, rotate through your class list again. If desired, grant the VIP extra privileges, such as selecting which class review game to play or receiving extra computer time.

Renee Guzak, St. Rose of Lima, Buffalo, NY

Timesaving Bulletin Boards

Looking for colorful, nonfading backgrounds for your **displays?** Buy inexpensive plastic rectangular tablecloths and trim them to fit your boards' dimensions. These durable plastic sheets can stay up all year and are reusable!

Kelly Melchi and Stephanie Ripoli
St. Laurence Catholic School, Elgin, IL

Borrowing Center

Keep students' desks less cluttered by storing shared **classroom supplies** in labeled, stackable plastic drawers. When a child needs a glue stick, a ruler, scissors, or a marker to complete an assignment, he knows just where to get (and return) the item.

Vicky Fioravante, P.S. 16, Staten Island, NY

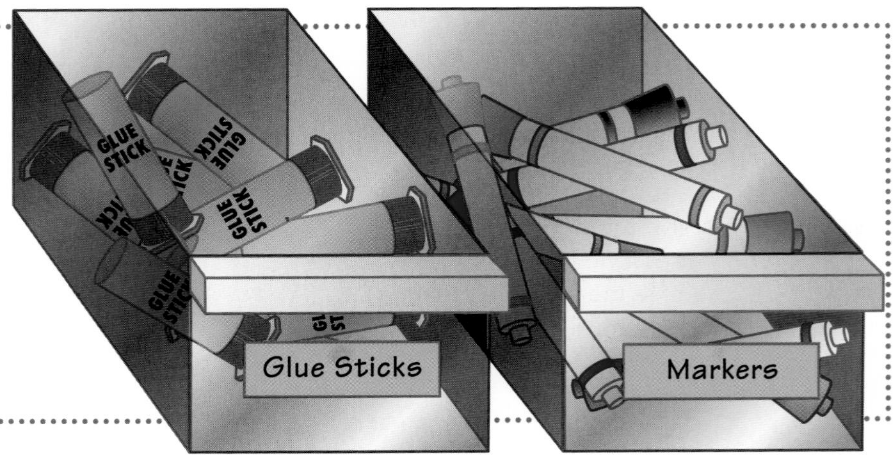

Management Tips and Timesavers

Homework? Check!

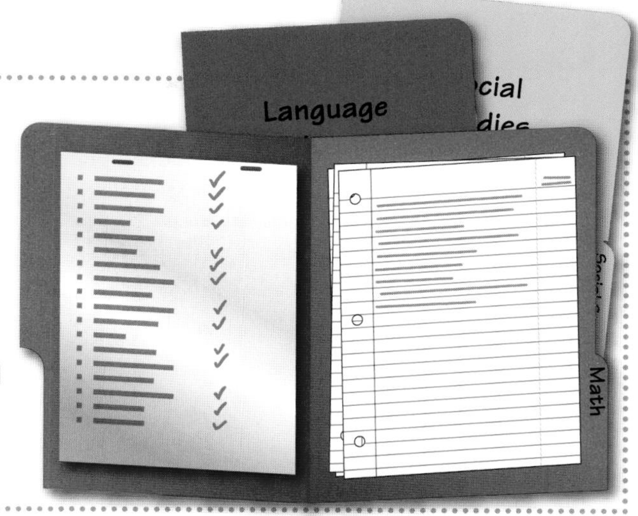

Here's a no-fuss idea for **collecting homework.** Create a folder for each subject and staple a laminated class list inside. Then, each morning, pass around the room a wipe-off marker and the folders for the subjects that have homework due. Each student who has completed his homework slips it in the appropriate folder, puts a check mark next to his name, and passes the folder and marker to the next student. Once the folders are returned, you can tell in an instant who turned in which assignments!

Renee Silliman, Spring Shadows Elementary, Houston, TX

A Parking Lot

Keep track of **class materials** with this simple tip! Place items such as staplers, hole punchers, and calculators in a central location called the parking lot. Then label each item's parking spot. At the end of the day, take a quick look at the parking lot and remind students to return any missing materials.

Diane Woodford, Covington Elementary, South Sioux City, NE

Absentee Assignments

Want a simple solution for keeping track of work for **absent students?** Try this! Keep a supply of the "While you were 'ooooout'" forms from page 288 handy. When you take attendance, label a slip for each absent student. Next, give the slip to another student and have him record the day's assignments for the missing classmate. At the end of the day, have the student return the slip. Cut off the coupon at the bottom, fill it in, and give it to the helper to thank him for his diligent work. Then tape the completed slip to the absent student's desk.

Amy Satkoski, Orchard Park Elementary, Indianapolis, IN

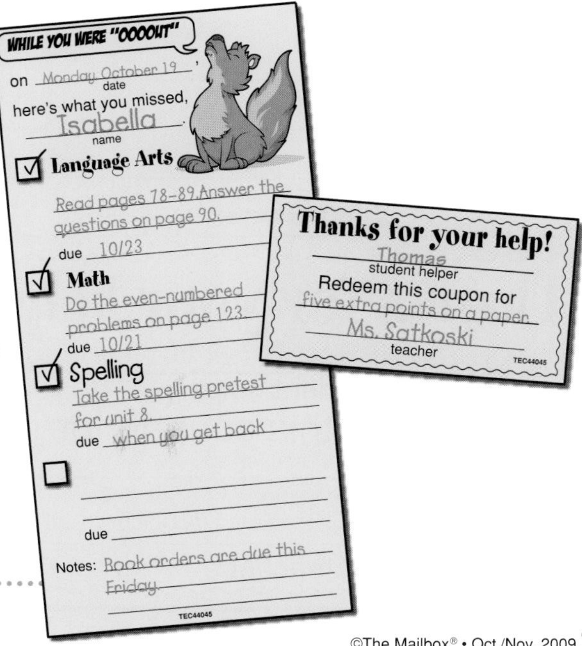

WHILE YOU WERE "OOOOUT"

on Monday, October 19,
date
here's what you missed,
Isabella.
name

☑ Language Arts
Read pages 78–89. Answer the questions on page 90.
due 10/23

☑ Math
Do the even-numbered problems on page 123.
due 10/21

☑ Spelling
Take the spelling pretest for unit 8.
due when you get back

☐
due

Notes: Book orders are due this Friday.

TEC44045

Thanks for your help!
Thomas
student helper
Redeem this coupon for
five extra points on a paper.
Ms. Satkoski
teacher
TEC44045

Absentee Assignment Slips

Use with "Absentee Assignments" on page 287.

WHILE YOU WERE "OOOOUT"

on ______________________,
date

here's what you missed,

______________________.
name

☐ **Language Arts**

____

____

due ______________________

☐ **Math**

____

____

due ______________________

☐

____

____

due ______________________

☐

____

____

due ______________________

Notes: ______________________

____

____

TEC44045

Thanks for your help!

____
student helper

Redeem this coupon for

____

____
teacher

TEC44045

WHILE YOU WERE "OOOOUT"

on ______________________,
date

here's what you missed,

______________________.
name

☐ **Language Arts**

____

____

due ______________________

☐ **Math**

____

____

due ______________________

☐

____

____

due ______________________

☐

____

____

due ______________________

Notes: ______________________

____

____

TEC44045

Thanks for your help!

____
student helper

Redeem this coupon for

____

____
teacher

TEC44045

Management Tips and Timesavers

A Bit More Practice

To help **early finishers** keep their skills sharp, make an extra copy of each reproducible you assign. Then put the extra page in a plastic sleeve along with a copy of the answer key. When a student finishes an assignment early, he studies the plastic-sleeved pages, chooses a topic or skill he needs to practice, and completes the page using a wipe-off marker. The child checks his work against the answer key, wipes the page clean, and takes another page as time allows.

adapted from ideas by Susan Appleton, Grove Park Elementary, Danville, VA, and Teresa Vilfer-Snyder, Fredericktown Intermediate, Fredericktown, OH

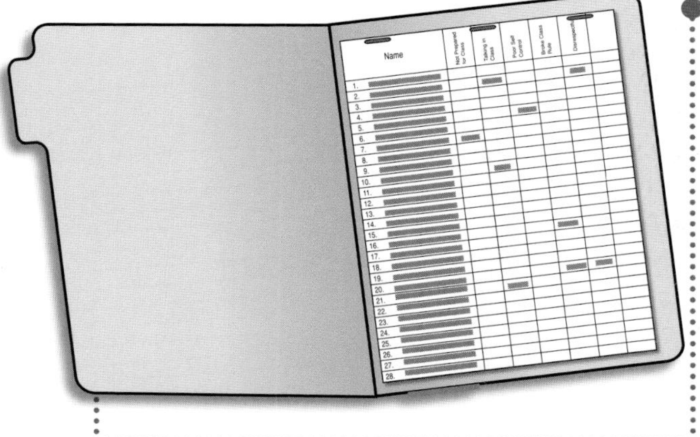

Class Conduct

Need to keep track of **students' behavior** when they change classes? Have each teacher staple a copy of her class list inside a folder and label the list with typical behavior concerns. When students change classes, each teacher hands her class's folder to the next teacher. If a student misbehaves during the class, the teacher initials and dates the appropriate column beside the child's name. At the end of the day, each teacher has a log of student behavior, which will come in handy for parent conferences or at report card time.

Sandy Fowler, High Point Christian Academy, High Point, NC

Efficiency Experts

Here's a tip that motivates students to **work quietly in groups.** Declare a daily contest by challenging each group of students to work more efficiently than the rest of the groups in the class. At the end of each day, announce the winning team, pointing out their positive behaviors, such as staying on task and keeping unnecessary talking to a minimum. Give each group member a small prize, such as a free homework pass, and then repeat the contest each day for a week or two. As student performance improves, increase the length of time between awards until you can count on first-rate group work!

Teresa Vilfer-Snyder

You Deserve a Break!
Pass—Good
Free Homework Excuse!
One Homework Assignment—Excused

Management Tips and Timesavers

Next!

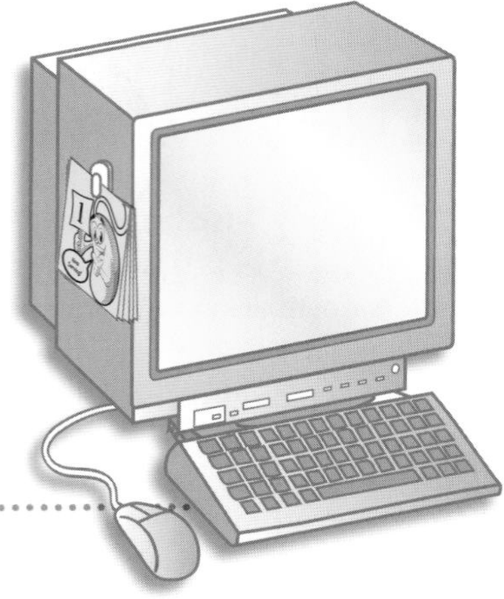

To manage students' **computer use,** stick a self-adhesive plastic hook on the side of each classroom computer. Next, copy and cut apart a different-colored set of number cards from page 291 for each computer. Then laminate and hole-punch the cards and hang a set from each hook. When a student is ready to use a computer, have him take a number card. For each computer, write a "1" on the board and have the student with that number card use the computer. When the child's time is up, he erases the "1" and writes a "2" on the board to let the student with that card know it's her turn.

Earning Kernels

This simple **reward system** will have students demonstrating good behavior all day long! Designate a small jar as your class behavior jar. Each time you catch a student being good, give her several uncooked kernels of popcorn to drop in the jar. When the jar is full, reward the class with a popcorn party or other incentive, such as a homework pass.

Marie E. Cecchini, West Dundee, IL

Fold and Return

Looking for an easy way to keep track of which **graded papers you've entered in your grade book?** After you record a student's grade, fold the graded paper in half vertically with the student's name on the outside. This trick makes it easy to return the papers to students too.

Louella Nygaard, Cordova, AK

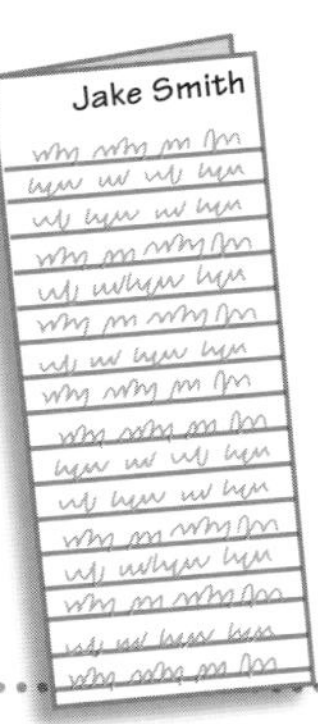

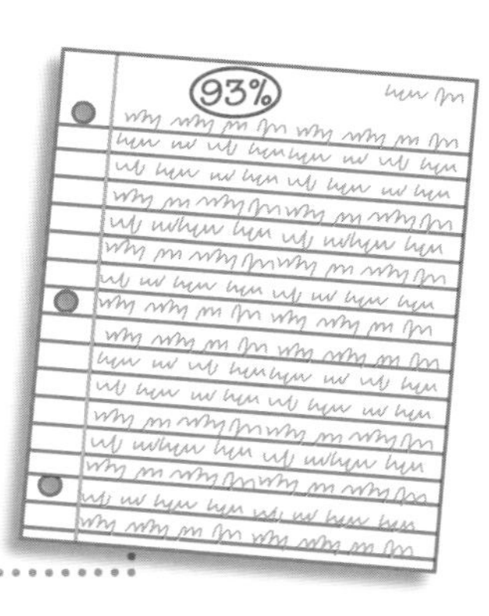

Just an Email Away!

Here's a tip for using email to stay in touch with parents even if they don't have email access! Gather parents' email addresses and create a group list that includes your email address. Then, when you email a note to the list and the message arrives in your inbox, print a hard copy for each parent who doesn't have email access and send the note home with her child.

Terry Healy, Marlatt Elementary, Manhattan, KS

Letters Made Easy

For **bulletin board letters** that are easy to make, use, and store, write each letter on a quarter sheet of colorful construction paper and laminate it. To title a bulletin board, simply post the letters you need. Then, for easy storage, file each set of letters in a report card–size envelope labeled with the title.

Christy Zepeda, Bradley Elementary, Watsonville, CA

Computer Cards

Use with "Next!" on page 290.

Management Tips and Timesavers

Breathe!

Post this acrostic poem to give students **stress-relieving tips** that will help them be rested and ready for standardized tests. Lead students to choral-read the poem with you and discuss the tips. Then have each child copy the poem on an index card, add a simple border, and take the card home to share with her parents. Follow up by rereading the poem with students the day before each testing session.

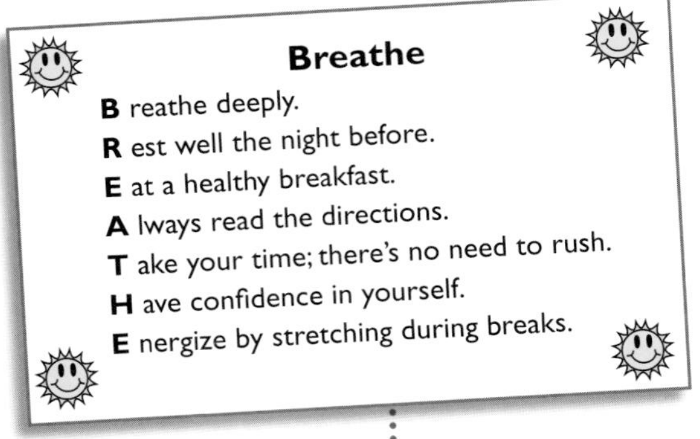
Breathe

B reathe deeply.
R est well the night before.
E at a healthy breakfast.
A lways read the directions.
T ake your time; there's no need to rush.
H ave confidence in yourself.
E nergize by stretching during breaks.

Susan Heywood, Benefield Elementary, Lawrenceville, GA

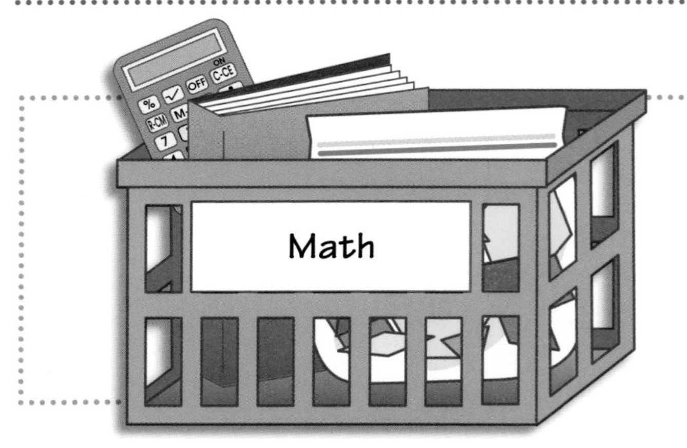

Baskets to Keep Them Busy

Need to keep **early finishers** on task? Label a tub or basket with each core subject you teach. Then fill each container with related practice pages, center activities, puzzles, books, and magazines. When a student finishes an assignment early, he simply chooses an activity and keeps on learning.

Minding the Master

Want to make sure you don't accidentally give a student your **master copy** of a skill sheet? Glue the answer key to its back. The thickness of the glued pages will remind you not to hand out the master, and you won't lose track of the key either!

Sally Dooley, Sunnycrest Elementary, Lake Stevens, WA

Sticky-Note Signal

To **keep students from interrupting group work** or individual conferences, have each child put a colorful sticky note in his agenda or journal. When the child needs help, he places the note at the top of his desk and continues working. With a quick glance, you can see who needs assistance. After you help the student, he returns the note to his journal and gets right back to work.

Lesanne Bohannon, Roosevelt Elementary, Nennah, WI

An Organizer That's Not All Wet!

Looking for a **space-saving** idea for setting up a center? Try this! Stock an inexpensive shower caddy with the center's materials. Then hang the caddy on a doorknob or hook. The center is accessible, you don't need an extra table or shelf, and it's easy to rotate different center materials in and out of the caddy!

Patricia D. Rodriguez, Bruni Elementary, Laredo, TX

Management Tips and Timesavers

Still Working?

Minimize interruptions during testing with this simple signal. Have each student fold and tape together a copy of the desk plate pattern from page 294. Then have the child position the desk plate on his desk to show his current status. With a quick glance, you'll see who's working, who needs help, and who's finished.

Colleen Dabney, Williamsburg, VA

Organized in a Zip!

Looking for a way to **organize and store your bulletin board items?** Try using extra large resealable plastic bags! For each bulletin board you use, put the letters and small shapes inside a sandwich-size bag and then store the bag and any larger items in an extra large bag. Label the bag with the topic or theme and stack or stand the bags in a cupboard. When it's time to put up a bulletin board, simply retrieve the bag you need and you're ready to decorate!

Diane Margolias, Arrowhead Elementary, Phoenix, AZ

Line Up!

Make **transition time** learning time! When you call a student to line up, first pose a question about a state capital, multiplication fact, vocabulary word, or spelling word. Have the child answer and get in line if she's correct. Students will review important skills while listening quietly for their names to be called.

Stephanie Affinito, Queensbury, NY

Marco! Polo!

Turn to everyone's favorite swimming pool game instead of clapping your hands to **grab your students' attention.** When you call out, "Marco," have your class answer, "Polo." You won't believe how quickly students will respond!

Michelle Berry, Leicester Elementary, Leicester, NC

Marco!

On the Hunt!

Turn **end-of-the-day cleanup** into a game! Secretly select a piece of trash on the floor or a classroom object that is out of place. Then tell students that you have identified a mystery object and the child who finds the item and puts it where it belongs will earn a small prize. Your classroom will be neat and tidy in no time!

Kristin Donahue, J. D. Mills Elementary, Austin, TX

Desk Plate Pattern

Use with "Still Working?" on page 293.

CAUTION:
WORK IN PROGRESS!

Tab

Our Readers Write

Slide Show Intro

I **introduce myself** to my new class with a simple computer slideshow that includes slides of my family, my favorite books, and what I did over the summer. For the last slide, I show students a picture of myself when I was their age. Then I have each student create a poster that includes the same information about himself to share with the class.

Rachel Pepe, River Place Elementary, Austin, TX

Nifty Notes

To take note of **student behavior,** I write each child's name at the top of a large index card. Throughout the grading period, I write the student's strengths on the front of his card and areas for improvement on the back. During parent conferences, I use the card as a reference and then send it home with the parents as a reminder of what we discussed.

Sister Mary Guadalupe, St. Joseph School, Lincoln, NE

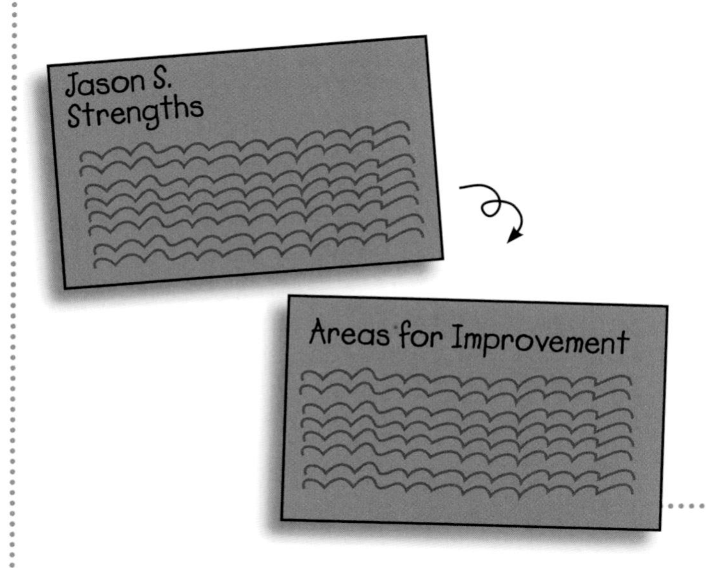

Name It!

To help my students tell the difference between the **place value** and the value of a digit, I have them respond aloud to statements like the ones shown. Then I explain that a digit's place value is always a word while the digit's value is always a number.

Meg Dowd, Cedar Hill Elementary, Lawrenceville, GA

Name a place to see animals. *(zoo, pet store, etc.)*
Name a place to exercise. *(park, gym, etc.)*
Name a place to swim. *(pool, lake, etc.)*
Every answer is a word. Every digit's place value is a word too.

Name the value of a CD. *(about $15.00)*
Name the value of a candy bar. *(about $1.00)*
Name the value of a video game. *(about $50.00)*
Every answer is a number. Every digit's value is a number too.

Handwriting Helper

I use this tasty saying to remind my students before they start to write that the **notebook paper** holes should be on the left side.

Allison Cohen, Happy Hollow Elementary, Wayland, MA

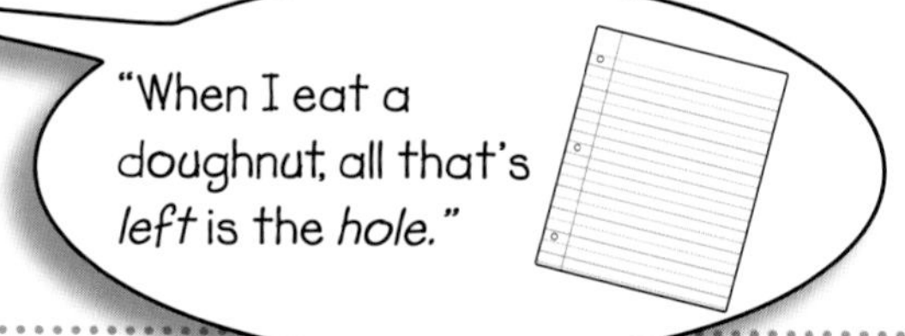

As All Around!

When my students behave like A-plus kids, I give each child a die-cut *A* as a **reward.** At the end of the week, I invite each student to exchange his *A*s for a fun treat.

adapted from an idea by Sandy Wells, John Paul II Catholic School, Gillette, WY

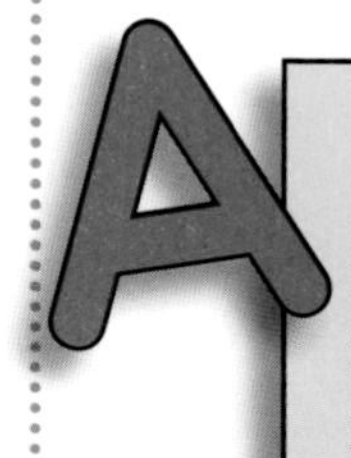

A+ Treats

5 *A*s = 15 minutes extra free time

10 *A*s = sit by a friend for a day

15 *A*s = lunch in the classroom

20 *A*s = homework pass

Singing Values

Place value practice is music to my students' ears when I have them sing this song to the tune of the theme song from *The Addams Family.* It helps students remember the order of numbers as well as how to read a number.

Mindy Fulmer, Lakeview Elementary, Little Elm, TX

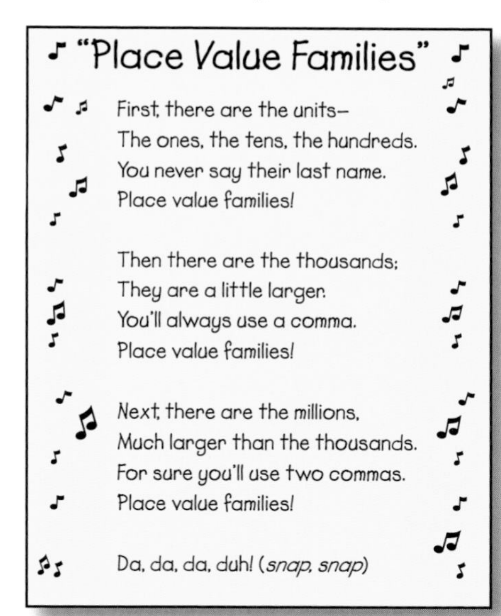

"Place Value Families"

First, there are the units—
The ones, the tens, the hundreds.
You never say their last name.
Place value families!

Then there are the thousands;
They are a little larger.
You'll always use a comma.
Place value families!

Next, there are the millions,
Much larger than the thousands.
For sure you'll use two commas.
Place value families!

Da, da, da, duh! (*snap, snap*)

The *I*s Have It

When my students have trouble remembering to **capitalize the pronoun *I*,** I give them a "black *I*." I simply use a black marker to write a capital *I* over each lowercase *i* on their papers. With this simple tip, my students laugh and learn at the same time.

Bonnie B. Boyd, Coquina Elementary, Titusville, FL

This year I would like to learn how to multiply large numbers. I would also like to learn how to do a fun science experiment.

Earth in 3-D

I have each small group of students use a foam ball and tempera paint to make its own **globe model** of Earth. Then I have them cut away a section of the ball and paint Earth's inner layers. Groups use their models throughout the year to learn everything from the continents to lines of latitude and longitude!

Janelle Biskup, Saint Stephen's Episcopal School, San Jose, CA

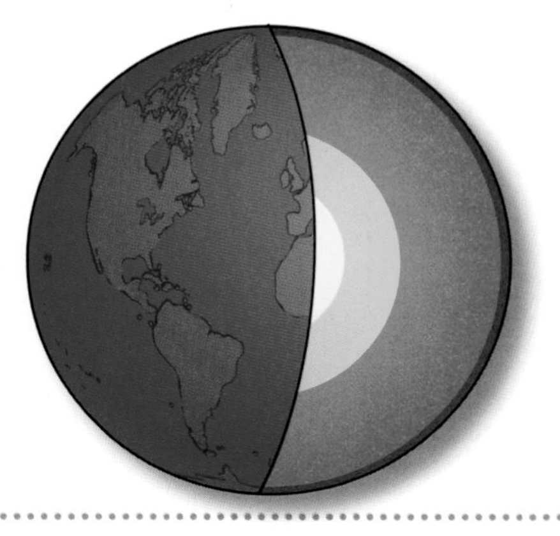

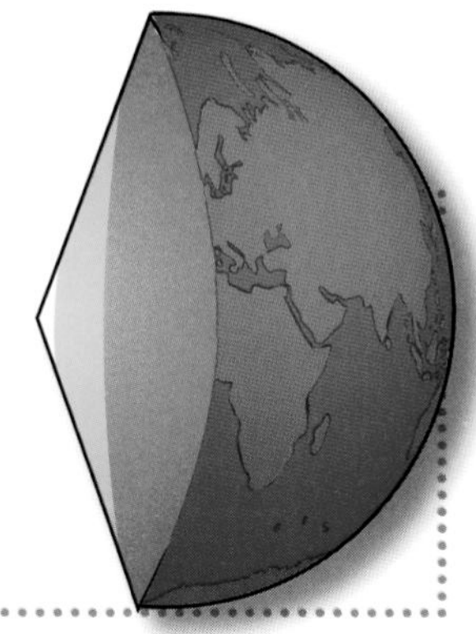

Prime and Composite Tic-Tac-Toe

For a quick review of **prime and composite numbers,** I have student pairs play tic-tac-toe. To play, each student chooses a different-colored marker. Player One writes a composite number on a square; then Player Two writes a prime number. The students continue taking turns until one gets three squares in a row, in a column, or diagonally. Once a winner has been declared, I have students switch places and repeat the game. I also use this game to review common and proper nouns or states and their capitals!

Linda Messner, Wilson Christian Academy, West Mifflin, PA

12	40	24
3	19	6
16	23	7

Reinforcing Covers

To prolong the lives of **magazines** my students love to read, I attach clear Con-Tact covering to the front and back covers. Now our classroom magazines last much longer, ensuring that all students have a chance to read them.

Camille Foreman, Red Bank Middle School, Red Bank, NJ

Put It to Music!

To help my students remember the **helping verbs**, we sing the song below. When former students visit, they tell me how much this song helped them even throughout high school!

Mary Beth Endicott, St. Joseph Elementary, Crescent Springs, KY

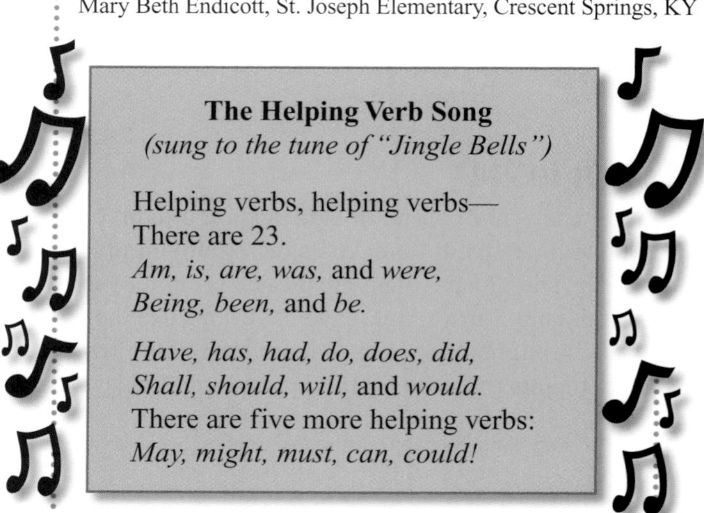

The Helping Verb Song
(sung to the tune of "Jingle Bells")

Helping verbs, helping verbs—
There are 23.
Am, is, are, was, and *were,*
Being, been, and *be.*

Have, has, had, do, does, did,
Shall, should, will, and *would.*
There are five more helping verbs:
May, might, must, can, could!

Lines of Noodles

To help my students learn **parallel, perpendicular, and intersecting lines,** we have fun with uncooked spaghetti noodles. After reviewing each type of line, I ask students to glue noodle models to construction paper and label each example. This activity is simple and can easily be used at a center.

Brooke Beverly, Dudley Elementary, Dudley, MA

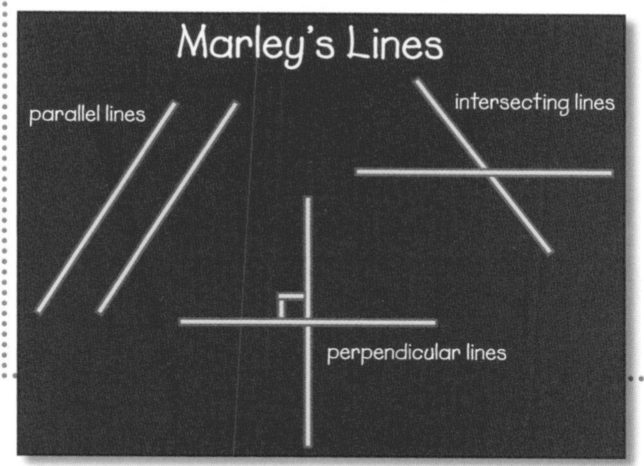

Pretty Cool Pointer

I use this one-of-a-kind **pointer,** made by one of my students, to keep my class's attention during lessons at the whiteboard. To make the pointer, fill a winter glove with pillow stuffing. Next, insert the shaft from an old golf club into the index finger of the glove and hot-glue the thumb and remaining three fingers down so it resembles a pointing hand. Finally, hot-glue the wrist of the glove to the shaft and tie the outside with ribbon. This inexpensive pointer far exceeds any store-bought one!

Belinda Anthony, Chukker Creek Elementary, Aiken, SC

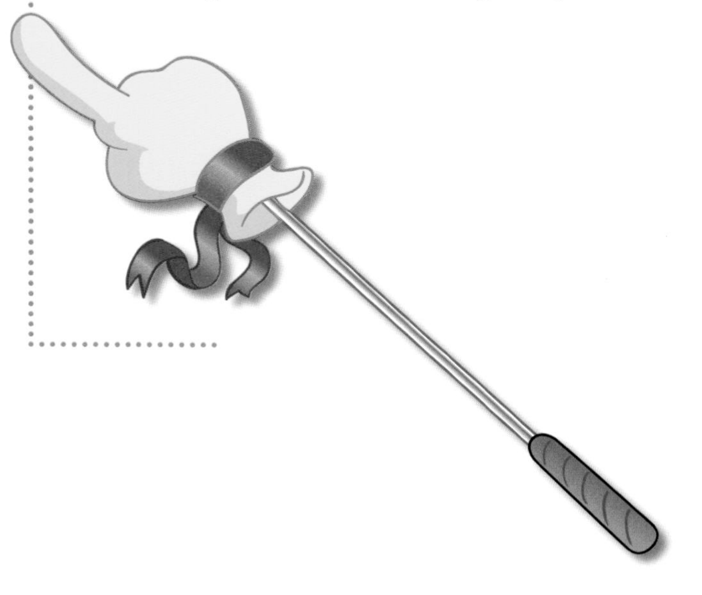

Books on Tape

This activity helps my students build reading **fluency** while providing learning materials for younger students. I have each student select a picture book, practice reading it until he is fluent, and then record himself reading the story. I also ask each student to attach a picture of himself to the cassette box. Then we place a copy of the book and the tape in a bag and donate it to our adopted kindergarten class. My students love this service project, and they have fun while working on their reading skills!

Carla Gay, Academy for Academic Excellence, Apple Valley, CA

Bookmarks From Borders

I make **bookmarks** from unused bulletin board borders by cutting them into rectangles and laminating them. Then I punch a hole in one end and tie it with a matching ribbon. My students can't wait to see the newest choices and choose their bookmarks.

Jennifer Harris, Live Oak Elementary, Castaic, CA

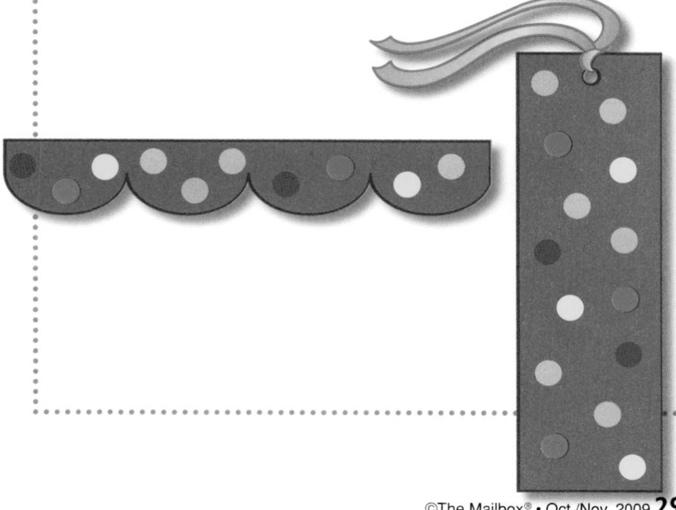

Guide Words Made Easy

I teach my students a simple strategy to determine which words fall between a pair of **guide words.** First, I have each student write the entry word choices in alphabetical order, skipping lines. Next, I ask the child to add the guide words beside the list alphabetically as shown. Then I have him circle the word or words that fall between the guide words.

Candy Schrack, Greenvale Elementary, Oklahoma City, OK

Long Division Dance

I introduce **long division** to my students with this simple cheer! First we chant, "Divide," and we each angle both arms together diagonally in front of our bodies. Next, we say, "Multiply," and make *X*s with our arms. Then we shout, "Subtract," and we each fold both arms in front of our bodies with fingertips touching to make a straight line. Next, we say, "Bring down," and bend over to touch the floor. Finally, we chant, "Again!" and jump up to start all over.

Alethea Setser, The O'Quinn School, James Island, SC

This Book Rates

My students love to rate our read-alouds and then analyze the **statistics.** After we finish a book, I have each student rate it on a scale of one star (not very good) to five stars (absolutely fantastic). I record the ratings on the board and guide students to calculate the mean, median, mode, and range of their numerical ratings. Then I post the book's title and statistics. At the end of the year, we compare all the statistics and award the book with the highest median "The Berris Prize" for the best read-aloud.

Debbie Berris, Poinciana Day School, West Palm Beach, FL

The BFG by Roald Dahl
Mean = 4.3
Median = 4
Mode = 4
Range = 2

Mark the Spot

For **inexpensive game pieces and counters,** I use pieces from puzzles that are no longer complete and puzzles I find on clearance. I put the pieces in small plastic bags for every two or three students and keep them handy for everyday use!

Kathryn Tucker, Bess Streeter Aldrich Elementary, Omaha, NE

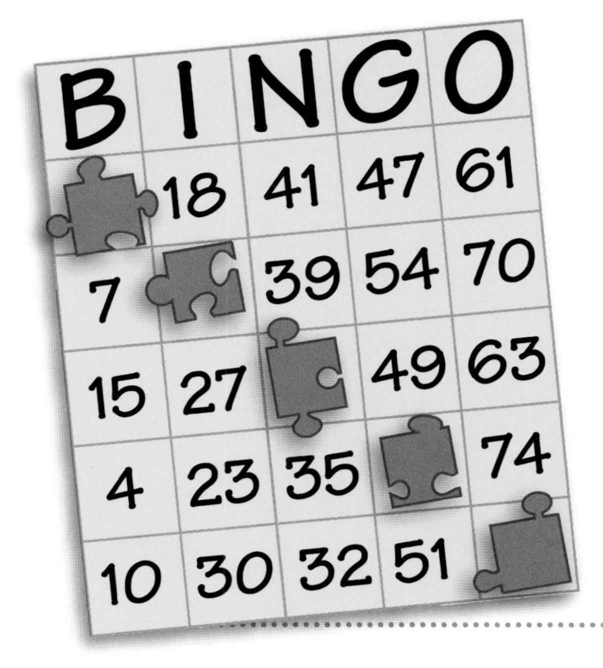

It's in the Name

To help my students remember what **parallel lines** are, I write the word *parallel* on the board and circle the two *l*'s. Then I show my students that parallel lines continue beside each other and never meet.

Jody Mineart, West Burlington Elementary, West Burlington, IA

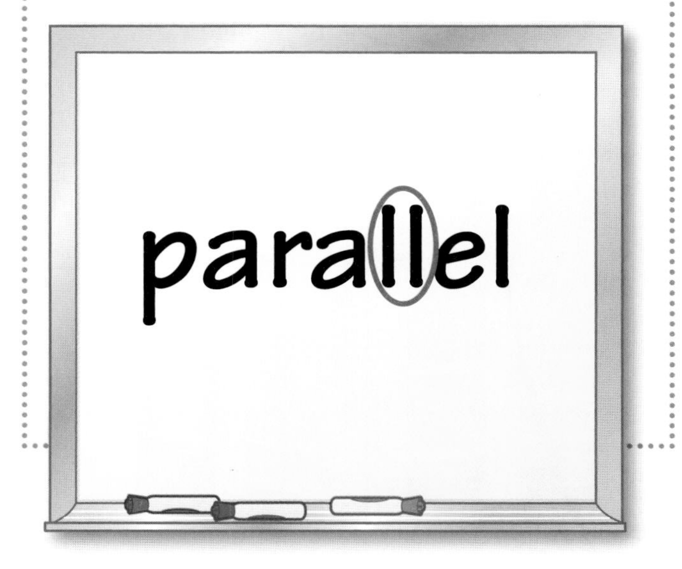

Speed It Up

I prevent the slowdown of having students copy each day's **journal prompt** by printing the prompts on labels. In the morning, I stick a label to the edge of each desk. When a student arrives, he places the label on the next page in his journal and begins writing.

Michelle Powell, Due Season Charter School, Camden, NJ

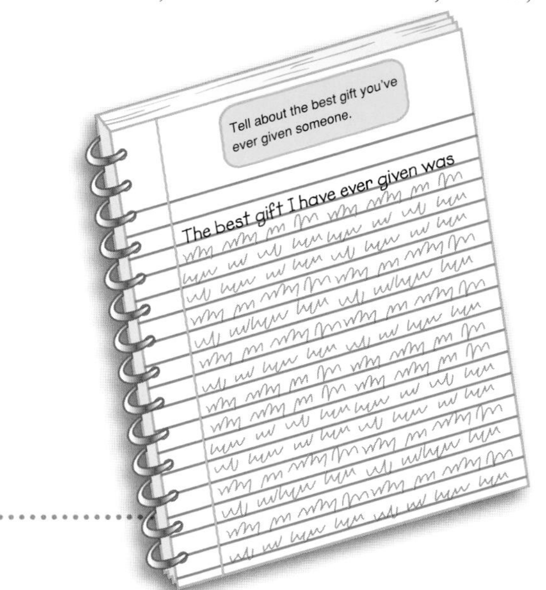

Math Melodies

For a harmonious way to help my students remember the difference between **prime and composite numbers,** I teach them the two songs shown.

Alison Renner, Dodge Literacy Magnet, Wichita, KS

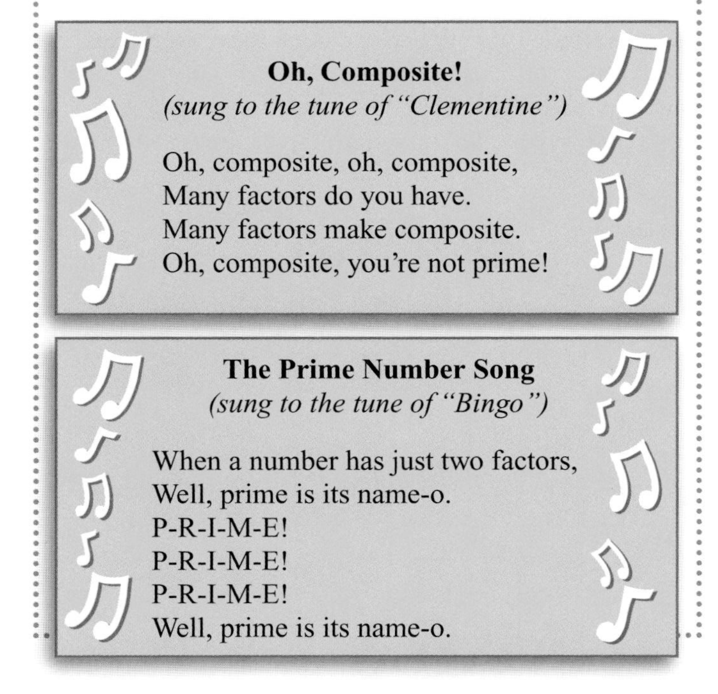

Oh, Composite!
(sung to the tune of "Clementine")

Oh, composite, oh, composite,
Many factors do you have.
Many factors make composite.
Oh, composite, you're not prime!

The Prime Number Song
(sung to the tune of "Bingo")

When a number has just two factors,
Well, prime is its name-o.
P-R-I-M-E!
P-R-I-M-E!
P-R-I-M-E!
Well, prime is its name-o.

Keys to Learning

To help my students remember important **math concepts and vocabulary,** I have them make these nifty rings. First, I have each child make a key-shaped construction paper cover, punch a hole in it, and slide it onto a metal ring. Each time I introduce a new topic, I guide the student to take notes on an index card. Then I have him punch a hole in the card and add it to his ring. To help each child keep his notes handy, I stick a self-adhesive hook on the side of his desk to hold his ring.

Karen Hall, S. S. Dixon Intermediate, Pace, FL

Bookmark Treasures

At the **end of the school year,** I give each student a bookmark memento. About a month before school lets out, I give each student a class list and have her write a positive comment beside each classmate's name. Then I collect the sheets and type a list of comments about each student. Next, I glue each list to a strip of construction paper, write a note on the back, laminate the strip, and add a bit of yarn. I love to watch my students' faces light up as they read their lists!

Nicole Weber,
Edna Ferber Elementary
Appleton, WI

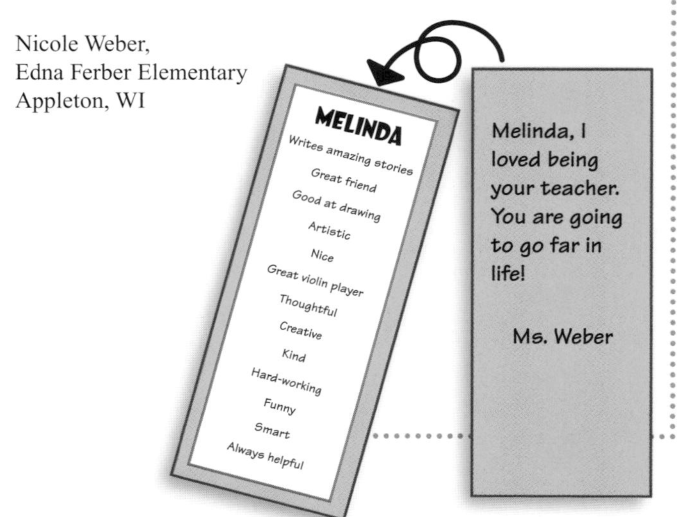

Color Collection

I made a color dictionary to encourage my students to **write creative descriptions.** I collected several paint sample strips with interesting color names, grouped them by color, and glued the strips onto sheets of paper. Then I slipped each sheet into a page protector and put the pages in a binder. When a student wants to add details to a description, he turns to the color dictionary for inspiration.

Patty Slagel
Ashburn Elementary
Ashburn, VA

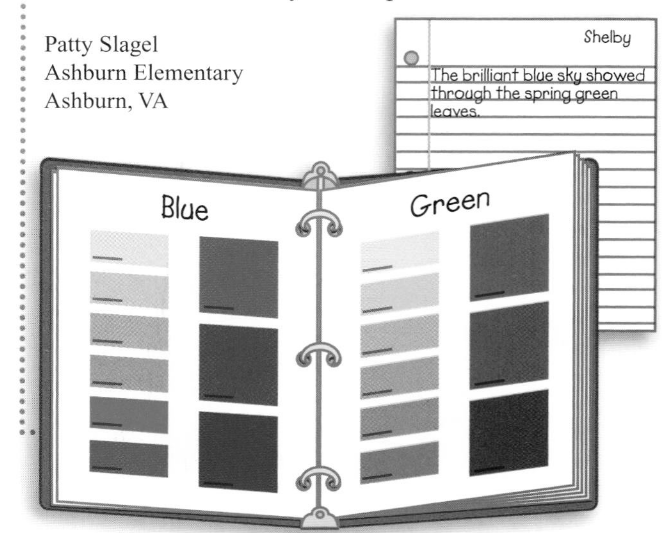

Create a Cube

I give my students hands-on experience with measuring **volume** with this homework idea. I have each student construct a cubic inch using materials he has at home. My students have used paper, clay, foam, needlepoint canvas, and even sponges. In class, we use students' cubic inches to explore the volume of classroom objects.

Sherwin Washburn, Cliffside Elementary, Shelby, NC

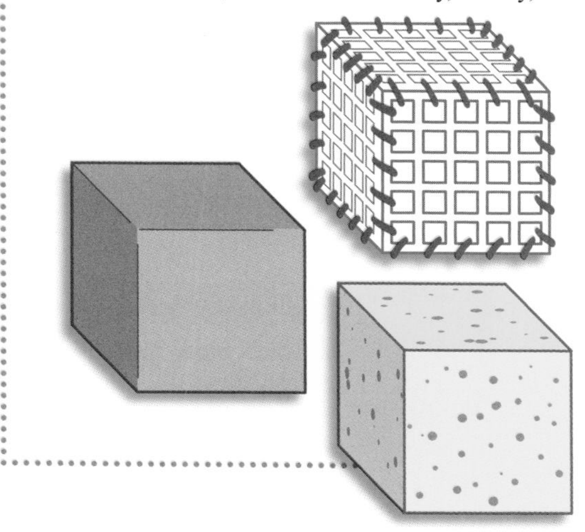

Take Two!

When a student has trouble **spelling** a word, I tell him to "take two." This means he makes two guesses, writing the word with two possible spellings. Then he uses his guesses as starting points for looking up the word in a dictionary. With this little trick, my students are learning to trust themselves and the dictionary!

Wendy Fosdick, Novi Meadows Elementary, Novi, MI

Catch!

To help my students **relax after a test session**, I program several beach balls with fun, open-ended questions. To play, I say a student's name, toss him the ball, and say, "Right thumb." The student catches the ball, reads aloud the question his right thumb is touching, and answers it. Then he throws the ball to another student and announces a different hand and finger. I periodically change balls to keep the questions fresh.

Sarah McBride, Wertheimer Middle School, Richmond, TX

Beach Ball Questions

If you won $10,000, what would you buy first?
If you could fly, where would you go?
What do you think fish think about cats?
What would you put in a time capsule that wouldn't be opened for 100 years?
Which food could you eat every day and never get tired of?
What do you know now that you wish you had known last year?
What do you think a dog is saying when it barks?
Which food do you hope you never eat again?

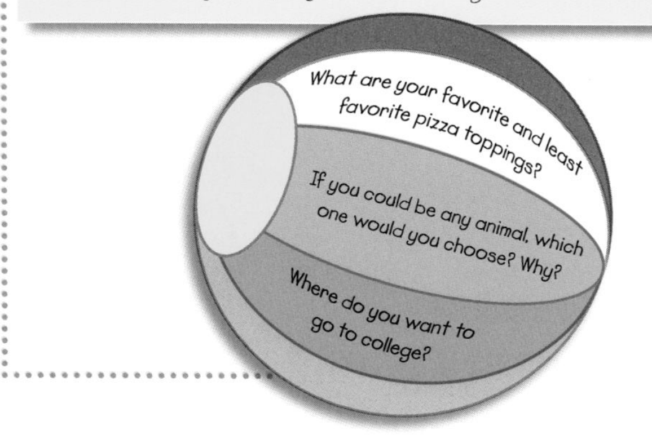

Best Foot Forward

When I introduce **division,** I teach my students to think of the divisor as a foot and the dividend as shoes. I write a problem on the board and ask students whether they could fit a foot the size of the divisor into a shoe the size of the dividend's first digit. If the foot would fit, I guide students to tell how many times it would fit. Then I guide students to solve the rest of the problem by fitting the divisor foot into each shoe in each step.

Nancy Komassa, Bryan Elementary, Plant City, FL

School Spirit!

To celebrate the **end of the year**, the teacher across the hall and I decorate our hall bulletin boards with school colors. We post pictures of our students from throughout the school year. Then I title my board "We've Got Spirit! Yes, We Do!" and she titles hers "We've Got Spirit! How 'bout You?"

Justin Woodard, Warren, AR

Spin and Spell!

My kids love to **review spelling words** because they get to stretch and move! I use a spinner and chart labeled as shown. I announce a word and spin to find out which action we'll use. Then it's time to move as we spell!

Christie Salcedo, Franke Park Elementary, Fort Wayne, IN

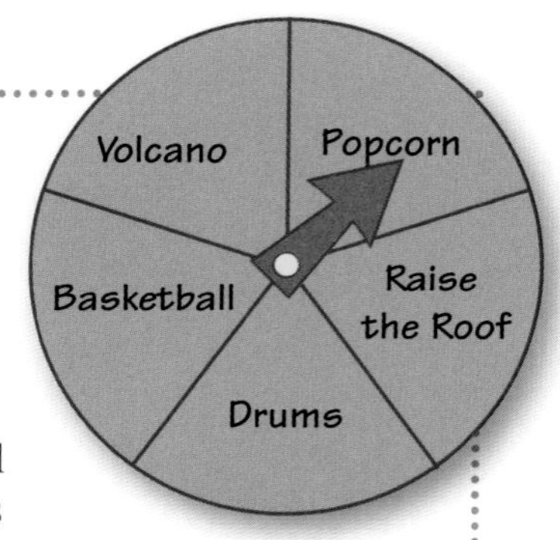

Activity	Actions
Popcorn	For each letter, stand quickly, say the letter, and sit back down.
Volcano	For each letter, raise your arms above your head and then move your arms down to represent lava coming from a volcano.
Basketball	For each letter, pretend to dribble a basketball and then pretend to shoot at the end of the word.
Raise the Roof	Push your hands up toward the ceiling as you say each letter.
Drums	As you say each letter, tap your desk to create a drumbeat.

Fraction Fudge

For a tasty way to practice using **fractions,** I have my students reduce this fudge recipe. I give each duo a copy of the recipe shown. Then I ask the partners to revise the recipe to make only one-fourth of a batch. Once I check each pair's reduced recipe, I give partners the ingredients, a quart-size resealable freezer bag, and waxed paper to make their own small batch.

Louanna Blackburn, Kingman Academy of Learning, Kingman, AZ

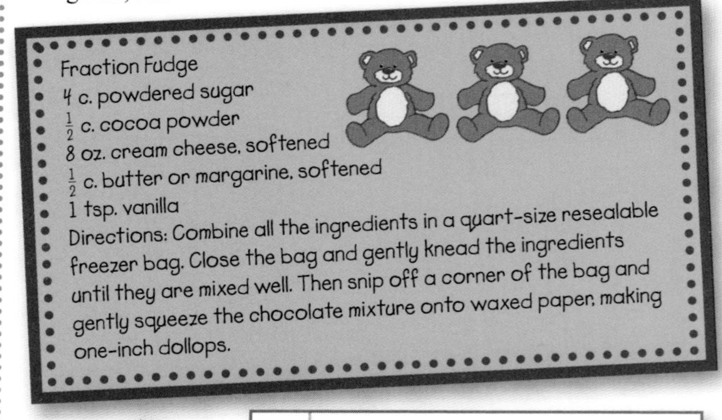
Fraction Fudge
4 c. powdered sugar
$\frac{1}{2}$ c. cocoa powder
8 oz. cream cheese, softened
$\frac{1}{2}$ c. butter or margarine, softened
1 tsp. vanilla
Directions: Combine all the ingredients in a quart-size resealable freezer bag. Close the bag and gently knead the ingredients until they are mixed well. Then snip off a corner of the bag and gently squeeze the chocolate mixture onto waxed paper, making one-inch dollops.

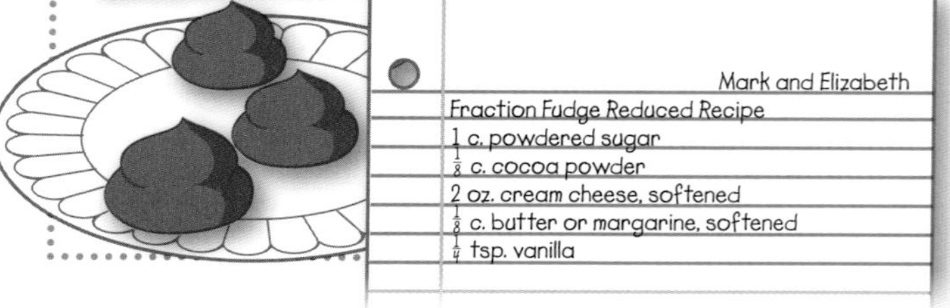
Mark and Elizabeth
Fraction Fudge Reduced Recipe
1 c. powdered sugar
$\frac{1}{8}$ c. cocoa powder
2 oz. cream cheese, softened
$\frac{1}{8}$ c. butter or margarine, softened
$\frac{1}{4}$ tsp. vanilla

Make and Take

I like to give each student a **keepsake** to help him remember our class. I buy an inexpensive clipboard for each student and use a permanent marker to write his name at the bottom. Then I give each child his board and set aside time for everyone to collect autographs from his classmates. Students love the memento, and parents say they're great for road trips!

Trisha Richmond, West Elementary, Wheatland, WY

Give It a Toss!

I've found a fun way to jazz up our **daily editing.** First, I write on the board sentences that contain several mistakes. Then I play music and have students toss a beach ball or small stress ball around the room. When I stop the music, the person holding the ball goes to the board and corrects one error. We continue until students have corrected all the mistakes.

Richard McCoy, Richland, MO

Scratch Paper Times Three!

To make sure my students line up their columns and make careful calculations when they take **math tests,** I make scratch paper pads! I staple together half sheets of lined paper, graph paper, and lattice grid paper for each student. When it's time for the test, I give each student a pad and remind her to do her best.

Missy Goldenberg, Overland Park, KS

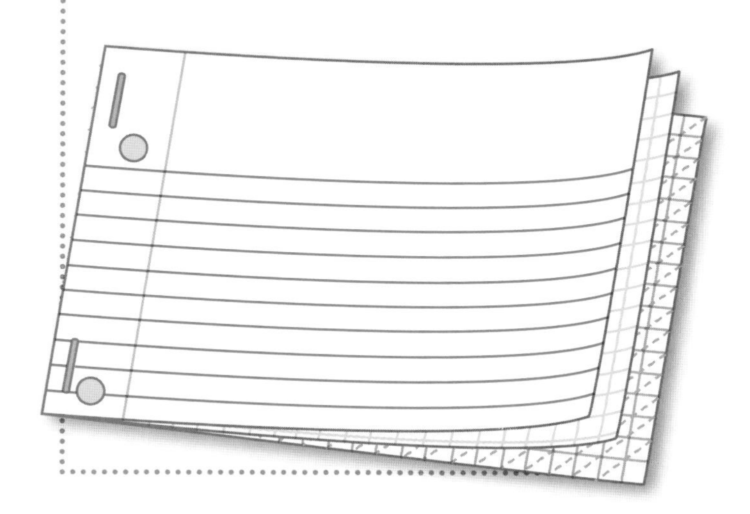

Here's the Deal!

For a quick **mixed number review,** I give each pair of students a deck of cards. I have the students remove the face cards and then draw two cards. Each partner uses the numbers to write an improper fraction and then converts the fraction to a mixed number. When all the cards have been used, students simply shuffle the cards and begin again.

Cynthia Mosley, Durham, NC

This Reminds Me Of...

Before independent reading sessions, I give my students preprinted **text-connection labels.** When a student makes a connection, he sticks the label inside his reading notebook and writes his example below it. My students love using the labels, and they're great reminders for the students to make connections as they read.

Michele Anszelowicz, Forest Lake Elementary, Wantagh, NY

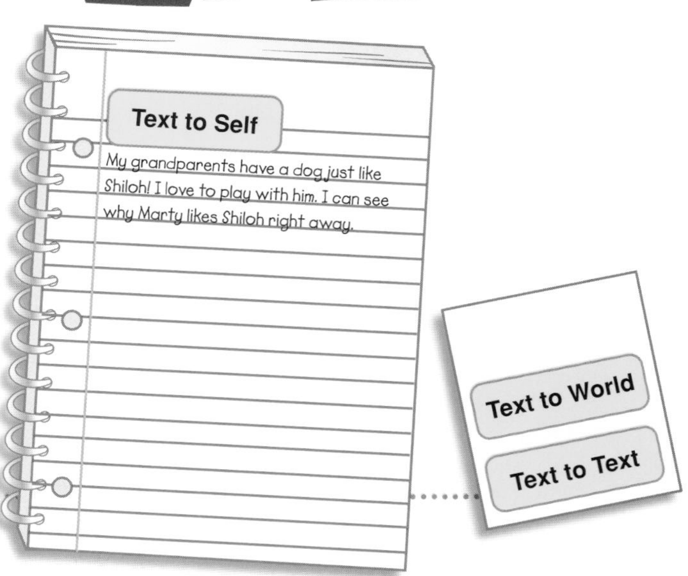

"PAWs" for Problem Solving

I use the acronym PAW as a **problem-solving reminder and rubric.** I explain what each letter stands for. PAW is easy to remember and, with it, my students can evaluate their work and make adjustments before they turn it in. Then, when I grade students' work, I award one point for each component.

Wendy Whitney Scherer, Eastman, WI

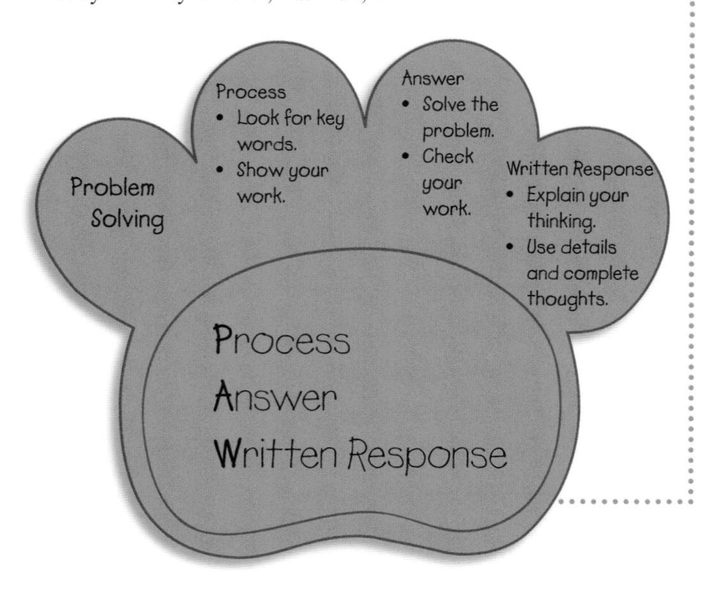

Today I Learned...

Here's what I do to spark **meaningful conversations** between my students and their parents! Once a week, I give each student an index card. I have her write on it a key word or phrase related to something she learned that day. Then I have her take the note home and share it with a parent or guardian. As the child explains the word or phrase, a conversation about school begins. For accountability, the adult initials the card. Then the child can turn it in for a small reward.

Dawn Young, Forest Hills Elementary, Lake Oswego, OR

Answer Keys

Page 8
We have some big problems!

Page 9

1. wait	6. cellar	11. fourth	16. ring
2. hour	7. clothes	12. weather	17. knew
3. horse	8. sells	13. sent	18. cash
4. build	9. principal	14. made	19. writes
5. whales	10. plane	15. week	20. current

Page 10

1. FLAG	9. 80,999
2. MEMORY	10. 29,880
3. STARS	11. 117,648
4. FREE	12. 3,780
5. NATION	13. 39,387
6. PRIDE	14. 119,905
7. STRONG	15. 330,081
8. BRAVE	16. 5,964

Page 12
Executive Branch: 1, 5, 8, 13, 15
Legislative Branch: 2, 6, 7, 9, 11, 12
Judicial Branch: 3, 4, 10, 14

Page 15

1. it	6. her	11. We
2. us	7. them	12. his
3. his	8. she	13. our
4. they	9. her	14. them
5. her	10. I	15. he

Page 16

1. D	6. H	11. I
2. S	7. R	12. M
3. G	8. O	13. U
4. L	9. J	14. F
5. E	10. N	15. B

HIS "GHOUL-FRIEND"

Page 17
The following turkeys should be colored:
1, 4, 6, 7, 9, 11, 14, 15.

Page 19
1. Answers may vary.
2. 7
3. 6
4. 6
5. 10
6. Yes, 14
7. Yes; It makes the mean smaller.
8. No; Six is still the most common number.
9. No; The middle of the data is still six.
10. 6

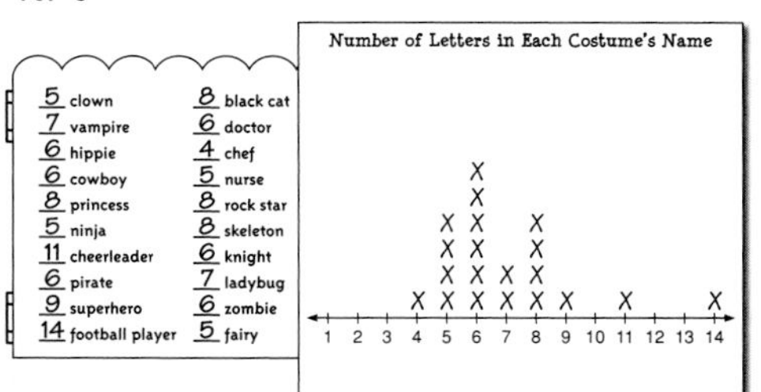

Page 22

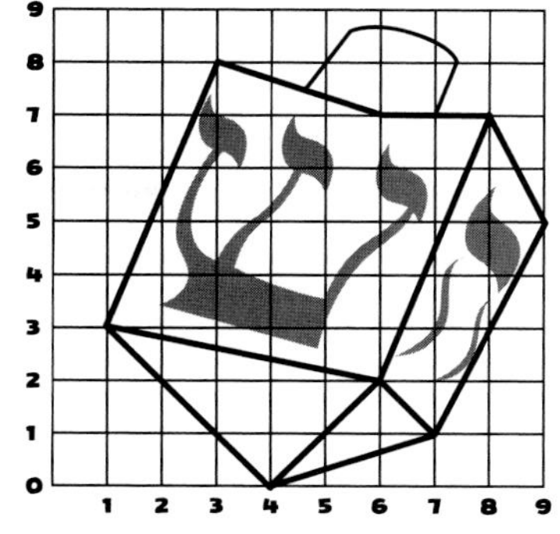

SPIN THE DREIDEL!
LIGHTING THE MENORAH

Bonus Box: Answers may vary. *eight nights* (5, 6), (5, 3), (1, 9), (4, 9), (8, 8), (3, 5), (5, 3), (1, 9), (4, 9), (2, 6), (2, 3); *oil* (6, 5), (5, 3), (1, 1); *candles* (7, 7), (7, 8), (3, 5), (4, 1), (1, 1), (5, 6), (2, 3); *shamash* (2, 3), (4, 9), (7, 8), (4, 7), (7, 8), (2, 3), (7, 2); *gifts* (1, 9), (5, 3), (9, 4), (8, 8), (2, 3)

Page 23

	LOCATION (where something is)	DIRECTION (where something is going)	TIME (when something takes place)
1. throughout the night			✓
2. into a winter wonderland		✓	
3. up the hill		✓	
4. until noon			✓
5. beside a tree	✓		
6. to their house		✓	
7. After that			✓
8. onto a snowball	✓		
9. down the hill		✓	
10. Before long			✓
11. toward the icy pond		✓	
12. at the pond's edge	✓		
13. in the water	✓		
14. For several seconds			✓
15. to the surface		✓	

Page 24
1. P = 24 yd., A = 20 yd.^{2}, Prancer
2. P = 24 yd., A = 26 yd.^{2}, Comet
3. P = 48 yd., A = 44 yd.^{2}, Dasher
4. P = 24 yd., A = 23 yd.^{2}, Blitzen
5. P = 72 yd., A = 168 yd.^{2}, Vixen
6. P = 40 yd., A = 48 yd.^{2}, Dancer
7. P = 38 yd., A = 66 yd.^{2}, Rudolph
8. P = 46 yd., A = 81 yd.^{2}, Donner
9. P = 32 yd., A = 34 yd.^{2}, Cupid

Page 25

						[1]m											
				[2]p	r	o	t	e	s	t	s						
						v											
						e											
[3]d	i	s	c	r	i	m	i	n	[4]a	t	e						
y						e			b								
n						n			o		[5]m	o	[6]u	r	n	e	d
[7]a	d	v	o	c	a	t	e		l				n				
m									i				i				
i				[8]a	s	s	a	s	s	i	n	a	t	e	d		
c									h				e				

Page 30

1. BANK	9. GROUND
2. JAM	10. PRESS
3. SEAL	11. DATE
4. RULER	12. FAN
5. STICK	13. OPEN
6. SINK	14. LIKE
7. POUND	15. RARE
8. MARCH	16. SPELL

GUION S. BLUFORD JR.
MAE C. JEMISON

Page 31
Monday: range = $27.00, median = $22.00, mode = $22.00, mean = $20.00
Tuesday: range = $21.00, median = $15.00, mode = $15.00, mean = $14.00
Wednesday: range = $19.00, median = $15.00, no mode, mean = $15.00
Thursday: range = $32.00, median = $15.00, mode = $12.00, mean = $19.00
Friday: range = $31.00, median = $24.00, mode = $14.00 and $24.00, mean = $27.00
Saturday: range = $40.00, median = $16.00, mode = $10.00 and $16.00, mean = $20.00

Page 32

1. right	5. right	9. perpendicular
2. obtuse	6. acute	10. parallel
3. obtuse	7. obtuse	11. intersecting
4. acute	8. right	12. perpendicular

Answers may vary and include the following:
13. $\overline{AB}$, $\overline{AE}$, $\overline{AH}$, $\overline{AG}$, $\overline{BC}$, $\overline{BQ}$, $\overline{BR}$, $\overline{BE}$, $\overline{BH}$, $\overline{BG}$
14. $\overrightarrow{NP}$, $\overrightarrow{NL}$, $\overrightarrow{HG}$, $\overrightarrow{ML}$, $\overrightarrow{QR}$, $\overrightarrow{QS}$, $\overrightarrow{OP}$, $\overrightarrow{IJ}$
15. $\overleftrightarrow{AG}$, $\overleftrightarrow{SF}$, $\overleftrightarrow{DJ}$

Page 33

1. fact	9. fact	16. fact
2. opinion	10. opinion	17. fact
3. fact	11. opinion	18. opinion
4. opinion	12. fact	19. opinion
5. fact	13. fact	20. fact
6. fact	14. fact	21. opinion
7. opinion	15. opinion	22. fact
8. opinion		

Page 34
L. r = 3 cm, d = 6 cm, C = 18.84 cm
M. r = 3.5 cm, d = 7 cm, C = 21.98 cm
N. r = 4.5 cm, d = 9 cm, C = 28.26 cm
O. r = 2 cm, d = 4 cm, C = 12.56 cm
P. r = 6.5 cm, d = 13 cm, C = 40.82 cm
Q. r = 2.5 cm , d = 5 cm, C = 15.7 cm

Page 37
1. $\frac{3}{10}$, $\frac{7}{10}$
2. $\frac{3}{8}$, $\frac{5}{8}$
3. $\frac{3}{4}$, $\frac{1}{4}$
4. $\frac{1}{7}$, $\frac{2}{7}$
5. $\frac{3}{4}$, $\frac{1}{4}$
6. $\frac{1}{6}$, $\frac{5}{6}$
7. $\frac{1}{4}$, $\frac{1}{2}$, $\frac{3}{4}$, $\frac{1}{12}$

Page 38
Answers may vary.
1. Although Lola Lavish could walk to work, she drives her car.
2. Ben Queasy added worms to his compost after he realized worms aren't gross.
3. When a tree in Ima Saver's yard died, she planted a new one.
4. Since Ben started recycling, there is less trash to take out on trash day.
5. Lola prefers to drive by herself, though she could save gas by carpooling.
6. If Ima gets a plastic shopping bag, she reuses it.
7. Because Ima wants to make a difference, she rides the bus instead of driving.
8. Ben plans his errands so that he doesn't waste gas driving all over town.
9. Ima walks to work nearly every day unless she rides her bike.
10. While Lola doesn't seem to care about the environment, she just isn't sure what to do first.

Page 39

1. R	7. T
2. E	8. D
3. H	9. G
4. A	10. Y
5. B	11. G
6. U	12. S

THE GETTYSBURG ADDRESS

Bonus Box: Answers may vary.

Page 44

1. 309 miles
2. 296 miles
3. 3,088 miles
4. 116 miles
5. 695 miles
6. 617 miles
7. 1,392 miles
8. 148 miles
9. 193 miles
10. $22.99
11. 2,626 miles
12. 222 miles
13. about 30 gallons
14. $121.73

3	0	4	5	3	0	9
2	3	1	4	8	2	1
6	1	2	1	7	3	2
2	6	1	7	2	9	2
6	7	1	3	9	2	2
1	1	6	8	6	9	5
1	9	5	2	2	9	9
3	3	3	0	8	8	4

Page 45

Explanations may vary.

1. no
2. no
3. yes
4. no
5. yes
6. no
7. yes
8. yes
9. no
10. no

Bonus Box:

1. In six days, about 1,080,000 people will visit the carnival.
2. Justin can buy 18 tickets with $25.00.
3. Two-thirds of 36 children is 24 children.
4. John's house is 26,400 feet from the carnival.
5. Abbie will get on the ride in 32 minutes.
6. The crew will sell 640 quarts.
7. Macy can fit 48 balloons in a row.
8. One-fourth of 2,360 children is 590 children.
9. Kaden sells 1,200 pounds of fries. One ton is 2,000 pounds.
10. Gena orders 73,500 bags. She needs 179 boxes.

Page 46

1. W 2. O 3. H
4. T 5. A 6. D
7. T 8. R 9. T
10. N 11. T 12. S
13. E 14 T 15. S

SHE WANTED TO TEST THE WATER!

Page 71

[A]There is trouble in the Cookie Kingdom. Princess Crumb has fallen into a deep sleep. The only way to wake her is with a mixture made from special cookies. The princess must be saved in less than two hours or she will sleep forever. King Crumb grabs his cell phone and calls Captain Snicker and his pal Doodle. He tells them which cookies they must find.

Captain Snicker flies off to find a butter cookie. He heads straight to Sweden. He arrives at a bakery and buys a butter cookie. He yells to the bakery owner, "Thank you!" Then he takes off for China.

Once in China, Captain Snicker begins searching for a fortune cookie. He flies around the Great Wall of China. He sees several dessert stands. He buys a fortune cookie in Beijing and heads back to the Cookie Kingdom.

[B]Meanwhile, Doodle picks up a shortbread cookie in Scotland. Then he zips off to the North Pole to grab an icebox cookie. From the North Pole, Doodle heads to America. He spots a bag of chocolate chip cookies near the Statue of Liberty. He grabs the bag and flies back to the Cookie Kingdom.

With only minutes to spare, Captain Snicker and Doodle present their cookies to the king. The king crushes the cookies and sprinkles them on his daughter. Princess Crumb awakens. Captain Snicker and Doodle save the princess and things in Cookie Kingdom are right once again.

Proper Nouns in Section A: Cookie Kingdom, Princess Crumb, King Crumb, Captain Snicker, Doodle, Captain Snicker, Sweden, China, China, Captain Snicker, Great Wall of China, Beijing, Cookie Kingdom

Proper Nouns in Section B: Doodle, Scotland, North Pole, North Pole, Doodle, America, Statue of Liberty, Cookie Kingdom, Captain Snicker, Doodle, Princess Crumb, Captain Snicker, Doodle, Cookie Kingdom

Page 72

People's Title: 5. Principal; 10. Mrs.; 18. Dr.
Holidays: 2. Thanksgiving Day; 7. Fourth of July; 17. Valentine's Day
Titles: 4. *Creative Cupcakes*; 11. *School Days*; 13. "Happy Birthday"
Months and Days: 3. Saturday; 9. June; 16. September
Names: 1. Wyoming; 8. Squeaky; 14. New York City
Correct: 6, 12, 15

Page 85

CHECKMATE!

Page 86

1. H
2. W
3. S
4. A
5. O
6. P
7. U
8. I
9. Y
10. G
11. J
12. M

When I say, "JUMP," YOU SAY, "HOW HIGH?"
Answers may vary. The idiom shows that one person controls the other.

Page 93

1. B
2. C
3. A
4. C
5. C

Page 95

1. J
2. D
3. G
4. A
5. I
6. C
7. B
8. E
9. H
10. F

F 11. misleading
T 12. breathless
F 13. blogger
T 14. careful
F 15. previews
T 16. reviewing
F 17. subway
T 18. misunderstood
F 19. unable
T 20. wooden
T 21. regenerate
F 22. preheat

Page 96

1. S
2. T
3. I
4. O
5. E
6. A
7. U
8. F
9. P
10. C
11. N
12. Y
13. H
14. D
15. R

YOU SPEND FIFTEEN DAYS OF EACH YEAR EATING!

Bonus Box: Answers may vary.

1. a unit of energy provided by food
2. fit
3. Vitamins help the body regulate chemicals that change food into energy.
4. consume
5. nutritious
6. The average adult male needs at least 2,900 calories per day. The average adult female needs about 2,200 calories per day.
7. KAHR-boh-HY-drayt
8. Milk has almost all the nutrients that are necessary for growth and good health.
9. No, fats are essential in small portions.
10. yes
11. sick
12. Cheese, eggs, fish, meat, and milk are high in protein.
13. yes
14. 2½ cups each day
15. ate

Page 103

1. B
2. C
3. A
4. C
5. B

Bonus Box: Answers will vary.

Page 104

1, 4–9. Answers may vary.

2.

When	Where	When or where
during	across	after
since	beneath	around
till	beside	before
until	outside	near
		throughout
		within

3. A. into B. about C. between D. during E. under F. across G. onto H. underneath I. behind J. outside K. past L. below

Page 105

Your NOSE!

gave	go / ate	fly	wrote	blow	open	type	tasted	knew	skipped	hike	swim
smiled	hid / run	try / were	made	will play	will sleep	will breathe	drew	move	shake	will make	will draw
washed	shout	flew / see	froze	will run	tear	will fly	sanded	packed	took	will go	catch
liked	break	work	rode	will eat	cook	will see	eat	fold	spoke	will learn	will practice
dive	play	bake	give	will walk	will write	will ride	ran	blew	washed	will open	take
hide	call	fall	skip	grow	look	sleep	speak	fold	come	will say	will bake

Bonus Box: went, flew, blew, opened, typed, hiked, swam, ran, tried, moved, shook, shouted, saw, tore, caught, broke, worked, cooked, ate, folded, dove, played, baked, gave, took, hid, called, fell, skipped, grew, looked, slept, spoke, folded, came

Page 113

1. B
2. C
3. B
4. A
5. C

Answers may vary for 6 and 7.

Page 114

Answers may vary for 2–4, 6, 7, and 9.

1. noun phrase, prepositional phrase, verb phrase, verb phrase, noun phrase; Sentences will vary.
5. Mom came, day ends, I ran, someone picks; Sentences will vary.
8. phrase, clause, phrase, clause, phrase; Sentences will vary.

Page 115

	Correct	Incorrect
1. Barney! the manager of the Paddle Inn rents paddleboats at the lake.	3,691	4,276
2. It costs $25.00 to rent a paddleboat for half an hour but it costs only $40.00 to rent one for an hour.	9,567	3,478
3. Emily, Kayla, Marcus, and Jason pool their money, $60.00, and rent a paddleboat for one hour.	2,901	3,475
4. Jason says, "I dont need a life jacket I'm a great swimmer"	17, 032	8,569
5. Barney glares at Jason and says, "Young man, if you don't wear a life jacket, you won't get on a boat."	6,397	2,983
6. Barney gives everyone a life jacket and makes sure they strap them on correctly.	6,989	7,555
7. Then he takes them to their paddleboat it has four paddles!	8,444	9,682
8. Without thinking Marcus steps in the lake instead of on the paddleboat.	955	1,099
9. Emily starts laughing so hard she falls in the lake too.	14,952	11,337
10. "That's why you have to wear a life jacket," Barney says as he chuckles.	5,324	4,736
11. Marcus climbs out of the lake and shakes the water from his hair all over Kayla.	19,766	23,789
12. Kayla squeals and ducks to get away from the water spray.	2,099	6,118
13. As she dodges the spray Kayla backs off the dock right into the lake.	1,714	1,003
14. So far Jason is the only one who hasn't fallen in the lake so he dives in!	2,413	2,500
15. Already dripping wet, Emily, Kayla, Marcus, and Jason climb into the boat and start paddling.	1,376	1,244

Page 116

Answers may vary.

1. nervous
2. talking
3. she was eavesdropping
4. will say yes
5. baseball
6. been under his bed
7. his feet have grown
8. messy
9. Destiny is home in her room. She's listening to music, walks through her doorway, and sees her brother.
10. Destiny is furious when she sees her brother. She squeals and glares at him.

Answers may vary for 11 and 12.

Page 119

Answers may vary. Possible words include the following:

bio: life
antibiotic, biology, biome
cred: to believe, to trust
accredited, credit, credible
form: shape
inform, formation, formula
hydr: water
hydrant, hydrated, hydrogen
meter/metr: measure
metric, diameter, perimeter
mono: one, single
monocle, monotone, monotonous
phon: sound
headphones, phonics, symphony
pol/polis: city, state
metropolis, police, politics
scrib/script: to write
describe, manuscript, prescription
sect/sec: cut
dissect, insect, intersection
struct: to build
construct, instruction, structure
techn: art, skill, craft
technical, technique, technology
therm: heat
geothermal, thermometer, thermostat
trac/tract: to drag, to pull
distract, trace, tractor
vid/vis: to see
invisible, video, vision
vor: to eat
carnivore, omnivore, voracious

Page 120

1. HOCKEY
2. Answers may vary.
3. tricky
4. a. fraction, action
   b. unique, beak
   c. bleak, creek
   d. frail, snail
5. Answers may vary.
6. a. Ulysses Grant
   b. Calvin Coolidge
   c. John Kennedy
   d. Ronald Reagan
7. COW
   COWSEE
   COSEE
   CHOSEE
   CHOESE
   CHEESE
8. If the shoe fits, wear it.

Page 121

1. Answers will vary. Possible answers include *strengths, flights, scratched,* and *stretched.*
2. a. foot
   b. hand
   c. eye
   d. arm, leg
   e. toe
3. One Hundred Cents
4. a. goose
   b. duck
   c. mare
   d. doe
   e. ewe
   f. pen
   g. falcon
   h. cow
5. Answers may vary.
6. a. delay or defer
   b. defeat
   c. decay
   d. delete
   e. daring
   f. damp or dank
7. a. stirrup
   b. runt
   c. watch
   d. has
   e. either
8. Alaska, Idaho, Iowa, Maine, Nevada, Ohio, Oklahoma, Wyoming

Page 122

1. Possible answers include *lane, road, drive, court,* and *route.*
2. Possible answers include the following:
   begin, brown, burnt, burst
   navel, novel
   towel, trail
3. **C**hristmas **E**ve is always interesting at our house**.** **G**randma insists on bringing **G**erman potato salad even though it gives my dad a rash**.** **A**unt **S**uzy brings boring store-bought cookies**,** and **U**ncle **J**im brings an empty stomach**.** **W**e always end up having to order **C**hinese food for dinner**.**
4. Possible answers include *butterfly, bluebird, rattlesnake, bumblebee,* and *hedgehog.*
6. A. object
   B. refuse
   C. perfect
   D. record
7. Answers may vary.
8. Possible answers include the following:
   Heated
   Oppressive
   Torrid
   Fleet
   Agile
   Speedy
   Timely

Page 123

1. Answers may vary.
2. George Washington, Bill Gates, Amelia Earhart, Thomas Edison, Abraham Lincoln, Michelle Obama, Eleanor Roosevelt, Harriet Tubman
3. **"**It was *or,***"** he said**, "**not *and.***"**
4. Answers may vary. Possible answers include the following: *jumpy, jolly, hoppy, hip, lumpy,* and *hilly.*
5. Answers may vary. Possible answers include the following:
   b. map, rot, use; mop, use, tar
   c. age, pin, rev
   d. tag, ill, oar
6. Answers may vary.
7. a. pride
   b. colony
   c. troop
   d. pod
   e. herd
   f. congregation
8. a. March
   b. sock
   c. shack
   d. cash
   e. marsh

Page 124

1. bend over backward, to try very hard to do something or please someone
   water under the bridge, something from the past that cannot be changed
2. Answers may vary. Possible answers include *about, after, at, for, of, on, onto, out, to, up,* and *upon.*
3. a) stop
   b) silent
   c) short
   d) spicy
   e) specific, sure
4. Answers may vary. Possible answers include *ancient, caffeine, efficient, either, foreign, heights, leisure, neither, protein,* and *weird.*
5. Answers may vary.
6. legend, patriot, partridge, format, mankind, message
7. a) maple
   b) birch
   c) spruce
   d) elm
8. *Charlie and the Chocolate Factory* by Roald Dahl
   Little House on the Prairie by Laura Ingalls Wilder
   Where the Wild Things Are by Maurice Sendak
   The New Kid on the Block by Jack Prelutsky

Page 125

Answers may vary for 1, 5, and 7.

2. A. winter + summer + spring + fall = 4 seasons
   B. Washington + Oregon + California = West Coast
   C. June + July + August = summer
   D. Texas + Louisiana + Mississippi + Alabama + Florida = Gulf Coast
3. The paragraph does not contain the letter e. Students' sentences will vary but should not include the letter e.
4. Answers may vary.
   A. hair; The other words name sense organs.
   B. soccer; In the other sports, an object is used to hit the ball.
   C. apple; An apple has seeds in its center, but each of the other fruits has a pit.
   D. shark; The shark is a fish, but the other animals are mammals.
6. A. Rome
   B. London
   C. Paris
   D. Berlin
8. Answers may vary. A possible answer is *dive, dove, dole, doll, poll, pool.*

Page 127

"Pepperoni Galore!"

Order may vary.

babies
heroes
sisters-in-law
anchovies
children
people
bunches
burritos
geese
loaves
chiefs
potatoes

Sentences will vary.

Page 128

"It's in the Name"

Answers may vary.

1. Dad
2. Mom
3. Ada, Ana, Anna
4. Bob
5. Elle, Eve

"Make Room for Me!"

smile, frown
lazy, energetic
fact, fiction
small, large
start, finish
first, last
left, right
kind, cruel

"There's a Flea on a Leaf"

Order may vary.

ape
cat
deer
rat
bat
wolf
goat
seal

"Have a Heart"

1. allowed/aloud
2. capitol/capital
3. principal/principle
4. feet/feat
5. piece/peace
6. threw/through

Page 130

"Use the Clues"

1. extremely happy
2. forms of illness
3. movable
4. started again
5. wild

Page 135

Introduction

The history and science of roller coasters are as amazing as a ride on one.

Roller Coaster History

Russians enjoyed one of the first roller coasters in the 1500s. They rode sleds down steep wooden slopes covered in ice.

The French made some changes. They built waxed slides and added wheels to the sleds. They also made a train of carts that moved along winding tracks.

The first American roller coaster was different from the French and Russian ones. It was a train of coal cars. Riders went slowly up a Pennsylvania mountain and had a thrilling ride back down.

Roller Coaster Science

Roller coasters move mostly by gravity and momentum since they have no engine.

To build momentum, a train of cars is usually pulled by a chain lift to the top of a track's first hill.

Gravity makes the roller coaster roll to the bottom of the hill. Then the coaster's momentum carries it (or a lift pulls it) to the top of the next hill.

Riding on a Roller Coaster

People on wooden roller coasters experience bumps and up-and-down motions.

In contrast, people on steel roller coasters glide smoothly on tubelike tracks. They also get to experience twists, turns, and complex loops.

The fun thing about modern roller coasters is that riders can sit, stand, or even be in a flying position.

Conclusion

Roller coaster fans of the future will no doubt see the rides become higher, faster, and more complex.

Page 170

1. 60
2. 500
3. 670
4. 1,360
5. 9,500
6. 15,900
7. 8,500
8. 12,800
9. 12,000
10. 598,000
11. 121,000
12. 6,000
13. 100,000
14. 50,000
15. 780,000
16. 1,190,000
17. 400,000
18. 500,000
19. 1,000,000
20. 600,000

Page 171

1. Carli
2. cafeteria food
3. pet peeves, TV commercials
4. text messaging and pet peeves
5. Charlie
6. 10 minutes
7. 30 minutes
8. Carli, 15 minutes

Page 179

1. 100 x 30 = 3,000
2. 200 x 60 = 12,000
3. 100 x 20 = 2,000
4. 200 x 40 = 8,000
5. 200 x 70 = 14,000
6. 200 x 70 = 14,000
7. 300 x 70 = 21,000
8. 500 x 50 = 25,000
9. 600 x 50 = 30,000
10. 800 x 60 = 48,000
11. 200 x 40 = 8,000
12. 700 x 90 = 63,000

The path leads to the first-place trophy.

Bonus Box:

1. 4,862
2. 9,164
3. 1,725
4. 7,128
5. 13,419
6. 15,275
7. 25,404
8. 24,516
9. 26,461
10. 42,460
11. 8,814
12. 61,115

Page 180

Order may vary.

$1/5 = 4/20, 3/15, 2/10$

$3/4 = 18/24, 15/20, 6/8, 21/28$

$1/2 = 2/4, 10/20, 3/6, 4/8$

$1 = 3/3, 5/5$

$1/4 = 5/20, 6/24, 7/28$

$3/8 = 6/16, 12/32, 9/24$

Bonus Box:

$1/5 = 0.2$

$3/4 = 0.75$

$1/2 = 0.5$

$1 = 1.0$

$1/4 = 0.25$

$3/8 = 0.375$

The lost book is $14/16$.

Page 184

9. True
10. True
11. False
12. False
13. True
14. False
15. True

Page 185

$3/4$ = T	$1/3$ = A	$8/9$ = S
$1/6$ = P	$4/5$ = F	$8/21$ = R
$17/20$ = H	$3/8$ = B	$4/7$ = Y
$1/5$ = M	$17/30$ = G	$9/20$ = I
$5/8$ = O	$1/15$ = D	$8/15$ = E

THE BASE OF THE GREAT PYRAMID in Egypt is as large as a parking lot for ten jumbo jets.

Page 187

$5\frac{1}{2}$ in. # 1 Initial here.	13.3 cm # 8 Initial here.	6.7 cm # 5 Initial here.	$2\frac{5}{8}$ in. # 5 Initial here.	5.4 cm # 10 Initial here.
9.3 cm # 3 Initial here.	$2\frac{1}{4}$ in. # 2 Initial here.	5.7 cm # 2 Initial here.	4.8 cm # 6 Initial here.	$\frac{7}{8}$ in. # 7 Initial here.
2.2 cm # 7 Initial here.	$3\frac{5}{8}$ in. # 3 Initial here.	$2\frac{1}{8}$ in. # 10 Initial here.	8.6 cm # 9 Initial here.	$5\frac{1}{4}$ in. # 8 Initial here.
$3\frac{3}{8}$ in. # 9 Initial here.	11.1 cm # 4 Initial here.	$1\frac{7}{8}$ in. # 6 Initial here.	13.9 cm # 1 Initial here.	$4\frac{3}{8}$ in. # 4 Initial here.

Page 191

Answers for 2, 5, and 8 may vary.

1. D. 3,872; E. 4,066; C. 46,585; A. 48,357; B. 53,056
3. A. 72,000; 77,162
   B. 28,000; 24,053
4. $75,330
6. A. 60,000; 73,315
   B. 180,000; 200,192
   C. 400,000; 381,456
7. one day, 18,945 pages; three days, 56,835 pages; five days, 94,725 pages
9. 4,567 x 42 = 191,814; 4,567 x 53 = 242,051; 4,567 x 68 = 310,556; 4,567 x 79 = 360,793
   2,389 x 42 = 100,338; 2,389 x 53 = 126,617; 2,389 x 68 = 162,452; 2,389 x 79 = 188,731

Page 192

- [x] [+] 1. 525 pounds
- [−] [+] 2. 22 pounds
- [+] [÷] 3. 7 days
- [+] [−] 4. 32 pounds
- [+] [÷] 5. 78 pounds
- [÷] [x] 6. 160 pounds
- [x] [x] 7. 10,220 pounds
- [x] [+] 8. $1,387

Page 193

1. cannonball
2. pike
3. cannonball, belly flop
4. 3 penguins
5. 17 penguins
6. 2 penguins
7. 773 dives
8. 20 penguins
9.

Number of Dives Per Penguin Per Day	
0	3, 6, 7, 8, 8, 9
1	1, 1, 2, 3, 4, 5, 6, 6
2	0, 0, 1, 2, 2, 4

10. 9 penguins

Page 200

Answers for 3, 5, 7, and 8 may vary.

1. A. 5 ft. B. 9 ft. C. 3 ft.
2. B
4. If each measurement is increased by 1 cm, the volume increases by 114 cm. If each measurement is decreased by 1 cm, the volume decreases by 78 cm.
6. A. V = 540 m^3 B. V = 425 m^3 C. V = 540 m^3 D. V = 480 m^3
9. 488 $in.^3$

Page 201

slide	180° turn	270° turn	90° turn	flip	360° turn	270° turn
360° turn	slide	flip	slide	180° turn	slide	360° turn
flip	270° turn	180° turn	90° turn	flip	flip	270° turn
360° turn	slide	90° turn	180° turn	90° turn	slide	270° turn
360° turn	180° turn	flip	360° turn	90° turn	270° turn	90° turn

Page 202

1. E	5. H	9. G
2. J	6. L	10. C
3. A	7. B	11. D
4. K	8. I	12. F

Bonus Box:

1. 19 in.	5. 12 in.	9. 20 in.
2. 4 in.	6. 17 in.	10. 22 in.
3. 32 in.	7. 9 in.	11. 8 in.
4. 48 in.	8. 13 in.	12. 14 in.

Page 203

1. –10	5. 1	9. 6	13. –8
2. 8	6. 2	10. 3	14. 4
3. –6	7. 7	11. –4	15. –11
4. –3	8. –5	12. 9	16. –1

BECAUSE THEY HAVE TWO LEFT FEET!

Page 204

1. 12	6. 18	11. $\frac{1}{12}$
2. $\frac{2}{5}$	7. $\frac{3}{16}$	12. 6
3. $\frac{1}{10}$	8. $\frac{5}{14}$	13. 4
4. 6	9. 10	14. $\frac{9}{14}$
5. $\frac{7}{12}$	10. $\frac{1}{22}$	15. $\frac{2}{7}$

The path leads to the hamster.

Page 209

1. Answers may vary.
2. 341 ÷ 6 = 56 R5, 452 ÷ 7 = 64 R4, 563 ÷ 8 = 70 R3, 674 ÷ 9 = 74 R8, 785 ÷ 10 = 78 R5
3. A. 4 (divisor), 196 (dividend), 49 (quotient)
   B. 5 (divisor), 165 (dividend), 33 (quotient)
   C. 6 (divisor), 474 (dividend), 79 (quotient)
   D. 7 (divisor), 448 (dividend), 64 (quotient)
4. Explanations may vary.
   A. 282
   B. 75 R1
   C. 64 R3
   D. 204
5. A. 145 R3, 145 x 5 = 725 + 3 = 728
   B. 231, 231 x 3 = 693
   C. 36, 36 x 12 = 432
   D. 11 R15, 11 x 54 = 594 + 15 = 609
6. B. 82
   A. 72
   D. 27
   C. 13
7. A. 6
   B. 1, 5, or 9
   C. 9
   D. 6
8. 789 ÷ 16 = 49 R5, 928 ÷ 16 = 58, 256 ÷ 16 = 16, 857 ÷ 16 = 53 R9
9. Answers may vary.

Page 210

Boxes with a base area greater than 11 square inches: B, D, E
Boxes with a base perimeter less than 20 inches: A, B, C
Boxes with a volume between 100 and 400 cubic inches: B, D, E

Page 211

Tiger, $t = 3$	Boots, $b = 1$
Cash, $c = 9$	Princess, $p = 13$
Callie, $c = 14$	Simba, $s = 7$
Patch, $p = 10$	Smoky, $s = 15$
Fluffy, $f = 2$	Midnight, $m = 6$
Toby, $t = 5$	Sophie, $s = 12$
Oliver, $o = 8$	Casper, $c = 11$
Butterscotch, $b = 4$	

Page 212

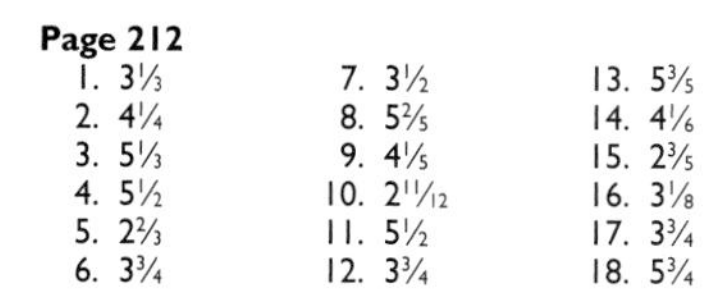

1. $3\frac{1}{3}$	7. $3\frac{1}{2}$	13. $5\frac{3}{5}$
2. $4\frac{1}{4}$	8. $5\frac{2}{5}$	14. $4\frac{1}{6}$
3. $5\frac{1}{3}$	9. $4\frac{1}{5}$	15. $2\frac{3}{5}$
4. $5\frac{1}{2}$	10. $2\frac{11}{12}$	16. $3\frac{1}{8}$
5. $2\frac{2}{3}$	11. $5\frac{1}{2}$	17. $3\frac{3}{4}$
6. $3\frac{3}{4}$	12. $3\frac{3}{4}$	18. $5\frac{3}{4}$

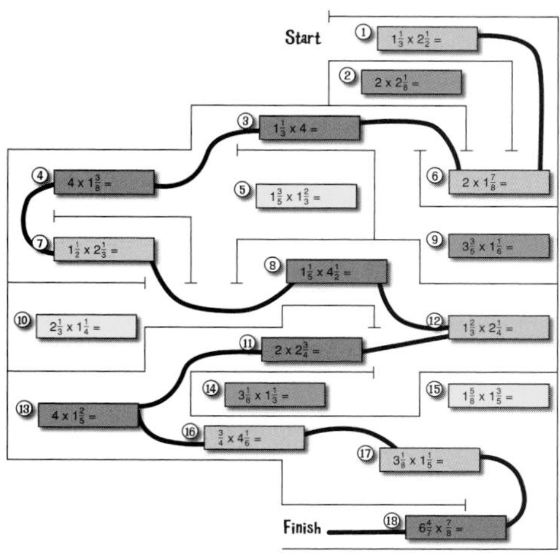

Page 214

A. 14 ÷ (2 + 5) = 2	I. (4 + 2) x 6 = 36
B. (10 – 3) x 4 = 28	J. 72 ÷ (6 + 3) = 8
C. 16 – (4 + 9) = 3	K. (14 – 6) ÷ 2 = 4
D. 14 – (7 + 5) = 2	L. 2 x (5 + 9) = 28
E. (12 – 4) ÷ 2 = 4	M. (9 + 2) x 5 = 55
F. 8 x (6 + 4) = 80	N. 24 ÷ (15 – 9) = 4
G. 3 x (6 – 2) = 12	O. 7 x (12 – 6) = 42
H. (5 + 7) x 6 = 72	P. (50 – 26) ÷ 3 = 8

Page 218

1.

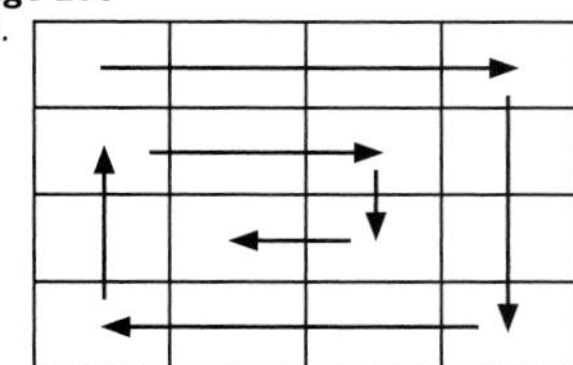

The pattern, which goes in a spiral, is add 6 and then subtract 2.
A = 30, B = 26, C = 34, D = 20, E = 22

2. 47
3. a and c
4. 9 nickels and 6 dimes
5. Problems will vary. Possible problems include the following: 314 + 658 = 972; 291 + 384 = 675; 259 + 614 = 873. The sum of the digits in the answer is always 18.
6. Monday
7. 512 tablespoons
8.

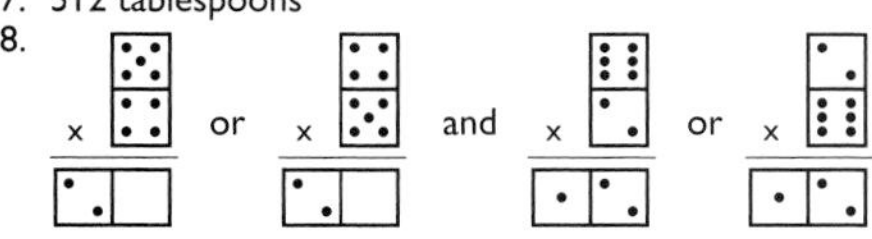

Page 219

1. 12
2. 25
3. 15 cows and 5 chickens
4. $2.52
5. 23
6. 71 x 53 = 3,763 or 53 x 71 = 3,763
7. The digits add up to 13.
8. a. LID
   b. MIX
   c. DIM
   d. LIVID

Page 220

1. 132; 34; 285
2. ½, ⅔
3. No. Rectangles of different areas can have the same perimeter.
4. Possible answers include the following:
   4 x 8 x (5 + 6) = 352
   (4 + 8) x 5 + 6 = 66
   4 x (8 – 5) x 6 = 72
5. 65¢, 83¢, $1.46
6. $x = 4$, $y = 2$ or $x = 8$, $y = 4$
7. possible answers include 40 = 17 + 23; 66 = 13 + 53; and 94 = 5 + 89
8. –16°F

Page 221

1. 
2. Answers may vary. Possible answers include the following:
   a. (4 x 4) – 4 + (4 ÷ 4) = 13
   b. [(6 x 6) ÷ (6 + 6)] + 6 = 9
   c. [(7 + 7 ÷ 7) x 7] ÷ 7 = 8
3. Answers may vary.

¼	⅞	¾
1⅛	⅝	⅛
½	⅜	1

4. Answers may vary. Possible answers include the following:
   a. 1 half-dollar and 5 dimes; 3 quarters, 2 dimes, and 1 nickel
   b. 3 quarters and 5 nickels; 2 quarters, 4 dimes, and 2 nickels
   c. 8 dimes and 4 nickels; 2 quarters and 10 nickels
5. 1:27 AM
6. Answers may vary. Possible answers include the following:

```
   974        951
+ 1,689    + 3,269
  2,663      4,220
```

7. a. lemon
   b. banana
   c. lemon
   d. banana
8. Dandy; Blaze ran one mile in 130 seconds, while Dandy ran one mile in 120 seconds.

Page 222

1. Answers may vary.

Coin/Bill	Approximate Mass
penny	2.5 g
dime	2.3 g
quarter	5.7 g
dollar bill	1 g

2. 2:45
3. The robin has 7 worms, and the woodpecker has 5.
4. A. 111 B. 222 C. 333 D. 12 E. 15 F. 21 G. 27
5. Answers may vary. One possible answer is [(5 + 10) x 20] ÷ 1 = 300
6. 32 7. 15 8. B, E

Page 223

1. 3 eggs, 5 eggs
2. Answers may vary.
3. ¼, ⅓
4. Answers may vary. Certain: rolling a sum greater than one, rolling a sum less than 13, rolling a number from one to six on each die. Impossible: rolling a sum less than two, rolling a sum greater than 13, rolling a sum with more than two digits, rolling a number greater than six on a die, rolling a zero on a die.
5. List B has the most numbers.
6. 8½ inches each day, 59½ inches in one week
7. 48
8. I x II = II or I + I – I = I

Page 226

"Cupid's Choices" 2/9

"Nothing But the Truth"

a. 11 kilograms = 11,000 grams, or 0.11 kilograms = 110 grams
b. 880 grams = 0.88 kilograms, or 88,000 grams = 88 kilograms
c. 7.5 kilometers = 7,500 meters, or 0.075 kilometers = 75 meters
d. 500 meters = 50,000 centimeters, or 0.05 meters = 5 centimeters
e. 6 millimeters = 0.6 centimeters, or 600 millimeters = 60 centimeters
f. 19 liters = 19,000 milliliters, or 0.19 liters = 190 milliliters
g. 40 liters = 40,000 milliliters, or 0.004 liters = 4 milliliters
h. 135 meters = 0.135 kilometers, or 13,500 meters = 13.5 kilometers
i. 60 centimeters = 0.6 meters, or 600 centimeters = 6 meters

Page 228

"Keepin' Cool"

Fractions converted to mixed numbers:	Mixed numbers converted to fractions:
13/3 = 4⅓	5⅔ = 17/3
7/2 = 3½	6¼ = 25/4
12/5 = 2⅖	9 3/7 = 66/7
9/5 = 1⅘	3⅖ = 17/5
8/7 = 1 1/7	7⅝ = 61/8
30/9 = 3⅓	8⅓ = 25/3
21/5 = 4⅕	2⅚ = 17/6
17/8 = 2⅛	4 8/9 = 44/9

Page 229

Level A

1. less than
2. yes
3. true
4. more
5. no
6. multiplication

Level B

1. 5
2. no
3. 5,124,628
4. 6-ton trailer
5. 0 and 3, 1 and 2
6. B, C, and F

Page 230

Level A

1. no
2. 6 minutes, 41.85 seconds
3. about 300 miles
4. false
5. about 55 crackers
6. 500

Level B

1. more than
2. yes
3. 27.63
4. Answers will vary.
5. The following sides are parallel: $\overline{AB}$ and $\overline{DC}$, $\overline{AD}$ and $\overline{BC}$.
   The following sides are perpendicular: $\overline{AB}$ and $\overline{BC}$, $\overline{AB}$ and $\overline{AD}$, $\overline{BC}$ and $\overline{DC}$, $\overline{DC}$ and $\overline{AD}$.
6. The recipe makes 4 gallons.

Page 231

Level A

1. 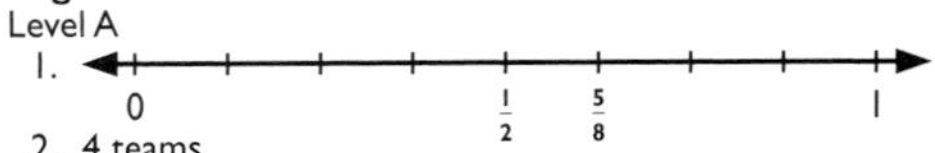

2. 4 teams
3. second place
4. Saturday
5. yes
6. B

Level B

1. more
2. no
3. 127.84, 721.84, 718.42, 817.42
4. True
5. 5/50, or 1/10
6. Both patterns follow the rule "add three, subtract two."

Page 232

Level A

1. Neither boy is correct. The greatest common factor is 18.
2. smaller
3. yes
4. 2.250 cm
5. rectangle
6. die

Level B

1. $70 skateboard discounted 35%
2. 3/16 cup of nuts
3. $0.30 and $0.50
4. 3 kg
5. =
6. 44 degrees

Page 233

Level A

1. 2 teams of 18, 3 teams of 12, 4 teams of 9, 6 teams of 6, 9 teams of 4, 12 teams of 3, 18 teams of 2
2. yes
3. yes; The club collected 4,602 cans this year.
4. no
5. Bruno eats 6 ounces. Fifi eats 2 ounces.
6. yes

Level B

1. More students are signed up for band. Two-fifths is equivalent to 14/35, and 3/7 is equivalent to 15/35.
2. C
3. no; Eighteen cows are brown.
4. length, height, and width = 3cm each, volume = 27 cm^3
5. 11 more children than teenagers; 12 more children than adults; 4 more children than adults and teenagers combined
6. no; The cars are 150 inches long, and the track is 108 inches long.

Page 234

Level A

1. multiplication (to find a common denominator), addition, and subtraction
2. 24 students
3. The greatest common factor is 5, and the least common multiple is 60.
4. 5 pints, 10 quarts, 5 gallons, 88 cups
5. In B, D, and E, n has a value of 7.
6. All perpendicular lines are intersecting lines. All intersecting lines are not perpendicular lines.

Level B

1. no; Kelly's family only used 49.9 fewer kilowatt hours.
2. 5.51, 5.505, 5.5, 5.150, 5.105, 5.1, 5.05
3. multiples of 2 < 30 multiples of 5 < 30

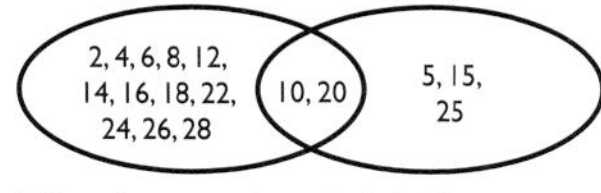

4. Values for x can be 6, 7, 8, 9, 10, 11, 12, 13, or 14.
5. $2\frac{1}{2}$ gallons, 20 pints, 320 fluid ounces
6. Answers may vary.

Page 237

The mystery animal for reptiles is TURTLE.
The mystery animal for fish is CATFISH.
The mystery animal for mammals is GIRAFFE.
The mystery animals for amphibians are TOADS.
The mystery animal for birds is PELICAN.

Page 248

1. over warm seas in the tropics
2. a. Rain clouds form.
   b. Winds start to blow in a circular pattern around a low-pressure area.
   c. Winds exceed 38 miles per hour.
   d. Winds exceed 74 miles per hour.
3. A *watch* means that conditions are right for a hurricane to hit within 36 hours. A *warning* means that a hurricane could strike an area in 24 hours or less.
4. They are different strengths. A Category 5 is the strongest, and a Category 1 is the weakest.
5. Answers may vary.

Page 249

1. renewable
2. geyser
3. core, hotter
4. erupts
5. can
6. world
7. steam, electricity, buildings

Bonus Box: Answers may vary.

Page 250

Explanations will vary.

1. The article is written to describe something.
2. Answers may vary.
3. arachnophobia
4. hunters
5. Spiders are arachnids that spin silk. They have two body parts, eight legs, no wings, and no antennae.

Page 251

Explanations will vary.

1. halite
2. heat and pressure
3. mineral
4. when magma cools
5. Limestone

Page 252

Answers may vary.

1. Layers of snow build up, packing together to form ice on the bottom. Over many years, the snow and ice create a large icy mass that is so big it starts to flow downhill.
2. About 17 football fields would fit on a glacier with an area of 100,000 square meters.
3. When a glacier flows downhill, it reshapes the land. A glacier erodes the rock and soil under it. It deposits some of the rock and soil in other places.
4. Glaciers can pick up huge boulders and deposit them in other places. There is no telling where a boulder will end up.
5. Answers may vary.

Page 253

1. The gravitational pull causes a black hole to trap objects.
2. Nothing can escape from a black hole, not even light.
3. Scientists measure the heat given off by these falling objects to locate a black hole.
4. Gases near a black hole swirl like water going down a bathtub drain.
5. Instruments on the Hubble Space Telescope help scientists measure the speed of the swirling gases around a black hole.
6. Answers may vary.

Black holes are the darkest spots in the universe. Would you believe that a black hole can begin as a gigantic shining star? Once that huge star uses all its fuel, it dies out. Then the star collapses inward because of the pull of its own gravity. This creates a black hole. The gravity of a black hole is so strong that it swallows everything that gets close to it. Any matter that falls into the black hole disappears from sight. Even light cannot escape from a black hole. This is why we cannot see a black hole.

So how do scientists know black holes exist? Dust, gases, and stars that are pulled toward a black hole become very hot. Scientists use instruments that detect this heat to locate a black hole. They also use the Hubble Space Telescope to find black holes. Gases near the black hole get pulled and swirl down to the black hole. This is like water swirling down a bathtub drain. Instruments on the telescope measure the speed of the swirling gases. Then scientists identify the black hole.

There is much more to learn about black holes. Most astronomers believe that millions of them lurk inside our galaxy.

Page 254

1. B
2. C
3. B
4. A

5, 6. Answers may vary.

Page 255

1. C
2. B
3. A
4. B
5. Answers may vary.

Bonus Box: Answers may vary.

Page 256

1. Zeus
2. common
3. Heat lightning
4. charges
5. always
6. features
7. hammer
8. branches
9. Ball lightning
10. cloud

Bonus Box: Answers may vary.

Page 265

A. bay
B. canyon
C. cape
D. channel
E. cliff
F. continent
G. delta
H. foothill
I. glacier
J. gulf
K. hill
L. isthmus
M. mesa
N. mountain range
O. mouth
P. peak
Q. peninsula
R. plain
S. plateau
T. prairie
U. strait
V. tundra
W. valley
X. volcano

Page 269

1. Dred Scott
2. free state
3. Henry Clay
4. John Brown
5. Abraham Lincoln
6. secede
7. South Carolina
8. Confederate States of America
9. Jefferson Davis
10. civil war
11. First Battle of Bull Run
12. Ulysses S. Grant
13. Robert E. Lee
14. Emancipation Proclamation
15. Clara Barton
16. the surrender of the Confederate forces

Page 270

1. Ponce de León was trained to be ~~an explorer~~ a knight.
2. As a page, Ponce de León learned the value of ~~youth~~ duty and honor.
3. People used to think Ponce de León ~~found~~ was looking for a Fountain of Youth.
4. In his training to become a knight, Ponce de León learned to ~~sail~~ read, write, use weapons, ride horses, and hunt.
5. Ponce de León first landed on the island of ~~Puerto Rico~~ Hispaniola.
6. Ponce de León ~~conquered~~ landed on Hispaniola in 1502.
7. Ponce de León is most famous for discovering ~~the Fountain of Youth~~ Florida.
8. Ponce de León found Florida when he was looking for an island called ~~Hispaniola~~ Bimini.

Page 271

1. emigrants found friendship and support.
2. is an emigrant.
3. the emigrants where to go.
4. land they could call their own.
5. pulled the covered wagons.
6. meant pioneers had to pack everything they would need.

Page 272

1. B
2. C
3. A
4. C
5. B
6. Answers may vary.

Page 273

1. C
2. B
3. A
4. B
5. B

Answers may vary for 6–8.

Page 274

1. STATUE
2. TABLET
3. LIBERTY
4. SYMBOL
5. FRIENDSHIP
6. DEMOCRACY
7. DESIGNED
8. COPPER
9. TRIBUTE
10. TYRANNY

FREEDOM

Bonus Box: *statue:* 3-D likeness of a person or animal made by an artist out of a solid material; *tablet:* pad or flat material with inscriptions; *liberty:* independence, or the condition of being free; *symbol:* object, mark, or sign that stands for an idea or quality; *friendship:* close feeling between friends; *democracy:* government in which the people hold the ruling power; *designed:* to have thought up and drawn plans for; *copper:* reddish-brown metal that is easy to shape; *tribute:* something that is done to show thanks or respect; *tyranny:* cruel and unfair use of power

INDEX